Financial Cultures and Crisis Dynamics

The recent financial crisis exposed both a naïve faith in mathematical models to manage risk and a crude culture of greed that embraces risk. This book explores cultures of finance in sites such as corporate governance, hedge funds, central banks, the City of London and Wall Street, and small and medium enterprises. It uses different methods to explore these cultures and their interaction with different financial orders to improve our understanding of financial crisis dynamics.

The introduction identifies types of cultural turn in studies of finance. Part I outlines relevant research methods, including comparison of national cultures viewed as independent variables, cultural political economy, and critical discourse and narrative policy analysis. Part II examines different institutional cultures of finance and the cult of entrepreneurship. Part III offers historical, comparative, and contemporary analyses of financial regimes and their significance for crisis dynamics. Part IV explores organizational cultures, modes of calculation, and financial practices and how they shape economic performance and guide crisis management. Part V considers crisis construals and responses in the European Union and China.

This book's great strength is its multi-faceted approach to cultures of finance. Contributors deploy the cultural turn creatively to enhance comparative and historical analysis of financial regimes, institutions, organizations, and practices as well as their roles in crisis generation, construal, and management. Developing different paradigms and methods and elaborating diverse case studies, the authors illustrate not only how and why 'culture matters' but also how its significance is shaped by different financial regimes and contexts.

Bob Jessop is Distinguished Professor of Sociology and Co-Director of the Cultural Political Economy Research Centre, Lancaster University, UK.

Brigitte Young is Professor for International Political Economy at the Institute of Political Science, University of Münster, Germany.

Christoph Scherrer is Professor of Political Science and Director of the International Center for Development and Decent Work, University of Kassel, Germany.

Routledge frontiers of political economy

Financial Cultures and Crisis Dynamics

Edited by
Bob Jessop, Brigitte Young, and
Christoph Scherrer

Routledge
Taylor & Francis Group

LONDON AND NEW YORK

First published 2015
by Routledge
2 Park Square, Milton Park, Abingdon, Oxfordshire OX14 4RN

and by Routledge
711 Third Avenue, New York, NY 10017

First issued in paperback 2016

Routledge is an imprint of the Taylor & Francis Group, an informa business

British Library Cataloguing in Publication Data
A catalogue record for this book is available from the British Library

Library of Congress Cataloging in Publication Data
Financial cultures and crisis dynamics / edited by Bob Jessop,
Brigitte Young, Christoph Scherrer.
  pages cm.
  1. Financial crises. 2. Financial risk management. I. Jessop, Bob.
  II. Young, Brigitte. III. Scherrer, Christoph.
  HB3722.F557 2014
  658.15'5–dc23   2014018107

ISBN 13: 978-1-138-22680-7 (pbk)
ISBN 13: 978-1-138-77604-3 (hbk)

Typeset in Times New Roman
by Wearset Ltd, Boldon, Tyne and Wear

Contents

Figures

Tables

Contributors

Stefan Beck studied Political Science at the Freie Universität Berlin. His research interests include political economy, the Varieties of Capitalism, and the dynamics of value chains. His dissertation about the German export model 'Vom Fordistischen zum kompetitiven Merkantilismus' was published in 2014 by Metropolis-Verlag (Marburg).

Raphaële Chappe is finalizing her PhD in Economics at The New School for Social Research. Her research interests include finance and risk management, law and economics, as well as the political, economic, and social implications of the evolution of the financial sector in the aftermath of the financial crisis. Her most recent publications include 'The Financial Crisis of 2008 as Cognitive Failure' co-authored with E. Nell and W. Semmler (forthcoming in *Berkeley Journal of Sociology*), and a chapter in Oxford University Press' *Handbook: The Economics of Climate Change* (2014). She is a member of The Cultures of Finance Working Group at the Institute For Public Knowledge (NYU). Prior to academia, she practiced as an attorney for eight years in the financial services industry. In her last position, she worked as a VP with Goldman Sachs in the Tax Department.

Charlie Dannreuther is a lecturer in European political economy at the University of Leeds. His interest in small business policy has informed contributions to international political economy, regulation theory, and European public policy. He recently chaired an EU-wide COST Action on Systemic Risk and the Financial Crisis (ISO 902), co-edited a special issue of *Capital & Class* on The Regulation Approach and the Crisis, and has been working with Professor Perren on the construction of economic concepts, like the small firm, in political discourse.

Eelke de Jong is Full Professor in International Economics at the Radboud University Nijmegen, The Netherlands. His research has dealt with various issues in the field of international monetary economics. Since 2000 the focus of his research has changed to the role of culture in the sense of norms and values for economics. These studies include cross-country studies and studies on the consequences of cultural differences for international cooperation, in particular for solving the European debt crisis. He has published ten books and several articles in national and international journals. The research on culture has been published in: *Culture and Economics: On Values, Economics and International Business* (Routledge, 2009).

Daniela Gabor is an associate professor in Economics at UWE Bristol. Her research explores discourses and practices of central banking through a critical political economy approach; the IMF's conditionality and advice on governance of cross-border financial interconnectedness particularly in relationship to global banks' market-based activities; shadow banking activities through the repo market, and the implications for central banking, sovereign bond markets, and regulatory activity, including Financial Transaction Taxes. Her research has been cited in the financial media, and received funding from European and British sources. Daniela has organized several conferences and workshops on critical finance questions. She disseminates her research through active blogging and tweeting activities, alongside traditional academic journal outlets (*Journal of Development Studies, Competition and Change, Development and Change, Review of Political Economy, Europe-Asia Studies*).

Mathis Heinrich is a PhD research student at the Cultural Political Economy Research Centre of the Sociology Department, Lancaster University, UK, and the Institute of Critical Social Analysis of the Rosa-Luxemburg Foundation Berlin, Germany. In his thesis, he is working on the role of transnational capital actors in the EU's economic and financial management of the current crises in Europe. He holds a Master's degree in political science and economics from the Philips-University Marburg and his main research interests cover international and comparative political economy, European integration, EU politics, and critical social theory.

Bob Jessop is Distinguished Professor of Sociology and Co-Director of the Cultural Political Economy Research Centre at Lancaster University, UK. He is best known for his work on state theory and his contributions to critical political economy (especially the regulation approach), the study of welfare state restructuring, and, most recently, the development of cultural political economy. He completed a three and a half year professorial research fellowship on the North Atlantic Financial Crisis in 2013 and is now writing up the results. Recent books are *Beyond the Regulation Approach* (2006), *State Power* (2007), *Towards a Cultural Political Economy* (2013, co-authored with Ngai-Ling Sum), and *The State: Past, Present and Future* (in press).

Oliver Kessler is Professor for International Relations at the University of Erfurt, Germany. His research draws from economic sociology, economic theory, and international political economy to explore the rationalities of risk and uncertainty in relation to financial practices, financial regulation, and stability in complex systems.

Amelie Kutter is Lecturer in European Politics and Discourse Studies and Marie Curie Fellow at European University Viadrina in Frankfurt (Oder). She holds a PhD (European University Viadrina) and an MA (Diplom, Freie Universität Berlin) in Political Science. She has lectured, researched, and published on the financial crisis, European integration, postsocialist transformation, and transnational political communication at Lancaster University, FU Berlin, European University Viadrina, TU Dresden, CERI/Sciences Po. She specializes in political discourse studies and methods of textual analysis.

Andrea Lagna is Associate Fellow at the Centre for Global Political Economy, University of Sussex, UK, and Visiting Lecturer at the University of Erfurt, Germany. He obtained a PhD in International Relations from the University of Sussex in 2013, focusing on the political economy of financial derivatives in present-day Italy. His current work explores the relationship between state power and financial innovation.

Daniel Mügge is Associate Professor of Political Economy at the University of Amsterdam. His research focuses on finance and its governance and the political economy of macroeconomic indicators. In the EU-funded GR:EEN project on Europe's role in the world (2011–2015) he leads the work on finance. In 2009 his dissertation was awarded the Jean Blondel prize for best European political science thesis of the year. Daniel was a visiting scholar at Harvard's Center for European Studies in 2012 and is lead-editor of the *Review of International Political Economy*.

Edward Nell serves as the Malcolm B. Smith Professor of Economics at the New School For Social Research in New York. Edward has served as an advisor to governments and NGOs, and he has taught and lectured at many universities in many countries. He has written articles ranging from philosophy and anthropology, through pure economic theory, to applied work and policy. Edward's contributions are in the field of macroeconomic theory, monetary analysis and finance, economic methodology and philosophy, transformational growth and development. He has written some 20 books, including *The General Theory of Transformational Growth: Keynes After Sraffa*, published by Cambridge University Press. His articles on economic theory and methodology have appeared in leading journals like *American Economic Review, Journal of Political Economy, Journal of Economic Literature, Cambridge Journal of Economics, Eastern Economic Journal, Review of Political Economy, Economic Development and Cultural Change, Analysis*, and *Social Research*.

Horacio Ortiz is a researcher at the Research Institute of Anthropology, East China Normal University. He obtained a PhD from the Ecole de Hautes Etudes en Sciences Sociales, Paris. He is the author of *Valeur financière et vérité. Enquête d'anthropologie politique sur l'évaluation des actions cotées* (Presses de Sciences Po, 2014). He is currently doing research on the financial industry in China.

Lew Perren is Professor of Management Research at the University of Brighton. His research into management and entrepreneurship has tended to be interdisciplinary in nature often drawing upon influences from linguistics, sociology, and philosophy. Lew is currently working with colleagues to explore the paradigms of management and political science using corpus analysis techniques.

Christoph Scherrer is Professor for Globalization and Politics and Executive Director of the International Center for Development and Decent Work at the University of Kassel and a member of the Steering Committee of the Global Labour University. He has recently received the Excellency in Teaching Award of the State of Hessia and the Excellence in Development Cooperation Award from the DAAD. Recent English language publications include: *Food Crisis: Implications for Labour* (2013, co-edited with D. Saha), *China's Labor Question* (2011, ed.), *The Role of Gender Knowledge in Policy Networks* (2010, co-edited with B. Young).

Willi Semmler is Henry Arnhold Professor of Economics, Department of Economics at the New School for Social Research, New York, and is associated with Bielefeld University, Germany. He was a visitor at Columbia University and Stanford University. He is the author or co-author of more than 90 articles in international journals and is author or co-author of 11 books. He has taught at, among other institutions, at the American University, Washington, DC, Bielefeld University, and UNAM, Mexico City. His recent book is *Asset Prices, Booms and Recessions* (Springer Publishing House, 2011). He is Research Fellow at the Schwartz Center for Economic Policy Analysis, New School, New York, and at the Centre for European Economic Research, Mannheim, Germany and is a member of the advisory board of the Society for Computational Economics.

Ngai-Ling Sum is Senior Lecturer in Politics and International Relations and Co-Director (with Bob Jessop) of the Cultural Political Economy Research Centre at Lancaster University, UK. She has research and teaching interests in international political economy; Gramsci and Foucault; globalization and competitiveness and transnational politics; and the Pearl River Delta region. She was awarded (with Bob Jessop) the Gunnar Myrdal Prize by the European Association of Evolutionary Political Economics for their co-authored book, *Beyond the Regulation Approach* (2006). She publishes in journals like *Critical Policy Studies, Development Dialogue, New Political Economy, Critical Asian Studies, Competition and Change, Capital & Class, Urban Studies,* and *Economy and Society* as well as edited collections.

Femke van Esch is Assistant Professor of European Integration at the Utrecht School of Governance (USG). She has expertise in European economic and monetary policy-making, EU leadership, and the method of comparative cognitive mapping. In her PhD thesis, she studied the role of political and financial leaders' beliefs in the establishment of the European Economic and

Monetary Union. Currently, Femke is studying the role and responsiveness of leaders' beliefs in the European response to the Euro-crisis. In addition to her academic work, Femke is a member of the Commission European Integration of the Advisory Council of International Affairs of the Dutch Ministry of Foreign Affairs.

Brigitte Young has been Professor of International Political Economy, Institute of Political Science, University of Münster, Germany since 1999. She held guest professorships at Science Politique in Paris, Science-Politique in Lille, Warwick University, UK, and Central European University, Budapest. Brigitte is a German delegate to the EU-COST project on 'Systemic Risks, Financial Crises and Credit' (2010–2014), and she is scientific advisor to the EU-FB7 FESSUD project (2011–2016). She is also a member of the expert group to advise the Minister of European Affairs of the state of North Rhine-Westphalia, Germany on the regional impact of the Eurozone crisis. Her research areas include economic globalization, European economic and monetary integration, world trade, global financial market governance, monetary policies, and heterodox economic theories. She has published widely in English and German. Her latest article is 'German Ordoliberalism as Agenda Setter for the Euro Crisis: Myth Trumps Reality', in: *Journal of Comparative European Policy*, Vol. 22: 3: 276– 287 (2014).

Preface

This book project is an outcome of the EU-COST Action ISO902 financed Project 'Systemic Risks, Financial Crisis and Credit – the Roots, Dynamics and Consequences of the Subprime Crisis' (2010–2014) under the leadership of Charlie Dannreuther, Leeds University, UK. The grant holder was Oliver Kessler, University of Erfurt, Germany. One of the three subthemes of the research activities covered was 'New Global Finance' led by Brigitte Young, University of Münster, and Christoph Scherrer, University of Kassel. At its first COST-meeting in Paris 2010, the work package membership decided to pursue the role of financial cultures from different theoretical and empirical perspectives with a view to publishing a joint book project. The reason for this specific focus on cultures in finance has to do with the sheer neglect of this topic in mainstream economics. Yet the financial crisis has provided a space for other social science disciplines to interrogate what went wrong with finance as well as a welcome, if belated, concern with cultures of finance in mainstream economics. As a result of the depth, scope, and duration of the crisis, the rational assumptions in the efficient market hypothesis and the belief in new technical innovations ushering in a new *Great Moderation* were strongly contested by other academic fields. Particularly in economic sociology, a cultural turn in finance, with its focus on the meanings attributed to social life and material objects, challenged the one-sided emphasis on the structural power of capital. It refocused attention on the interconnectedness between interpretive-cultural meanings and structural material properties and practices.

Thus we were delighted that Bob Jessop, as one of the leading advocates of Cultural Political Economy, and Ngai-Ling Sum, the co-director of the Cultural Political Economy Research Centre at the University of Lancaster, UK, joined the project at an early stage and contributed in various ways to the realization of the book project. Bob Jessop invested a great deal of time and effort as co-editor to give superb guidance to most authors or co-authors to reformulate their arguments to give the book a more coherent theoretical structure. Last but not least, we much appreciate Bob Jessop's grammatical corrections and improvements of many of the non-English native speakers' texts. In many respects, the majority of individual book chapters bear to some extent the footprint of the Cultural Political Economy (CPE) approach.

The edited papers in this volume are the result of drafts presented at workshops at the Central European University, Budapest, Hungary in 2012, at COST conferences at the University of Kassel and Berlin both in 2013. We want to express our appreciation to the individual contributors of the chapters for the stimulating discussion at the workshops, for their responsiveness to our frequent calls for re-writes, for their patience, and for submitting subsequently the innovative papers on financial cultures and the dynamics of crises.

A special note of appreciation goes to Oliver Kessler and Charlie Dannreuther, both contributing authors to this volume, for their support of the project. We also want to thank Dorothee Bohle, Central European University, Budapest, for hosting the book drafting meeting in 2012. We are also grateful for the financial and organization support offered by the International Center of Development and Decent Work (ICDD), University of Kassel.

We also owe a tremendous debt to Anil Shah, University of Kassel, who with great diligence and attentiveness prepared the final manuscript for submission, generated the index, and followed meticulously the instructions of the publisher's handbook. The financial support of the University of Kassel for the final preparation of the manuscript is gratefully acknowledged. Christoph Scherrer would particularly like to thank the team of the DFG Research Group Landnahme, Acceleration, Activation. Dynamics and (De)stabilisation of Modern Growth Societies for providing an inspiring, yet tranquil environment at their villa.

Brigitte Young and Christoph Scherrer
Working Package Leader: New Global Finance

Abbreviations

AIG	American International Group
BERR	Department for Business and Enterprise Regulatory Reform
BIS	Bank for International Settlement
BRIC	Brazil, Russia, India, China
CAPM	Capital Asset Pricing Model
CB	Central Bank
CCA	Compliance Cost Assessment
CCM	Comparative Cognitive Mapping
CD	Certificate of Deposit
CDA	Critical Discourse Analysis
CDO	Collateralized Debt Obligations
CDS	Credit Default Swaps
CEO	Chief Executive Officer
CFMA	Commodities Futures Modernization Act
CFTC	Commodities Futures Trading Commission
CME	Coordinated Market Economies
CML	Capital Market Liberalization
CONSOB	Commisione Nazionale per la Società e la Borsa (Italian Securities and Exchange Commission)
CPE	Cultural Political Economy
CRA	Community Reinvestment Act
DTB	Deutsche Terminbörse
ECB	European Central Bank
EMS	European Monetary System
EMU	(European) Economic and Monetary Union
ERT	European Round Table of Industrialists
ETF	Exchange Traded Fund
EU	European Union
FDIC	Federal Deposit Insurance Corporation
Fed	Federal Reserve System
FSA	Financial Services Authority
FSB	Financial Stability Board
FSOC	Financial Services Oversight Council

GDP	Gross Domestic Product
GEM	Global Entrepreneurship Monitor
GIPS	Greece, Ireland, Portugal, Spain
IC	Individualism-Collectivism
IFCF	Industrial and Commercial Finance Corporation
IMF	International Monetary Fund
LIBOR	London Interbank Offered Rate
LME	Liberal Market Economies
LTCM	Long-Term Capital Management
LTRO	Long-term Refinancing Operation
MATIF	Marché à Terme International de France (French derivatives exchange)
MBS	Mortgage Backed Securities
MINT	Mexico, Indonesia, Nigeria, Turkey
MPT	Modern Portfolio Theory
MSCI	Morgan Stanley Capital Index
NAFC	North Atlantic Financial Crisis
OECD	Organisation of Economic Co-operation and Development
OMT	Outright Monetary Transaction
OTC	Over the Counter
PD	Power Distance
QE	Quantitative Easing
RIA	Regulatory Impact Assessment
R&D	Research & Development
RMB	Renminbi
SDR	Special Drawing Rights
SEC	Securities and Exchange Commission
SFIT	Small Firms Impact Test
SIV	Structured Investment Vehicle
SME	Small and Medium-sized Enterprise
SOE	State-owned Enterprise
SPV	Special Purpose Vehicle
SSF	Social Studies on Finance
TSLF	Term Securities Lending Facility
TUF	Testo Unico della Finanza (Finance Consolidation Act)
UA	Uncertainty Avoidance
UK	United Kingdom
UN	United Nations
UNEP	United Nations Environment Programme
USA	United States of America
VAR	Value at Risk
VoC	Varieties of Capitalism
WB	World Bank
WTO	World Trade Organization

Introduction

Bob Jessop and Christoph Scherrer

Banks like to invest in culture. Deutsche Bank boasts more than 56,000 pieces of artwork. Banks also like to sponsor culture. ING bank is 'the most important sponsor of the Rijksmuseum' in Amsterdam (van de Water 2007: 7). But finance as a field has long been portrayed by various commentators as being devoid of specific cultural traits. For example, insiders emphasize the rationality of decision-making in finance. Many are highly trained professionals, some with PhDs in physics or mathematics. From the outside they seem to epitomize 'economic man', the rational utility maximizer. From a cultural political economy perspective, however, both of these depictions could be seen to involve a distinctive culture of economic rationality and dispassionate economic calculation. For other commentators, however, finance as a field has been characterized by distinctive traits, for example, a culture originally based on trust that has transformed into a culture of risk (see Chappe *et al.*, this volume) or as markets based on status (see Kessler, this volume).

The recent financial crisis-cum-Great Recession has challenged this perception of rationality and market perfection even among those who previously endorsed or accepted it. Public comments on the origin of the crisis were loaded with cultural references. A popular explanation for the emergence of the crisis was 'greed' incentivized by the 'bonus culture' in the financial sector; and the popular epithet 'bankster' clearly connotes a culture and activities bordering on the criminal. The media and public opinion distinguish between 'Main Street' and 'Wall Street' cultures and discuss the increasing separation and, indeed, antagonism between these two economic and social worlds as a result of financialization. In this context, there is talk about the distinct culture of investment banking or how the 'quants', that is, professional investors using mathematical and statistical models to drive their trades, have changed the culture of finance, not necessarily to the better (for example, Patterson 2011).

As a final example, albeit extended, Christine Lagarde, then French Finance Minister (and now Managing Director of the IMF) once remarked that the global financial crisis would not have occurred had Lehman Brothers been Lehman Sisters (Lagarde 2010; cf. Kristof 2010 on 'Mistresses of the Universe'). This self-described 'quip' reflects the wider re-signification of the recurrent 'myth' of prudent woman and irresponsible man, which disguises broader economic and political dynamics behind the crisis (Prügl 2012; more generally, see Tett 2013). Looking beyond the general 'myth', the issue of a gendered dimension to financial and trading cultures has been widely debated (and contested) from many perspectives and, in addition to earlier organizational ethnographies (for example, McDowell 1997, 2010) has also generated a wide-ranging body of post-crisis research into whether there are significant gendered differences in individual or organizational financial cultures (for example, intriguingly, the study by a neuroscientist with several years' trading experience with Goldman Sachs: Coates 2012).[1]

The opening three paragraphs already contain several notions of culture. The first notion of culture used above, which is also common in everyday understandings, identifies it with artistic activity and art objects. The second pertains to shared habits of thought, mental models, modes of calculation, or patterns of conduct that characterize an identifiable set of individuals, groups, organizations, or broader social community. This could be a dominant, sub-, or counter-culture. A third meaning, building on the second, is that this culture is somehow deviant or harmful, such as a culture of greed, a testosterone-fuelled culture of high-risk trading, or indifference to the harms caused by one's activities. Fourth, and conversely, for those who want to set themselves apart from 'the crowd', culture can also be invoked in a more positive sense, for example, of high culture, nonconformism, a spirit of innovation, or entrepreneurial culture (on the last of these, see, for example, Dannreuther and Perren, this volume). We will introduce further meanings of culture below but we should emphasize here that it is not the aim of this introduction to our volume to provide a comprehensive survey of all of the main approaches, let alone all approaches, to culture that might be relevant to finance, financial institutions, financial practice, financial systems, or financial crises. We highlight those most relevant to the contributions that derive from the COST project and how they fit within the cultural turn.[2]

Economics as an academic discipline in its dominant, neo-classical guise largely tries to evade recognition of cultural differences, i.e. particular cultural settings (a third meaning of culture), by positing universal and transhistorical economic laws that operate regardless of context (for a nuanced historical and contemporary overview of the place of culture in economics, which addresses classical political economy, neo-classical economics, and a thematic cultural turn in recent economics, see Beugelsdijk and Maseland 2011). In this sense, if cultural differences existed, they would be seen as frictions that obstruct rational economic action and should be assumed away, or even removed as unwarranted obstacles to perfect competition. Orthodox Marxist analyses may also lead to neglect of culture in so far as they trace the financial crisis to the rise of financialization in response to operation of the tendency of the rate of profit to fall (e.g. Potts 2010). The recurrent financial crises in the last three decades have, however, attracted the interest of other disciplines that were already more attuned, or 'pre-adapted', to one or another kind of cultural turn in the social sciences (e.g. the various contributions in Callon 1998; or the excellent review of recent developments in the sociology of markets in Fourcade 2007).

The most recent North Atlantic Financial Crisis (NAFC) also made the field of finance more accessible to these other disciplines by diminishing the power of the previous academic gatekeepers to control the allocation research money on financial matters – gatekeepers who had endorsed the efficient market hypothesis as the operating principle of modern finance. In addition, the post-crisis blame game produced many insider accounts of what went wrong. Congressional or parliamentary hearings and court cases have also required the disclosure of further material that makes the sector, its actors, and its conduct more transparent. As these new financial actors and their practices become more visible, their commonalities and the differences in how they see their roles and places in their specialized fields and society more generally also become discernible. The new visibility reveals the obvious, namely, that 'economic man' even in international finance does not conform to the economic textbook ideal of a rational utility maximizer. And even when their behaviour comes close to it, it is not an automatic outcome of market forces but of the confluence of a specific socialization reinforced by many practices.

An interest in the cultural aspects of economics, including industry and finance, was a characteristic of nineteenth-century political economy (e.g. the early generations of the German Historical School), of the old institutionalisms (e.g. Veblen, Commons), and classical sociology (see respectively, for example, Shionaya 2001; Camic and Hodgson 2013; Swedberg 2003). The institutionalization of the disciplinary separation between economics and other social sciences undermined this interest. The pioneers of the recent 'cultural turn' (on which, see below) in analysing finance come from diverse fields and currents in the social sciences. In the last 20 years or so, in sociology, for example, the work of Pierre Bourdieu has influenced many (e.g. Adkins 2011; Bourdieu 2005); and Viviana Zelizer has pioneered research on neglected aspects of value and values in organizing and limiting market economies and market arrangements (e.g. Zelizer 1994). Donald MacKenzie's analysis of the role of the efficient market hypothesis for modern financial markets is a path-breaking contribution from the social studies of science tradition (e.g. Mac-Kenzie 2006; MacKenzie *et al.* 2007). In the field of economic sociology and critical accounting studies, the Centre for Research on Socio-Cultural Change (CRESC) at the University of Manchester has done some pioneering work on the culture of private equity (e.g. Froud and Williams 2007). Studies that emphasize different kinds of calculation and measurement have also influenced the study of finance, especially technologies of calculation (e.g. Amato *et al.* 2010). The cultural turn can also be found among post-structuralist authors. For example, Marieke de Goede 'discusses some of the moral, religious and political transformations that have slowly constructed the domain of finance as a legitimate, rational, and above all, natural practice (2005: x). Likewise Paul Langley's inquiry into everyday finance directed attention away from the cultures in finance to the financial behaviour of ordinary people (Langley 2008; see also Aitken 2007; Hobson and Seabrooke 2007).

In many of these works we find another notion of culture: 'in its broad sense of the meanings that we give social life and material objects, and the concrete practices that they enable and depend on for their sustenance' (Best and Paterson 2010: 3; and, for an influential approach in terms of alternative justifications of economic conduct, see Boltanski and Chiapello 1999). From the perspective of culture in this general sociological sense, the initial development of political economy can also be interpreted as a cultural project – a domain of meaning and ethical purpose – that surreptitiously constructs a specific 'moral economy' – a domain of moral sentiments and norms (Blaney and Inayatullah 2010: 32; for contrasting approaches to later developments in political economy and/or economics, see, for example, Fourcade 2009; Mirowski 2002). Recognizing this turn has encouraged several scholars to generate research agendas for cultural economy or cultural political economy (for example, Amin and Thrift 2004; Babe 2009; Best and Paterson 2010; du Gay and Pryke 2002; Ray and Sayer 1999). A common feature of these agendas is their call to examine discourses as well as material practices. This provides a powerful means both to critique and to contextualize recent claims about the 'culturalization' of economic life in the new economy – seeing these claims as elements within a new economic imaginary with a potentially performative impact as well as a belated (mis)recognition of the semiotic dimensions of all economic activities (for sometimes contrasting views on the 'culturalization thesis', see Du Gay and Pryke 2002; Ray and Sayer 1999).

This conclusion is all the more justified because, while every social practice is semiotic (in so far as social practices entail meaning), no social practice is reducible to its semiotic moments. Semiosis involves more than the play of differences among networks of signs and is therefore never a purely intra-semiotic matter without external reference. It cannot be understood or explained without identifying and exploring the extra-semiotic conditions that make semiosis possible and make it more or less effective – including its embedding in material practices and their relation to the constraints and affordances of the natural and social world (Fairclough *et al.* 2004). This highlights the role of variation, selection, and retention in the development and consolidation of some construals rather than others and their embedding in practices that transform the natural and social world (cf. Sayer 2000; Sum and Jessop 2013).

On cultural turns

So far we have explored some possible meanings of culture in regard to finance and some of the ways in which social scientists (especially in anthropology, ethnography, geography, global and international political economy, international relations, political economy, political science, social studies of science, and sociology) have studied some 'cultural' aspects of financial institutions, organizations, and everyday life. Now we consider more systematically the nature of the cultural turn. The latter subsumes a wide range of (re-)discoveries – at least as compared with previous neglect in some humanities and social science fields – of the important role of semiosis in social life. For present purposes, semiosis serves as an umbrella concept for diverse forms of the production of meaning oriented to communication among social agents, individual or collective. It includes argumentation, discourse, ethics, framing, hermeneutics, historicity (the use of history to make history), iconography, identity formation and activation, narrative, performativity, rhetoric, and subjectivation (on different approaches, see Bachman-Medick 2006; de Jong 2009; Fairclough 2003; Hoppe 2007; McCloskey 1998; see also the general overview in Sum and Jessop 2013). From this plethora of turns, the studies presented in this volume are primarily oriented to discourse analysis, framing, linguistic analysis, narrative policy analysis, and performativity (or its explanatory limits) which are the most relevant to our concern in the COST Action with cultures of finance (for details, see chapter summaries).

In this context it is useful to distinguish four types of cultural turn: thematic, methodological, ontological, and reflexive. In brief, a cultural turn could address previously neglected themes (thematic), propose a new entry point into social analysis (methodological), discover that 'culture' is actually foundational to the social world (ontological), or, lastly, apply one or more of the preceding turns to reflect upon the development of, or resistance to, the making of cultural turns (reflexive) (Sum and Jessop 2013: 13, 72–113). Examples of all four turns can be found in the study of finance (see Table I.1). Different chapters in the present volume provide examples of the first three, albeit with different emphases and sometimes in combination. For example, Lagna's chapter takes a theme (derivatives in markets for corporate control) to present a critique of performativity theories and constructivism (a methodological critique of two kinds of methodological turn) in order to justify a different methodological entry-point with ontological commitments about the nature of capitalism (namely, 'political Marxism').

In thematic terms, there is innovative work on the culture of hedge funds and private equity firms, with special reference to their modus operandi and modes of calculation, regulatory imaginaries, and their distinctive contribution to new cultures of finance (Ortiz, this volume). Another chapter explores the collusive culture in the City of London and draws parallels to status markets known in the field of art (Kessler, this volume); and there is a complementary chapter that contrasts cultures of trust and cultures of risk in US banking and the contribution of the latter to the sub-prime crisis (Chappe *et al.*, this volume). Two other contributions examine the plausibility of varieties of capitalism. One tests the impact of national culture on investors' behaviour and on the institutional form of the financial system (de Jong, this volume), the other questions a simple juxtaposition of market-based and bank-based financial systems (Beck and Scherrer, this volume). In making this thematic turn, some authors also make a cultural turn in the use of research methods and/or aim to uncover new features of finance as a social reality.

Likewise, in methodological terms, there is a chapter on the role of mental models and political cultures in shaping international coordination among different varieties of capitalism – with special reference to techniques of mapping mental models that can also be applied fruitfully in other contexts (de Jong and

Table I.1 Cultural turns and financial relations

Cultural turns	Definition	Examples from the field of finance
Thematic	Studies 'cultural' themes that have previously been neglected in given discipline, scientific approach, or field of inquiry	Organizational culture in financial agencies Modes of financial calculation Financialization of everyday life Organizational learning from financial crises Varieties of financial culture Regulatory imaginaries Crisis narratives and construals
Methodological	Adopts new methodological approach or analytical technique concerned with semiosis (more or less broadly or narrowly defined) as best entry point into a given field of inquiry	Mental models Narrative turn Metaphors of crisis-management Corpus linguistic analysis of financial crisis journalism Technologies of securitization Rhetorics of regulatory reform
Ontological	Argues that semiosis is a basic constitutive or co-constitutive feature of the social world and so must always be included in any analysis of social phenomena that aims both to interpret and explain such phenomena	Role of economic and financial imaginaries in defining economic practices Economists make markets Formation of financial subjects Neo-liberalism as a class project Valuation as constitutive of moral economy Greed, fear, confidence, animal spirits, etc. Americanism and Fordism à la Gramsci
Reflexive	Applies one or more of the above turns to the rise of a given discipline, approach, or field of analysis in order to interpret and/or explain its adoption of the cultural turn	Financial economics as a cultural field Critique of economic categories à la Marx Cultural history of economics Origins of the cultural turn in economics Critical genealogy of the law and economics movement

Note
The examples given in the right-hand column are exemplified in individual chapters (see chapter summaries below) or in the discussion and references in this introduction.

van Esch, this volume). Another chapter demonstrates the importance of taking seriously the motivations, cost-benefit calculations, and understandings of competitive advantage of financial service providers and their supporters when it comes to making choices about regulatory regimes at a pan-regional or supranational level (Mügge, this volume). Other approaches to reading the cultural moment in terms of sense- and meaning-making are critical discourse analysis (Dannreuther and Perren, this volume), critical discourse analysis (or CDA) plus discursive policy studies (Kutter and Jessop, this volume), and CDA combined with narrative policy analysis of the crisis-responses and their legitimations pursued by central banks (Gabor and Jessop, this volume). Last but not least, one contribution provides an analysis of successive economic imaginaries and their articulation to financial, fiscal, and political imaginaries and then traces their consequences for stability and crisis (Young, this volume). This involves both a thematic and a methodological innovation in terms of the way in which it analyses and contextualizes these imaginaries and their effects. We should note in this respect that, whereas a methodological cultural turn is most visible when the relevant analysis also takes some aspect of culture as its entry point, it can also occur, less visibly, when the analysis introduces cultural aspects at a later stage in the analysis in order to provide a more adequate interpretation and explanation of its object of inquiry. Provided that this is not just a residual 'X factor' introduced as a catch-all explanation for what is otherwise left unexplained but is properly integrated into the analysis, this could also be counted as part of the broader cultural turn.

The ontological turn is expounded by Sum and Jessop in Chapter 1 (see also below). This is also evident in the chapters on the performative role of financial imaginaries in the BRIC economies (Sum, this volume) and on the significance of selective interpretation patterns of an imagined economic world as well as the differential power of specific economic interests (Heinrich and Jessop, this volume). This turn is also implicit in several other chapters (notably, Lagna, Ortiz, and de Jong and van Esch). More generally, a concern with the role of imaginaries in making sense of a complex world is shared by all authors. Some explore the performative power of imaginaries (e.g. Sum; Young), others the selective qualities of imaginaries (e.g. Kutter and Jessop; Gabor and Jessop), their strategic use (e.g. Dannreuther and Perren; Heinrich and Jessop), their use in academia (e.g. Beck and Scherrer), their role in the reduction of complexity and uncertainty in processes of interest formation (e.g. Mügge), and the conflict between imaginaries (e.g. Ortiz, de Jong). The authors' specific contributions are summarized in the next section.

Five contributions to this volume are informed by one specific variant of Cultural Political Economy (CPE). This strand of the cultural turn understands culture in the above-mentioned general semiotic sense, that is, in ontological terms as a concern with the social production of intersubjective meaning and its constitutive role in social life (see Sum and Jessop, this volume; Sum and Jessop 2013). This approach integrates the cultural turn with the analysis of instituted economic and political relations and their social embedding. Instead of arguing that all social phenomena have interpretative-cultural and structural-material properties, the CPE approach seeks to reveal their interconnection and co-evolution in constructing social relations. Key influences in Sum and Jessop's development of CPE are Marx's critique of political economy, which is concerned with the economic categories that organize capital as a social relation as well as with the emergent structural properties of that relation, and Gramsci's analyses of the 'determinate market' (historically specific accumulation regimes and their modes of regulation) and the 'historical bloc' (a specific, reciprocally determined relation between what orthodox Marxists would describe as 'base' and 'superstructure'). This approach also draws on Foucault's analyses of governmentality, technologies of governance, and genealogy of political economy, including neo-liberalism (Foucault 2008a, 2008b). Overall, in line with its articulation to the regulation approach (Jessop and Sum 2006), CPE stresses the historical contingency and spatio-temporal specificity of accumulation regimes and their co-constitution through struggles for political, intellectual, and moral leadership (hegemony) and to institute partial, provisional institutional and spatio-temporal fixes to stabilize accumulation despite the contradictions and crisis-tendencies inherent in the capital relation. Key concepts in this regard are economic imaginaries, their translation into hegemonic projects, their institutionalization in specific structures and practices, and their relationship to specific forms of subjectivation as well as specific objects of economic and political governance. While these themes are highlighted in the chapter by Sum and Jessop, other chapters that draw on the CPE approach select just some themes without necessarily committing their authors to all of the concepts, propositions, and explanatory principles associated therewith. In this sense, CPE can be seen as a toolkit for research on cultures of finance and crisis dynamics that can be utilized selectively.

One of the key differences between CPE and other approaches that make a cultural turn is its explicit integration of the general evolutionary mechanisms of variation, selection, and retention into semiotic analysis. This does not entail the sort of evolutionism that posits predetermined sequences. Rather, an evolutionary turn highlights the dialectic of path-dependency and path-shaping that emerges from the contingent co-evolution of semiotic and extra-semiotic processes that make some meaningful efforts at complexity reduction more resonant than others. It should be noted here that the semiotic and extra-semiotic space for variation, selection, and retention is contingent, not pre-given. This also holds for the various and varying semiotic and material elements whose selection and retention occur in this 'ecological' space. This indicates the need for a clear distinction between social construal and social construction (cf. Sayer 2000: 90–3). All actors are forced to construe the world selectively as a condition of going on within it. But, while all construals are equal before complexity, some are more equal than others. Given the potential for infinite variation in construals, it is important to explore how their selection and retention are shaped by emergent, non-semiotic features of social structure as well as by inherently semiotic factors.

The CPE perspective is far from the only one employed below. Indeed, the diversity of perspectives on culture in finance and the methods applied makes this volume unique and illustrates the networking and dialoguing effects of the COST Action. The cultural political economy approach, with its emphasis on combining semiotic and structural analysis, as presented in chapter 1 and elaborated in several other chapters, is not the only one employed below. Indeed, the diversity of perspectives on the significance of culture in finance and the range of methods applied make this volume unique and illustrate the networking and dialoguing effects of the COST Action. It also confirms another key principle of CPE, namely: given the complexity of the real world, no single theoretical perspective or methodological entry point can do justice to that complexity. This requires the adoption of different approaches and methods to reveal different aspects of that complexity. It also calls for space to debate different approaches and compare their theoretical, empirical and policy implications. COST gave us this space.

Summary of chapters

The first part of the book 'Researching Cultures of Finance: Theoretical Foundations and Methods' looks at some theoretical foundations and methods for researching cultures of finance and/or the cultural moments of finance. The theoretical foundations stretch from taking culture as a set of persistent shared beliefs of a specific collectivity, mostly the national state, to taking culture as a discursive process and product. Likewise, the methods range from operationalizing cultural differences as independent variables for quantitative analysis through discourse and narrative policy analysis to specific case studies of institutional and organizational discourse.

In the first chapter, entitled 'Sense- and Meaning-making in the Critique of Political Economy' Ngai-Ling Sum and Bob Jessop flag their 'cultural turn' as ontological and reflexive. Their theoretical frame differs from other approaches to culture because they argue that all social phenomena have both semiotic and material properties. This requires an approach that navigates a tricky course between a one-sided constructivism that highlights the role of ideas, discourses, or culture in making and remaking economic reality and a one-sided structuralism that reifies economic institutions, market forces, and 'iron laws' and minimizes the scope for ideas and agents to make a difference. In short, the chapter emphasizes the structural coupling and co-evolution of sense- and meaning-making, on the one hand, and the character and emergent properties of economic (and other) relations, on the other hand.

In other words, the Sum-Jessop approach to CPE aims to show how the economic field is socially constructed, acquires its specific emergent features and distinctive logic and dynamics, and remains vulnerable to disruption and dislocation. In this context, the authors set out the key concepts of their approach. In particular, they highlight the role of sense- and meaning-making (illustrated through rival 'economic imaginaries') in enabling social agents to 'go on' in a complex world; examine the disorienting impact of crises as objectively overdetermined, subjectively indeterminate moments in economic development; and discuss some of the ways in which social agents learn in, through, and from crises. These points are complemented by a discussion of the specificity of capitalist social relations and their crisis-tendencies. While cultural political economy applies the cultural turn, as its name implies, in the field of political economy, the general propositions and heuristic that inform its analysis can be applied elsewhere by combining them with concepts appropriate to other social forms, fields, institutional dynamics, and social practices. In this sense, their chapter is both a contribution to the critique of political economy that is compatible with much recent work in the sociology of finance and a more general contribution to the critical analysis of social relations and social dynamics, broadly understood.

Rooted in management studies, Eelke de Jong is mainly concerned about the possibility of miscommunication between people from different cultures/countries. In 'The Cultural View on Financial Markets', therefore, he presents cross-country comparisons with a definition of culture as a set of common values of a group that shapes individuals' beliefs and actions. These values are transmitted from generation to generation and, thus, are quite persistent. Language, education, and religion facilitate the transmission of values. Their persistence constitutes a deeper layer on which institutions are built. In other words their explanatory power is prior to and, therefore, contextualizes institutional approaches. While institutional approaches are said to implicitly assume that formal institutions lead to a particular behaviour, according to de Jong, the underlying value system drives the behaviour of the economic actors.

For measuring the impact of a country's culture on the institutional form of its financial system, de Jong operationalizes culture on the six well-known cultural dimensions of Geert Hofstede: individualism versus collectivism, uncertainty avoidance, masculinity versus femininity, power distance, long-term orientation, and indulgence versus restraint. His econometric tests make use of extensive data sets. The results that he reports in 'The Cultural View on Financial Markets' show that most cultural dimensions significantly explain differences in the patterns and rhythms of stock market capitalization in Western countries for the 1990s. This effect wears thin in the first decade of this century. Instead, the institutional set-up of the pension system together with investors' behaviour explain cross-country variations in the financial system. The regression analysis reveals a national component in the non-rational, behavioural explanations of stock price movements. This national component is also visible if one compares the national origin of investors in one country. Foreign investors frequently misunderstand their counterparts as shown, for example, in the way that German investment banks took an AAA rating for American bonds at face value. He explains this behaviour in terms of the German culture of respect for rules.

The contribution by Amelie Kutter and Bob Jessop: 'Culture as Discursive Practice: Combining Cultural Political Economy and Discursive Political Studies in Investigations of the Financial Crisis' illustrates another approach to the cultural turn in the field of the political economy. For their part, they reject essentializing classifications of culture and the resulting stereotyping of reified national cultures.

A particularly useful aspect of this chapter, given the overall objectives of this volume, is the wide-ranging survey of alternative approaches to the analysis of culture. This said, the authors' framework builds on Cultural Political Economy as laid out in Chapter 1 by Sum and Jessop and complements it with insights drawn from the now well-established field of critical discourse analysis and from the emerging field of discourse policy studies. This framework conceptualizes the co-evolution and structural coupling of meaning-making and structuration in terms of the three generic processes of variation, selection, and retention. Of the four modes of selectivity involved in social evolution (structural, discursive, technological, and agential) involved in these processes, Kutter and Jessop focus on the discursive mode. Deploying critical discourse analysis, they explore the discursive genre of financial journalism and its structural, agential, and technological selectivities.

The authors combine (linguistic) critical discourse analysis and narrative policy studies to explain the specific approaches to crisis-management, such as the EU's prioritizing of Eurozone financial stability over recovery at the periphery. They examine the discursive strategies used to streamline and simplify crisis construals through privileged metanarratives and causal stories and the use of legitimation strategies to narrow down crisis construals and make some crisis-management proposals more persuasive and legitimate than others. Taking the example of editorials from the German business daily, *Handelsblatt*, the authors show how the financial press sought to frame and constrain the German government's response to the Eurozone crisis at a time (early 2010) when EU institutions were apparently embarking, hesitantly, on measures to address the crisis that seemed likely to contradict the Ordoliberal principles associated with post-war German economic and political practice. Three features of these texts are particularly interesting. The first is the role of the cautionary tale of the Greek crisis and the general economic policy lessons that the press drew from its specific (and less moralizing) narration of this crisis about the general need to reduce public debt and to redesign the regulatory aspects of Economic and Monetary Union. Second, *Handelsblatt* op-eds were typical of the editorial genre, presenting pointed commentary in tune with the paper's general editorial line. And, third, they took the form of policy advice, moving from problem-definition and problem-analysis to problem-solution. Enhanced by pleas to translate 'lesson-drawing' directly into policy, *Handelsblatt* journalists amplified and legitimized the view that policy-making should be conducted in a technocratic matter, finding a fix that responds to the (naturalized) logic of financial markets. In this sense, the form of discourse matters as much as basic content in the relative success of efforts to shape and guide official responses to financial crisis.

The second part of the book examines specific cultures of finance. It begins with the contribution entitled 'What Price Culture? Calculation, Commensuration, Contingency, and Authority in Financial Practices' by Oliver Kessler. This uses the LIBOR scandal, that is, the rigging of one of the main reference interest rates, the London Interbank Offered Rate (LIBOR), to illustrate the specifics of contemporary financial (and financialized) cultures. The scandal made visible the social dimensions of price determination. Prices are supposedly the main source or signal of information for market transactions. They are said to equilibrate supply and demand and, therefore, should emerge from the impersonal play of the forces of demand and supply. However, the scandal revealed that the daily determination of the LIBOR was not a snapshot of market activities at 11 o'clock, but the result of ties between bankers and brokers that reached beyond the mere professional interaction envisioned in textbooks. This rested on an entanglement of gifts, services, and favours. In the ensuing hearings in the House of Commons, culture served as a key concept to make sense of what happened. The question was whether the collusion among traders was typical of the culture in the participating banks or just actions of 'a few bad apples'. Whatever the merits of these alternative interpretations, Kessler observes that for one price in a market to be possible, an entire set of institutions, conventions, subjectivities, and rules must exist. Culture refers to the stabilization of the social context for prices to be formable. If the formation of prices is a matter of culture, how can one differentiate the financial culture from an industrial culture, as both operate on the basis of prices? To answer his own question Kessler introduces Patrik Aspers' differentiation between standard markets and status markets. In a standard market, the scale of valuation is set and the market participants orient themselves primarily to this standard. In contrast, in the status market, valuation is not independent of the actors' status. The price of the traded commodity or service will reflect the status of the market participants. As the prices of banking (interest rates and fees) are based on a network of personal ties, calculative practices, and the status of the actors, financial markets, according to Kessler, correspond more to status than to standard markets. This has ramifications for attempts to regulate financial activities. Actors will interpret the rules according to the 'imperatives of the culture', that is, their own particular way of sense-making. Regulation will achieve little, if it does not account for the specific culture. This implies that calculative practices of organizations need to be subject to regulation. This calls for regulators to become experts in this field, to acquire not only knowledge about the technical issues, but also about the social 'fabric' that characterizes the market. This makes the regulators part of the field, however, and thereby limits their ability to rein in finance.

While Kessler discovers signs of a collusive culture in the City of London (as an international centre for international finance), the dominant discourse in British politics and the business press sees it as one site of the culture of entrepreneurship that is necessary to competitiveness and needs nurturing throughout the UK economy. In their contribution 'Financialization and the Enterprise Decoy', Charlie Dannreuther and Lew Perren analyse how the term entrepreneur has been used to pave the way for major financial reforms since the 1980s in the UK and has been invoked again after the crisis to justify risky financial behaviour. Making use of discourse analysis, they highlight the function of the term entrepreneurship as a floating signifier with no intrinsic relation between actual economic praxis and what is signified as entrepreneurial. Drawing on a longitudinal study of meanings associated with the entrepreneurial sign in debates in the United Kingdom Parliament, they can show how the denotation and connotations of the entrepreneur changed over time. The shifting usages of the term reveal how the sign of the entrepreneur diverted political attention from the social and political tensions generated by financialization and direct it towards the promotion of entrepreneurship as a multipurpose 'Swiss Army knife' that could solve the complex demands of policy-making. The entrepreneurial signifier, Dannreuther and Perren argue, could be used to coordinate a wide range of political actions. Its promotion legitimized the deregulation of financial activities, which in turn fostered financialization. Concrete measures to increase financial access for small entrepreneurs, such as the promotion of short-term venture capital or small firm credit scoring, however, failed to realize their objective. Instead it led to abuses of privileged information by banks in their lending decisions and encouraged speculative finance into new areas. Thus the term enterprise works as a decoy and not as an adequate description of the culture and practice of British banking.

Whereas Kessler's analysis is more synchronic, distinguishing economic cultures in terms of enduring differences in the mechanisms for price formation, Raphaële Chappe, Edward Nell, and Willi Semmler focus on changes in financial culture in the United States over the post-war period. Their contribution 'Booms, Busts and the Culture of Risk' identifies a shift from a culture of trust in banking to a culture of risk where uncertainty is considered to be manageable to the extent that it can be transformed into calculable risks. Like de Jong, they define culture as a set of commonly shared attitudes; however, unlike de Jong, they see culture as a process that varies over time rather than treating it as a deeper, change-resistant layer of values. The new culture of risk consists of a reckless attitude towards risk-taking and is manifested in overconfidence, a sense of entitlement to excessive compensation, a focus on the short term, and a reliance on models of risk management that are seriously flawed. This culture emerged in the wake of deregulation and globalization and played a critical role in the recent financial crisis by exacerbating the mechanisms of boom-bust cycles.

Since a microeconomic level analysis fails to explain the formation of preferences that underlie the decision-making of key financial actors, the authors prefer to analyse decision-making in finance at the meso level, that is, at the level of context and structure that predetermines the way choices are made. This is where Chappe, Nell, and Semmler locate culture. At the macro level they work out the links between the financial crisis and macroeconomic trends. Structural changes in the financial sector, especially increasing international competition and the rise of unregulated alternative investment vehicles such as private equity firms and hedge funds, changed the culture of investment banking. Traditionally, investment banking had been relationship-driven but, as corporate clients made use of the increased competition to diversify sources of investment, financial services, and advice, it became more transaction-driven. The investment banks compensated for the loss of income by engaging more in proprietary trading financed by high levels of debt. This was accompanied by a change in the organizational structure of investment banking. The traditional partnership-type organizational structure was based on trust, loyalty, and little employee mobility between firms. In the new era, investment banks took on the corporate organizational form and competed for professional staff, which changed the forms of compensation. It also transformed the financial image that actors sought to convey of themselves from trustworthy and prudent stewards of other people's money to guides to wealth. In effect, they became gamblers. This culture was reinforced on the one hand by increased competition and on the other hand by a lack of economic penalty thanks to government bailouts and, we might add, the decision not to prosecute those responsible for fraud or failure. The current reforms have yet to provide a structure that disincentivizes this risk-taking culture.

Part III, titled 'Cultural Factors in Financial Crisis Generation', takes a critical look at economic imaginaries. It starts with an account of the succession of economic imaginaries oriented to the pursuit of financial stability. The following two contributions focus on contemporary imaginaries. The first one criticizes a popular academic classification of capitalist societies, the Varieties of Capitalism approach, mainly on the basis of its misconception of the role of finance in the respective types of capitalism. The second criticizes this approach for its neglect of agency and moves on to highlight the roles of imaginaries in processes of companies' interest formation.

Brigitte Young provides a historical perspective on economic imaginaries in her contribution, titled 'Financial Stability and Technological Fixes as Imaginaries across Phases of Capitalism'. She identifies four successive economic imaginaries that are each closely articulated and intertwined with distinctive monetary, fisco-financial, and political understandings and practices. These imaginaries are: the nineteenth-century gold standard with its deflationary bias, which eventually broke down in the interwar period; the State Keynesianism associated with postwar Atlantic Fordism with its stagflationary bias and associated crises in public debt, which broke down in the 1970s; the rise of monetarism in the 1970s and 1980s with its focus on reducing public debt and public spending more generally – which was succeeded by privatized Keynesianism and reliance on private debt from the 1990s onwards to maintain a finance-led growth regime premised on deregulated and innovative financial markets embedded in a financialized neoliberal society. These different imaginaries represent four contrasting hegemonic meaning systems that, in their different ways, anticipated and adumbrated future economic shifts that served to guide business and political leaders and to create subjects whose identities and redefined interests would fit the new logic of capitalist accumulation. In each case the author describes briefly the genesis and key features of the economic imaginary, its leading financial contradiction, its effects in successive historical crisis situations, and the efforts made to transcend these crises by promoting new imaginaries along with the interests of those who promote it.

In addition to its concern with the specificities of each economic imaginary and how it was eventually embedded, at least for a time, in a relatively stable economic and political order, the author also identifies the technological supports and innovative practices that helped to consolidate and extend the imaginary.

Indeed, constructing these new meaning systems was based on the irrational praise of technological fixes that would in different historical conjunctures ensure financial stability. Moreover, as different as these economic and financial imaginaries were, they had in common the unshakable belief that technological innovations can provide once and for all the conditions for financial stability.

In their contribution, titled 'Varieties of Capitalism: Beyond Simple Dichotomies', Stefan Beck and Christoph Scherrer focus on a typology that is popular in comparative political economy: the liberal and coordinated market economies of the Varieties of Capitalism approach popularized by Peter Hall and David Soskice. The concept of Varieties of Capitalism has challenged mainstream economics by a differentiated view of capitalist economies. Its great strength lies in making visible the compatibility between these two different forms of capitalism. Despite the alleged homogenizing force of globalization, the two forms can coexist because their institutional settings reflect the historically evolved specialization in the product and service markets. However, from a cultural political economy perspective the approach comes with some fundamental limitations that are mainly the result of its reductionist way of making sense of the complex, dynamic interactions among territorially defined economic spaces. Its dichotomous ideal types are a-historic, static, and, especially in the case of the liberal market economies modelled according to their self-representation but not to real-life practices. Beck and Scherrer argue that the Varieties of Capitalism typology does not take sufficient account of the evolution of these variants of capitalism with the result that it over-emphasizes differences between the banking systems of the coordinated and the liberal market economies. It also overlooks functional equivalencies in the respective financial systems, such as public loan guarantees instead of public banks.

Beck and Scherrer also challenge the common claim in the Varieties of Capitalism literature that financialization emanated from the liberal market economies. Taking the United States and Germany as exemplars of the two main variants of capitalism, they show that the financialization of the liberal market economies was brought about not least by strong competition of companies headquartered in the coordinated market economies. Furthermore, the financial system of the liberal market economy was ascribed attributes such as transparency and the diversification of risk, which are not empirically recognizable. Market-based systems exhibit a distinct lack of transparency, a high concentration of risk, and liquidity squeezes due to the oligopolistic character of financial markets. The Varieties of Capitalism literature of the Hall and Soskice variant have uncritically adopted the imaginaries guiding the protagonists of so-called free markets. Beck and Scherrer conclude that the reduction of global capitalism to two ideal types, centring social strategies on production firms, assuming a one-dimensional rationality, and taking national boundaries for granted, fails to capture the dynamics of the two ideal types. It also neglects the interplay of more or less universal dynamics resulting from prevalent basic capitalist relations and the variety in not always nation-centred business and political cultures.

Daniel Mügge's chapter titled 'Competitive Concerns and Imaginaries in the Liberalization of European Finance' combines the two themes of the previous contributions: a critique of the Varieties of Capitalism approach and the role of imaginaries. He criticizes the Varieties of Capitalism approach for neglecting the agency of economic actors in bringing about change in the respective types of capitalism. He points out that economic actors operate at different scales and that, therefore, not all actors are exposed to international competition. In addition, changes are not just forced upon the specific type of capitalism from the outside – internal actors may also push for reforms.

These internal change-agents, however, are not driven by some pre-given objective interests since it is uncertain what their interests are and whether what looks to be in their short-term interest is also good in the long term. Therefore, their motivation might be better explained by the way they make sense of their particular position in the context of competition. Mügge argues that the firms' regulatory preferences are strongly inspired by imaginaries, by commonly shared narratives about what the future will hold. They help in reducing complexity. These imaginaries give guidance about the most relevant trends to which business and political strategies should be adapted. Taking two contrasting examples of coordinated market economies, France and Germany, he shows that major financial firms and policymakers took their cue for financial market policy preferences and policies from narratives such as 'the inevitable rise of investment banking', 'the dissolution of national financial markets', 'the need for global presence in order to survive', or 'finance as engine of growth'. Not all of these imaginaries proved correct. The unexpected outcomes underline that the financial players were attempting to pursue their interests on an unknown terrain – making it essential for them to work with imaginaries that reduced complexity and served as guides for the interest formation as a basis for their ability to 'go on' in a complex, uncertain economic and political world.

Part IV highlights the role of economic imaginaries and modes of financial calculations for crisis dynamics. Horacio Ortiz picks up the concept of imaginaries but shows that imaginaries not only guide actors' preference formation but can also be strategically used. In his contribution, entitled 'Hedge Funds and the Limits of Market Efficiency as a Regulatory Concept', he takes the self-image of hedge funds as an example. Hedge funds convey an image of independence. They are supposed to be run by gifted individuals who must be left free to choose their investment strategy and change it according to their reading of the market. However, as Ortiz shows, most hedge funds are either owned by institutional investors or handle institutional investors' money under close monitoring. While the image of the lone sagacious investor serves to keep the regulators away, the discrepancy between the image and the demands of institutional investors' bureaucratic procedures presents hedge funds managers with a dilemma. As the author was able to observe at first-hand, hedge fund professionals seeking to attract money for their investment strategies are forced to struggle with contradictory expectations. On the one hand, they have to stick to the myth of independence, the myth of being able to beat the market. On the other hand they are not allowed to claim that markets are not efficient because this would not only conflict with the conventional wisdom at the time (which may still hold) but also with the expectations of their potential clients, who, for monitoring purposes, favoured investment strategies based on mathematical models that are premised on the efficient market hypothesis. However, after the financial crisis, the hedge fund managers observed in this case study engaged in the intellectual challenge of relating their own strategy to these expectations learnt that the institutional investors had now started to favour fundamental analysis. The author enriches our understanding of imaginaries. They can guide actors' preference formation and actions, they can be used strategically for maintaining autonomy, but they can also come into conflict with other prevalent imaginaries and lead to confusion.

An even greater emphasis on strategic behaviour is seen in the contribution by Andrea Lagna. His contribution 'Derivatives as Weapons of Mass Deception and Elite Contestation: The Case of FIAT' criticizes the social studies of finance school for the neglect of active agency. While he acknowledges that the ethnographic studies of this school have uncovered the role of conventional habits and discourses for the constitution of financial markets, he points out that they overlook the strategic environment in which actors experience their existence as well as the power differentials which mark this environment. Taking a cue from political Marxism and critical institutionalism Lagna, through the example of the modernization of Italian finance, shows the fruitfulness of combining an analysis of the role of imaginaries for institutional change with an analysis of strategic behaviour directed at subverting these changes for one's own gains.

The post-war Italian economic system was characterized by an alliance of private business oligarchies and expanding public enterprises. In 1996, inspired by the imaginary of market-oriented strategies of modernization, a coalition of pro-market technocrats and left-leaning politicians attempted to break this traditional structure by introducing financial market reforms. One especially effective tool in this campaign was expected to be the strengthening of the rights of minority shareholders. It was aimed at limiting cross shareholding practices that block-holders traditionally used to consolidate and enforce their relations of mutual trust. What was intended to constrain business oligarchies, however, turned out, as the case study demonstrates, to enable one particularly powerful industrial family, the Agnellis, to stay in control at the car manufacturer (FIAT) in the middle of a crisis. The deregulation of the financial market made the financial instrument of stock swaps available to investors in Italy. By making clever but not completely lawful use of swaps, the Agnellis stayed owners and controllers of FIAT.

In a further exploration of financial imaginaries and their translation into practice, Ngai-Ling Sum's chapter applies a CPE approach to discourses on the 'BRIC' countries (Brazil, Russia, India, and China). This acronym was coined in 2001 by Jim O'Neill – then Chief Economist at Goldman Sachs – and is an excellent example of how a series of economic and financial imaginaries can be condensed into a powerful signifier that gives sense and meaning to a changing

– and uncertain – global conjuncture. The author first identifies some key questions from a CPE entry-point regarding the construction of economic imaginaries. She then examines the role of (trans-)national forces in making and remaking the 'BRIC' as a 'growth' and 'hope' object and notes how the resonance of this imaginary depends not only on trends in the financial and real economies but also on specific discourses, practices, and knowledging technologies. The 'BRIC' discourses were recontextualized in the Sinophone world as 'four golden brick countries' to signify 'strength' and 'greatness at last' and the author shows how China, as one of the major 'golden bricks', was eager to showcase its strength after the outbreak of the 2007 financial crisis and its repercussions on China's economic performance. In particular, a vast stimulus package has posed tremendous fiscal challenges, especially to its regional-local authorities, which increasingly rely on land as collateral for loans and as a source of revenue. This intensified land-based accumulation and inflated the 'property bubble', with severe impacts on subaltern classes and groups. The chapter concludes by noting new economic imaginaries for emerging markets that have been proposed in the light of the declining economic performance of the 'BRIC' economies. Overall, it illustrates powerfully the construction of economic imaginaries, the role of discursive, technological, and agential selectivities in selecting and retaining some among many competing imaginaries, their mobilization and recontextualization for diverse economic and political purposes in different conjunctures and spatial contexts, their translation into economic and political strategies and policies, and, finally, the ways in which these in turn generate resistance, in this instance, at the local level.

The last part of the book 'Crisis Construals and Responses to Financial Crisis in Europe' explores the European Central Bank's meaning-making frames for its responses to the financial crisis. In line with his introductory chapter on different financial cultures among developed market economies, Eelke de Jong together with Femke van Esch develop this approach in their contribution 'Culture Matters: French-German Conflicts on European Central Bank Independence and Crisis Resolution'. They test the extent to which the conflict within the European Central Bank (ECB) between France and Germany about the bank's crisis policies can be traced to their different political cultures. Employing the same operationalization of national culture (especially the different attitudes about 'Power Distance', i.e. the levels of accepted inequalities), they are able to confirm that there is a fit between the expected position of these countries' representatives based on their respective political culture and the actual positions that they express in official speeches.

In addition, they develop a new method for identifying whether the actual representatives express merely the interests of their governments (even though they are formally independent after having been nominated to their positions on the board of the ECB) or whether their respective position is in line with their government because of a shared culture. For this, they employ the technique of comparative cognitive mapping. A cognitive map on the basis of public speeches, statements, or writings enables the systematic qualitative and quantitative comparison of their leaders' beliefs. This mapping for the German former president of the Bundesbank, Axel Weber, and the French former president of the ECB, Jean-Claude Trichet, reveals that the cognitive maps of these two leaders correspond with the hypotheses as derived from national culture. The authors take this as evidence in support of their claim that cultural differences were at the root of the conflicts on the ECB's board.

In the next chapter, Mathis Heinrich and Bob Jessop write on crisis construals and the power of construal in the EU crisis. Building on CPE, they distinguish between interpretive power and interpretive authority, the former indicating the capacity to construe crises and propose solutions and the latter denoting the formal authority to translate crisis construals into specific crisis-management policies. This distinction matters when it comes to the right to declare a state of economic emergency and undertake emergency measures as part of the overall crisis response. Before illustrating the relevance of their CPE approach, the authors sketch the necessary background to the crisis in the political economy of the European Union within a world market context. They note the increasing heterogeneity in the varieties of capitalism in the European Union, the divergence in growth dynamics and economic competitiveness, and the constraints on economic adjustment imposed by Economic and Monetary Union. These conflicts can be traced back to divergences between the national accumulation regimes, modes of regulation, social power constellations and economic imaginaries within the EU, the ambiguities of the euro as a master and negotiated currency in the world market, and the interests of different fractions of capital within and beyond European economic space. They also distinguish the economic strategies corresponding to profit-producing (industrial) and interest-bearing capital and the tensions rooted in. All of these factors are reflected in rival narratives about the nature of the crisis in the Eurozone and appropriate crisis-management strategies.

The authors explore crisis interpretations and policy initiatives in three areas: (1) the European rescue and guarantee measures for member states with serious payment difficulties; (2) the ECB's monetary policy and the non-standard measures it has taken to address the crisis; and (3) reforms of European governance structures concerned with tightening fiscal discipline and boosting global competitiveness by reducing macroeconomic imbalances. Although various measures have been implemented, they have reproduced and reinforced a crisis of crisis management. Heinrich and Jessop also remark how the crisis has reinforced previous economic and political patterns and policies, notably, the Lisbon Agenda strategy and the emphasis on measures to boost national and regional competitiveness. An important conclusion of this CPE-inspired analysis of the euro crisis is that the limits on effective crisis management can be traced back to selective interpretation patterns of an imagined economic world as well as to the more obvious differential power of specific economic interests.

Finally, Daniela Gabor and Bob Jessop, in 'Mark my Words: Discursive Central Banking in Crisis', apply a version of CPE, which is inspired in part by Karl Niebyl's history of monetary theory, to economic imaginaries that have shaped monetary policy. They consider the 'New Keynesian' consensus during the 'Great Moderation' (itself an 'imagined' phase of economic development); the disorientation produced therein by the unexpected and massive North Atlantic Financial Crisis and its repercussions in the Eurozone; the resort to non-standard monetary measures in the resulting 'state of economic emergency'; and, lately, the efforts to find exit strategies to enable a return to New Keynesian 'business as usual' despite the new and massive role of state-produced 'collateral' in recent efforts at crisis-management. Of particular interest is that central banks act as if they see their task in discursive terms, that is, to confirm dominant economic imaginaries, maintain a shared economic imaginary among key market actors (creating an 'epistemic community'), stabilize the expectations of banks and governments in a world of radical uncertainty, and restore confidence during (inherently temporary) periods of crisis.

Indeed, Gabor and Jessop remark that the crisis reveals that central banking is not a technocratic exercise but deeply political and ideological. The crisis produced a new set of emergency measures that have since posed problems about how to return to pre-crisis 'business as usual' central banking practices based on the narrative and institutional re-instatement of the efficient market hypothesis. This is complicated by the development of collateralized finance, which has progressively undermined the authority and policy instruments of central banks. Previously relying on interest rate policy, the central bank resort to outright monetary purchases suggests that it is willing in extremis to stand ready to intervene in sovereign bond markets to reassure markets when worries about public debt threaten collateral-driven demand. Interestingly, despite the crucial role of these new practices, central banks hardly mention collateral-based finance in their narratives because this would challenge the conventional narrative. In addition, crisis narratives blame failures of regulation rather than economic policies or financialization and marginalize the extent to which central banks have taken exceptional measures to restore finance-dominated accumulation. This helps to prepare the return to business as usual. The key lesson that emerges from this analysis is that the integration of the analysis of economic imaginaries and discursive practices with conventional economic analysis reveals the extent to which policies are contested and contingent, linking struggles over the construction of the 'crisis' and its 'solutions' to configurations of power and interest groups in policy spaces. In short, as the CPE approach suggests, economic sense- and meaning-making, economic policy, and economic reality are mutually constitutive.

As a brief conclusion to what has proved to be a long introduction, we would like to remind our readers that highlighting the significance of sense- and meaning-making, the role of economic imaginaries, or the specificities of economic cultures or sub-cultures to the analysis of finance, financial institutions, and financial practices is not the same as claiming that the cultural turn is the only valid approach to financial matters or, less vaingloriously, that the cultural turn is always the best starting point for analysing such issues. It is an argument that financial affairs cannot be adequately interpreted and explained without regard to themes, methods, and substantive claims posed in recent decades by the cultural turn. But, as the proof of the pudding is in the eating, we now invite our readers to test the wares prepared in the cultural turn kitchen by sampling the following chapters or partaking in the whole feast.

Notes

1 Coates explores testosterone levels in traders and their role in the over-reaching of hyper-successful traders, leading to exceptional losses. More broadly, and for our purposes, more importantly, the re-signification of the essentializing 'myth' prompted more research on gendered differences – or lack thereof – in board room behaviour. There is also important research on the gendered impact of the crisis and crisis-management measures, especially austerity but these generally reflect a 'gender turn' rather than explicitly 'cultural turn' in economic analysis.
2 We offer apologies in advance, therefore, to those whose work we neglect that would otherwise claim a prominent position in any survey of the broader fields of economics and culture or culture and economics.

References

Adkins, L. (2011) Practice as temporalisation: Bourdieu and economic crisis, in S. Susen and B.S. Turner (eds), *The Legacy of Pierre Bourdieu*, London: Anthem Press.

Aitken, R. (2007) *Performing Capital: Toward a Cultural Economy of Popular and Global Finance*, Basingstoke: Macmillan.

Amato, M., Doria, L., and Fantacci, L. (eds) (2010) *Money and Calculation: Economic and Sociological Perspectives*, Basingstoke: Palgrave Macmillan.

Amin, A. and Thrift, N. (2004) Introduction, in idem (eds), *The Blackwell Cultural Economy Reader*, Oxford: Blackwell.

Babe, R.E. (2009) *Cultural Studies and Political Economy: Toward a New Integration*, Oxford: Lexington Books.

Bachmann-Medick, D. (2006) *Cultural Turns: Neuorientierungen in den Kulturwissenschaften*, Reinbeck bei Hamburg: Rowolt.

Best, J. and Paterson, M. (2010) Understanding Cultural Political Economy, in idem (eds), *Cultural Political Economy*, London: Routledge.

Beugelsdijk, S. and Maseland, R. (2011) *Culture in Economics: History, Methodological Reflections, and Contemporary Applications*, Cambridge: Cambridge University Press.

Blaney, D. and Inayatullah, N. (2010) Undressing the wound of wealth, in J. Best and M. Paterson (eds), *Cultural Political Economy*, London: Routledge.

Boltanski, L. and Chiapello, E. (1999) *Le nouvel ésprit du capitalisme*, Paris: Gallimard.

Bourdieu, P (2005) *The Social Structures of the Economy*, Cambridge: Polity.

Callon, M. (ed.) (1998) *The Laws of the Market*, Oxford: Blackwell.

Camic, C. and Hodgson, G.M. (eds) (2013) *Essential Writings of Thorstein Veblen*, London: Routledge.

Coates, J. (2012) *The Hour between the Dog and the Wolf: Risk Taking, Gut Feelings, and the Biology of Boom and Bust*, London: Penguin.

De Goede, M. (2005) *Virtue, Fortune, and Faith: A Genealogy of Finance*, Minneapolis: University of Minnesota Press.

De Jong, E. (2009) *Culture and Economics. On Values, Economics and International Business*, London: Routledge.

Du Gay, P. and Pryke, M. (eds) (2002) *Cultural Economy: Cultural Analysis and Commercial Life*, London: SAGE.

Fairclough, N. (2003) *Language and Power in Social Life*, Harlow: Longman.

Fairclough, N., Jessop, B., and Sayer, A. (2004) Critical realism and semologic, in J.M. Roberts and J. Joseph (eds), *Realism, Discourse and Deconstruction*, London: Routledge.

Foucault, M. (2008a) *Security, Territory, Population, Lectures at the Collège de France, 1977–1978*, Basingstoke: Palgrave.

Foucault, M. (2008b) *The Birth of Biopolitics: Lectures at the Collège de France, 1978–1979*, Basingstoke: Palgrave.

Fourcade, M. (2007) Theories of markets and theories of society, *American Behavioral Scientist*, 50(8): 1015–34.

Fourcade, M. (2009) *Economists and Societies: Discipline and Profession in the United States, Britain and France, 1890s–1990s*, Princeton: Princeton University Press.

Froud, J. and Williams, K. (2007) Private equity and the culture of value extraction, *New Political Economy*, 12(3): 405–20.

Hobson, J.M. and Seabrooke, L. (eds) (2007) *Everyday Politics of the World Economy*, Cambridge: Cambridge University Press.

Hoppe, R. (2007) Applied cultural theory: tool for policy analysis, in F. Fischer, G.J. Miller, and M.S. Sidney (eds), *Handbook of Public Policy Analysis*, Boca Raton, FL: CRC Press.

Jessop, B. and Sum, N.L. (2006) *Beyond the Regulation Approach: Putting the Capitalist Economy in its Place*, Cheltenham: Edward Elgar.

Kristof, N.D. (2010) 'Mistresses of the Universe', *New York Times*, 7 February.

Lagarde, C. (2010) What if it had been Lehman Sisters? *International Herald Tribune*, 11 May. http://dealbook.nytimes.com/2010/05/11/lagarde-what-if-it-had-been-lehman-sisters/.

Langley, P. (2008) *The Everyday Life of Global Finance*, Oxford: Oxford University Press.

McCloskey, D.N. (1998) *The Rhetoric of Economics*, 2nd edn. Madison: University of Wisconsin Press.

McDowell, L. (1997) *Capital Culture: Gender at Work in the City*, Oxford: Blackwell.

McDowell, L (2010) Capital culture revisited, *International Journal of Urban and Regional Research*, 34: 652–8.

McDowell, L. (2011) Making a drama out of a crisis: representing financial failure, or a tragedy in five acts, *Transactions of the Institute of British Geographers*, 36(2): 193–205.

MacKenzie, D.J. (2006) *An Engine, Not a Camera: How Financial Models Shape Markets*, Cambridge, MA: MIT Press.

MacKenzie, D.J., Muniesa, F. and Siu, L. (eds) (2007) *Do Economists Make Markets? On the Performativity of Economics*, Princeton: Princeton University Press.

Mirowski, P. (2002) *Machine Dreams: Economics Becomes a Cyborg Science*, Cambridge: Cambridge University Press.

Patterson, S. (2011) *The Quants: How a New Breed of Math Whizzes Conquered Wall Street and Nearly Destroyed It*, New York: Crown.

Potts, N. (2010) Surplus capital: the ultimate cause of the crisis?, *Critique*, 38(1): 35–49.

Prügl, E. (2012) 'If Lehman Brothers had been Lehman Sisters…': gender and myth in the aftermath of the financial crisis, *International Political Sociology*, 5(1): 21–35.

Ray, L. and Sayer, A. (eds) (1999) *Culture and Economy after the Cultural Turn*, London: SAGE.

Sayer, A. (2000) *Realism and Social Science*, London: SAGE.

Shionoya, Y. (ed.) (2001) *The German Historical School: The Historical and Ethical Approach to Economics*, London: Routledge.

Sum, N.L. and Jessop, B. (2013) *Toward a Cultural Political Economy: Putting Culture in its Place in Political Economy*, Cheltenham: Edward Elgar.

Swedberg, R. (2003) *Principles of Economic Sociology*, Princeton: Princeton University Press.

Tett, G. (2013) Central banking: still a man's world, *Financial Times*, 9 August.

Van de Water, M. (2007) Sponsoring of art and culture by banks in the Netherlands. A research into the motivations of Dutch banks to support the arts. MA Thesis, Faculty of History and Arts, Erasmus University Rotterdam. thesis.eur.nl/pub/.../Master%20 Thesis%20Maarten%20vd%20Water.pdf.

Zelizer, V. (1994) *The Social Meaning of Money*, Princeton: Princeton University Press.

Part I

Researching cultures of finance

Theoretical foundations and methods

1 Sense- and meaning-making in the critique of political economy

Ngai-Ling Sum and Bob Jessop

The introduction to this volume argued for the intellectual use-value of the cultural turn in political economy and, in particular, its relevance to the analysis of finance. This chapter introduces one distinctive approach to the cultural turn that affirms its crucial contribution to political economy but also insists on the continued importance of taking seriously the specificity of social relations and their emergent dynamic in the field of political economy. While cultural political economy (hereafter CPE) applies the cultural turn, as its name implies, in the field of political economy, the general propositions and heuristic that inform its analysis can be applied elsewhere by combining them with concepts appropriate to other social forms, fields, institutional dynamics, and social practices. Given the concern of this volume with cultures of finance, we focus on the role of semiosis, that is, sense- and meaning-making, in the organization of economic and political relations and provide some comments on their structural aspects.

Cultural political economy

CPE is a distinctive and still evolving approach in the humanities and social sciences that highlights the contribution of the cultural turn (a concern with semiosis considered as sense- and meaning-making) to the analysis of the economic and the political, their articulation, and their embedding in wider sets of social relations in capitalist social formations at different scales up to and including world society. It has six features that *together* distinguish it from other versions of CPE that address similar topics: (1) the grounding of its version of the cultural turn, that is, its interest in semiosis or meaning-making, in the existential necessity of complexity reduction; (2) its interest in the mechanisms that shape the movement from social *construal* to social *construction* and their implications for the production and contestation of social relations of domination and hegemony; (3) its concern with the interdependence and co-evolution of the semiotic and extra-semiotic in general and in specific contexts and conjunctures; (4) its integration of individual, organizational, and societal learning into the dialectic of semiosis and structuration and, by extension, of path-shaping and path-dependency; (5) its analysis of the role of technologies, in a broadly Foucauldian sense, in shaping domination and hegemony; and (6) its de-naturalization of social imaginaries as part of a broader *Ideologie-* and *Hegemoniekritik*. This chapter focuses on themes one to four, with the first and third meriting most attention (for extended analysis of all themes, see Sum and Jessop 2013).

The editors' introduction identified four types of cultural turn: thematic, methodological, ontological, and reflexive. The present authors identify mainly with the third and fourth. We do not confine CPE to the study of 'cultural' topics in political economy (for example, the economics of art markets, the creative industries, professional culture, the cultural influence of the mass media, the culturalization of the economy or economization of culture); nor do we argue that social scientific investigation should generally begin with meaning-making (for example, by starting with the analysis of discourse and discursive practices) as opposed to another entry-point (such as social structure or individual or collective agency). Rather we argue that, whether one starts with meaning-making or another analytical entry-point, an adequate explanation of political economy dynamics must *sooner or later* integrate semiosis into the analysis because intersubjective meaning-making is foundational to social practice. And, in terms of reflexivity, our approach not only critiques the categories and methods of orthodox political economy but also emphasizes the contextuality and historicity of its claims to knowledge. The North Atlantic Financial Crisis (or NAFC) illustrates this well as it casts doubt on (and should also prompt self-doubt about) orthodox economics and neo-liberal views of the self-regulating market. It follows that a self-consistent CPE calls for reflexivity on the part of social scientists about the conditions of their own practices. In this sense, CPE does not seek to add 'culture' to economics and politics as if each comprised a distinct area of social life and, *a fortiori*, entailed distinct objects for theoretical and empirical analysis that might then be explored in terms of their external interactions or mutual conditioning in specific situations.

Instead, arguing that all social phenomena have both semiotic and material properties, CPE studies their interconnections and co-evolution in structuring as well as construing social relations. Accordingly CPE aims to steer a path between two complementary theoretical temptations: 'hard political economy' and 'soft cultural economics'. We refer to these for the sake of alliteration as well as contrast as the structuralist Scylla and constructivist Charybdis of political economy (for a summary, see Table 1.1). While the former reifies formal, market-rational, calculative activities and analyses them apart from their discursive significance and broader extra-economic context and supports, the latter subsumes economic activities under broad generalizations about social and cultural life (especially their inevitably semiotic character). Hard political economy tends to establish a rigid demarcation between the economic and the cultural, reifying economic objects, naturalizing *homo economicus*, and proposing rigid economic laws. At best, therefore, culture is regarded merely as an optional supplement in political economic analysis. At its most extreme, this leads to universalizing, transhistorical claims valid for all forms of material (or 'economic') provisioning. This is common in mainstream economics premised on reified and naturalized universal categories and rationalities as well as in orthodox Marxism

Table 1.1 Constructivist Charybdis and structuralist Scylla

Constructivist Charybdis	Structuralist Scylla
Grasps the semiotic-material construction of social relations, reveals their social embedding, and notes the performative impact of semiosis	Grasps the *distinctiveness* of specific economic categories, forms, and social relations and their structured/structuring nature in wider social formations
But finds it hard to define specificity of economic relations vis-à-vis other relations – because they are all equally discursive in character	But reifies such categories, regards economic structures as natural, and views agents as mere *Träger* (passive bearers) of economic logics
Strong risk of idealism, defining economic relations in terms of their manifest *semiotic content*	Strong risk of economic determinism, explaining economic processes in terms of *'iron laws'*
'Soft Economic Sociology'	*'Hard Political Economy'*

with its essentialization of 'iron' economic laws. In other cases, mainstream economics tends to separate economizing activities from their extra-economic supports, to regard the economy as a self-reproducing, self-expanding system with its own laws, and to provide thereby the theoretical underpinnings for economic reductionism. This leads to thin accounts of how subjects and subjectivities are formed and how different modes of calculation emerge, come to be institutionalized, and get modified. In contrast, CPE follows critical political economists and, curiously, actor-network theory, in regarding capital not as a thing but as 'a social relation between persons, established by the instrumentality of things' (Marx 1967: 717). CPE interprets the latter broadly to include not only natural resources, tools and machines, commodities, and so on, but also social resources, discursive practices, social technologies, organizational forms, and the like. For technical and economic objects are always socially constructed, historically specific, more or less socially embedded in – or disembedded from – broader networks of social relations and institutional ensembles, more or less embodied and habituated in individuals, and more or less institutionalized and routinized in collective agencies.

The second temptation is the sociological imperialism of radical social constructivism, according to which social reality is reducible to participants' collectively created and reproduced meanings and understandings of their social world. Unfortunately, while such currents correctly reject a sharp division between the cultural and material and also stress the cultural dimensions of material life, they tend to lose sight of the specificity of economic forms, contradictions, institutions, and so on. This makes it hard to distinguish *in material terms* between capitalist and non-capitalist economic practices, institutions, and formations – they all become equally discursive and can only be differentiated through their respective semiotic practices, meanings, and contexts and their performative impact. This can lead to an arbitrary account of the social world that ignores the unacknowledged conditions of action as well as the many and varied emergent properties of action that go un- or mis-recognized by the relevant actors. It also ignores the many and varied struggles to transform the conditions of action, to alter actors' meanings and understandings, and to modify emergent properties (and their feedback effects on the social world).

In contrast to the tendency in cultural studies to neglect the specificity and logic of economic as opposed to other social categories, CPE aims to show how the economic field is socially constructed, acquires its specific emergent features and distinctive logic and dynamics, and remains vulnerable to disruption and dislocation. Moreover, in revealing the socially constructed nature of the phenomena of political economy, CPE involves a form of political intervention that goes beyond *Ideologiekritik*. The *latter* serves at best to reveal the immanent contradictions and inconsistencies in relatively coherent meaning systems, to uncover the ideal and material interests behind meaning systems and ideologies more generally, and to contribute to the re-politicization of sedimented, taken-for-granted discourses and practices. A rigorous pursuit of CPE would also explore the semiotic and extra-semiotic mechanisms involved in selecting and consolidating the dominance and/ or hegemony of some meaning systems and ideologies over others. This in turn offers more solid foundations to understand the nature of different forms of social domination and to critique them (*Herrschaftskritik*).

In offering a 'third way' CPE, as presented here and in the authors' individual chapters, emphasizes the importance of specific modes of material (or economic) provisioning and allocation and their associated economic forms, modes of calculation, social agents, and so forth. For us, it is especially important to consider the series of economic forms (the commodity form, money, wages, prices, property, and so on) associated with the capitalist mode of production. These have their own effects that must be analysed as such and that contribute to the selection and retention of competing economic imaginaries. In regard to the dynamics of financial crisis, for example, one must consider not only economic and financial imaginaries and their associated cultures but also the development of new money forms, functions, and changing currency pyramids and their articulation to finance capital, financialization, and finance-dominated accumulation.

In addition, as many theorists have noted in various contexts (and adherents of 'hard political economy' sometimes forget), the reproduction of the basic forms of the capital relation and their particular instantiation in different social formations cannot be secured purely through the objective logic of the market or a domination that operates 'behind the backs of the producers'. For capital's laws of motion are doubly tendential and depend on contingent social practices that extend well beyond what is from time to time construed and/or constructed as economic. CPE provides a corrective to these problems too. In part this comes from its emphasis on the constitutive material role of the extra-economic supports of market forces. But it also emphasizes how different economic imaginaries serve to demarcate economic from extra-economic activities, institutions, and orders and, hence, how semiosis is also constitutive in securing the conditions for capital accumulation.

Semiosis and structuration

The importance of semiosis and structuration are rooted in the hypercomplexity of social relations and the cognate importance of complexity reduction as a condition of social action. Indeed, the sum of all social activities (including interactions with nature) often verges on, or tips into, chaos. In contemporary conditions, where the ultimate horizon of social action is 'world society', this excludes any possibility that 'society' in its entirety can be observed in real time – or ever. This forces actors to engage in selective sense- and meaning-making based on discursively selective '*imaginaries*' and efforts at *structuration* that limit compossible combinations of social relations. Together these reduce the complexity that actors must handle – albeit at the price of neglecting other features of the natural and social worlds. We now address semiosis in terms of the role of imaginaries and will then discuss structuration in terms of compossibility.

An imaginary is a semiotic ensemble (or meaning system) that frames individual subjects' lived experience of an inordinately complex world and/or guides collective calculation about that world. There are many imaginaries and most are loosely bounded and have links to other imaginaries within the broad field of semiotic practices. They comprise a specific configuration of genres, discourses, and styles and thereby constitute the semiotic moment of a network of social practices in a given social field, institutional order, or wider social formation (Fairclough 2003). Genres are distinctive ways of acting and interacting viewed in their specifically semiotic aspect and, as such, they serve to regularize (inter) action. Examples include initial public offering documents, political party manifestos, and university mission statements. Discourses represent other social practices (and themselves too) together with relevant aspects of the material world from the vantage point of particular positions in the social world. Illustrations include particular economic discourses, such as mercantilism, liberalism, the 'social market economy', or revolutionary syndicalism. Styles are ways of being, identities in their specifically semiotic (as opposed to bodily/material) aspect. Two instances are the 'new' managerial style depicted by Boltanski and Chiapello (2007) and the flexible, entrepreneurial, risk-taking, self-responsible individual of advanced liberalism (Miller and Rose 2008). Genres, discourses, and styles are dialectically related. Thus discourses may be enacted as genres and inculcated as styles and, in addition, get externalized in a range of objective social and/or material facts (for example, nature as modified by human action, physical infrastructure, new technologies, and new institutional orders).

Imaginaries exist at different sites and scales of action – from individual agents to world society (Althusser 1977; Taylor 2003). Without them, individuals cannot 'go on' in the world and collective actors (such as organizations) could not relate to their environments, make decisions, or engage in strategic action. In this sense, imaginaries are an important semiotic moment of the network of social practices in a given social field, institutional order, or wider social formation (Fairclough 2003). Indeed, if social phenomena are discursively constituted, it is inherently improbably that they are ever fully constituted and continually reproduced through appropriate discursive and social practices. On the contrary, discursive relations are polysemic and heteroglossic, i.e. have alternative meanings and involve different voices and agents; subjectivities are plural and changeable, and extra-semiotic properties are liable to material disturbances as well as discursive transformation. For example, capitalist relations are always articulated with other production relations and are, at most, relatively dominant; moreover, their operation is always vulnerable to disruption through internal contradictions, the intrusion of relations anchored in other institutional orders and the lifeworld (civil society), and resistance rooted in conflicting interests, competing identities, and rival modes of calculation. Combined with critical political economy, critical semiotic analysis has much to offer in exploring this dynamic.

Discourses are most powerful where they operate across many sites and scales and can establish and connect local hegemonies into a more encompassing hegemonic project. These discourses will be *retained* (discursively reproduced, incorporated into individual routines, and institutionally embedded) when they are able to reorganize the balance of forces and guide supportive structural transformation. Although any given economic or political imaginary is only ever partially realized, those that succeed, at least in part, have their own performative, constitutive force in the material world – especially when they correspond to (or successfully shape) underlying material transformations, can mobilize different elites to form a new power bloc, can organize popular support, disorganize opposition, and marginalize resistance. In short, discourses and their related discursive chains can generate variation, have selective effects – reinforcing some discourses, filtering others out – and contribute to the differential retention and/ or institutionalization of social relations through the recursive selection of certain imaginaries. In a complex world there are many sites and scales on which such processes operate. So it matters how local sites and scales come to be articulated to form more encompassing sites and scales and how the latter in turn frame, constrain, and enable local possibilities. These interrelations are themselves shaped by the ongoing interaction between semiotic and extra-semiotic processes. This poses intriguing questions about the articulation of micro-social diversity to produce relatively stable macro-social configurations (Jessop and Sum 2006).

A second aspect of complexity reduction concerns the emergent pattern of social interactions, including direct or indirect human interactions with the natural world. If these are not to be random, unpredictable, and chaotic, it is essential that possible connections and sequences of action are limited so that expectations are stabilized and patterns of action become institutionalized. Whereas structuration refers to a complex, contingent, tendential process that is mediated through action but produces results that no actors can be said to have willed, structure refers to the contingently necessary outcome of diverse structuration efforts. In this sense, structuration creates a complex assemblage of asymmetrical opportunities for social action, privileging some actors over others, some identities over others, some ideal and material interests over others, some spatio-temporal horizons of action over others, some coalition possibilities over others, some strategies over others, and so on. Structural constraints always operate selectively: they are not absolute and unconditional but always temporally, spatially, agency-, and strategy-specific. Conversely, to the extent that agents are reflexive, capable of reformulating within limits their own identities and interests, and able to engage in strategic calculation about their current situation, there is scope for strategic action to alter the strategic selectivity of current structural configurations and thereby modify strategically selective constraints (see Jessop 2007).

Where semiosis and structuration as forms of complexity reduction are complementary, they transform meaningless and unstructured complexity into meaningful and structured complexity (Glynos and Howarth 2007). The social and natural world becomes relatively meaningful and orderly for actors (and observers) in so far as not all *possible* social interactions are *compossible* in a given spatio-temporal matrix of time-space envelope. Many other meanings are thereby excluded and so are many other possible social worlds. This does not exclude competing imaginaries concerning different scales and fields of social action or, indeed, rival principles of societalization more generally. Because complexity reduction has both semiotic and structural aspects, we should treat the 'cultural' and the 'social' as dialectically related moments of the social world. Its cultural moment refers to sense- and meaning-making and the resulting properties of discursive formations (such as distinct discourses, genres, genre chains, styles, or inter-textuality) regardless of their condensation, or otherwise, in social structures. And its social moment concerns the extra-semiotic features of social practices and the resulting properties of social interaction (such as social cohesion and institutional integration, dilemmas and contradictions, and institutional logics) that operate 'behind the backs' of agents and may not correspond to their sense- and meaning-making efforts. The scope for disjunction and non-correspondence between the cultural and social moments makes it necessary to study both in their articulation.

Combining these arguments, our approach to CPE does not explain the selection of some meaning systems over others purely in intra-semiotic terms. It also refers to other forms of selectivity. Specifically, construal and construction have four interrelated aspects: semiosis, structuration, agency, and technologies. Their interaction is important in explaining how semiosis contributes to social construction. While the first three are fairly intuitive, technologies merit a brief comment. They include diverse social practices that are mediated through specific instruments of classification, registration, calculation, and so on, that may discipline social action (cf. Foucault 1975; Miller and Rose 2008). Technologies have a key role in the selection and retention of specific imaginaries in so far as they provide reference points not only in meaning-making but also in the coordination of actions within and across specific personal interactions, organizations and networks, and institutional orders. In this sense they are important meaning-making instruments deployed by agents to translate specific social construals into social construction and hence to structure social life. Relevant examples for present purposes include accounting practices, the construction and use of competitiveness indexes, techniques of securitization, regulatory practices, and other forms of economic governmentalization.

Another way to think about the movement from construal to construction is in terms of sedimentation. For present purposes, this covers all forms of routinization that lead, inter alia, to forgetting the contested origins of discourses, practices, processes, and structures. This gives them the form of objective facts of life. In turn, politicization covers challenges to such objectivation that aim to denaturalize the semiotic and material (extra-semiotic) features of what has been sedimented. In exploring the dialectic of sedimentation and re-politicization, CPE draws extensively on the concepts and tools of critical discourse analysis and critical political economy. Inter alia this helps to reveal that ideology is most effective when least visible rather than self-evidently manipulative or propagandistic (Fairclough 1989: 84–6). Finally, for the sake of clarity, we note that sedimentation and (re-)politicization are not confined to a specific 'political' domain (separate from other social domains) – they are contingent aspects of all social life (Glynos and Howarth 2007).

Imaginaries and their significance

Semiotic and structuring practices can be classified in terms of: (1) their system relevance; (2) their relation to spheres of life; (3) their spatio-temporal location and horizons of action; and (4) their associated types of social agency. Although presented sequentially, these features are intertwined. To explore them, we focus on economic imaginaries. In other contexts one might discuss other socially construed and/or constructed fields of practice, such as technology, economics, law, politics, education, science, or religion, and other aspects of the lifeworld, such as gender, sexual orientation, ethnicity, national identity, or generation. Indeed, nothing in our approach entails that the logic of capital accumulation determines the dominant mode of societal organization. This is a historically contingent question even where the capital relation is economically dominant – which is never guaranteed merely by the presence of capitalist relations of production. Different social forces mobilized behind other societal visions may contest the primacy of capital accumulation as a mode of societalization and seek to contain its role in the development of world society. Alternative logics include national security, religious fundamentalism, ecological sustainability, or democratic citizenship.

In this sense, in so far as the economy cannot be 'determinant in the last instance' but only more or less dominant within limits set by various institutional rivalries and the balance of social forces, the scope for the cultural turn in economics becomes even greater. One must then explain why capital accumulation could ever become the dominant principle of societal organization as well as specify the conditions under which this happens. This said, we should note at once that the economy is a historically constituted category with changing denotation and connotations and that its meaning is heavily contested (on its history as an economic category, see, for example, Burkhardt 1992; Fey 1936; Finley 1973; Foucault 2008; Marx 1963; Tribe 1978). Nonetheless its use simplifies a complex social world and has semiotic and material consequences in making sense of that world and organizing economic activities. In addition, through variation, selection, and retention, economic ideas may have a performative, constitutive force in shaping economic relations (see Callon 1998; MacKenzie *et al.*, 2007; Mirowski 1994; and, for a critique of performativity, Lagna, this volume).

First, system relevance concerns features of the social world grasped in terms of the emergent, tendential structured coherence of their instituted properties. This can be illustrated from economic imaginaries and their relation to imagined economies. CPE distinguishes the 'actually existing economy' as the chaotic sum of all economic activities (broadly defined as concerned with the social appropriation and transformation of nature for the purposes of material provisioning) from the 'economy' (or, better, 'economies' in the plural) as an imaginatively narrated, more or less coherent subset of these activities occurring within specific spatio-temporal frameworks. The totality of economic activities is so unstructured and complex that it cannot be an object of effective calculation, management, governance, or guidance. Instead such practices are always oriented to subsets of economic relations (economic systems, subsystems, or ensembles) that have been semiotically and, perhaps organizationally and institutionally, fixed as appropriate objects of intervention. Economic imaginaries have a crucial constitutive role in this regard in so far as they give meaning and shape to the 'economic' field. They identify, privilege, and seek to stabilize some economic activities from the totality of economic relations and transform them into objects of observation, calculation, and governance. The 'knowledge-based economy', for example, can be read as a distinctive semiotic order organized around and in support of a novel economic strategy, state project, and hegemonic vision (see Sum and Jessop 2013). The 'BRIC' imaginary (initially a hunch that Brazil, Russia, India, and China would become the new engine of economic growth in the first decades of the twentieth century) is another telling example because it guided economic strategies and had performative effects until the early 2010s (see Sum, this volume). But it is also clear that this imaginary was not a perfect 'self-fulfilling prophecy' but just one among several competing imaginaries that was obliged to face the audit of the world market. The dynamism of the BRIC economies has been influenced by crisis-management in the North Atlantic region, the contagion effects of the NAFC, and the flight to safety in the light of the anticipated tapering of quantitative easing in the USA – all of which have reinforced specific local and national economic crisis-tendencies in the BRIC economies themselves. In short, economic imaginaries give meaning and shape to the 'economic' field or aspects thereof and, as such, exclude elements – usually unintentionally – vital to the subsequent overall performance of the identified subset of economic (and extra-economic) relations.

Economic imaginaries are always selectively defined – due to limited cognitive capacities and to the discursive and material biases of specific epistemes and economic paradigms. They typically exclude elements – usually unintentionally – that are vital to the overall performance of the subset of economic (and extra-economic) relations that have been identified. Such exclusions limit in turn the efficacy of economic forecasting, management, planning, guidance, or governance, because such practices do not (indeed, cannot) take account of excluded elements and their impact. Moreover, if they are to prove more than 'arbitrary, rationalistic, and willed' (Gramsci 1971: 376–7), they must have some significant, albeit necessarily partial, correspondence to real material interdependencies in the actually existing economy and/or in the relations between economic and extra-economic activities. Conversely, where an imaginary is successfully operationalized and institutionalized, it transforms and naturalizes these elements and instrumentalities into the moments of a specific economy with specific emergent properties. This process is mediated through the interaction among specific economic imaginaries, appropriately supportive economic agents – individual or collective – with appropriate modes of calculation and behavioural or operational dispositions, specific technologies that sustain and confirm these imaginaries (for example, statistics, indexes, benchmarks, records), and structural constellations that limit the pursuit of contrary or antagonistic imaginaries, activities, or technologies.

When an imaginary is operationalized and institutionalized, it transforms and naturalizes the included elements as parts (moments) of a specific, instituted economy. An instituted economy comprises subsets of economic relations that have been organizationally and institutionally fixed as appropriate objects of observation, calculation, management, governance, or guidance. This process of institution (or structuration) sets limits to compossible combinations of social relations and thereby renders them more predictable and manageable as objects of social action. However, by virtue of competing economic imaginaries, competing efforts to institute them materially, and an inevitable incompleteness in the specification of their respective economic and extra-economic preconditions, each 'imagined economy' is only ever partially constituted. Moreover, there are always interstitial, residual, marginal, irrelevant, recalcitrant and plain contradictory semiotic and extra-semiotic elements that escape any attempt to identify, govern, and stabilize a given 'economic arrangement' or broader 'economic order'. These can disrupt the smooth performance of instituted economies and provide important sources of resistance. But, they also help preserve a reservoir of semiotic and material resources – sources of redundancy and flexibility – that enable dominant systems (through the agency of their associated social forces) to adapt to new challenges through their re-articulation and recombination in the service of power. Similar arguments would apply, with appropriate changes, to so-called meso- or micro-level economic phenomena, such as industrial districts or individual enterprises. The recursive selection of semiotic practices and extra-semiotic processes tends to secure the 'requisite variety' (constrained heterogeneity rather than simple uniformity) behind the structural coherence of economic activities.

Second, while many social activities are appropriately observed in terms of instituted systems and, indeed, some, such as the payment of taxes, could be ascribed to several systems, other social activities lack direct system relevance. This holds especially for activities that are not anchored in particular system logics but relate to other identities and interests that are transversal to these logics. Examples include the national and/or regional identity of an imagined community (Anderson 1983), gender and sexual orientation, socially constructed 'racial' identities, or the formation of political generations rooted in shared experiences. By virtue of this lack of direct system relevance, these could be referred to various spheres of life, the 'lifeworld' (broadly interpreted) or, again, to 'civil society' (as long as this is not equated with 'bourgeois' society). They may nonetheless acquire system-relevance through their articulation into the operation of system logics (for example, the use of gender to segment the labour force or the mobilization of 'racial' identities to justify educational exclusion). System-relevant and lifeworld imaginaries provide the basis for agential identities and interests, whether individual, group, movement, or organizational. Agents normally have multiple identities, privileging some over others in different contexts. This is the basis for social scientific interest in 'intersectionalism', that is, the effects of different combinations of system-relevant and 'lifeworld' identities.

Third, imagined economies (or their equivalents for other systems) are discursively constituted and materially reproduced on many sites and scales, in different spatio-temporal contexts, and over various spatio-temporal horizons. This is well illustrated in the chapter by Andrea Lagna (this volume), on the role of municipalities as well as national reformist governments in creating the financial crisis in Italy. Imaginaries inform economic phenomena from one-off transactions through stable economic organizations, networks, and clusters to 'macroeconomic' regimes. While there is often massive scope for variation in individual transactions, the medium- to long-term semiotic and material reproduction demands of meso-complexes and macroeconomic regimes narrow this scope considerably. Recursive selection of semiotic practices and extra-semiotic processes at these scales tends to reduce inappropriate variation and thereby secure the 'requisite variety' (constrained heterogeneity rather than simple uniformity) that supports the structural coherence of economic activities. Stable semiotic orders, discursive selectivities, social learning, path-dependencies, power relations, patterned complementarities, and material selectivities all become more significant, the more that material interdependencies and/or issues of spatial and intertemporal articulation increase within and across diverse functional systems and the lifeworld. Yet this growing set of constraints also reveals the fragility and, indeed, improbability of the smooth reproduction of complex social orders.

Fourth, the relation between semiotic and structuring practices can be classified in terms of their associated types of social agency. Everyone is involved in semiosis because meaning-making is the basis of lived experience. However, just as Gramsci observed that, while everyone is an intellectual, not everyone performs the function of an intellectual, we suggest there is no equality in individual contributions to meaning-making. Each system and the different spheres of the 'lifeworld' have their own semiotic divisions of labour that overlay, differentially draw on, and feed into lived experience. There are individuals and/or collective intellectuals (such as political parties and old and new social movements) who are particularly active in bridging these different systems and spheres of life and attempting to create hegemonic meaning systems or develop sub- or counter-hegemonic meaning systems. And, of course, increasingly, semiosis is heavily 'mediatized', that is, influenced by the mass media and social media. Given the diversity of systems and the plurality of identities in the 'lifeworld', one should not privilege *a priori* one type of social actor as the leading force in semiosis in general or in building hegemony in particular. Similar points hold for structuring practices to the extent that there are competing societalization principles and no *a priori* guarantee that one principle will dominate the others. Nonetheless, as a working hypothesis at the level of world society, a case can be made that the profit-oriented, market-mediated logic of differential capital accumulation is becoming more dominant as the world market has been increasingly integrated under the logic of neo-liberalism and, in particular, of finance-dominated accumulation.

Comments on learning

Semiosis as meaning-making does not fall from heaven. While actors are forced to reduce complexity through meaning-making as a condition of going on in the world, they are able, within limits, to modify meanings and interpretations in the light of individual lived experience, organizational learning, institutional experimentation, and macro-social change. In this context learning is an important aspect in the variation, selection, and retention of imaginaries and, hence, in the changing relation between semiosis and structuration. Learning has the same selectivities (semiotic, structural, technological, and agential) as semiosis more generally. This is especially evident in crises, which tend to throw established patterns of meaning into crisis too, provoking profound disorientation. Nonetheless a crisis does not automatically lead to learning: cognitive capacities may be lacking or the situation may be too unstructured (chaotic); or, again, lessons learnt are irrelevant because the situation is too turbulent to apply them. Learning depends on a dialectics of *Erlebnis* and *Erfahrung* that has its own temporalities, shaped by crisis dynamics. *Erlebnis* refers to *immediate experience* in the face of disorientation and associated attempts to make sense of disorienting events/processes. *Erfahrung* refers to the lessons learnt from this disorientation and sense-making. Importantly, it typically includes an element of the objective dimensions of the crisis – lessons must be adequate to the crisis, not just idiosyncratic reactions.

When crises throw established modes of learning into crisis, three stages in learning can occur: learning in crisis, learning about crisis, and learning from crisis (Ji 1996). Each stage is likely to involve different balances of semiosis and structuration. It can also involve different degrees of reflexivity, that is, learning about learning. The latter requires that actors recognize the need for new imaginaries because inherited approaches have not worked well in crisis situations and that they reorganize information collection, calculation, and embodied and/or collective memory. Shifts in strategic learning and knowledge production often require a shift in the balance of forces in wider social relations.

Crises of a given system, hence crises of crisis-management, are especially likely to disrupt learnt strategic behaviour and lead to an initial trial-and-error 'muddling-through' approach. *Learning in crisis* occurs in the immediacy of experiencing crisis, considered as a moment of profound disorientation, and is oriented to the phenomenal forms of crisis. It involves attempts to make sense of an initial disorientation (at some level of everyday life, organizational and/or institutional and/or policy paradigms, disciplinary or theoretical framing, and meta-narrative) in order to 'go on' in the face of the crisis as it is experienced (*Erlebnis*). Three points merit attention here. First, social actors have different social, spatial, and temporal positions as well as reflexive capacities and past and will live the crisis in different ways. In this sense, actors' strategic learning does not come directly from the crisis as a whole, but from their own circumstances and crisis experiences. This can lead to different strategic responses (strategic variation); and their results vary in terms of success or survival under certain structural and conjunctural conditions (strategic selection). Second, actors vary in their capacities to 'read' the crisis, to respond to it in the 'short term', and, once we allow for power differentials, to impose their readings and solutions on others. Lastly, learning in crisis is more likely to address the empirical and actual dimensions of the crisis than to deal with its real causes (especially in terms of their spatio-temporal breadth and depth).

Learning about crisis occurs as a crisis unfolds, often in unexpected ways, with lags in real time as actors begin to relate the symptoms of crisis to underlying mechanisms and dynamics. This stage differs from learning in crisis because it takes more time to dig beneath phenomenal features (if it did not, then this would not be a 'crisis' that is disorienting at the level of theoretical or policy paradigm and it would be possible to engage in routine crisis-management routines) and/or to scan the environment for analogous events in past or present. Social actors learn through 'trial-and error' in specific conditions and, in this sense, through 'learning about crisis' they also embark on learning from crisis. In this sense, learning about crisis goes beyond the 'phenomenal' features of a crisis to its objectively overdetermined causes (including the role of specific actors and actions in producing it). Often these causes only become apparent through reflexive trial-and-error experimentation based on particular theoretical and policy paradigms. A major obstacle in learning about crisis is the existence of power relations and structural constraints that mean that the powerful do not need to learn from their mistakes but can impose the costs of these mistakes on others.

Learning from crisis occurs after a crisis is (temporarily) resolved (or changes its form, for example, from liquidity crisis to sovereign debt crisis or fiscal crisis) and includes preventive or prudential actions to prevent repetition, to improve crisis-management routines, and so on. It may lead to revisions in imaginaries, whether these take the form of meta-narratives, theoretical frameworks, policy paradigms, or everyday expectations and routines. In this phase, strategic lessons are retained after the surviving social actors have had time to reflect on the new, post-crisis realities. Only then is overall strategic reorientation and path-breaking likely to be accomplished.

Lessons from the past are often invoked in the course of all three learning types. This involves the use of history to make history or, put differently, the effort to define appropriate historical parallels as a basis for responding effectively to the crisis in real time. Such lessons often interact with 'spatial' dimensions, such as policy transfer across different fields, sites, levels, and scales of policy-making.

CPE on crises

A CPE approach to crisis builds on the insight that crises are objectively overdetermined but subjectively indeterminate (Debray 1973: 113). It combines semiotic and material analyses to examine: (1) how crises emerge when established patterns of dealing with structural contradictions, their crisis-tendencies, and strategic dilemmas no longer work as expected and, indeed, when continued reliance thereon may aggravate matters; (2) how contestation over the meaning of the crisis shapes responses through processes of variation, selection, and retention that are mediated through a changing mix of semiotic and extra-semiotic mechanisms. Indeed, because they are never purely objective, extra-semiotic events or processes, crises offer a real-time laboratory to study the dialectic of semiosis and materiality.

Economic imaginaries and their sedimentation are always liable to dislocation with the result that '[t]he development of an accumulation regime is all the time implicitly open' (Scherrer 1995: 480, our translation). Crises often create profound cognitive and strategic disorientation and trigger proliferation in interpretations and proposed solutions. In cases of dislocation, subjects are obliged to adopt new identities and translate them into new structures of action. An interesting area for CPE analysis is the proliferation of efforts to interpret economic crises, the selection of some interpretations to shape policy-making and other strategic reactions, and the retention and institutionalization of some responses as the basis for new, sedimented routines, organizations, and institutions (Sum and Jessop 2013). Crises create deep cognitive, strategic, and practical disorientation by disrupting actors' taken-for-granted, sedimented views of the world and how to 'go on' in it. This opens space for path-shaping interventions rather than 'muddling through' in the hope that the situation may resolve itself. In developing a new 'imaginary', they can give new meanings to inherited structures and seek to transform or replace them. Nonetheless, in so far as individuals and collective agencies remain embedded in structures, crises can never be fully open situations. Thus both the reproduction of a given accumulation regime and the outcome of its crises depend on the reciprocal subversion of contingency and necessity as these are established in and through discursive practices (Scherrer 1995).

A crisis is most acute when crisis-tendencies and tensions accumulate across interrelated moments of a given structure or system, limiting manoeuvre in regard to any particular problem. Shifts in the balance of forces may also intensify crisis-tendencies by weakening or resisting established modes of crisis-management (Offe 1984: 35–64). This creates a situation of more or less acute crisis, a potential moment of decisive transformation, and an opportunity for decisive intervention. This opens space for strategic interventions to significantly redirect the course of events rather than 'muddle through' in the (perhaps forlorn) hope that the situation will eventually resolve itself. Moreover, as Milton Friedman (1962: 32) put it hyperbolically but tellingly: '[o]nly a crisis produces real change. When that crisis occurs, the actions that are taken depend on the ideas that are lying around'. This indicates that a 'war of position', that is, preparing the cultural and social ground for crisis-induced strategic interventions, will also prove important to the nature and outcome of crisis-management and crisis response. In short, crises are potentially path-shaping moments that provoke responses that are mediated through semiotic-cum-material processes of variation, selection, and retention.

Crises never produce a particular response or outcome alone but are mediated via the construals and proposed responses of relevant social forces. The role of economic imaginaries is crucial in all three moments of variation, selection, and retention. Their role in complexity reduction is never wholly innocent. It is intimately connected to diverse forms of social contestation, alliance building, and forms of domination. Thus a crisis is a moment for contestation and struggle to make sense of it and inform individual and collective responses. This involves, among other issues, delimiting the origins of a crisis in space-time and its uneven spatio-temporal incidence; identifying – rightly or wrongly – purported causes (agential, structural, discursive, and technical – in various senses of this last word) at different scales, over different time horizons, in different fields of social practice, and at different levels of social organization from nameless or named individuals through social networks, formal organizations, institutional arrangements, specific social forms, or even the dynamic of a global society; determining its scope and effects, assessing whether it is a crisis 'in' or 'of' the relevant system(s); reducing its complexities to identifiable causes that could be targeted to find solutions; charting alternative futures; and promoting specific lines of action for socially identified forces over differently constructed horizons of action (cf. Gramsci's comments on the complexity of the origins of the Great Depression and, hence, the difficulties of identifying them (1995: 219); and, for a study of the 1997 'Asian' crisis in South Korea on these lines, see Ji 2006). It follows that, given a crisis in/of a given social order, the emergence and consolidation of a new economic regime does not occur purely through technological innovation and changes in the labour process, enterprise forms, and forms of competition. Wider ideational and institutional innovation going beyond the economy narrowly conceived is needed, promoted, and supported by political, intellectual, and moral leadership. This includes a new 'economic imaginary' that is articulated to new state projects and hegemonic visions that can be translated into material, social, and spatio-temporal fixes that would jointly underpin a relative 'structured coherence' to support continued accumulation.

Conclusions

Our approach to CPE takes the cultural turn seriously, highlighting the relations between meanings and practices. In so far as semiosis is studied apart from its extra-semiotic context, resulting accounts of social causation will be incomplete, leading to semiotic reductionism and/or imperialism. Conversely, in so far as material transformation is studied apart from its semiotic dimensions and mediations, explanations of stability and change risk oscillating between objective necessity and sheer contingency. On this basis, we outlined six interrelated features of CPE, introduced the notion of 'economic imaginary' as a useful general concept for analysing the co-evolution of semiosis and structuration, and provided a simplified (of course!) account of some of the implications of CPE for the analysis of crisis and crisis-management. We apply this approach in our individual chapters to illustrate its heuristic and explanatory potential. Overall, the evolutionary and institutional approach to semiosis advocated here enables us to recognize the semiotic dimensions of political economy at the same time as indicating how and why only some economic imaginaries among the many that circulate actually come to be selected and institutionalized. And the semiotic and evolutionary approach to political economy enables us to identify the contradictions and conflicts that make capital accumulation inherently improbable and crisis-prone, creating the space for economic imaginaries to play a role in stabilizing accumulation in specific spatio-temporal fixes and/or pointing the way forward from recurrent crises.

References

Althusser, L. (1977) *Lenin and Philosophy and Other Essays*, London: Verso.
Anderson, B. (1983) *Imagined Communities: Reflections on the Origin and Spread of Nationalism*, London: Verso.
Boltanski, L. and Chiapello, E. (2007) *The New Spirit of Capitalism*, London: Verso.
Burkhardt, J. (1992) Wirtschaft, in O. Brunner, W. Conze and R. Koselleck (eds), *Geschichtliche Grundbegriffe. Historisches Lexikon zur politisch-sozialen Sprache in Deutschland. Band 7*, Stuttgart: Klett-Cotta.
Callon, M. (ed.) (1998) *The Laws of the Markets*, Oxford: Blackwell.
Debray, R. (1973) *Prison Writings*, London: Allen Lane.
Fairclough, N. (1989) *Language and Power in Social Life*, Harlow: Longman.
Fairclough, N. (2003) *Analysing Discourse*, London: Routledge.
Fey, A. (1936) *Der Homo Oeconomicus in der klassischen Nationalökonomie und seine Kritik durch den Historismus*, Limburg: Limburger Verdruckerei.
Finley, M.I. (1973) *The Ancient Economy*, Berkeley: University of California Press.
Foucault, M. (1975) *Discipline and Punish*, Harmondsworth: Penguin.

Foucault, M. (2008) *Security, Territory, Population. Course at the Collège de France, 1977–1978*, Basingstoke: Palgrave Macmillan.

Friedman, M. (1962) *Capitalism and Freedom*, Chicago: University of Chicago Press.

Glynos, J. and Howarth, D. (2007) *Logics of Critical Explanation in Social and Political Theory*, London: Routledge.

Gramsci, A. (1971) *Selections from the Prison Notebooks*, London: Lawrence & Wishart.

Gramsci, A. (1995) *Further Selections from the Prison Notebooks*, London: Lawrence & Wishart.

Jessop, B. (2007) *State Power: A Strategic-Relational Approach*, Cambridge: Polity.

Jessop, B. and Sum, N-L. (2006) *Beyond the Regulation Approach: Putting Capitalist Economies in their Place*, Cheltenham: Edward Elgar.

Ji, J-H. (2006) *Learning from Crisis: Political Economy, Spatio-Temporality, and Crisis Management in South Korea, 1961–2002*, Thesis (PhD) Lancaster University.

Mackenzie, D., Muniesa, F., and Siu, L. (eds) (2007) *Do Economists Make Markets? On the Performativity of Economics*, Princeton: Princeton University Press.

Marx, K. (1963) *Theories of Surplus Value*, 3 volumes, London: Lawrence & Wishart.

Marx, K. (1967) *Capital, Volume I*, London: Lawrence & Wishart.

Miller, P. and Rose, N. (2008) *Governing the Present: Administering Economic, Social and Personal Life*, Cambridge: Polity.

Mirowski, P. (ed.) (1994) *Natural Images in Economic Thought: 'Markets Red in Tooth and Claw'*, Cambridge: Cambridge University Press.

Offe, C. (1984) *Contradictions of the Welfare State*, London: Hutchinson.

Scherrer, C. (1995) Eine diskursanalytische Kritik der Regulationstheorie, *Prokla*, 100: 457–82.

Sum, N.L. and Jessop, B. (2013) *Towards a Cultural Political Economy: Putting Culture in its Place in Political Economy*, Cheltenham: Edward Elgar.

Taylor, C. (2003) *Modern Social Imaginaries*, Durham, NC: Duke University Press.

Tribe, K. (1978) *Land, Labour and Economic Discourse*, London: Routledge & Kegan Paul.

2 The cultural view on financial markets

Eelke de Jong

The literature on Varieties of Capitalism (VoC) tends to focus on non-financial sectors (see Hall and Soskice 2001). It regards formal institutions (in particular law) as an important determinant for the good performance of economies. This literature tends to classify economies in groups. Although these typologies can be very useful for didactical purposes, they do no justice to the heterogeneity within each group of countries. Often one economy can be regarded as typical of that particular class. The other members in the group deviate to a greater or lesser extent from this benchmark. Moreover some countries, including The Netherlands, are hard to incorporate in any group. The VoC literature compares countries and implicitly assumes that the same institutional structure will lead to the same results. One can question this assumption. Common European regulations, for example, do not always lead to the same results in each member state. Finally, this literature largely ignores the interaction between individuals and institutions from different countries.

This chapter illustrates the advantages of a cultural approach over the VoC literature. Culture is at least a set of common values of a group.[1] These values are transmitted from one generation to the next. They are formed over centuries, so that culture is often quite persistent. It does not change that easily, although I allow that extreme collective events (such as a period of war) can lead to sudden changes. Culture can be regarded as the deeper layers on which institutions are built (see, for example, Williamson 2000). In this respect, culture digs deeper than the institutional approach in explaining comparative economic phenomena. Differences in value patterns can lead to differences in behaviour although the formal institutions are the same. Finally, value differences can cause miscommunication between people from different cultures, leading to very detrimental effects (see below).

This chapter has four main sections. The first briefly discusses three approaches for explaining cross-country differences in financial systems: institutional or legal, the political approach, and some cultural approaches. In my view, many of these approaches lack a sound theoretical argumentation. The next section provides a theory for the cultural approach and the following section illustrates this empirically. Together these sections address the structure of the financial sector. The third section addresses investors' behaviour in two steps:

first, I discuss cross-country differences in investment strategy resulting from differences in culture and, second, I illustrate how misunderstandings associated with different financial systems (cultures) can contribute to crises. Some concluding remarks follow.

Different explanations of cross-country differences in financial systems

There are three main approaches for explaining cross-country differences in financial systems: the legal approach, the political approach, and the cultural view. The legal approach holds that the key precondition for the development of equity markets is the extent of protection of outside investors through the legal system (La Porta *et al.* 1997 and 1998). The authors construct indicators of minority-shareholder rights protection and show that stock market development is significantly related to these indicators. An investor will consider an investment in shares more attractive if legal provisions are more flexible and adapt more quickly to changing economic conditions and contracting needs of the agents (Beck *et al.* 2003).

The political approach claims that political structures explain cross-country differences in stock market developments (Rajan and Zingales 2003; Pagano and Volpin 2005). In particular, Rajan and Zingales argue that markets and the resulting competition do not respect the value of incumbency and can destroy some forms of insurance provided by social and economic institutions. When political groups that are adversely affected by this become strong, the political system might suppress the development of markets. The disadvantages of their study are that they do not explain systematically why this suppression differs so much across countries. Thus they treat some countries as exceptions and providing different rationales for emergence of these exceptions: political and cultural factors for the USA and economic arguments for the UK. Pagano and Volpin (2005) model the interaction among entrepreneurs, rentiers, and workers when these three groups have to agree upon the degree on investor protection and the employers' freedom to fire workers. Depending on the strength of the workers' preference for working with the same employer, this political process leads to a low level or a high level of protection of investors. The two corresponding equilibriums are labelled corporatist and non-corporatist equilibrium, respectively. Their work does not explain, however, why one country ends in the corporatist equilibrium and the other in the non-corporatist one. Cultural characteristics could help in this respect.

The cultural approach argues that cross-country differences can be explained by differences between national cultures, defined as systems of beliefs that shape individuals' actions. On the macro-level these beliefs are assumed to be important determinants of the legal and political system. Studies belonging to this group are Stulz and Williamson (2003), Licht *et al.* (2005), Kwok and Tadessa (2006), and Aggarwal and Goodell (2009 and 2010). The studies differ in how they represent culture. Stulz and Williamson approximate culture by the dominant language and the dominant religion in a country. A common language facilitates communication about beliefs. This can facilitate the creation of common values but may also disclose differences. But it does not entail specific values. However, where religious leaders have expressed their view on certain topics, one can explore if there is a relation between religion and economic phenomena. This is not always possible, however, since the opinions of adherents of a particular religion can differ widely on economic issues (see Iannacone 1992).

The other studies use cultural dimensions which refer to specific values and have a continuous scale. The dimensions used are those derived by Hofstede (2001) and by Schwartz (1994). Both sets of dimensions are based on survey data of IBM employees (Hofstede) or teachers and students (Schwartz). Since the cultural dimensions refer to specific values they can be used in a theory that connects values (culture) with institutions and practices (see, for example, de Jong 2009: passim). Nonetheless, many of the studies are exploratory. An exception is de Jong and Semenov (2009a) in that it presents a quite extensive theoretical framework for the relation between the importance of financial markets, institutions, and culture.

The legal approach and cultural approaches that use dominant language and religion as proxies for culture enable us to distinguish varieties of capitalism: a country has a common law or a civil law system or is predominantly Protestant. It is hard to incorporate different sub-types within these broad categories as well as countries that combine features from different varieties of capitalism. As stated earlier, the political approach does not provide a systematic analysis. Thus I use the cultural approach based on cultural dimensions for deriving plausible relations among culture, institutions, and financial systems. This method allows for a variegated capitalism in the sense that, although common forces are identified, each country is still unique.

Cross-country differences in financial systems: a theoretical framework

This section uses the general framework of the relations among economic performance, governance, institutions, and culture as set out in Chapter 3 of de Jong (2009) and represented here by Figure 2.1. In this framework, economic performance refers to the relative importance of stock markets; governance to the way conflicts are dealt with and people behave; institutions to the written regulations; and culture to the common set of beliefs/values. An extensive description of the relations relevant for financial markets can be found in de Jong and Semenov (2009a), a concise one in Chapter 5 of de Jong (2009). This section relies on these studies. My argument starts at the right-hand sight of the figure. Although I will refer to stereotypes to facilitate the description, I have a continuum in mind.

Financial systems are often classified as market- or bank-based systems. In market-based systems, firms are financed by bonds and equity traded on markets. Investors who buy these financial products do not have a close relationship with

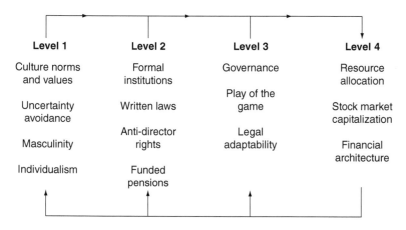

Figure 2.1 Theoretical framework financial market.

the firm, so that this system is also characterized as an at arms'-length system. Since many investors lack direct contact with firms' management, other mechanisms are put in place in order to ensure that each and every investor is informed about the firms' performance. First of all regulation requires that firms provide extensive accounting reports of their activities and expected future performance. Moreover, this information must be shared by all investors. Consequently, a strict anti-insider trading legislation is in place. Firms have a dispersed ownership; an individual investor owes only a small share of the firm and has no direct influence on the firm's management. In principle this gives management much room to manoeuvre, which can easily lead to a misuse if it is power for own benefit. This misuse can be restricted by law, so that management is held more accountable to the interests of the shareholders. The quality of bonds is assessed by rating agencies.

In a bank (or intermediaries) based system, companies are primarily financed by bank loans and equity provided by a few large investors; often families. Close ties between the different firms (cross-holdings) and financiers exist, so that this is also known as the network-based system or relationship finance. Often a few (dominant) owners finance a firm. The financiers obtain the information they need through regular visits to the firm or from their position as a member of the firm's board or supervisory board. Consequently, the reporting requirements are much less strict than in a market-based system. Legislation about insider trading is lacking or, if it exists, its implementation is weak. As financiers are often involved in management, there is no need to restrict management's room for manoeuvre as occurs in a market-based system.

The establishment of a market is costly. The infrastructure of a well-functioning market comprises the market organization itself and the regulation and supervisory organizations that ensure that every participant is treated fairly. As a consequence, market-based systems are more common in developed than developing countries. Naturally, a financial system starts as a bank- or relatives-based system and can then evolve into a more market-based system. Legislation often lags behind these developments, which implies that there is a tendency to protect the rights of existing owners. If judges can interpret laws in accordance with new circumstances, this will stimulate new investors; their rights can be protected even though these are not yet included in a law. So a high degree of legal adaptability stimulates financial markets. Of course markets can only flourish if there are enough investors with sufficient capital. In this respect, institutional investors and, in particular, the nature of pension systems are important (Roëll 1996). Pension funds are more important in countries with a funded pension system than in those with a pay-as-you-go system.

Financial systems provide money for risky investments. In intermediaries-based systems, the intermediary must take care of all the depositors who have entrusted their money in the hands of the intermediary. This leads to a risk-averse attitude. Consequently, the investments are predominantly in relatively safe activities. In a financial markets-based system, each investor is free to decide in which company he or she invests. Investors with a relatively low level of risk or ambiguity aversion can decide to invest in risky assets with a potentially high return. These will be more innovative products (Allen and Gale 2000, especially Chapter 13).

Finally, two system-wide phenomena appear to be relevant: attitudes to competition and to uncertainty. A network system is characterized by close relationships. These relations shield the participants from competition by others. In a markets-based system competition dominates in financial markets as well as in product markets. So one expects that the attitude towards competition (and maybe also foreign influences) is more positive in a markets-based system. Share prices can fluctuate widely. Of even more importance is that financial markets are vulnerable to systematic risk: long periods of low prices. Hence, markets-based systems are more characterized by uncertainty.[2]

The various characteristics of the financial systems can be related to the cultural dimensions of Hofstede. Hofstede distinguishes five dimensions: Individualism versus Collectivism, Uncertainty Avoidance, Masculinity versus Femininity, Power Distance, and Long-term Orientation.

Individualism-Collectivism (IC) reflects whether people look only after themselves and their immediate family, or belong to in-groups that look after them in exchange for loyalty. People in collectivist societies have a 'We' consciousness; for them collective interests prevail. In individualist societies, people have an 'I' consciousness; for them individual interests prevail. One expects that a high score on Individualism is more in favour of markets-based systems since in these systems an individual can choose what he or she wants, whereas in a bank-based system the interests of the collectivity are more important.

Uncertainty Avoidance (UA) refers to the extent to which people feel threatened by uncertainty and ambiguity and try to avoid it and/or protect themselves against it. People in societies with a high score on Uncertainty Avoidance have difficulty in accepting uncertainty inherent in life and avoid conflict and competition. We therefore expect that high Uncertainty Avoidance is associated with close relationships of firms with their stakeholders; a regulatory environment that hinders competition in the financial system and in particular the development of stock markets; and judicial decisions have to be based on written law.

Femininity-Masculinity deals with the relative emphasis in society on caring for others and quality of life on the one hand, and achievement and success on the other. Feminine societies stress equality and solidarity and are therefore likely to favour a comprehensive system of pension provision by the state (a pay-as-you-go system). In a masculine society competition is more accepted. All these characteristics suggest that masculinity is associated with a markets-based system.

Power Distance (PD) refers to the extent to which the society accepts that power within its organizations and the society as a whole is distributed unequally. In high Power Distance societies power and wealth are concentrated; a characteristic of a bank-based system. However, in such societies cooperation between different partners is difficult and close relationships between a firm and a stakeholder are less likely. This suggests a positive impact of Power Distance on capital market development. Consequently the expected sign of Power Distance is ambiguous.

In a later study a group of Asian researchers (Chinese Culture Connection 1987) came with a fifth dimensions *Long-term Orientation*. Long-term oriented societies stress future rewards, in particular saving, persistence, and adapting to changing circumstances. Short-term oriented societies foster virtues related to the past and present such as national pride, respect for tradition, preservation of 'face', and fulfilling social obligations. Hence, the values related to this dimension influence stock market development in opposite directions: negatively through the regulatory environment and positively through the character of relationships with shareholders. Given this, as with Power Distance, we make no definite prediction about the influence of the country's position on Long-term Orientation.

Finally, Minkov has derived a sixth dimension from the World Values Survey, which is presented as the sixth dimensions in the latest version of Hofstede's book *Cultures and Organizations* (Hofstede *et al.* 2010). This dimension is called *Indulgence versus Restraint*. Indulgence stands for a society that allows 'relatively free gratification of basic and natural human drives related to enjoying life and having fun' (Hofstede *et al.* 2010: 281). Restraint stands for a society that suppresses gratification of needs and regulates it by means of strict social norms. Since stock markets leave more room for individual choice, I expect a positive correlation between indulgence and stock market capitalization. On the basis of this analysis we would expect stock markets to be more developed in societies with lower Uncertainty Avoidance and in societies with higher Masculinity, Individualism, and Indulgence.

Cross-country differences in financial systems: empirical evidence

Many empirical studies use a number of countries for the analysis without much argumentation. De Jong and Semenov (2009b) is an exception to this rule. They base their analysis on a group of 17 countries, which they call Western economies. In their view this group is to be preferred for several reasons. First, the theoretical analysis is based on assumptions and experiments conducted in Western economies. Some of the concepts used might not be correct in other societies. Uncertainty, for example, and the need to avoid it are concepts which are more present in the cognitive frame of Western people than of Asian people. Second, in many occasions Hofstede (2001) finds a significantly different relation between culture and economic characteristics for groups of developed and developing countries. Since the establishment of a market is costly, this might be true for stock market development too. Finally, the concentration on a group of similar countries reduces the omitted variables bias. As a control group de Jong and Semenov also use a large group of both developed and developing countries. They find that cultural influences are more diverse and important in their small group of Western countries than in the large control group. From this they conclude that culture is more important to explain cross-country differences in groups of otherwise homogenous countries. The differences in a set of heterogeneous countries are more likely to be dominated by material circumstances such as income per capita.

In the following analysis, I distinguish three groups of countries: Western economies – the countries considered in de Jong and Semenov (2009b), a group of OECD countries, and a group consisting of both developed and developing countries (see Appendix for details).

By considering these different groups I can test the robustness of de Jong and Semenov's finding that culture is more important for explaining differences in a group of homogenous countries. The relations are estimated for two periods, 1990–1999 and 2000–2009. Two different dependent variables are used. The first is stock market capitalization as a percentage of GDP, which is the dependent variable in de Jong and Semenov (2009b). The second is called financial architecture and measures the size, the activity, and the efficiency of the stock market. This variable is used in Kwok and Tadesse (2006). The Appendix contains a description of the variables and of the estimation procedure used. The estimation procedure consists of two steps. In the first step I only consider cultural dimensions as possible explanatory variables, whereas in the second step other explanatory variables are also considered. The statistically significant coefficients are presented in Tables 2.1 and 2.2 (stock market capitalization) and 2.3 and 2.4 (financial architecture).

During the 1990s four cultural dimensions significantly affect stock market capitalization in the group of Western countries: Masculinity, Power Distance, Uncertainty Avoidance, and Indulgence versus Restraint (Table 2.1, part A). All four have the expected sign. Uncertainty Avoidance negatively affects stock

Table 2.1 Stock market capitalization, 1989–1999

	Western	OECD	Large sample	
A: Cultural dimensions only				
uai	−0.011*		−0.009**	
	(0.06)		(0.00)	
mas	0.006*			
	(0.06)			
ivr	0.013*	0.011***	0.006**	
	(0.07)	(0.00)	(0.01)	
pdi	0.016**			
	(0.02)			
idv		0.006**		
		(0.03)		
ltowvs		0.007**	0.006**	
		(0.03)	(0.01)	
_cons	−0.432	−0.901***	0.384	
	(0.49)	(0.01)	(0.13)	
N	17	32	60	
adj. R-sq	0.448	0.369	0.328	
B: Including other explanatory variables				
uai	−0.010**			−0.006***
	(0.03)			(0.00)
mas	0.004*			
	(0.09)			
pdi	0.011**			
	(0.03)			
Pension	0.005***	0.003**	0.004**	
fund	(0.00)	(0.03)	(0.02)	
gdpcap		0.000***	0.000***	0.000***
		(0.00)	(0.00)	(0.00)
_cons	0.332*	−0.039	0.050	0.472***
	(0.09)	(0.66)	(0.44)	(0.00)
N	17	33	54	65
adj. R-sq	0.689	0.553	0.448	0.587

Notes
p-values between parentheses
* P-value < 0.1, ** P-value < 0.05, *** P-value < 0.01.

market capitalization, whereas the other dimensions have a positive effect. Indulgence versus Restraint is also significant in the other two groups and Uncertainty Avoidance in the large group of developed and developing countries. Individualism versus Collectivism stimulates stock markets in the group of OECD countries and Long-term Orientation positively affects stock market capitalization in the OECD countries and in the larger group. In the second step, the importance of funded pensions and GDP per capita appear to be the only other variables with significant coefficients (Table 2.1, part B). Uncertainty Avoidance, Masculinity, and Power Distance are still significant in the group of Western countries. Uncertainty Avoidance is significant in the large group if only income per capita

Table 2.2 Stock market capitalization, 2000–2009

	Western	OECD	Large sample	
A: Cultural dimensions only				
ivr		0.013**		
		(0.02)		
uai			−0.012***	
			(0.00)	
_cons		0.144	1.483***	
		(0.63)	(0.00)	
N		33	68	
adj. R-sq		0.140	0.139	
B: Including other explanatory variables				
uai			−0.007***	−0.006**
			(0.00)	(0.00)
Pension fund	0.010***	0.007***		
	(0.00)	(0.00)		
gdpcap		0.000***		0.000***
		(0.00)		(0.00)
checks			0.065***	
			(0.04)	
_cons	0.615***	0.103	0.557***	0.472***
	(0.00)	(0.44)	(0.00)	(0.00)
N	17	33	65	65
adj. R-sq	0.552	0.603	0.244	0.587

Notes
p-values between parentheses.
* P-value < 0.1, ** P-value < 0.05, *** P-value < 0.01.

is the other explanatory variable. The inclusion of the funded pensions reduces the number of observations (compare the last two columns of Table 2.1, part A). These results indicate that at least during the 1990s several cultural variables had plausible and significant effects on the relative importance of stock markets. There is also some evidence that cultural variables are more important for explaining the differences within a group of homogenous countries.

The results are quite different for the first decade of this century. No cultural dimension has a significant effect in the group of Western countries (Table 2.2). Indulgence versus Restraint is important for explaining differences within the group of OECD countries and Uncertainty Avoidance in the large group. The importance of funded pension systems is the only significant explanatory factor in the group of Western countries. Along with GDP per capita it also explains the differences in the group of OECD countries (Table 2.2, part B, second column). Uncertainty Avoidance explains the differences within the large group. Income per head or checks is the other significant variable. These results show that cultural differences are much less important during this decade. Moreover, the idea that cultural dimensions are in particular important for explaining differences within a homogenous set of countries is not confirmed.

Table 2.3 Financial architecture, 1989–1999

	Western	OECD	OECD	Large	Large
A: Cultural dimension only					
uai	−0.012***		−0.005***	−0.004***	−0.004***
	(0.00)		(0.00)	(0.00)	(0.00)
pdi	0.009**			−0.002**	
	(0.05)			(0.04)	
idv		0.003*			0.002**
		(0.06)			(0.04)
ivr		0.004**			0.002*
		(0.03)			(0.08)
cons	0.714***	−0.116	0.656***	0.624***	0.344***
	(0.00)	(0.35)	(0.00)	(0.00)	(0.00)
N	17	32	33	69	62
adj. R-sq	0.471	0.240	0.324	0.318	0.333
B: Including other explanatory variables					
uai			−0.004**	−0.002**	−0.004***
			(0.01)	(0.02)	(0.00)
Pension fund			0.002**	0.002**	
			(0.04)	(0.02)	
gdpcap				0.000***	0.000***
				(0.01)	(0.00)
_cons			0.499***	0.293***	0.387***
			(0.00)	(0.00)	(0.00)
N			32	49	68
adj. R-sq			0.391	0.468	0.472

How would the results change if I used another variable as an indicator for the importance of financial markets, namely the indicator financial markets architecture? This variable measures the size, activity, and efficiency of financial markets. The regressions with financial architecture as an explanatory variable confirm the results found with stock market capitalization. Cultural differences were important explanatory factors in the 1990s and much less so in the first decade of this century (see Table 2.3 and 2.4). For the group of Western countries it is even extreme in the sense that while during the 1990s the cultural dimensions Uncertainty Avoidance and Power Distance were the only significant explanatory variables, during the subsequent decade the non-cultural variables were the only significant ones. Another finding is that in both periods *Uncertainty Avoidance* is the only significant cultural dimension if non-cultural variables are also included in the set of explanatory variables (bottom part of Table 2.3 and 2.4). The funded pensions' assets as a percentage of GDP is the most important non-cultural explanation. The importance of this variable increases over time. During the 1990s and a great part of the first decade of the twenty-first century stocks markets grew at a high rate. It is interesting to know whether the growth rates of these markets were such that the stock markets' importance converges across countries or that cultural factors hamper the movement towards dominance by financial markets.

Table 2.4 Financial architecture, 2000–2009

	Western	OECD	Large	Large
A: Period 2000–2009: Cultural variables only				
ivr		0.007*		
		(0.08)		
uai			−0.005**	−0.004**
			(0.01)	(0.04)
idv				0.004*
				(0.08)
_cons		0.159	0.808***	0.599***
		(0.49)	(0.00)	(0.00)
N		33	69	69
adj. R-sq		0.067	0.074	0.104
B: Period 2000–2009: Cultural dimensions and other variables				
uai				−0.003*
				(0.08)
Pension fund	0.007**	0.006***	0.006***	
	(0.03)	(0.00)	(0.00)	
gdpcap				0.000***
				(0.00)
_cons	0.440**	0.393***	0.387***	0.550***
	(0.02)	(0.00)	(0.00)	(0.00)
N	17	33	56	68
adj. R-sq	0.228	0.207	0.192	0.196

Notes
p-values between parentheses.
* P-value < 0.1, ** P-value < 0.05, *** P-value < 0.01.

In order to investigate this I have estimated traditional growth equations in which the growth rate of stock market capitalization is explained by the level of stock market capitalization at the beginning of the period and cultural dimensions and institutional variables. These equations are estimated for two periods, namely 1990–1999 and 2000–2009. Once again the relation is estimated for the three groups of countries separately.

Except for the group of OECD countries in the first decade of this century, the level of stock market capitalization at the beginning of the period has a negative effect on the growth of stock market capitalization in the subsequent decade (Table 2.5). This implies that within these groups of countries the importance of stock markets converges and the differences between countries decrease. This conclusion is confirmed by the fact that the coefficients of the cultural variables Uncertainty Avoidance and Individualism have signs opposite to the ones expected for a larger share of equity markets. This suggests that stock markets grow relatively more in more collectivistic countries and countries scoring high on uncertainty avoidance. The importance of a funded pension system is positively related to the relative growth of stock markets. Note that due to data availability the group of OECD countries and the larger group differ considerably between the two periods. The

Table 2.5 Growth of stock market

	Western	Western	OECD	Large
A: Period 1990–1999				
stmkt~1990	−16.609*	−18.495**	−20.670***	−15.750***
	(0.08)	(0.04)	(0.00)	(0.00)
Pension fund	0.087*	0.106**	0.104**	
	(0.07)	(0.02)	(0.03)	
gdpgrowth		−4.295*	–	
		(0.08)		
uai			0.156**	
			(0.03)	
idv				−0.119**
				(0.05)
_cons	13.544***	22.446***	(0.05)	26.073***
	(0.00)	(0.28)	(0.00)	(0.0)
N	17	17	24	39
adj. R-sq	0.133	0.268	0.467	0.326
B: Period 2000–2009				
stmkt~2000	−5.641**			−3.507**
	(0.02)			(0.03)
idv	−0.385***		−0.178***	−0.106**
	(0.00)		(0.01)	(0.04)
Pension fund	0.091*			
	(0.07)			
_cons	35.862***		17.484**	17.091***
	(0.00)		(0.00)	(0.00)
N	17		32	57
adj. R-sq	0.468		0.183	0.171

group of Western countries is the same in both periods. In this group of Western countries stock markets grow faster in countries with funded pension systems and during the period 2000–2010 less in relatively individualistic countries.

Investors' behaviour

So far I have focused on the relation between culture and the degree to which financial systems operate at arm's-length. I now turn to three cases concerning the relation between differences in culture and behaviour by investors. One case is the influence of individualism on investment strategies; two cases illustrate the problems that can emerge as investors used to a particular system enter a market in which another system dominates.

Individualism and trading strategies

Often one assumes implicitly that traders on financial markets behave in more or less the same way. Recent empirical studies challenge the idea that traders are uniform and thus can be modelled by a representative agent. For example, women are often more cautious and take less speculative positions than male colleagues (Barber and Odean 2001). Another assumption from traditional theory is that securities are rationally priced in the sense that they reflect all publicly available information. Stock prices, however, show systematic patterns that contradict this assumption. Two such anomalies are short-term momentum and long-term reversal. While the former means that stock prices show positive short-term autocorrelation, the latter means that prices return after a while to their fundamental values. Daniel *et al.* (1998) develop a model to explain these anomalies in terms of investor overconfidence and biased self–attribution. An overconfident investor overestimates the precision of his private information relative to the public information accessible to all investors. According to the self-attribution theory, people tend to attribute events that confirm their actions to their own ability and disconfirming to external noise (bad luck). Assume that, based on private information, an investor buys a stock. If, during later periods, public information confirms this choice, his confidence will rise; if it does not, then it will only have a small effect on his confidence. Only after many disconfirming signals will he choose the opposite strategy. This behaviour leads to short-run autocorrelation (short-term momentum) and, eventually, to reversal. In addition, overconfident investors trade more, leading to greater volatility in asset prices.

The psychological literature links overconfidence, over-optimism, and self-attribution bias to individualism (see the references in Chui *et al.* 2010). In particular, Nurmi (1992: 72) concludes that 'cross-cultural differences in self-attribution is typically explained by Western individualism and the collectivist orientation of Eastern cultures'. Chui *et al.* (2010) link these results to those of Daniel *et al.* (1998) and investigate whether momentum profits and return reversals are stronger in more individualistic countries than collectivistic ones. They use Hofstede's Individualism index. Their sample consists of monthly data on stock returns and trading volumes from February 1980 (for some countries) to June 2003. These figures are collected for more than 20,000 individual stocks from 41 countries. They find that trading volume and volatility of stock prices increase with Individualism. These results remain significant when other variables are taken into account. These returns are then used to construct so-called momentum portfolios for each country: in brief, based on returns in the last six months, stocks are chosen for the next six months. So a winner portfolio consists of the one-third of stocks that had the highest return in the last semester and these are held for the next six months and the return on this portfolio is calculated. Likewise, a loser portfolio is constructed from the stocks with the lowest return over the last six months. It appears that, except for four countries, the return on the winners' portfolio is significantly higher than that on the losers' portfolio. This indicates that momentum strategy is profitable. Moreover, the return on momentum portfolios increases monotonically with scores on the Individualism index (Chui *et al.* 2010: 378). Once again, this result is robust after allowing for other explanatory variables and for changes in the sample size (such as excluding Asian countries, small firms or large firms). After some periods, however, returns on the winners' portfolio become negative and lower than that on the other portfolios. This is in line with the reversal hypothesis. The effect appears to be related to Individualism; higher Individualism leads to larger reversals.

These results show that there is a national component to non-rational, behavioural explanations of stock price movements. Even in financial markets, part of investors' behaviour is related to the values ingrained in them during their formative years. This is exactly what culture is about: the values transmitted from one generation to the other. In less individualistic countries, children's education stresses the value of the collectivity and supports less self-esteem and uniqueness of the individual. The adult investor trained in such a society puts more weight on collectively available information than his colleague born and raised in an individualistic country. As this section has shown, these differences in culture have real consequences even in financial markets, which are often regarded as to be world-wide and driven by universal rules.

When two cultures of finance clash

I have dealt so far with differences between systems. However, increasingly people from different systems (cultures) meet each other. What are the consequences if a firm or an individual comes in contact with persons from other cultures? This question is intensively studied in the field of International Business. Almost every issue of the *Journal of International Business Studies* contains at least one article in which culture has a dominant place. Traditionally much attention is paid to the questions about the consequences of cultural differences for a firm's entry mode of foreign markets. Should it only sell its products to the foreign market or should it develop a more committing strategy, such as a joint venture or building a new plant? Less attention is paid to the consequences of cultural differences for financial issues and in particular international capital flows.[3]

This section discusses two publications that deal with cultural differences for foreign investments and, in particular, their contribution to financial crises. In his book, *Fault Lines*, Raghuram G. Rajan describes hidden fractures that, in his view, threaten the world economy. One of these fault lines arises when investors from countries with an at-arm's-length financial system invest in countries with a relationship-based financial system. These investors are used to select their investments by means of publicly available information. This information is not available in the countries with relationship-finance. In these countries, close ties between financial institutions and firms provide the information needed by the investors. Moreover, if necessary, these domestic investors can influence board members to change the firms' policy. Foreign investors are confronted with the 'liability of foreignness'; they cannot obtain the information contained in the relations between different domestic actors (investors and firms' management). They therefore look for other mechanisms which can protect their investments.

In the 1990s, according to Rajan (2010: 77), foreign loans had three characteristics that increased the chance for foreign investors to recover their investment without precise knowledge of borrowers' creditworthiness. These loans were (1) short-term, (2) denominated in the foreign currency (mostly US dollars), and (3) provided via domestic banks rather than lent directly to end-users. The short maturity ensured that foreign investors could withdraw their loans quickly. The denomination in the investor's currency protects the investor against adverse exchange rate movements. By providing the loans through domestic banks, foreign investors expected to obtain a government guarantee in case of a crisis. They foresaw that in crisis situations the government would not let their own banks go bankrupt. Some investors invested in equity and expected that they could sell at reasonable prices if necessary.

These investment strategies have played an important role in the Mexican crisis of 1994/1995 and the Asian crisis in 1997. According to Rajan both cases were characterized by overinvestment. In the Mexican case the investments were mainly in government debt. During the year before the crisis the maturity of government debt was shortened[4] and increasingly guaranteed in US dollars (the so called *tesobonus*). In the Asian case the money went to the private sector. In both situations a fragile situation arose in which adverse events could easily trigger a huge outflow of money. In Mexico the trigger was a sudden devaluation of the Mexican peso in December 1994, after the incoming government had lifted capital controls. In Asia the devaluation of the Japanese yen and the fact that the overambitious investments did not perform well led to the crisis.

An important conclusion from these cases is that foreign capital can be so fluid that it does not enhance economic prosperity. This position contrasts with the conclusion of classical theory, which assumes that capital flows from capital-abundant countries to capital-scarce countries. In this way capital is supposed to boost the production capacity of the capital-receiving countries. Short-term capital flows, however, do not end up in productive capacity but in non-productive speculative investments, such as real estate. Prasad *et al.* (2007) suggest that the conclusion that foreign capital is used for unproductive activities is more generally valid. They find that developing countries that have relied more on foreign capital than have their counterparts fare less well in terms of growth per capita. This result is robust to including other determinants of growth in the regression as well as different groups of countries and different time periods. This relation does not hold for developed countries. This contrast between developed and developing countries suggests that the differences in financial cultures (systems) between these two groups of countries are significantly larger than those between individual members within the group of developed countries.

My next example shows that the differences in financial systems (culture) can be very relevant within developed countries. Michael Lewis (2011: 157–65) reports how the differences between German and American financial culture contributed to the failure of IKB, a German bank located in Düsseldorf. The Germans are used to Ordoliberalism (see also the chapter by de Jong and van Esch). In this system, rules are important and everyone is expected to adhere to the rules. In accordance with this idea, the German investment bankers took an AAA rating at face value and interpreted it as a sign of a riskless investment. As a consequence, IKB management did not invest in a system that would track what was behind the complex bonds they were purchasing; triple A tells enough. Another consequence was that German investors were still buying toxic assets when everybody else had realized that the sub-prime mortgage market was collapsing. 'The last buyer in *the entire world*, several people on Wall Street have told me, were these wilfully oblivious Germans' (Lewis 2011: 161). In addition, whereas the American investment bankers obtained huge bonuses, their German counterparts earned a meagre annual salary equivalent to US$100,000 with a bonus of US$50,000. Yet 'they are treated by the German public as crooks' (ibid: 162). Lewis suggests that the respect the Germans showed for the rules led them to believe that triple A implies riskless and to miss the selfish conduct of American investment bankers. Thus they let their own banks down.

Concluding remarks

This chapter addressed the relation among culture, financial systems, and investors' behaviour. In fact, it relates culture to differences between financial systems, between individuals' behaviour within a system, and the possible consequences of individuals from different cultures interacting with each other. In this sense, it deals with comparative and international studies. In my view, this approach has some advantages over the institutional approach. The institutional approach implicitly assumes that formal institutions lead to a particular behaviour. The cultural approach questions this automatism and argues that institutions should reflect underlying value systems to be effective. So it is important to study the relation between culture (in the sense of dominant values) and the institutional structure. The same institutional structure can lead to differences in behaviour depending on actors' value systems. This item is dealt with in the section on individualism and stock price behaviour.

Finally, unexpected consequences can arise if people from different cultures have to cooperate. I illustrated this in terms of how misunderstandings and reactions thereto can contribute to crises. In my view, the relevance of culture for the disciplines of economics and political science will increase in the near future. Within Europe the legislation is increasingly becoming uniform, often with the aim of establishing a level playing-field. This will not be the result if the member states implement EU rules differently. For example, there is evidence that some Southern countries protect their domestic industries more than the Northern countries. This is in particular the case for cross-border acquisitions; Italy and France are inclined to define and protect national champions whereas the UK and Dutch governments, for example, are inclined to leave these processes to market forces. These differences can be traced to cultural differences. International transactions in the broadest sense are another area where cultural factors play an important role. This is why culture plays such an important role in the field of International Business Studies. It is more surprising that it has at most a minor position in international economics and politics, where, in my view, it is also relevant. Sobis and De Vries (2009), for example, show that the policy advice given to a Polish city highly depends on the advisors' nationality. These differences can be traced once again to cultural differences.

Assuming that culture is becoming more important for political and economic topics, it is important to have a guideline for good studies in this field. The need for these guidelines is even more pressing since the concept of culture can be very broad and vague (de Jong 2009: 5–9). I therefore recommend starting with the economic or political phenomenon. Use the existing literature in economics and political science to derive a clear description of it. Then relate these characteristics to the cultural dimensions. Psychological and sociological literature can be of help for deriving these relations. When the conceptual model is finished one should put it to an empirical test, the final step.

Appendix estimation procedure and data

The relations in Tables 2.1–2.4 have been estimated by the following procedure. First the dependent variable (stock market capitalization or financial architecture) is regressed on all six cultural dimensions. From this step, I obtain those cultural dimensions that have a significant impact on the dependent variable. These results are reported in the upper part of the tables. In the second step, capital market capitalization is regressed on the cultural dimension(s) that proved significant in step one, with regard to each of the explanatory variables listed below. The most significant ones were added to the list of explanatory variables. From this list I subsequently dropped the most insignificant one, until all variables included in the regressions are significant at the level of at least 10 per cent. These results are reported in the bottom part of the tables.

The dependent variables are:

Stock market capitalization as a percentage of Gross Domestic Product. Source: Beck and Demirgüç-Kunt (2009).
Financial architecture is the average of the three architecture series: (size+activity+efficiency)/3.
Size is market capitalization of domestic stocks to GDP divided by the claims of the banking sector against the private real sector as a percentage of GDP. Source: Beck and Demirgüç-Kunt (2009).
Activity is the total value of stocks trade as a percentage of GDP divided by bank credit ratio. Source: Beck and Demirgüç-Kunt (2009).
Efficiency is the product of total value traded ratio and overhead ratio. Source: Beck and Demirgüç-Kunt (2009).

Explanatory variables

Uncertainty Avoidance Source: Hofstede *et al.* (2010).
Individualism versus Collectivism Source: Hofstede *et al.* (2010).

Power Distance Source: Hofstede *et al.* (2010).

Femininity versus Masculinity Source: Hofstede *et al.* (2010).

Long-term Orientation Source: Hofstede *et al.* (2010).

Indulgence versus Restraint Source: Hofstede *et al.* (2010).

GDP per capita GDP per capita, constant 2000 USD, average 1990–2010. Source: World Development Indicators.

Rule of law is the assessment of the law and order tradition in the country by experts of country-risk rating agency 'International Country Risk'. It takes into account two components: (1) military interference in rule of law and in the political process; and (2) integrity of the legal system. Averages for 1982–1995. Source: La Porta *et al.* (1998).

Anti director rights: Source La Porta *et al.* (1999).

Legal justification The index measures the level of legal justification required in the process. The index is formed by the normalized sum of: (i) complaint must be legally justified, (ii) judgment must be legally justified, and (iii) judgment must be based on law (not on equity principles). Source Djankov *et al.* (2003).

Funded pensions indicator Autonomous pension funds' assets as % of GDP, average 2000–2010. Source: OECD.

Growth GDP growth, annual %, average 1990–2010. Source: World Development Indicators.

Openness is the sum of export and import of goods and services relative to GDP, average 1985–1995. Source: World Development Indicators.

Checks is a measure of the number of veto-players in the political decision process. Source: Beck *et al.* (2003).

Supreme Court power is a dummy equal to one if Supreme Court judges have both life-long tenure and power over administrative cases, and zero otherwise. Source: Beck *et al.* (2003).

Interest rate is the deposit interest rate. Source: World Development Indicators.

The following countries comprise the set of Western and OECD countries:

Western countries: Australia, Austria, Belgium, Canada, Denmark, Finland, France, Germany, Italy, The Netherlands, New Zealand, Norway, Spain, Sweden, Switzerland, United Kingdom, and United States of America.

The set of OECD countries includes the Western countries and Chile, the Czech Republic, Estonia, Greece, Hungary, Iceland, Ireland, Israel, Japan, South Korea, Luxembourg, Mexico, Poland, Slovak Republic, Slovenia, and Turkey.

Notes

1 There are many definitions of culture, see for example de Jong (2009: 5–9). In anthropology, in particular, the definition is very broad.

2 Uncertainty is associated with ambiguity and fear, whereas risk is associated with probability and refers to cognitive processes of calculation. Another often used distinction is that in the case of risk we know the distribution, whereas in that of uncertainty or ambiguity the distribution of the outcome is unknown. See for example Knight ([1921] 1971).
3 The exception is the home bias of investments, i.e. that the share of domestic assets in many portfolios is significantly higher than one would expect from optimal portfolio allocation.
4 The shortening of maturities is a phenomenon frequently observed during the period just before the outbreak of a crisis.

References

Aggarwal, R. and J.W. Goodell (2009) Markets and institutions in financial intermediation: national characteristics as determinants, *Journal of Banking and Finance*, 33: 1770–80.

Aggarwal, R. and J.W. Goodell (2010) Financial markets versus institutions in European countries: influence of culture and other national characteristics, *International Business Review*, 19: 502–20.

Allen, F and D. Gale (2000) *Comparing Financial Systems*, Cambridge, MA: MIT Press.

Barber, B.M. and T. Odean (2001) Boys will be boys: gender, overconfidence, and common stock investment, *Quarterly Journal of Economics*, 1: 261–92.

Beck, T. and A. Demirgüç-Kunt (2009) Financial Institutions and Markets Across Countries and Over Time: Data and Analysis, *World Bank Policy Research Working Paper* No. 4943, May 2009.

Beck, T., A. Demirgüç-Kunt, and R. Levine (2003) Law and finance: why does legal origin matter?, *Journal of Comparative Economics*, 31(4): 653–75.

Chinese Culture Connection (1987) Chinese values and the search for culture-free dimensions of culture, *Journal of Cross-Cultural Psychology*, 18: 143–74.

Chui, A.C.W., S. Titman, and K.C.J. Wei (2010) Individualism and momentum around the world, *The Journal of Finance*, 65(1): 361–92.

Daniel, K., D. Hirshleifer, and A. Subrahmanyam (1998) Investor psychology and security market under- and overreaction, *Journal of Finance*, 53(6): 1839–85.

de Jong, E. (2009) *Culture and Economics: On Values, Economics and International Business*, London: Routledge.

de Jong, E. and R. Semenov (2009a) Cultural determinants of financial behaviour. In P. Mooslechner, V. Redak, M. Schürz, and E. Springler (eds), *Auf der Suche nach dem Selbst*, Marburg: Metropolis.

de Jong E. and R. Semenov (2009b) *A Theory on Cultural Determinants of Stock Market Development: Its Strength and Limits*, paper presented at the 21st Annual EAEPE Conference, 6–8 November in Amsterdam.

Djankov, S., R. LaPorta, F. Lopez-de-Silanes, and A. Shleifer (2003) Courts. *Quarterly Journal of Economics*, 118(2): 453–517.

Hall, P.A. and D. Soskice (2001) *Varieties of Capitalism: The Institutional Foundations of Comparative Advantage*, Oxford: Oxford University Press.

Hofstede, G. (2001) *Culture's Consequences*, 2nd edn, London: Sage.

Hofstede, G., G.J. Hofstede, and M. Minkov (2010) *Cultures and Organizations: Software of the Mind*, New York: McGraw Hill.

Iannaccone, L.R. (1992) Heirs to the Protestant ethic? The economics of American fundamentalists. In M.E. Marty and R. Scott Appleby (eds) *Fundamentalisms and the State: Remaking Politics, Economics, and Militance*, Chicago: University of Chicago Press.

Knight, F.H. ([1921] 1971) *Risk, Uncertainty and Profit*, Chicago: University of Chicago Press.

Kwok, C.C.Y. and Tadesse, S. (2006) National culture and financial systems, *Journal of International Business Studies*, 37: 227–47.

La Porta, R., F. Lopez-De-Silanes, A. Shleifer, and R.W. Vishny (1997) Legal determinants of external finance, *Journal of Finance*, 52: 1131–50.

La Porta, R., F. Lopez-De-Silanes, A. Shleifer, and R.W. Vishny (1998) Law and finance, *Journal of Political Economy*, 106: 1113–55.

LaPorta, R., F. Lopez-de-Silanes, A. Shleifer, and R.W. Vishny (1999) The quality of government, *Journal of Law, Economics and Organization*, 15(1): 222–79.

Lewis, M. (2011) *Boomerang; Travels in the New Third World*, New York: W.W. Norton.

Licht, A.N, Goldschmith, C. and Schwartz, S.H. (2005) Culture, law, and corporate governance, *International Review of Law and Economics*, 25: 229–55.

Nurmi, J.-E. (1992) Cross-cultural differences in self-serving bias: responses to the attributional style questionnaire by American and Finnish students, *Journal of Social Psychology*, 132: 69–76.

Pagano, M. and P.F. Volpin (2005) The political economy of corporate governance, *The American Economic Review*, 95(4): 1005–30.

Prasad, E.S., Rajan, R.G., and A. Subramanian (2007) Foreign capital and economic growth, *Brookings Papers on Economic Activity*, 1: 153–229.

Rajan, R.G. (2010) *Fault Lines: How Hidden Fractures Still Threaten the World Economy*, Princeton: Princeton University Press.

Rajan R.G. and L. Zingales (2003) The great reversals: the politics of financial development in the 20th century, *Journal of Financial Economics*, 69: 5–50.

Röell, A. (1996) The decision to go public: an overview, *European Economic Review*, 40: 1071–81.

Schwartz, S.H. (1994) Beyond individualism/collectivism: new cultural dimensions of values. In U. Kim, H.C. Triandis, C. Kagitçibasi, S.C. Choi, and G. Yoon (eds), *Individualism and Collectivism: Theory, Method, and Applications*, London: Sage, 85–119.

Sobis, I. and de Vries, M. (2009) *The Story behind Western Advice to Central Europe during its Transition Period*, Bratrislava: NISPAcee.

Stulz, R.M. and R. Williamson (2003) Culture, openness, and finance, *Journal of Financial Economics*, 70: 313–49.

Williamson, O.E. (2000) The new institutional economics: taking stock, looking ahead, *Journal of Economic Literature*, 38. 595–613.

3 Culture as discursive practice

Combining cultural political economy
and discursive political studies in
investigations of the financial crisis

Amelie Kutter and Bob Jessop

Since the North Atlantic Financial Crisis became evident in 2007, arguments in terms of culture (broadly understood) have become more prominent in public debate and academic analysis. In public debate, for example, the emergence or persistence of crisis has been explained in terms of 'greed' as a human disposition, the 'bonus culture' in the financial sector, or the hegemony of the 'efficient' market hypothesis in theoretical and policy paradigms. Similar trends are found in academic debates. In mainstream economics, for example, there is growing interest in behavioural economics; the Keynesian critique of 'Casino capitalism' has been revived; and there was renewed interest in Minsky's arguments about the psychology of speculative and Ponzi finance. Likewise, in political economy, we can observe how the history of economic ideas and economic sociology are mobilized to explain weaknesses in accumulation strategies and economic policy. In their different ways, these approaches all indicate that 'culture matters'. While looking beyond prevailing mainstream perspectives to cultural factors is certainly timely, it cannot provide a blank cheque for any and all kinds of cultural explanations. Indeed, there are real pitfalls facing those who make 'cultural turns'.

First, one may easily fall into soft economic sociology and constructivism. They counter-pose culture, broadly interpreted, to 'hard' rationalist, institutionalist, or economistic explanations as an entry point and/or explanatory factor. In so doing, they privilege culturalist interpretations and explanations and overlook the mutual constitution of meaning-making and structuration (Sum and Jessop, this volume, for a discussion). Another potential trap resides in hasty generalization and essentializing classification. For instance, it was common in 2008 to identify ad hoc measures of crisis management with paradigmatic choices, reading liquidity injections and short-term stimulus packages as a return to the post-war Keynesian policy paradigm. The fact that German politicians and regulators rejected any deviation from the prevailing EU monetarist consensus during negotiations on Eurozone crisis management has often been identified with an essentially German policy tradition or national economic culture. While economic paradigms and national policy traditions will certainly be relevant during policy-formulation, it is questionable whether they can be straightforwardly read into heterogeneous contemporary debate and whether they take on the content suggested by conventions of academic disciplines, be that the concern with para-digms of economic theory in political economy or the concern with national identity and tradition of economic thought in comparative studies. In fact, by identifying culture with substantive-ideational content or by associating it with some essential characteristics of a national collective, one might run the risk of stereotyping culture, failing to grasp its contentiousness, multiplicity, and transformation.

These considerations are partially motivated by the findings that emerged from the study of German financial commentary on the Eurozone crisis pre-sented in this chapter. The study revealed that, in the important conjuncture of early 2010 when the EU's approach to crisis management was not settled yet, an opinion-priming segment of mediatized debate – the financial press – was reluctant to support the German government's policies. Commentators con-demned the government's (slowly diminishing) opposition to the rescue of indebted Eurozone members, debt restructuring, debt-targeting by the European Central Bank, or comprehensive EMU reform. They did so with reference to plurality of theoretical traditions, while distancing themselves from a 'German model', be that identified with a superior growth model, German Ordoliberalism, or prudent fiscal management. Still, their portrayals and causal stories of the crisis would lend plausibility to the overall approach to crisis management that largely enhanced the German government's preferences.

This chapter uses this puzzle to illustrate the dilemmas of interpretation facing those who take an interest in a cultural turn in political economy. The chapter shows how to make a cultural turn without falling into 'soft' interpretative studies and without stereotyping or essentializing culture. We propose a combi-nation of two approaches that have proved fruitful in exploring the financial crisis and its management: Cultural Political Economy and Discursive Political Studies.[1] The first conceives of culture as complexes of meaning-making and highlights the mutual conditioning of two equally necessary modes of complex-ity reduction: sense- and meaning-making and structuration. This excludes one-sided cultural or structural explanations and draws attention to the articulation of economic imaginaries and institutional and spatio-temporal fixes in a variegated economic and political space (see Introduction; and Heinrich and Jessop, this volume). The second approach uses the knowledge-theoretical insights of the linguistic turn and the specific epistemology of Critical Discourse Analysis to establish that discourse is a 'hard' fact reality that takes on its own dynamics (Kutter forthcoming-a). It is shown how, drawing on Critical Discourse Ana-lysis, one can develop a reflexive method of interpretation that highlights the discursive aspect of complexity reduction without losing sight of agential, struc-tural, and technological dimensions highlighted in CPE.

The chapter outlines the insights generated in CPE and Discursive Political Studies to then develop a discourse-theoretical entry point to the CPE agenda. The Eurozone crisis is introduced as a disorienting moment in which established spatio-temporal fixes fail to contain crisis dynamics and give way to struggles over the definition of future fixes. Drawing on the example of the German financial press, and editorials from the business daily *Handelsblatt* more particularly, we show how discourse matters in complexity reduction, not only by streamlining representations of the crisis, but by bringing these representations in line with the practice of financial journalism and its agential, technological, and structural modes of selection. The chapter concludes with some reflections on that (thought) experiment.

Cultural political economy on variation, selection, and retention

A key argument of CPE is that no individual or collective agent can ever comprehend the totality of all economic (and economically relevant) activities in all its complexity – let alone in real time. This is why it focuses on economic imaginaries as enforced efforts to reduce that complexity as a condition of going on in the world. What actors (and observers) conceive of as an 'economy' (or some of its constituent parts) is the result of complexity reduction that emerges through sense- and meaning-making and structuration within and across specific spatio-temporal horizons. CPE interprets culture as sense- and meaning-making, which is a universal feature of social interaction rather than a distinct field or sub-system of the social world. It regards 'culture' as 'the ensemble of social processes by which meanings are produced, circulated and exchanged' (Thwaites *et al.* 1994: 1). As such, culture turns the inordinate complex economic world into intelligible objects of calculation, management, and intervention. And it is this that justifies, indeed, necessitates, a cultural turn in disciplines that neglect the crucial, ontologically foundational nature of sense- and meaning-making in social life. Structuration, on the other hand, refers to the setting of limits to com-possible combinations of social relations and stabilizing the expectations and actions of diverse individual and collective actors. It reduces the complexity of the economic world by establishing temporary fixes in time and space that allow for continued accumulation (Sum and Jessop 2013 and this volume).

Although every social practice is semiotic (in so far as social practices entail meaning), no social practice is reducible to its semiotic moments. Semiosis involves more than the play of differences among networks of signs and is therefore never a purely intra-semiotic matter without external reference. It cannot be understood or explained without identifying and exploring the extra-semiotic conditions that make semiosis possible and make it more or less effective – including its embedding in material practices and their relation to the constraints and affordances of the natural and social world. This highlights the role of variation, selection, and retention in the development and consolidation of some construals rather than others and their embedding in practices that transform the natural and social world. This poses several methodological challenges on how to analyse discourse without falling into voluntarism or discursive imperialism and, at the same time, without falling into the structuralist view that the requirements of institutions and/or systems determine which ideas get adopted and become hegemonic in terms of their ideational adequacy to system reproduction.

CPE conceptualizes the co-evolution and structural coupling of meaning-making and structuration in terms of the three generic processes of variation, selection, and retention. It posits a greater variety of potential economic imaginaries and accumulation strategies than could co-exist in practice within a given spatio-temporal envelope. Thus makes it necessary to explore the manner in which specific imaginaries and strategies are *selected* through discursive and material mechanisms and translated into strategies and policies; and that shape the process of *retention* when these strategies and policies prove more or less effective and become sedimented into taken-for-granted imaginaries and relatively coherent sets of social relations. Sum and Jessop have proposed four such mechanisms involved in this complex, overlapping, and recursive process of variation, selection, and retention. These are summarized in Table 3.1, which is largely self-explanatory (for a more detailed explication, see Sum and Jessop 2013).

This research strategy can be applied in at least two ways. One strategy is to pursue an analysis that integrates all four modes of selectivity within the broader CPE framework and uses them to interpret and explain a specific phenomenon drawing on a Foucauldian-type archive of various materials. Sum's tracing of the constitution and translation of competitiveness discourses across territorial scales and her investigations in the 'BRIC' story are impressive examples of this comprehensive, integral strategy (Sum 2009 and this volume respectively; for partial realizations see Heinrich and Kutter 2013, and Heinrich and Jessop, this volume). These applications integrate concepts from interpretive studies and Foucauldian governmentality in an eclectic-productive manner. The other strategy is to privilege one of the four entry points and to develop a consistent framework that captures this particular mode of selectivity and guides its in-depth primary analysis. At the same time, the conditioning of this mode of selectivity by the other modes would be made explicit, both at the level of conceptualization and description. This second option is pursued below, with Discursive Political Studies – and linguistic Critical Discourse Analysis in particular – being the privileged entry point.

Discursive political studies

Adopting 'discourse' as the primary analytical entry point to a CPE agenda while avoiding, at the same time, the pitfalls of thin interpretation, implies taking the knowledge-theoretical assumptions of discourse approaches seriously and putting them into dialogue with the overall assumptions of CPE. Robust, theoretically substantiated, discourse approaches are distinguished by an epistemological linguistic turn. They not only assume that language and discourse matter in cognition and social construction but also seek to understand social and political reality in and through their linguistic-discursive constitution, adapting concepts from linguistics and literary studies (on epistemological turns, see Bachmann-Medick 2009: 30). Through such linguistic turn, ideas, agents, or structures turn into points of intersection of discourses. The focus of attention shifts towards

Table 3.1 The four modes of selectivity and their effects

Mode	Grounded in	Effects
Structural	Contested reproduction of basic social forms (e.g. capital relation, nature-society relations, patriarchy, racism), their specific instantiations in different institutional orders and organizational forms, and in specific interaction contexts.	Structures favour some interests, identities, agents, spatio-temporal horizons, strategies, and tactics over others. Focuses on how path-dependency limits scope for path-shaping. Structure is not an absolute constraint that applies equally to all actors. Selectivities are relative, relational, and asymmetrical.
Discursive	Semiosis as sense- and meaning-making that is grounded in enforced selection in the face of complexity. Operates at all scales from the micropores of everyday life to self-descriptions of world society.	Semiosis provides and articulates elements of meaning-making and thereby shapes perception and social communication. Discursive selectivity frames and limits possible imaginaries, discourses, genre chains, arguments, subjectivities, social and personal identities, and the scope for hegemony, sub-hegemonies, and counter-hegemonies.
Technological	Technologies regarded as assemblages of information and categories, disciplinary and governmental rationalities, sites and mechanisms of calculated intervention, and social relations for transforming nature and/or governing social relations.	Involve specific modes of objectivation, subjectivation, knowledging technologies, interwoven dispositives, and social coordination. As well as their differential capacities to transform nature, technologies shape social relations through (1) horizontal and vertical divisions of labour and knowledge, (2) their material effects (e.g. the built environment or anatomo- and biopolitics), and (3) their epistemological effects ('truth regimes'). Shape choices, capacities to act, distribute resources and harms, and convey legitimacy through technical rationality and effectivity.
Agential	Specific capacities of specific social agents (or sets of agents) to 'make a difference' in particular conjunctures thanks to idiosyncratic abilities to exploit structural, discursive, and technological selectivities.	'Agents make their own history but not in circumstances of their own choosing.' Making a difference depends on abilities to (1) read conjunctures and identify potentials for action; (2) re-politicize sedimented discourses and re-articulate them; (3) invent new social technologies or recombine extant technologies; (4) deploy strategies and tactics to shift the balance of forces in space-time.

understanding the discursive construction of ideas, agents, and structures and the social-political implications of such construction. We will briefly recall the knowledge-theoretical foundations of this linguistic turn and the variety of discourse theories it produced in the field of political studies broadly understood. Recognizing the differences between discourse theories and their philosophical roots is a prerequisite for developing a discourse-theoretical entry point to the CPE agenda.

Knowledge-theoretical foundations

The linguistic turn is the result of an ongoing discussion in the humanities on the knowledge-theoretical implications of modern language philosophy that posits that all cognition is conditioned by language. In the social sciences, the debate has taken two routes (see Kutter forthcoming-a, ch. 3, for an elaboration of the following). On the one hand, the linguistic turn stimulated reflection upon adequate conceptions of interpretation. Drawing on Wittgenstein and Heidegger, scholars in hermeneutics moved beyond the inherited opposition between a hermeneutics of recovery, which focused on uncovering the intended meaning, and a hermeneutics of suspicion, which focused on uncovering the true meaning behind the apparent, distorted understandings of society. Instead, they proposed a reflexive hermeneutics, one that gives expression to social imaginaries in which language and social practices are embedded, making them a subject of moral and political reflection and dialogue (Gibbons 2008).

On the other hand, the linguistic turn was driven by the adoption of linguistic structuralism in the social sciences and associated criticisms directed at this approach, formulated from the viewpoint of (post-Marxist) social theory, sociolinguistics, literary intertextuality studies, and interpretive studies broadly understood. Advocates of a structuralist semiotics of social relations suggested that social reality was to be understood and studied as a synchronous system of signs whose meaning is given by their differential position within the system, following Ferdinand de Saussure's structuralist theory of language. Critics questioned the one-sided focus on structure (the language system; *langue*) and highlighted meaning-constitution through linguistic interaction, communication, performance (the language event; *parole*); thus paving the way for various 'post-structuralist' cultural turns (Bachmann-Medick 2009: 34–6).[2] In contrast to reflexive hermeneutics, this current suggests that any communication or dialogue is embedded or implicated in power-immanent formations and practices of discourse. It implies that their performativity can only be disentangled through deconstructive-reconstructive methods.

Discourse theories

The lasting contribution of the linguistic turn is to have de-naturalized assumptions about social reality, culture, and scientific truth and to have produced a range of post-positivist epistemologies. More specifically, the linguistic turn has generated what could be called Discursive Political Studies: a set of distinct theories that conceptualize the political in its broadest sense from a discourse-theoretical angle. Only some of them will be presented here to illustrate the potential that these approaches, as *discourse theories*, offer for the study of political-economic phenomena. They each address different aspects of the political and rest on diverging assumptions about how the discursive construction of these phenomena works and how it should be studied (Kutter, forthcoming-a, ch. 3).

The three most prominent are: deliberative studies; Foucauldian discourse studies; and discourse studies of hegemony. Deliberative studies examine the role of practical reasoning in building political-societal consensus, drawing on Jürgen Habermas' adoption of speech act theory in a reflexive hermeneutics that is situated in the tradition of the Frankfurt school (Habermas 1984). Deliberative studies conceive of discourse as 'debate' and focus on the conditions and procedures, such as quality of argumentation and the speech act situation, which are assumed to enhance the mediation of dominant and marginal proposals for the solving of collective problems (see, for example, Fischer 2003). Foucauldian discourse studies, on the other hand, explore discursive modes of discipline and government, drawing on Michel Foucault's discourse archeology and study of governmentality with their specific roots in (post-)structuralist semiotics and the French history of mentalities (Foucault 1997). These studies conceive of discourse as power-immanent 'formation of knowledge'. They investigate operations of signification and complexes of semiotic practices that enact inclusion or exclusion and implicate the individual in specific modes of government (see, for example, Angermüller and van Dyk 2010). Discourse studies of hegemony, finally, explore discursive modes of shifting and maintaining social-political power under conditions of overdetermination and contestation. They draw on Ernesto Laclau and Chantal Mouffe's discourse-analytical account of radical democratic politics that integrates elements of Gramsci's ideas on hegemony to post-structuralist semiotics (Laclau and Mouffe 2001). The crucial moment of discursive construction is here seen in operations of signification that make a particular political-economic project partially hegemonic. The discourse analysis of such 'hegemonic articulations' usually focuses on how chains of equivalence between 'elements' of signification are established and dissolved (see for example Howarth and Griggs 2012).

The three approaches all strive for grand explanation of the political as such and seek to grasp discourse phenomena at a high level of abstraction. However, there are important variants of smaller-range discourse theories that address discursive construction at the micro and meso level of social organization. They focus on discourse phenomena at a lower level of abstraction, such as the framing of a scenario of action or generic patterns of linguistic interaction specific of a field of social practice. For instance, interpretive policy studies focus on how a situation is grasped emotionally-conceptually and transformed into a scenario of political intervention in public-political debate. They conceive of discourse as 'collective mental constructs' and expect them to be revealed in 'narratives', 'frames', or 'concepts' as defined in interpretive and narrative sociology, usually referring to the hermeneutic tradition (see for example Conolly 1993 or Stone 2012). Yet another conceptual framework is provided by linguistic Critical Discourse Analysis (CDA). This current conceives of discourse as linguistic interaction (language in use) that is specific of a particular political setting or field of social practice. Drawing on socio-linguistics, critical linguistics, systemic functional linguistics, or intertextuality studies, CDA expects social inclusion or exclusion to be revealed in the linguistic-discursive features of texts produced in these specific contexts (Fairclough and Wodak 1997).

This overview over selected discourse theories demonstrates that 'discourse' can mean very different things. A robust discourse study will always have to make explicit which epistemological universe (or combination of theories) it is borrowing. It will have to consider the limits of the chosen approach implied by its theoretical tradition (hermeneutics, (post-)structuralist semiotics, linguistics) and level of abstraction. Ignorance of these differences has caused misunderstandings, according to which 'grand' discourse theories suffer from obfuscating abstractionism, interpretive and linguistic discourse approaches cling to linguistic and phenomenological positivism and are useful, at best, as methods. Once one engages in actual discourse analysis, however, it will soon become apparent that conceptual work at all levels of abstraction is necessary. In short, a robust discourse study involves developing a discourse-analytical strategy that conceptualizes the subject under investigation from a specific theoretical perspective and makes such conceptualization consistent and transparent across levels of abstraction and analysis (Kutter forthcoming-a, ch. 3).

Culture as discursive practice: using CDA as privileged entry point

In this chapter, the discourse theory of linguistic Critical Discourse Analysis is used as a starting point for formulating an analytical strategy that corresponds to the overall framework of CPE and which is suited to investigate complexity reduction in crisis debate. Drawing on CDA, one can investigate the discursive mode of selectivity in-depth without losing sight of the other modes of selectivity outlined in CPE. In addition, the perspective of CDA provides an original way of addressing the challenges of a 'cultural turn' mentioned in the introduction, such as the danger to soften and to essentialize culture.

As outlined before, CDA assumes that intersubjective meaning (and hence culture in the understanding of CPE) is constituted through context-dependent linguistic interaction. It can be studied in the correspondence between linguistic features of texts of an utterance, such as textual, grammatical, or semantic characteristics, and the context of expression. The context, in turn, has its own discursive features: the pragmatic and cognitive underpinnings of the interactional setting, the generic discursive practice of the social-institutional field in question, or intertexts and voices that invoke events or accustomed lines of interpretation (for text-context heuristics in CDA see Wodak 2008: 11–14). By enacting these contextual dimensions, a single utterance becomes meaningful to the participants. At the same time, it acquires new meaning when recontextualized within another setting or specialized field of social practice.

Using the discourse theory of CDA has several implications (Kutter forthcoming-a, ch. 3). First, investigating 'culture' here implies reconstructing 'situated discursive practice', which ranges from events of linguistic interaction (the act of signification) to conventionalized linguistic-discursive routines that form part of a broader social practice such as financial journalism. Collective understandings of the political or the economy cannot be revealed independently of discourse agency and its specific 'situatedness'. The second conclusion is that other modes of selectivity outlined by CPE are implicated in such discursive practice. They are partially identifiable in concrete texts when these are carefully put in context. For instance, agential modes of selectivity, which stem from agents' relational positioning and differential capacity, can be discerned from self- and other representations of social actors in the text and the pragmatics of the text. Thus, predication (characterizations), mitigation, or argumentation will convey the speaker's effort at positioning herself and persuading the (imagined) interlocutor (van Leeuwen and Wodak 1999). The technological mode of selectivity can be identified when focusing on genre, that is on various aspects of text organization that are specific of a specialized social practice (Fairclough 2003: 67). The structural mode of selectivity comes into play rather intermediately, when considering how generic patterns of linguistic interaction enact macro-level modes of governance or fractioning of capital (see section 'Investigating complexity reduction'). Taking the stance of CDA, third, implies an increased awareness of the way one makes inferences from texts. Text analysts following an interpretive-hermeneutic framework usually focus on identifying content (such as proposals, claims, scenarios of action) and take this content as indicative of a specific theoretical paradigm or political-economic ideology. A critical discourse analysis, instead, explores the way this content is shaped, accentuated, and transformed through textual composition and strategic use of a variety of means, such as lexis, argumentation, or genre. The sensitivity towards the materiality and performativity of texts and the conditioning contexts facilitates the development of methods of critical-reflexive reading. It allows distancing oneself from the categories suggested by academic discipline and contemporary political debate.

A discourse-analytical strategy for investigating complexity reduction

To examine the complexity reduction involved in representations of crisis and crisis management, an analytical strategy was adopted that combines insights from narrative policy studies and CDA. While concepts of narrative policy studies capture how specific approaches to crisis management are constructed discursively, concepts from CDA grasp how such constructions are rendered persuasive within a specific setting of linguistic interaction. While CDA provided the theory and epistemology for studying text in context, narrative policy studies suggested what aspects of linguistic interaction were relevant for the discursive construction of scenarios of political intervention.

Following narrative policy studies, scenarios of political intervention, such as crisis management, are generated through arguments that identify causes, consequences, and responsibility for past events and, in so doing, move a situation from the realm of fate to the realm of human agency (Stone 1989: 283). Once mobilized in public, such 'causal stories' can set and shift agendas, challenge or perpetuate social order, place the burden of losses and adjustment, empower 'fixers', enforce a programme that happens to be high on the agenda, or restructure alliances (Stone 1989: 297). Hence, in causal stories of crisis, one can identify a first instance of complexity reduction: they highlight (only) certain crisis phenomena and attribute causation and responsibility in specific ways.

Considering the mediatization of politics in late modern societies, Hay points to processes of meta-narration that emerge from mass mediation and may delimit the space in which causal stories about crisis can be told and politically contested. By meta-narration, Hay refers to abstractions in media coverage that replace the specific attributions of agency and causality in individual stories by more general attributions and that integrate disparate events by identifying some common essence of crisis. Drawing on the example of media discourse during the Winter of Discontent in the United Kingdom in 1978–1979, he shows how individual accounts of strikes against wage-cuts were assimilated into a major story. According to this story, the strikes were indicative of 'a crisis of an overloaded state held to ransom by the trade unions and brought to this condition by its reliance on moribund Keynesian techniques' (Hay 2010: 447). Drawing inspiration from this narrative reading of the Winter of Discontent, one could identify further instances of complexity reduction involved in mediatized crisis representation; three moments of generalizing abstraction: the accentuation of certain crisis phenomena rather than others; their construction as indicative and symptomatic of a more general and complex failure; and the extrapolation from a range of disrupting events to a threat that affects a larger collective in existential ways requiring immediate action. While the first two moves of abstraction lend plausibility to a certain scenario of action, the latter mobilizes support for its implementation. Thus, complexity is likely to be reduced not only by specific causal stories that integrate experiences of disruption into scenarios of political intervention, but also by moves of abstraction that lend plausibility to some causal stories rather than to others (for a discussion see Kutter forthcoming-b).

These assumptions were implemented in a critical discourse analysis that triangulated a range of text-analytical methods. A qualitative content analysis identified major elements of crisis-related causal stories, including the highlighted crisis phenomenon, cause, blame-taker, and proposal for an exit strategy. A rough argumentation analysis scrutinized the argumentative construction of individual causal stories focussing on the claim, the grounds, and warrants they were based on (Toulmin 2003). Finally, the analysis of legitimation strategies revealed the less obvious means by which the author's general communicative plan was rendered persuasive, e.g. through justifying reference to reason, authority, or morals; or by means of plausibilization, such as rhetorical figures, allusion, (linguistic forms of) narration, or wordplay (Kutter, forthcoming-a, ch. 3; van Leeuwen and Wodak 1999). The subsequent synoptic analysis, aided by the software *atlas.ti*, revealed recurrent types of causal stories and types of generalizing abstraction regularly linked to some of them. It also brought to light how structural, agential, and technological selectivities were textually enacted (for examples see Kutter 2014). The following sections will show how the analytical strategy can be brought to bear in a CPE of the Eurozone crisis.

The Eurozone crisis as a disorienting moment

Crises occur when a set of social relations (including their connection to the natural world) cannot be reproduced (cannot 'go on') in the old way. They may be manageable through routine forms of crisis management (including muddling through, displacement, or deferral) or provoke a crisis in crisis management. A crisis is most acute when crisis tendencies and tensions accumulate across interrelated moments of a given structure or system, limiting manoeuvre in regard to any particular problem. Shifts in the balance of forces may also intensify crisis tendencies by weakening or resisting established modes of crisis management (Offe 1984: 35–64). Nonetheless, a crisis is never a purely objective, extra-semiotic event or process that automatically produces a definite response or outcome. Without subjective indeterminacy, there is no crisis – merely chaos, disaster, or catastrophe and, perhaps, fatalism or stoicism. Crises are a potential moment of decisive intervention and transformation, where, rather than muddling through, decisive action can repair broken social relations, lead to change via piecemeal adaptation, or produce radical innovation. In short, crises are potentially path-shaping moments (Jessop 2013b). Crises often produce profound cognitive, strategic, and practical disorientation by disrupting actors' sedimented views of the world. They disturb prevailing meta-narratives, theoretical frameworks, policy paradigms, and/or everyday life and open the space for proliferation (*variation*) in crisis interpretations, only some of which get *selected* as the basis for 'imagined recoveries' that are translated into economic strategies and policies – and, of these, only some prove effective and are *retained* (Jessop 2013a, 2013b).

The Eurozone crisis can be considered an acute crisis of this kind and disorienting moment. Devaluation dynamics on bond markets produced sovereign debt crises, in particular in those recession-struck countries whose growth models had suffered from the 2007/2008 financial crisis and who could not buffer pressures by currency devaluation due to Eurozone membership, such as Greece, Ireland, Portugal, and Spain (GIPS). This situation invited financial speculation on GIPS' default and Euro devaluation and threatened to extend losses to holders of GIPS' bonds in the financial centres of the European Union. As EU representatives were divided on measures of crisis management, the financial crisis was paralleled and reinforced by impasse in multilateral negotiation. Intergovernmental polarization was fuelled by media panics that pitched national audiences or social groups against each other as good compliant vs bad non-compliant Europeans or prudent vs parasite members of society (Kutter 2014). These multiple crisis tendencies impaired the routines of managing Eurozone stability and produced a crisis of crisis management within the European Union (Heinrich and Jessop, this volume). In this initial period of disorientation, several alternative exit strategies were voiced. However, thanks to the coordinated agenda-setting at EU level, dissent was channelled into a relatively consistent approach to crisis management oriented on established objectives of EU economic integration. The approach centred on maintaining financial stability within the Eurozone by means of fiscal consolidation, to be achieved through austerity (cuts in public expenditure), deflationary policies (for example, wage cuts), and competition-oriented restructuring at the national level; enhanced by central coordination and oversight at EU level; and enforced by credit conditionality following the example of the International Monetary Fund (IMF) towards members that faced solvency issues (Kutter 2014). When examining the current outcome of crisis management from a CPE perspective, the question arises about the modes of selectivity (structural, discursive, technological, and agential) through which this temporary 'fix' was produced (for a combined examination see Heinrich and Kutter 2013). When choosing the discursive mode as privileged entry point to analysis, as done here, the question is how discursive dynamics contributed to selection and retention.

Investigating the selective dynamics of crisis debate in the financial press

This question will be assessed by examining how the Eurozone crisis was constructed and explained in public debate, drawing on the particular example of the German financial press. The investigation started from the assumption that financial journalists, by providing expert opinion about adequate strategies of crisis management in the context of high uncertainty, contribute to the selection and retention of specific approaches to crisis management. Given that their interpretive authority increased with continuing financialization of economic and social relations and given their high visibility as 'crisis readers of first resort', financial journalists are likely to have influenced the general course of debate, though rather in the role of a crisis explainer than an agenda-setter. Since they professionally mediate between the specialist discourse of economics and the common sense of a larger national audience, they are also likely to normalize and streamline the debate by recontextualizing events and proposals in established categories of debate on economic policy.

This particular contribution of financial journalists is studied drawing on a sample of 50 editorials published on the Greek and Eurozone crisis in the major German business daily *Handelsblatt* in 2010. The articles were taken from a larger sample of financial commentary on macroeconomic policy (Kutter 2013a). Within this spectrum, *Handelsblatt* represents an important voice. It is the German business daily with the highest distribution, which provides expert opinion on business and financial news with special emphasis on individual sectors and firms.

Handelsblatt targets an educated readership and praises itself for being read by the higher ranks in business and politics. During the period of investigation, *Handelsblatt* competed for this prestige and audience with the financial daily *Financial Times Deutschland* (*FTD*) and specialist pages in national general opinion papers such as *Frankfurter Allgemeine Zeitung* (*FAZ*) or *Süddeutsche Zeitung* (*SZ*), all run by different publishing houses. While *FTD*, modelled on the British *Financial Times*, highlighted international financial markets and took a more holistic view on capitalist economies, *SZ* and *FAZ* privileged the perspective of small investors and the different stakeholders of German economic and social policy.[3]

The editorials in *Handelsblatt* certainly reflect this constellation. They promoted an editorial line slightly different from that of the other papers. Similar to commentaries in *FTD*, they distanced themselves from Greece-bashing that was predominant in tabloid and general opinion papers in 2010. Just as *FTD* commentaries, they harshly criticized the German government's policies and came up with alternative suggestions. But *Handelsblatt* editorials would not advocate stimulus as an exit strategy and would not refer to Keynesian theorems of aggregate demand when pointing out Germany's contribution to the disaster as did some commentators in *FTD* (for voices of *FT/FTD* see also Young and Semmler 2011). *Handelsblatt* editorials stood out with their consistent plea for a comprehensive restructuring of Greek debt, to be combined with quick, but conditional, bailout and 'structural reforms'. They also campaigned for a decisive deepening of economic and currency union before the reform of the Economic and Monetary Union (EMU) was placed on the political agenda. However different the *Handelsblatt* proposals seemed from those of the German government, they still enhanced the overall direction that EU representatives took from March 2010 on: a crisis management that relied upon coercive fiscal consolidation and enhanced central coordination of EU economic governance. In order to understand how *Handelsblatt*'s crisis representations were involved in locking-in this approach it is necessary to move beyond the editorialists' explicit stances or relational positioning and reconstruct the complexity reduction implied in crisis narratives and financial commentary. Below, the findings are presented that were produced with the help of the discourse-analytical strategy outlined before (see section 'Culture as discursive practice').

Complexity reduction through causal stories and generalizing abstraction

The in-depth analysis of the (meta-)narrative construction of *Handelsblatt*'s crisis-management proposals revealed that these were embedded in two dominant causal stories. The story of excessive government debt (debt story), which was predominant during the first half of 2010, highlighted problems of public finances, attributed causation to expansionary fiscal policy or neglect of competitiveness, put the blame on national governments and called for 'smart' (competitiveness-enhancing) austerity. It portrayed the sovereign debt crises in the Eurozone as resulting from national policy failure. The story of the flawed system of the European Economic and Monetary Union (EMU story), which gained salience from March 2010 on, highlighted problems with the institutional design of the EMU. It attributed causation to overly 'soft' budgeting rules, missing instruments for their enforcement and for state or bank rescue. EU heads of government and state took the blame for erroneously optimistic assumptions about the viability of such institutional design, for politically capturing the existing instruments of EU economic governance, and for delaying necessary reform towards a deepening of economic integration.

However, the debt story and the EMU story were not uncontested. In fact, they were challenged by contradicting stories. Thus, the story of flawed banking foregrounded problems of private finances and attributed causation to flawed financial regulation and corporate culture. The story of financial market dynamics highlighted the logics of financial speculation as overruling any prudent fiscal policy. And individual editorials called into question the assumption that a stringent design of regulatory policy alone would do the job of stabilizing the Eurozone, pointing to a necessary adjustment of the role of the European Central Bank or the interdependency of various European and global financial zones.

The greater appeal of the *debt story* and the *EMU story* resides above all in moves of generalizing abstraction and objectifying depictions of financialization rationalized with reference to neoclassic economics. The persuasiveness of the two stories is derived from the particular way journalists constructed the Greek situation as a 'case' informing crisis management in more general ways. With reference to the Greek case, of which editorialists assumed that it was characterized by high structural government debt that triggered devaluation spirals on financial markets and affected the whole of the Eurozone, a specific notion of crisis was established. The Greek crisis appeared as symptomatic of a general failure of fiscal policy applying to all EU member states; and as revealing systemic failure in the regulatory design of the EMU. As journalists conjured up the threat of metastasis and Eurozone or EU break-up (and thus an existential threat for the EU collective as such), coercive fiscal consolidation and enhanced central governance became compelling solutions. The threat of contagion and system breakdown, which lend plausibility to extraordinary EU-wide political intervention, was rendered palpable by drawing an analogy to the financial crisis in 2007–2008. The point of comparison was constructed by reference to theorems of information asymmetries (and particularly moral hazard) and by naturalizing depictions of financial markets. The latter were seen to establish the 'truth' about the viability of an economy or financial system. Their verdict was treated as factual constraint and the maintenance of (financial) 'market confidence' as imperative against which any measure of state rescue or EMU reform was to be evaluated (for the full study see Kutter 2014).

Complexity reduction through selectivities of financial commentary

The streamlining effect of causal stories and meta-narration was supported by features of the specific practice of financial journalism with its structural, agential, and technological selectivities. Financial journalism is an institutionalized profession that draws, on the one hand, on mass media practices and, hence, classifies and processes knowledge according to the news value (controversy, celebrity, proximity) assumed to attract the attention of the (national) target audience and appeal to its assumed ideological preferences. On the other hand, the profession employs specialist knowledge of finances and business when rationalizing economic developments, following debates in international specialist communities. In financial commentary, economic developments, including crisis tendencies, are mediatized in line with this professional practice (structural selectivity at the meso-level). The investigated commentaries consistently foregrounded those proposals for crisis management that triggered controversy and were voiced by influential national and EU politicians or representatives of important regulatory bodies such as the Federal Reserve, the ECB, the Bundesbank, or the IMF that all followed the same conception of growth promotion, financial conditionality, and intergovernmental coordination. In addition, the journalists highlighted those aspects of the crisis that could be rationalized with reference to theorems of (mainly orthodox) economics, as demonstrated in the previous section.

With the continuing financialization, financial journalism has become more significant, both in terms of references made to financial commentary outside of the profession and in terms of the space attributed to financial news and commentary within business and general opinion media. This trend has endowed financial journalists with interpretive authority and positioned them in strategic ways. They are seen to belong to a transnational class that consistently pushed for the efficiency of financial markets and, correlatively, called for the retreat of state intervention. However, since the 2007–2008 financial crisis, financial journalists have taken the blame for acting as a mouthpiece of financial interests and failing to expose malfunctions and malfeasance. The investigated commentaries reflect some re-positioning along these lines (agential selectivity). They integrated criticism and alternative views, while keeping up the ideological-editorial profile of the paper vis-à-vis competitors. For instance, *Handelsblatt* editorialists did not hesitate to identify pre-crisis financial policies as misallocation resulting from regulatory capture by financial interests. At the same time, they would insist on only modest re-regulation of financial markets, conjuring up the threat of renewed red tape or 'socialism'. And while they castigated the existing design of the EMU, they confined criticism to the institutional set-up, rather than bring up the issue of EU-promoted financialization and the dependencies among unsustainable growth models that it created. Hence, alternative views were co-opted, rather than used for shifting established (orthodox) schemes of interpretation. This can be shown in strategies of mitigation that qualified a deviating view or downplayed the blame attributed to financial actors or (captured) regulators (Kutter 2013b).

Finally, the practice of commenting on finances and macroeconomic policy is selective due to the specific techniques of text composition and the more general tendencies of governmentality that it employs (technological selectivity). Thus, the editorials analysed showed features of a classic journalistic opinion piece, providing pointed commentary in line with an editorial preference. At the same time, they evoked the structure of policy advice, moving from problem-definition and problem-analysis to problem-solution. Through this evocation of the practice of policy advice, enhanced by pleas for 'lesson-drawing' to be straightforwardly implemented in policy, financial journalists gave resonance and legitimacy to the 'rationality project' (Stone 2012: 9–11). They suggested that policy-making should be a technocratic matter of finding the adequate fix; a fix that responds to (naturalized) logics of financial markets.

Conclusions

The overall aim of this chapter was to demonstrate how 'culture' could be integrated in political economy without falling into 'soft' interpretative studies and without stereotyping or essentializing culture. We proposed a combination of two approaches that have proved fruitful in exploring the financial crisis and its management: Cultural Political Economy and Discursive Political Studies. CPE provides theoretical and analytical tools for addressing crisis construals without losing sight of the lessons of critical political economy about the basic (material) features of capitalism, its foundational contradictions, its crisis tendencies, and the dynamics of differential accumulation. It suggests conceiving of culture as process of sense- and meaning-making that is analytically and empirically distinct from, but nonetheless coupled with, structuration as a process of setting limits to possible combinations of social relations (here economic and financial relations). As such, culture is expected to impact on (or be implicated in) crisis and crisis management through processes of variation, selection, and retention. In the course of this evolutionary process, the complexity of the totality of economic relations is reduced to calculable and manageable objects. Drawing on these assumptions, we proposed to explain specific outcomes of crisis management, such as the EU's prioritizing of Eurozone financial stability over recovery at the periphery, as a product of such complexity-reduction; to be revealed in structural, discursive, technological, and agential modes of selectivity.

Discursive Political Studies, on the other hand, help to specify this research programme with regards to the crucial question of the discursive mode of selectivity. They provide post-positivist epistemologies through which the construction of specific aspects of the political can be studied, including the selective construction of scenarios of political intervention and crisis response. By combining two theoretical strands in Discursive Political Studies, namely, narrative policy studies and linguistic Critical Discourse Analysis, we developed an analytical strategy that addressed discursive modes of complexity-reduction in public debate on the Eurozone crisis, and in financial commentary published in the German business daily *Handelsblatt* in 2010 more specifically. Drawing on middle-range theories such as 'causal stories' and 'meta-narration' (narrative policy studies) and 'legitimation strategies' or 'genre' (CDA), we showed how varying and contradictory representations of crisis were discursively narrowed down so that some proposals for crisis management became more persuasive than others. This streamlining was not only driven by dynamics of mediatized crisis debate, that is, thanks to recurrent generalizing abstraction from the 'Greek case' as being symptomatic of general failure of fiscal policy and EMU institutional design. It was also produced by the specific generic linguistic-discursive practice of financial journalism and the structural, agential, and technological selectivities it enacts. It is these features of complexity-reduction, rather than some essential and substantive ideational content, that lends authority to specific approaches to crisis management.

Overall, the study invites us to consider the foundational character of meaning-making (or: culture) and expose it as a 'hard fact' reality that is implied in, rather than juxtaposed to, any political-economic activity. The combination of CPE and Discursive Political Studies ensured that the investigation of culture qua sense- and meaning-making followed consistently a *via media* between 'soft economic sociology' and interpretation, which one-sidedly emphasize the constructivist features of economic activities and their greater or lesser social embedding in wider sets of social relations, and a 'hard political economy', which one-sidedly naturalizes and reifies the basic economic categories and 'laws of motion' of the profit-oriented, market-mediated economy.

Notes

1 The chapter results from the authors' collaboration within the framework of the project 'A Cultural Political Economy of Crisis and Crisis Management' directed by Bob Jessop at Lancaster University 2010–2013 and funded by the ESRC (RES-051–27–0303). The discourse analysis of *Handelsblatt* editorials on the Eurozone crisis was possible thanks to Seed Money awarded to Amelie Kutter by the European University Viadrina in 2013–2014. We are indebted to the editors for their helpful remarks and to Sophia Grunert and Mathis Heinrich for their research support.
2 Post-structuralism here refers exclusively to the critique of adoptions of linguistic, de Saussurian, structuralism; this critique is shared by most discourse approaches from Foucault on. Even though theory evolution overlaps historically, this variant of post-structuralism should not be conflated with a constructivist critique of structural Marxism.
3 The varying profiles of the newspapers emerged from a corpus analysis of the word frequencies and word clusters. On media data and reader surveys at the time of the research, see 'Leseranalyse Entscheidungsträger in Wirtschaft und Verwaltung (LAE)', www.m-cloud.de/LAE2011/. Note that *FTD* went bankrupt in December 2012.

References

Angermüller, J. and van Dyk, S. (2010) (eds) *Diskursanalyse meets Gouvernementalitätsforschung. Perspektiven auf das Verhältnis von Subjekt, Sprache, Macht und Wissen*, Frankfurt/M.: Campus.
Bachmann-Medick, D. (2009) *Cultural Turns. Neuorientierungen in der Kulturwissenschaft* (3rd, rev. edn), Reinbek bei Hamburg: Rowohlt.
Conolly, W. E. (1993) *The Terms of Political Discourse*. 3rd edn, Oxford: Blackwell.
Fairclough, N. (2003) *Analysing Discourse: Textual Analysis for Social Research*, London: Routledge.

Fairclough, N. and Wodak, R. (1997) Critical Discourse Analysis. In T.A. van Dijk (ed.), *Discourse as Social Interaction*, London: Sage.

Fischer, F. (2003) *Reframing Public Policy: Discursive Politics and Deliberative Practices*, Oxford: Oxford University Press.

Foucault, M. (1997) *Essential Works of Foucault, 1954–1984*. Edited by P. Rabinow, New York: The New Press.

Gibbons, M. T. (2008) Hermeneutics. In W. A. J. Darity (ed.), *International Encyclopedia of the Social Sciences*, Detroit, MI: Thompson Sale.

Habermas, J. (1984) *The Theory of Communicative Action*. Translated by T. McCarthy. Boston: Beacon.

Hay, C. (2010) Chronicles of a death foretold: the Winter of Discontent and the construction of the crisis of British Keynesianism, *Parliamentary Affairs*, 63: 446–70.

Heinrich, M. and Kutter, A. (2013) A critical juncture in EU integration? The Eurozone crisis and its management 2010–2012. In F. Panizza and G. Philip (eds), *The Politics of Financial Crises*, London: Routledge.

Howarth, D. and Griggs, S. (2012) Poststructuralist policy analysis. Discourse, hegemony and critical explanation. In F. Fischer and H. Gottweis (eds), *The Argumentative Turn Revisited: Public Policy as Communicative Practice*, Durham/NC: Duke University Press.

Jessop, B. (2013a) A cultural political economy of crisis construals in the North Atlantic Financial Crisis. In M. Wengeler and A. Ziem (eds), *Sprachliche Konstruktionen von Krisen*, Bremen: Hempen.

Jessop, B. (2013b) Recovered imaginaries, imagined recoveries. In M. Benner (ed.), *Before and Beyond the Global Economic Crisis*, Cheltenham: Edward Elgar.

Kutter, A. (2013a) Zur Analyse von Krisendiskursen: korpusgestütze Explorationen der nordatlantischen Finanzkrise aus politisch-ökonomischer Perspektive [Analysing crisis discourse: corpus-based explorations of the North-Atlantic Financial Crisis]. In M. Wengeler and A. Ziem (eds), *Sprachliche Konstruktionen von Krisen*, Bremen: Hempen.

Kutter, A. (2013b) Totgesagte leben länger. Die Fortschreibung ökonomischer Ordnung in Krisenlektionen der deutschen Finanzpresse [Their death was prematurely reported: constructions of social-economic formation in the German financial press]. In J. Maeße (ed.), *Ökonomie, Diskurs, Regierung: Interdisziplinäre Perspektiven*, Wiesbaden: VS Verlag.

Kutter, A. (2014) A catalytic moment: the Greek crisis in the German financial press, *Discourse & Society*, 25.

Kutter, A. (forthcoming-a) *Polity-Construction: Discourse and Legitimation in the European Union*.

Kutter, A. (forthcoming-b) Others are to blame: crisis narratives in the financial press, *Critical Policy Studies*.

Laclau, E. and Mouffe, C. (2001) *Hegemony and Socialist Strategy. Towards a Radical Democratic Politics*. 2nd edn, London: Verso.

Offe, C. (1984) *Contradictions of the Welfare State*, London: Hutchinson.

Stone, D. (1989) Causal stories and the formation of policy agendas, *Political Science Quarterly*, 104: 281–300.

Stone, D. (2012) *Policy Paradox: The Art of Political Decision Making*, 3rd rev. edn, New York: W. W. Norton.

Sum, N. L. (2009) The production of hegemonic policy discourses: 'competitiveness' as a knowledge brand and its (re-)contextualizations, *Critical Policy Studies*, 3: 184–203.

Sum, N. L. and Jessop, B. (2013) *Towards a Cultural Political Economy: Putting Culture in its Place in Political Economy*, Cheltenham: Edward Elgar.

Thwaites, T., Davis, L., and Mules, W. (1994) *Tools for Cultural Studies*, Basingstoke: Palgrave Macmillan.

Toulmin, S. (2003) *The Uses of Argument*, Cambridge: Cambridge University Press.

van Leeuwen, T. and Wodak, R. (1999) Legitimizing immigration control: a discourse-historical analysis, *Discourse Studies*, 1: 83–118.

Wodak, R. (2008) Introduction: discourse studies – important concepts and terms. In R. Wodak and M. Krzyzanowski (eds), *Qualitative Discourse Analysis in the Social Sciences*, Basingstoke: Palgrave.

Young, B. and Semmler, W. (2011) The European sovereign debt crisis. Is Germany to blame?, *German Politics and Society*, 29: 1–24.

Part II
Cultures of finance

4 What price culture?

Calculation, commensuration, contingency, and authority in financial practices[1]

Oliver Kessler

The North Atlantic economic malaise, which eventually turned into a global economic crisis, will certainly be remembered as a defining moment in global finance. Gone is the heady discourse of unfettered globalization and light-touch regulation that marked the pre-crisis period from the mid-1970s to the mid-2000s. Given the magnitude and duration of the crisis, it is no surprise that a plethora of narratives, interpretations, data, and suggestions for technical fixes are currently up in the air. Even though the G20, the International Monetary Fund (IMF), the Financial Stability Board (FSB), and the Bank for International Settlement (BIS) still cling to the idea of the inherent rationality of finance and, accordingly, attribute the crisis to all sorts of exogenous shocks, asymmetric information, misaligned incentives, or regulatory failures (FSB 2009a, 2009b, 2010a, 2010b, 2011; FSB/IMF 2010; FSB/IMF/BIS 2010; FSF 2008a, 2008b; IMF 2008a, 2008b), this strategy has become increasingly unconvincing to many, even in the circles that once advocated for it. For this strategy not only repeats the efficient market hypothesis and legitimizes the search for 'technical fixes',[2] but also disregards the transformative dynamics within financial markets that preceded (and helped to precipitate) the crisis.

Meanwhile, outside the core regulatory network, these changes are addressed under the heading of financialization, finance-led, or finance-dominated capitalism, a rubric that implies that more is at stake than regulatory or market failures (see Deutschmann 2011; Engelen *et al.* 2010, 2011; Ertürk *et al.* 2008; French *et al.* 2011; Kessler and Wilhelm 2013). The crisis was not simply a 'failure' of otherwise stable markets. Rather, the crisis demonstrates that we have to understand both the internal dynamics of financial practices and the changing constellation of finance vis-à-vis other sectors before we can begin to explain what happened and is happening. Without financialization and the advent of the new network of actors, models, and financial instruments, the crisis would not have occurred. From this perspective, the crisis points to a *social* dimension in the valuation processes of markets themselves that must be understood in its own terms (cf. Best 2009; Hall 2009; Jessop 2004; Kessler 2012; Leander 2009; Sinclair 2009; and Tsingou and Seabrooke 2009). Consequently, the question of how to reform financial markets is not just a question of introducing simple technical fixes to a technical problem but, rather, one that requires a conceptual discussion on 'the social' in finance, i.e. its character as a set of instituted social relations, and its potential consequences for the nature, scope, and effectiveness of regulatory measures. It is necessary to develop a different social theory that allows us to see and assess things differently before we mobilize to change things or think about scientific 'tests' or 'proofs'. Otherwise, we are bound to repeat yesterday's mistakes (in so far as these were due to the neglect of 'the social') and implement reforms that will be invalidated (or shown to be inadequate) by the next crisis.

In this light, my contribution pursues three different, albeit interrelated, arguments. First, the concept of prices provides a more promising vantage point than risk for exploring economic or financial cultures and crises, that is, helps us to better understand, describe, and frame financial contingency. Specifically, it reveals where culture becomes relevant in the modes of calculation around price formation and its role as a signalling mechanism. Second, authority is linked to the 'art of contingency management' and related to knowledge claims about contingency and this notion can be fruitfully applied in the economic and, especially, financial domains, especially in an era when finance-led or finance-dominated accumulation has become crucial. Third and finally, the reconstruction of boundaries between systems, symbolic media (including money), and so on, allows cultural political economists to get a better handle on the limits of regulation and the 'function' of 'critique'.[3]

The chapter has three main sections. The first reconstructs some *problematiques* and dimensions of 'cultural finance' by discussing the recent LIBOR scandal to inform my later discussion of conceptual questions related to culture in the second section. In particular, the latter proposes that prices rather than risk allow us to describe financial contingency. The third section indicates further avenues that the cultural political economy approach could pursue: the management of contingency through authority and the reconstruction of constitutive boundaries in the context of regulation and critique.

Bringing culture back in

To approach, conceptualize and frame the social in finance, the notion of culture appears promising (cf. Best and Paterson 2010; Sum and Jessop 2013). The 'revival' of culture is not attributable to some higher force within the dynamic of IPE as a transdisciplinary enterprise nor is it due to some recent empirical proof of an *ex-ante* formulated hypothesis or to some other 'empirical' necessity. Its rationale is far more 'practical' and pragmatic: the notion of culture is widely used in the media, public, and policy circles. It is used when there is talk about differences between Main Street and Wall Street; about the necessary split of retail (or 'normal') from investment banking as they constitute distinct 'cultures'; or about how the 'quants' have changed finance. It also arises when someone notes that previously non-economic fields have been colonized through finance.[4]

There is certainly much to the claim that we face a crisis of a specific financial culture. Culture is, of course, a hopelessly vague and fuzzy term.[5] Its uses

include a way of doing business, a possibility to have a career within a surrounding network of relationships, identities, and expectations, a specific set of authorities, rationalities, social ties, material objects, and 'legitimate' practices (cf. the
editors' introduction).[6] Thus there is an obvious risk that, in invoking culture
without further specification, we speak past each other. Yet this is eventually
also one reason why the notion of culture is so appealing: it allows us to talk
about processes, changes, and problems we do not yet understand without over-
simplifying our conceptual apparatus.

Given that the transformative dynamics in advanced capitalist economies
during the last 20–30 years have rested on, reinforced, and generalized a new
financial culture, the million-dollar question now is, of course: how can we
understand culture in general and 'financial' culture in particular? At once we
face a conceptual problem. The question of 'culture' is too often posed in essen-
tialist terms, that is, when we ask what ultimately unifies a given 'culture' and
distinguishes it from other cultures. Yet all such searches have ended in fiasco
and the notion of culture has been replaced by other concepts, such as routines
or conventions.

Of course, everybody familiar with social theory will instantly realize that no
ultimate solution to this challenge is possible. Culture has no core, no stronghold or
ground from where it can be tamed. For example, with the notion of culture, we
touch upon the old micro-macro problem and would have to differentiate between
culture on the micro and macro level. On the micro level, it is used to describe the
changing internal organization and everyday interactions within finance itself
(Knorr-Cetina 1999; Knorr-Cetina and Bruegger 2002). In macro-terms, culture is
either used to denote the changed perception, (dis)embedding, legitimacy, and influence of finance vis-à-vis other spheres – in addition to any other structural changes
that might have occurred (see financialization above). Yet we know that the micro-
macro *problematique* has no final solution and it is futile to seek one. Rather this
contribution proposes to change perspective. Instead of searching for the 'stuff' of
cultures, the germ from which cultures emerge, emanate, and decay, I propose to
understand 'culture' in relational terms by linking it to the concept of *contingency*.
Contingency describes the realm between the necessary and impossible. This realm
of the possible (and compossible), however, is not a natural object or thing subject
to physical laws. As the crisis has shown, what is possible or impossible changes in
tandem with the network of actors, models, and instruments. Contingency is a social
product of this mutual observing, thinking, evaluating, acting, and knowing. Generally speaking, *culture describes the specific type of contingency within a field*. In
order to be identifiable as a distinct culture, finance has to be separated from other
things, areas, or rationalities: it needs to be separated from legal cultures, security
cultures, or political cultures. Instead of asking what culture is, the primary question
posed here is *how are cultures differentiated*, that is, how are their boundaries set
and reproduced in such a way as to allow for the emergence of the specific kind of
complexity that characterizes that field and for the specific ways in which that complexity is reduced in that field? This is not to engage in a new form of essentialism,
but to ask for the 'condition of possibility' for a specific culture and its associated

contingency.[7] It points to a reconstruction of constitutive rules, intersubjective meanings, and the specific operations and observations of finance.

In this context I want to ask what it is about the operation of financial markets that links it (and them) to economics and not to, say, literary studies. This something is, I suggest, the price mechanism. Accordingly, my contribution proposes that from the perspective sketched in the previous paragraph, a cultural political economy of price discovery and formation and its performativity can help us to understand what kind of contingency (and operations) we are dealing with in finance, how this contingency is managed through specific forms of knowledge and authority, and how distinctive cultures of finance that emerge on this basis problematize attempts at regulation and critique. More specifically, I argue that contingency in finance, its 'rules of formation' and its operations, can be explored in terms of the operation of a distinctive kind of *price formation*. It is common knowledge, of course, that prices are both a condition of economic rationality and its characteristic representation. But there is nothing automatic or spontaneous about the price mechanism, especially in the financial system. We must ask how prices for financial products are enabled, how they interconnect, how the operation of price mechanism is secured, and how prices 'perform' their functions in the financial system and the wider economic order. In this regard I want to argue that it is the 'authority' of economists and, especially, financial economists, with its system-specific 'imaginary', codes and programmes, that stabilizes the field within which prices are formed and within which they can connect. Indeed, given the widespread acceptance among practitioners and academics alike that Lionel Robbins (1932) was right to characterize 'economics' as the 'science of trade-offs and prices', we can understand how they gain the capacity and legitimacy to provide the 'relevant' knowledge and background for the formation of financial expertise and to apply it within the regulation discourse. Prices enable us to link authority, in the sense of the acknowledged expertise and institutionalized capacity to manage contingency, in the economic and financial sphere. For it is overwhelmingly economists who are key experts, hold key administrative positions, and are the key commentators in this field – not anthropologists, sociologists, or historians.

This conceptual move allows us to see two things. First, the concept of prices links the micro with the macro: it points to cultures of validation, calculative practices, and the 'mutual observation' of financial participants. Second, the notion of culture is unavoidably tied to sense- and meaning-making (semiosis) and also involves a specific take on the problem of 'the production of the normal' (structuration). To explore this avenue, the next section turns to the recent LIBOR scandal.

LIBOR and the culture of banking

Within the banking sector, the application of the models, devices, calculative practices, and mutual observations between actors is not the same as 20 years ago. It is fair to say that with these changes came a new culture of banking. In the eye of the wider public this 'new culture' has bred corruption, cynicism, and fraud. What is true is that an entire economy of symbionts and parasites has emerged around the pleasures and needs of over-paid bankers. This is not to feed into another round of accusations about greed and corruption, but cultures do have their own criteria and standards of what is normal or deviant behaviour.[8] Inside and outside perspectives thus necessarily differ on their evaluation of the same 'action' or the same set of practices. This clash of perspectives is quite visible in the significant rise of financial scandals and frauds over the last years. It does not seem completely outrageous to believe that financial actors have developed a distinct culture that not only makes these practices possible, but that made them acceptable (see Chappe *et al.*, this volume). The vastly different ways in which these actions or practices can be evaluated has been demonstrated recently in the contestation and negotiation that has occurred in public hearings where interrogators, bankers, and the wider public confront each other in apparently mutual incomprehension (one cannot see what one cannot see). I will try to reconstruct these clashes by looking at one of the biggest financial frauds of the entire post-war economy: the manipulation of the London Interbank Offered Rate (LIBOR) and other, similar rates.

The LIBOR is a benchmark to reflect at what rates banks could borrow unsecured funds from each other. It is an estimate based on daily reports. The banks are asked to answer the question 'At what rate could you borrow funds, were you to do so by asking for and then accepting inter-bank offers in a reasonable market size just prior to 11 am London time?' At exactly 11 am every day, 16 banks report their expected costs on 10 currencies and 15 maturities. From these reports, the lowest and highest 25 per cent are discarded and the LIBOR is calculated as the median of the remaining 8 reports for each maturity. Ever since its introduction back in 1986, the LIBOR has become one of the key references in financial markets. According to recent estimates, the LIBOR serves as a reference for more than 10 trillion USD of loans (mortgages, credit cards, car loans, student loans, etc.) and more than 350 trillion USD of swaps. It is fair to say that the LIBOR (and equivalent rates in other financial markets) is at the heart of the circulation of capitalist credit money, interest-bearing capital, and ever more rarefied derivatives. If capitalist credit money is at the heart of modern capitalism (Ingham 2004), LIBOR is its nervous system.

The LIBOR scandal

The LIBOR scandal unfolded back in 2008. An article in the *Wall Street Journal* on 16 April 2008 openly questioned the accuracy of LIBOR and set off a machinery of investigations, public outcry, and stigmatizations.[9] During these investigations, it became known that the LIBOR was systematically manipulated and that all those who had their mortgage or credit linked to the LIBOR had to pay the price for this (sometimes benefitting, sometimes losing). In particular, the US authorities compiled several reports and demanded steps from the Bank of England to restore LIBOR's credibility. Finally, in June 2012, Barclays admitted that the reporting system was manipulated and accepted a fine of 290m GBP.[10] In July, a parliamentary inquiry was ordered in the United Kingdom and two executives of Barclays resigned (including the previously untouchable CEO, Bob Diamond). Two facts are very disturbing: first, the LIBOR scandal was long in the making. Already back in 2007, there was growing concern within the FSA and the Federal Reserve that the submitted LIBOR rates did not reflect the true costs of money. At that time, first unofficial reports that questioned the reported figures were sent to the British Bankers' Association (responsible at the time for setting LIBOR) and to the US Commodity Futures Trading Commission. Yet it took several years before actions were actually taken.

The second disturbing feature is how easy it was to manipulate the LIBOR: it is based on estimates stated in reports supplied by the banks themselves and, if they report wrong numbers, then LIBOR is set at a wrong price. Currently, it is unclear whether the manipulation was coordinated by an insider group or the result of a 'gentlemen's agreement'. But what appears to have happened is that key players (such as Bittar from Deutsche Bank or Hayes from Barclays or Danziger of Royal Bank of Scotland) were able to manipulate the LIBOR in two ways:[11] first, they were able to report wrong prices through their banks by influencing the report panel; and they used their good ties with brokers to get them to report wrong market information to support the numbers given in the reports. In return, the banks would order so-called wash-trades, the simultaneous buying and selling of one asset, which would leave a nice fee with the brokers. All it took were a couple of emails. See, for example, the following conversation:[12]

JEZRI MOHIDEEN (then the bank's head of yen products in Singapore): 'What's the call on LIBOR', in a 21 August 2007 chat.
DANZIGER: 'Where would you like it, LIBOR that is'
UNKNOWN TRADER: 'Mixed feelings, but mostly I'd like it all lower so the world starts to make a little sense'
TAN CHI MIN: 'The whole HF world will be kissing you instead of calling me if LIBOR move lower' (HF= hedge funds)
DANZIGER: 'OK, I will move the curve down 1 basis point, maybe more if I can.'

This conversation not only shows how simple it was to manipulate the rate (assuming that it worked in this instance) but how this was done with no sense of wrong-doing. For them, it was as exciting as buying onions in the supermarket. At the same time, it was an easy way to make money: the trading floors could bet against the movement – and make millions; it was like playing poker where only one player sees the hands of the other players.

What makes the LIBOR fraud fascinating is not just its magnitude but also because it is just one of many ways to manipulate indices and benchmarks: energy indices, oil prices, CDS prices, and even Fortex. Everywhere where regulators do not set the rate themselves, but ask for reports from the industry, one can expect that prices are systematically reported wrongly. One could say that this is against the free market ideology, that the free market forces would have led to the right numbers and that therefore this illustrates the need for less rather than more regulation. However, I think that this is exactly the wrong lesson to be learned: it has become clear that the Bank of England itself is a weak regulator de-coupled from important information streams and the Financial Service Authority (FSA) is notoriously unwilling to enforce tight regulations. This 'absence' allowed the 'culture' to spread where this behaviour was now regarded as being normal. Even though I do not want to rationalize this behaviour or to feed common arguments about greed, this scandal shows that the way *numbers* are produced points to a cultural dimension of finance: the fraud was embedded in a system of mutual favours, of recognition, help, assistance, and solidarity.[13] The ties between bankers and brokers for example reaches beyond the mere professional interaction that economists envision: an entire economy of gifts, services, and favours has emerged, including paid prostitutes, horse races, travels, and freely available cocaine. Through this manipulation, one could help traders in distress to get their quotas and signal solidarity.

However, the story of the LIBOR scandal goes beyond the story of collusion among a group of bankers. The LIBOR scandal reflects the transformative dynamics of banking in the last 20 years: it touches upon the end of Glass-Steagall and the separation of investment from credit units within a bank; the kind of regulation set in place, the financialization of Western economies, and the ties between traders, brokers, and regulators in specific ways. The LIBOR scandal is a story made possible by the advent of the current culture of banking. Much has been written on these changes, the decline of the gentlemanly capitalist ethos of 'my word, my bond' within these circles in favour of more ruthless profit-making and rent-seeking. However, this is not the most interesting way to explore: instead, it shows that the spread of a culture is linked to an institutional arrangement, the link between actors and rests 'between' them: this is what constructs a specific contingency and makes these practices possible. The question to be asked at this point is what culture tells us about the 'contingency' in finance. The hearing with Bob Diamond is very instructive.

The hearing

Interestingly enough, the issue of culture was raised at the hearing of Bob Diamond, former CEO of Barclays. In fact, the notion of culture appears throughout the hearing and shows how culture links up with questions of what is perceived to be possible, the limits of regulation and solidarity between the actors. The hearing starts with several questions about Diamond's resignation and the chain of events preceding it. Already question 8 by the Chair of the hearing committee raises the issue of whether there was not a problem with the culture at Barclays. The following questions again and again refer back to the problem of culture, the centralized management structure within Barclays. Question 114 turns the question of culture to the question of the role of banking in today's society. The commission uses culture to show that this behaviour was accepted and consequently known to Diamond whereas Diamond stresses that this was the wrong-doing of a few that does not represent the culture of Barclays.[14] Rather, the culture of Barclays helped to cooperate fully with regulators and wipe out this behaviour.[15] In this exchange, culture serves as a key concept to make sense of what has happened, to allocate guilt, knowledge, and thus responsibility. This becomes very clear in Question 136 where the questioner suggests to Diamond that:

> Mr Diamond, you seem to be inhabiting a slightly parallel universe, because you talk about the culture of Barclays as if that is the thing that saved Barclays, but that is the thing that is the problem. Surely you must realise how enraged people are at the criminality. You talk about reprehensible behaviour, but it is actually criminality. There is certainly a lot of talk that you have been unapproachable and that that is part of the reason for this. We also know that the absolute motivation for those traders prior to the financial crisis was their own personal gain, presumably because their personal reward was only linked to the profitability of their book and not to the profitability of the bank. What would you say to that?

Yet soon after this more 'micro' perspective on the culture of Barclays, the hearing takes an interesting turn. The question of responsibility, guilt, and culture is taken to a macro level. The following exchange is worth quoting at length:

Q175 MR LOVE: Taking the conversation that we have had so far, do you accept there is something wrong with the culture of the banking industry in this country?

BOB DIAMOND: Andrew, that is an appropriate question, given the financial crisis, given what I have had to deal with in a short time as chief executive, from the PPI scandal to swap mis-selling with small companies, to the LIBOR scandal. I think there are aspects to the culture of financial services that are changing post-financial crisis, and appropriately changing and evolving. Andrew's point – not the bad behaviour, which is wrong at any time, in any age in any business, but the context of people being rewarded more broadly on firm results, for example, is something we do even more of now. I think that –

Q176 MR LOVE: Sorry to interrupt, but can all the problems that you have just highlighted, plus the one we are here to discuss, be answered by changes in regulation? Surely something much deeper is the problem with our banking industry. Would you accept that?

BOB DIAMOND: Andrew, there were problems with the banking industry that led to PPIs, for example. Today, one of the difficult things for bank chief executives is to recognize that there were problems like PPI that happened many years ago over a period of time, but we still have to fix it today. The best we can do is recognize where there those problems were, be completely transparent with the regulators and, internally, understand exactly what the impact was, learn from those mistakes, and if customers or clients were impacted, put it right.

...

Q178 MR LOVE: But that's merely a regulatory change – superficial. I sympathize and support your call for regulatory change, but there is something much deeper at work here, and that has to be ventilated. I am asking whether you think there will be a positive result for the UK banking industry. Will it re-establish trust and confidence and make you more transparent? Would that benefit the banking industry?

BOB DIAMOND: I think in many of these things, it is a balance between how it is done, who does it, what the results are, how intrusive it is and is it impacting our ability to do business with our customers. It is hard to give a simple answer.

In this exchange, the key question turns out to be whether it is possible to 'regulate' a specific culture. This question is interesting not only from the rather technical debates one usually gets in these hearings and the public reports, but also because it essentially puts the question of culture in a more comprehensive context of *authority, regulation, and the possibility of 'critique'*.[16] How can one evaluate those practices? How can one assess what was known or not known; what is seen as normal or deviant behaviour? Who controlled contingency – and how, on that basis, can one allocate responsibility, guilt, and accountability? To pursue this, the LIBOR scandal points to two further questions that this contribution will raise – and that shed some light on the themes, subjects, and thrust of the cultural political economy. First, how can we conceptualize this link between culture and responsibility in the light of the LIBOR scandal (this is related to the question of how the concept of culture can be conceptualized in the light of the LIBOR scandal). This brings us to the question of authority and the 'management' of contingency. And, second, what are the consequences for financial regulation, that is, what could a cultural political economy tell us about the prospects and limits of regulation? The first question is addressed in the next section before we talk about financial regulation in the narrow sense.

Cultures of contingency: risk or prices?

When there is talk about culture, responsibility, or blame in social theory, the key concept commonly used nowadays to understand this relationship is that of risk. For example, Mary Douglas and Aaron Wildavsky have developed a grid-group model to show how societies allocate responsibility differently on the bases of their culturally informed concepts and understandings of 'nature' (Douglas 1992; Douglas and Wildavsky 1982). According to Douglas and Wildavsky, societies treat risk differently according to their degree of social cohesion (group) and 'imposition of rules' (grid). Risk therefore is not a cognitive category, but related to how societies deal with blame and shame. 'Critical political economists' have also turned to the concept of risk to denote the particular behaviour, identities, interactions, and interests within the economy (Amoore 2004; de Goede 2004; Langley 2013). Risk and uncertainty are also used to highlight differences between orthodox and heterodox economic thought.[17] Whereas orthodox rationality-based explanations evade uncertainty and start from given categories, identities, and strategies (minimax, tit-for-tat, and so on), heterodox approaches have in recent years highlighted the distinctive rationality of uncertainty to examine how economic actors reduce it to risk (an example of what the editors call complexity reduction) through the invocation of economic categories, definitions, and imaginaries.[18]

In contrast to these quite common lines of contestation, the LIBOR scandal points to 'structuration' through prices. That is: it is not the notion of risk or the absorption of uncertainty into risk that seems to characterize the specific 'contingency' and its spatial and temporal manifestation. Instead, it is the notion of price.[19] To ask for a description of this contingency that makes practices possible implies that the above-mentioned favours, solidarity, and, shall we say, 'economy of gifts' are not the expression of some general human disposition to create club goods. These ties are there for a reason and 'function' in a specific way that separates them from ties and nodes in religious groups, political parties, or football clubs. What is possible, how links are formed and perpetuated is different in finance from other areas. This is what is implied to talk about a specific financial culture. I suspect that – as the LIBOR example shows – these ties, practices, and 'the advent of new possibilities' can be explained and made intelligible by looking at the *formation of prices in financial markets* (especially in rarefied forms such as derivatives, CDOs, and so on). In contrast to legal judgments or political decisions, this network of actors, models, practices, and 'gifts' circled around (fictitious) prices and how they were formed (in the materiality of the LIBOR). Prices reduce complexity and at the same time produce a specific contingency. They can only change in certain ways, they have specific social, factual, and temporal consequences and need to connect in particular ways to make new prices possible. Hence, the concept of prices appears promising to understand what was going on, to put it in the context of economic rationale and financialization.

When it comes to prices, however, we have become accustomed to understand them in rather economic terms: prices are said to equilibrate supply and demand. That is essentially already everything that economists can tell us. Deviations from the common story that lower prices increase demand and lower supply (and vice versa), are then framed in terms of paradoxes or effects, that is, for example the classic observation that higher prices often increase demand due to assumed quality effects. Within this economic setting, prices operate mechanistically and within a naturalized concept of economic orders. They 'function' as 'signals' and trigger economic decisions: yet prices are actually epiphenomenal as it is this decision (on the basis of some utilization- or cost-function-based rules) and thus the economic actor who stands behind the operations of economic structures.[20]

This rather mechanistic and rational approach to prices seems to miss the lesson to be learned from the LIBOR scandal. Prices are not simply 'there' nor do they operate freely in a naturalistic systemic environment. To make use of prices for a cultural political economy, we need to leave these confines behind and re-locate them into the context of sociology and 'critical political economy'. For example, one only needs to remember that objects need to be made comparable (commensurated) in order to link them through the price mechanism: prices do have social-temporal and factual consequences: they have social consequences in so far as expectations are formed on the basis of possible payments; they have their own temporality (how fast prices can be produced is linked to the technical infrastructure of the economy, think about the impact of computer trading, etc.); and they have factual consequences as 'things' and objects change their meaning once they are subject to the 'logic of prices'.

For one price in a market to be possible, an entire set of institutions, conventions, subjectivities, and rules need to be in place. Just imagine what actually enters the picture when we look at the (artificial but real) price of money, that is, interest rates. The price is not simply the product of supply and demand, or some negotiation between economic agents on the spot. Even though we might think that it's only two persons in a room setting the interest rate, there is more to it: this 'price' links together the entire set of Banking Regulations (in particular Basle II), the institutional settings of Central Banks, that is, whether they are independent or subject to political commands, the internal regulations within banks that relate profiles of the customers to proposed interests, the production of ratings (through scores or ratings), and material objects like desktop (that produces the number once it is filled with all the information), the internet protocols which allow for the extraction of the scores and ratings for this company, person, or object on the spot, paper, pens, and so on.[21] Similarly, a price for a Collateralized Debt Obligation depended upon various regulations for the relevant actors, the ratings, and various 'class categories' for the different slices. Without the entire legal arrangement, it would not have been possible to price those 'rights'.[22]

This process of 'making prices possible' or 'price formation', the constellation of necessary institutions, models, and actors could be named *economization*. This relates to the 'quantification' of communication (some authors may speak of 'framing' at this point). Desires, beliefs, essentially the entire perceived complexity of the environment are reduced to a single number – the price. This form constructs a specific expertise, memory, temporality, and specific dynamics of instability (in the form of solvency and less of over-capacities or reduction of sales) in markets. Yet this closure is never complete: especially as prices are the 'product' of financial markets, a focus on prices is always flanked by an observation of the behaviour of others. The memory of financial markets is predominantly stored in numbers, but especially when expectations break down and financial crises occur, a different and more personalized set of memories of past trades, episodes of instability and chaos become relevant.

In the context of prices, we can now assess the role of culture: culture is not attributable to an organization, the economy as a whole or some mystic 'stuff'.

Rather, culture refers to the stabilization of this social 'context' for prices to be formable. This 'stabilization' of 'links' between them might include aspects of 'gifts', status, and solidarity. For example, one can think that if one actor has violated fundamental 'rules of the game' other actors refuse to do business and thus no price can be 'made'. Hence a change in actors, models, practices, and material devices is linked to changes in the 'culture'.[23] Through this continuous link (or reproduction) of prices – certain memories, imaginaries, identities, and subjectivities are formed. Before we can explore what this means for regulation, we must answer the prior question how – on the basis of prices – it becomes possible to separate a financial from an industrial culture – as both operate on the basis of prices?

At this point, Patrik Aspers distinguishes standard markets from status markets. These are ideal types and, in reality, we always find mixtures of both. Yet the distinction allows us to see how price formation can follow different logics in how expectations are formed. Within standard markets, there exists a 'convention' or 'generally accepted' standard. This is based on specific characteristics – quality conventions – according to which different qualities of the traded good can be differentiated. These set of characteristics are used to evaluate the material and non-material dimensions. For example, there are conventions that enable actors to differentiate qualities of raw materials, foodstuff, or homogenous commodities. Hence, it is possible to produce a vertical order of goods around these characteristics. This also implies that to be 'in' the market requires common knowledge about the standard. Yet, as Aspers points out:

> Standard market cannot – be reduced to the commodity – as any market is also about its actors. In a market ordered by standard, markets actors are positioned as a result of how well they perform according to the established scale of valuation, that is, the standard. In this type of market, it matters little who the actors are. What matters is what they do. If there is a standard entrenched in the market, actors on both sides of the market orient themselves primarily to this.
>
> (Aspers 2009: 115)

Hence, the knowledge needed to orient oneself in the market and to make informed decisions is based on the observation of other actors vis-à-vis the standard.

Such standards are (1) separate from and (2) more stable than the identities of the actors in that market (ibid: 123). Standard markets, then, in a sense correspond to the 'classic' story told in economics where the price simply makes an exchange easier.[24] The basic operation within this process is the payment from one party to the other. Through the payment a 'tacit contract' is sealed where the offer is accepted (or rejected in the case one comes to the decision not to pay the price). Payments then make future payments possible or impossible. Payments reproduce the economy while everything that makes them 'possible' (desires, demand, production, and so on) is 'beyond' the economic system, i.e. to be found in its environment (see Baecker 1988: 67; also Luhmann 1988). In this context, mainstream economic theory assumes that prices refer to goods, services, or demands: they ease the process of exchange and reduce the amount of necessary knowledge to a minimum: one only needs to know the price and compare it with one's own preferences. Knowledge about the internal organization of companies, the impact for the wider economy, or the production process is simply not *necessary* (even though this might impact on one's decisions) when we can observe a price. A price is simply a 'tag' attached to goods or services. Following this line, from this perspective, the function of prices is to reduce transaction costs. Instead of an exchange of butter for bread, one 'buys' bread and 'sells' butter on the 'market'. The logic, however, is the same and simply results from individual preferences and the exchange between economic actors.

Status markets follow a different logic. Status markets prevail where there is no 'objective' standard and aesthetic judgments are dominant. Consider, for example, the art market or that for luxury goods. In these markets, the ranking between actors is not determined by the quality of characteristics (for example the quality of wool) they produce. Rather, valuation is not independent of the actors' status themselves (Aspers 2009: 116). The exchange of goods and services is directly related to the rank order of identities of the market actors (ibid: 117). The identity of the actors is 'within' the products themselves. The values of products (prices) are 'constructed' independently from labour, exploitation, or false consciousness. Rather, as Patrik Aspers has noted, the quality of products is inherently intertwined with *who* the actors are. 'What is traded in this kind of market is a function of the participant actors' (Aspers 2009: 117). The knowledge relevant to make informed decisions is then directed towards the social order ('status') in the market and the identities of the participants. In this sense, the social 'differentiation' in the market is more stable than the goods, as we can easily find it, for example in the fashion market.

I assume that price formation in financial markets correspond more to status markets than to standard markets. Even though certain products are certainly 'standardized', the discussion above suggests that the 'culture' in banking is based on the network of personal ties, employed instruments, and calculative practices – including their status.

The similarity of financial markets to status markets is linked to the kind of expectations actors need to form. Within financial markets, we find that second-order expectations, that is, the expectations of (future) payments reproduce the system.[25] One buys or sells shares, credit or other financial products on the basis of expectations of future payments. The financial market does not produce 'commodities' independent of the identities in the market. One can say that *prices operate self-referentially here as they only refer to themselves.*[26] Consequently, the social, temporal, and factual consequences are different from commodity markets. The social consequences, for example, that someone cannot pay for some good right now, can be transformed into a temporal problem in so far as one can 'buy' the capacity to buy now and sell it later, that is, pay interest on a loan. The temporal conditions change because the temporality of the economy is not linked to production chains, harvests, or business cycles, but to the temporality of financial products, that is, settlement dates of derivatives, the 'waves' of financial indices, and so on. The factual consequences are linked to what 'individual' things, markets, or objects 'mean' within the economy: through the operation of the financial markets, the very meaning of an object (food, war, and so forth) changes: wheat in financial markets is something different from the actual physical product.

The consequences are far-reaching: already when we look at how profits are generated, then the motive of profit is usually related to differences between costs and prices. How profits are generated in standard markets depends on what actors do, how they behave, and how they evaluate quality differences. Profits with financial products are directly related to the identities of participants, for example, the ratings of the Rating Agencies or the verdict of financial analysts that all 'reveal' and 'structure' expectations about expected future payments. Prices in financial markets are a social product emerging from the set of mutual observations, the ascription of authority and expertise, and epistemic uncertainty about the value of the derivate that is closed or reduced to risk through performative processes of economic models (MacKenzie et al. 2008). Prices themselves become the material bases of financial markets and stimulate the innovation of financial products (Callon 1998; Muniesa 2007).

Hence, we can assume that how prices work within standard markets and financial markets as status markets affects the possible technological and material infrastructure, the logic of interaction, processes of semiosis and structuration, and thus their 'cultures'. Just think about the dependence of finance of fibre optic cables, the opening and closing auctions, the meaning-making processes of objects, and the authority of financial gurus and ratings – that tell us something about the future of the economy. This dependence on the future, the kind of authority necessary to run a business or satisfy demands, and the temporality of production chains is different within the real economy.[27] On this basis, for example, we often also differentiate between two 'circulations' within finance: financial streams that 'operate' according to the 'logic' of manufacturing and simply make their operations smoother by providing credit for investments; and the 'logic' of proprietary trading of banks for their own profit and own 'circulations'. Hence, the claim that banks provide crucial services to the 'real' economy – and therefore need to be rescued when in distress – exactly misses the point about 'culture' as a status market. This last point about knowledge and authority and the two different financial streams brings us back to the question of how culture allows us to assess differently the possibility of financial regulation.

Contingency, authority, and the limits of regulation

To assess the consequences for how a cultural political economy allows us to see differently the possibility of financial regulation, let us go back to the LIBOR scandal for a moment. So far, the discussion of the LIBOR scandal has shown how actors, models, and regulations were linked in specific ways to enable the manipulation of price formation (or discovery), how that was premised on an 'institutional arrangement' and specific links based on contingency. Taking the discussion of prices on board, we can now see that financialization is more than simply an extension of the logic of financial markets or of the relevance of financial profits for companies. Financialization is linked to questions of authority (the expertise, capacity, and legitimacy to manage contingency) and hence to power and, on this basis, ultimately to critique.

The question about authority can draw from the discussion on prices: while financial markets are now constituted on mathematically operating and automatic price mechanism, the meaning of prices is always referred back to epistemic authorities: these authorities can be personal like financial gurus like Soros or Druckermiller) or institutionalized like rating agencies. In any case, the constitution of authority is irremediably linked to the price mechanism and the 'making' sense of prices: authorities tell us about how contingency works, how the 'noise' can be translated, and thus we ascribe them the capacity to tell us something about the future. Crucially, any account of authority in a financialized world needs to take account of the specific operationality of financial markets. That is why the Catholic Church, football or rock stars, or even politicians are not considered to have the necessary expertise to act as an authority in financial markets (exceptions prove the rule): they deal with a different contingency.

Financialization and the spread of a financialized culture hence comes with a new 'set' of rules that allow for the ascription of authority: authority within finance is said to say something about the 'very logic' of financial markets, about the meaning of prices, and thus the future evolution of financial markets themselves. Hence authorities always control what others know and do not know. They control contingency. Rating agencies control what counts as economic knowledge, what kind of knowledge, and what kind of non-knowledge is regarded as relevant, what practices are seen as 'good' or 'bad' for the viability of companies, countries, or certain products. Authorities control the 'links' between actors and hence help to stabilize the background for prices. They are part of the social matrix of financial markets.

That said, the cultural political economy approach is far more sceptical about the *regulation* of financial markets than other approaches, for three reasons. First, as the scandal evidently shows, the regulation of individual sectors or types of actors is not enough in itself. From this perspective, the entire language of incentives, asymmetric information, and 'shocks' is hopelessly naïve in terms of its legal theory. This language assumes that regulations can make incentives 'mutually consistent', that economic agents aim to meet efficient criteria (rather than, for example, engage in control fraud), to make information symmetric by making everything transparent. Regulations cannot make markets effective by just laying out what is allowed and what is not. Yet from the discussion above, we can see that if regulations try to steer financial contingency, then the system reproduces itself: it recreates links – simply by interpreting the rules according to the 'imperatives of the culture', that is, their own particular way of sense-making.

It is not feasible to stabilize banks by simply giving them more rules to constrain them. If regulations are said to stabilize markets, then it is futile to focus on actors if they are assumed to be rule-followers rather than rule-benders or rule-breakers. Rather what needs scrutiny is how the nature of price formation and the correlative links *between* actors are stabilized (through semiosis and structuration) to allow for prices to emerge in the first place (assuming that these are not perfect markets as defined by neoclassical economics, where every actor is a price-taker rather than some being price-makers). This implies that calculative practices of organizations (which structure what and how actors mutually observe themselves) need to be subject to regulation. That said, on the sceptical side, it is obvious that even the cursory attempt to de-couple certain links will inevitably lead to counter-reactions within the system that produce new links faster than can be accounted for by regulatory bodies. The system has an incredible capacity to regenerate itself. If specific 'links' are not wanted, then one needs to simply forbid them completely. Third, the common excuse that 'one needs to have a sound banking system to have a vibrant economy' essentially confuses two circulations and does not see the different 'price logics' at play within the real and financial economy. To take them into consideration would mean that they need to be de-coupled institutionally and/or that proprietary trading within banks should be forbidden.

That brings us to the question of critique. To link culture to price formation which at the same time links questions of authority and regulation shows the hopeless situation for the 'wider public' and for the possibility of 'critique'. Any critique of current practices would need to take the position from 'within the culture', i.e. the financialized 'price formation'. Yet that requires already to become an expert in this field and to communicate within the logic of the market.[28] That implies knowledge not only about the product that is traded on the market, but also the identities and social 'fabric' that characterizes the market. At the same time, the question of critique in the sense of what the financial markets are for, the function and contribution finance makes for society, necessarily escapes this logic as it cannot be captured within this code. Critique from outside the cultural context will not be understood, it will be taken as 'illiteracy' and assumed to be based on a wrong image of what financial markets do. These two different communications – from within and outside financial culture – will only lead to mutual irritation, but not understanding.

Conclusion

This contribution pursued three interrelated objectives. Apart from a conceptual interest in the notion of culture and how it could be linked to financial markets, this contribution intended to demonstrate the need to look closer at apparent economic concepts like prices, free them from their economistic meaning, and re-locate them in the context of a cultural political economy. This contribution started with a discussion of the LIBOR scandal to show how the advent and diffusion of a culture made specific practices possible, i.e. that cultures draw a boundary between inside and outside where different criteria for evaluating actions, socialization, and soce-tialization (*Vergesellschaftung*) prevail. This 'closure' was referred to as the 'con-struction of specific contingency'. At the same time, this contribution asked how financial cultures differ from other cultures through the specific 'logic' of price for-mation and the kind of contingency they allow for. To pursue this question about contingency, this contribution suggested that culture can be grasped conceptually as the semiotic and structural modalities of the stabilization of the context of prices as a precondition for price formation (and, indeed, manipulation). On that basis, this contribution suggested that real markets and financial markets (especially in fictitious money, fictitious credit, and fictitious capital) are differentiated by their operationality of prices, especially in the context of finance-dominated accumula-tion. This distinction was then used to explore the limits of financial regulation, the constitution of authority, and the limits of critique.

Notes

1 Bob Jessop provided valuable feedback on different iterations of this chapter.
2 As the G20 has recently argued,

> [we] have agreed and are implementing a broad range of financial reforms to address the major fault lines that caused the crisis. We are building more resilient financial institutions, making substantial progress towards ending too-big-to-fail, increasing transparency and market integrity, filling regulatory gaps and address-ing the risks from shadow banking. We will pursue our work to build a safe, reli-able financial system responsive to the needs of our citizens

G20 (2013)

3 In particular, note the limits of a critique of investment banking and of a critique of 'economics': the former because it essentially has fed a culture that will remain some time yet; and the latter because of its constitutive blindness: their concept of crises does not lead us astray, it leads nowhere.
4 Just think about the fact that nobody knows the best credit sales person, but the best investors are global stars. This 'colonization' of the credit culture by the investment bank was highlighted several times when policy makers argued for a return to 'boring' banking, when it was emphasized that banking has to serve the real economy and not vice versa.
5 See for example Zelizer (2010).
6 In this context, see also the literature on performativity like McKenzie and Millo (2003).
7 One caveat is in order, as Bob Jessop pointed out in a private conversation: there are at least two kinds of contingency – the contingency of *choices* made by more or less reflexive agents in the light of their cognitive, appreciative, and normative sense- and meaning-making systems, as framed by structural contexts, and the contingency in structures (the degrees of interdependence, co-evolutionary constraint, compossibili-ties, and lack of complementarities, etc.). Interestingly, crisis is a moment of strategic disorientation and unstructured complexity – hence of greater contingency.
8 One might recall drugs as a cultural device in the arts in the 1970s – and maybe even today.
9 See www.bbc.co.uk/news/business-18671255.
10 It has become clear that the Bank of England itself is a weak regulator de-coupled from important information streams; the FSA is notoriously unwilling to enforce tight regulations.

11 It is said that Barclays, the Royal Bank of Scotland (RBS), UBS, and Deutsche Bank strategically lied about their real costs of borrowing.

12 Exchange is reported at: www.bloomberg.com/news/2012–09–25/rbs-instant-messages-show-LIBOR-rates-skewed-for-traders.html.

13 In contrast to many classic analyses from Weber to Habermas, finance does not seem to represent the prime example for 'individualized' action, but shows deep traits of common actions and 'communality'. The collusive behaviour of hedge funds and their joint dinners are eventually another example worth exploring in some detail.

14

> Q 135: One wonders how much more noise there has to be in the firm about it, before it does, as you put it, come out. When you have derivatives traders shouting out their positions across the trading floor 'to confirm that other traders had no conflicting preference prior to making a request to the Submitters' – that is paragraph 54 of the FSA report – does that not say something about the culture in Barclays?

15

> A 133: I am sorry to come back to it again, but it is a sign of the culture of Barclays that we were willing to be first, we were willing to be fast and we were willing to come out with it. That does not excuse the behaviour.
> A 134: I think that the culture has shown that when we have a problem, we get all over it. As soon as it was known, it was dealt with. I think that that is an important thing. There is a reason why an industry-wide problem is coming out now.

16 Culture is used to criticize the purely economic rationality.

17 Kessler (2008, 2012).

18 For an intriguing discussion on ignorance see McGoey (2012).

19 See here again Luhmann (1988). Also Kalthoff (2005) and his idea of 'cultures of economic calculation'.

20 In modern economics, the concept of prices has been extended to include almost everything that can be framed in terms of incentives: reputation, solidarity, or what have you.

21 See Luhmann (1988); see also Veblen (1994 [1899]) on the leisure class.

22 At the same time, as will be argued later, it points to the relations and relational underpinnings, not the individual actors themselves. The point is not that we need better banking regulations but, rather, that banking practices are strongly interconnected with other fields and rules.

23 Witness the change of the technological infrastructure of financial markets, how computer trading has replaced the outcry models in stock exchanges; how computer-based trading changes the culture of finance more generally. That means, however, that even the perceived absence of culture, the technological communication, style, professionalization, and 'technological episteme' of the field – is nevertheless a culture. This is eventually one of the basic paradoxes of cultural political economy: one cannot evade a culture and step outside of it. Cultures are always there. Being in the world is always being with others, as Heidegger would put it.

24 This and the next paragraph focus on the 'common' story. I am aware that even this rather simple story demands further qualifications but I discuss this story to highlight the one distinction between prices in commodity and in financial markets. A full story would need to consider the performative consequences of prices in commodity markets as well. Likewise, in mentioning price, I do not want to commit myself to any particular theory of money. For good discussions, see Jessop (2013) and Pahl (2008).

25 The economics of convention approach talks about a self-referentiality of financial markets (cf. Orléans 2001).

26 This does not mean financial prices have no effects on the real economy. This paragraph focuses on price formation, not on possible performative consequences.

27 In the context of contingency, we can say that authority is ascribed 'art of contingency management'.

28 One can differentiate here internal and external critiques. An external critique will identify the societal consequences of financialization (for example, in terms of the kind of inequality it creates). An internal view needs to 'rationalize' practices from 'within' the culture. My argument concerns the moment of change: if one wants to change a culture, it cannot be done by simply imposing certain regulations as the 'connectivities' that stabilize that culture will simply reorganize. This implies that frauds cannot be excused by simply referring to some 'function' the banking system fulfils for the entire economy.

References

Amoore, L. (2004) Risk, reward and discipline at work, *Economy and Society*, 33(2): 174–96.

Aspers, P. (2009) Knowledge and valuation in markets. *Theory and Society*, 38(2): 111–31.

Baecker, D. (1988) *Markt und Information*, Frankfurt/Main: Suhrkamp.

Best, J. (2009) How to make a bubble: toward a cultural political economy of the financial crisis, *International Political Sociology*, 3(4): 461–5.

Best, J. and Paterson, M. (eds) (2010) *Cultural Political Economy*, London: Routledge.

Callon, M. (ed.) (1998) *The Laws of the Market*, Oxford: Blackwell.

Deutschmann, C. (2011) Limits to financialization, *European Journal of Sociology*, 52(3): 347–89.

Douglas, M. (1992) *Risk and Blame: Essays in Cultural Theory*, London: Routledge.

Douglas, M. and Wildavsky, A. (1982) *Risk and Culture*, Berkeley, CA: University of California Press.

Engelen, E., Ertürk, I., Froud, J., and Williams, K. (2010) Reconceptualizing financial innovation: frame, conjuncture and bricolage, *Economy and Society*, 39(1): 33–63.

Engelen, E., Ertürk, I., Froud, J., Johal, S., Leaver, A., Moran, M., Nilsson, A., and Williams, K. (2011) *After the Great Complacence. Financial Crisis and the Politics of Reform*, Oxford: Oxford University Press.

Ertürk, I., Froud, J., Johal, S., Leaver, A., and Williams, K. (eds) (2008) *Financialisation at Work: Key Texts and Commentary*, London: Routledge.

Financial Stability Board (2009a) *Improving Financial Regulation*. Report of the Financial Stability Board to G20 Leaders, 25 September.

Financial Stability Board (2009b) *Progress Since the Pittsburgh Summit in Implementing the G20 Recommendations for Strengthening Financial Stability*, 9 November.

Financial Stability Board (2010a) Press Release: Financial Stability Board meets on the Financial Reform Agenda, 9 January.

Financial Stability Board (2010b) Promoting Global Adherence to International Cooperation and Information Exchange Standards, 10 March.

Financial Stability Board (2011) Shadow Banking. Scoping the Issues. Available at: www.financialstabilityboard.org/publications/r_110412a.pdf, last visited 5 February 2014.

Financial Stability Board/International Monetary Fund (2010) *The Financial Crisis and Information Gaps*, Basel: FSB.

Financial Stability Board/International Monetary Fund/Bank for International Settlement (2010) *Report to G20 Finance Ministers and Governance, Guidance to Assess the Systemic Importance of Financial Institutions, Markets and Instruments: Initial Considerations*, Basel: Bank for International Settlement.

Financial Stability Forum (2008a) *Report of the Financial Stability Forum on Enhancing Market and Institutional Resilience*, Basel: Bank for International Settlements, available at www.fsforum.org/publications/r_0804.pdf, last visited 5 February 2014.

Financial Stability Forum (2008b) *Report of the Financial Stability Forum on Enhancing Market and Institutional Resilience, Follow-up on Implementation*, Basel: Bank for International Settlements.

French, S., Leyshon, A., and Wainwright, T. (2011) Financializing space, spacing financialization, *Progress in Human Geography*, 35(6): 798–819.

G20 (2013) *G20 Leader's Declaration*. Available at: https://www.g20.org/sites/default/files/g20_resources/library/Saint_Petersburg_Declaration_ENG.pdf, last visited 28 February 2014.

de Goede, M. (2004) Repoliticizing financial risk, *Economy and Society*, 33(2): 197–217.

Hall, B.R. (2009) Intersubjective expectations and performativity in global financial governance, *International Political Sociology*, 3(4): 453–7.

Ingham, G.K. (2004) *The Nature of Money*, Cambridge: Polity.

International Monetary Fund (2008a) *Global Financial Stability Report April 2009*. Washington, DC: International Monetary Fund.

International Monetary Fund (2008b) *Global Financial Stability Report October 2009*. Washington, DC: International Monetary Fund.

Jessop, B. (2004) Critical semiotic analysis and cultural political economy, *Critical Discourse Studies*, 1(2): 159–74.

Jessop, B. (2013) Credit money, fiat money and currency pyramids: reflections on financial crisis and sovereign debt, in Jocelyn Pixley and Geoff Harcourt (eds), *Financial Crises and the Nature of Capitalist Money: Mutual Developments from the Work of Geoffrey Ingham*, Basingstoke: Palgrave Macmillan.

Kalthoff, Herbert (2005) Practices of calculation: economic representation and risk management, *Theory, Culture & Society*, 22(2): 69–97.

Kessler, O. (2008) *Die Internationale Politische Ökonomie des Risikos*, Wiesbaden: VS-Verlag.

Kessler, O. (2012) On constructivism, Hayek and the current economic crisis, *Review of International Studies*, 38(3): 275–99.

Kessler, O. and Wilhelm, B. (2013) The three utopias of shadow banking, *Competition and Change*, 17(3): 248–64.

Knorr-Cetina, K. (1999) *Epistemic Cultures: How the Sciences Make Knowledge*, Cambridge, MA: Harvard University Press.

Knorr-Cetina, K. and Bruegger, U. (2002) Global Microstructures. The Virtual Societies of Financial Markets, *American Journal of Sociology*, 107(4): 905–50.

Langley, P. (2013) Anticipating Uncertainty. Reviving Risk? On the stress testing of finance in crisis, *Economy and Society*, 42(1): 51–73.

Leander, A. (2009) Close Range: Targeting Regulatory Reform', *International Political Sociology*, 3(4): 465–68.

Luhmann, N. (1988) *Die Wirtschaft der Gesellschaft*, Frankfurt/Main: Suhrkamp.

McGoey, L. (2012) Strategic unknowns: towards a sociology of ignorance, *Economy and Society*, 41(1): 1–16.

MacKenzie, D. and Millo, Y. (2003) Constructing a market, performing theory, *American Journal of Sociology*, 109(1): 107–45.

MacKenzie, D., Beunza, D., and Hardie, I. (2008) A price is a social thing: towards a material sociology of arbitrage, in J. Beckert, R. Diaz-Bone, and H. Ganßmann (eds) *Material Markets: How Economic Agents Are Constructed*, Clarendon Lectures in Management Studies. Oxford: Oxford University Press, 85–109.

Muniesa, F. (2007) Market technologies and the pragmatics of prices, *Economy and Society*, 36(2): 377–95.

Orléans, A. (2001) The self-centered logic of financial markets, in P. Petit (ed.), *Economics and Information*, Dordrecht: Kluwer Academic Publishers.

Pahl, H. (2008) *Das Geld in der modernen Wirtschaft. Marx und Luhmann im Vergleich*, Frankfurt/Main: Campus.

Robbins, L. (1932) *An Essay on the Nature and Significance of Economic Science*, London: Macmillan.

Sinclair, T. (2009) Let's get it right this time: why regulation will not solve or prevent global financial crises, *International Political Sociology*, 3(4): 450–3.

Sum, N.L. and Jessop, B. (2013) *Towards a Cultural Political Economy: Putting Culture in its Place in Political Economy*, Cheltenham: Edward Elgar.

Tsingou, E. and Seabrooke, L. (2009) Power elites and everyday politics in international financial reform, *International Political Sociology*, 3(4): 457–61.

Veblen, T. (1994 [1899]) *The Theory of the Leisure Class: An Economic Study of Institutions*, New York: Penguin Books.

Zelizer, V. (2010) *Economic Lives: How Culture Shapes the Economy*, Princeton: Princeton University Press.

5 Financialization and the enterprise decoy

Charlie Dannreuther and Lew Perren

Introduction

The crucial question that British politicians need to ask themselves and, frankly, they ought to be asking the public too, is: do we think that finance should be a utility and simply serve the rest of the economy or do we think that finance should be an *enterprise* in its own right.

But if you want finance to be a utility then you're not going to have the profits and the dynamism and frankly the *entrepreneurial drive* that has made London so vibrant in recent years.

And you are also not going to have a big part of the British economy that has been producing taxes and driving forward growth. However if you say well actually I do want finance to be a profit-seeking *enterprise* and to have London as a crossroad of global finance then that comes with risk attached.

(Gillian Tett of the *Financial Times*, 2013, emphasis added)

Since the financial crisis broke out, there has been a broad political consensus among leading parties and key commentators that the financial sector needs to perform more like a utility. But despite stubbornly high levels of complaints regularly upheld by the Financial Ombudsman Service (FOS 2009), progress in this regard has been limited. In the UK, governments have been far more squeamish about regulating this sector because of its national champion status in the UK economy and because of the ideological conflict surrounding regulation in a liberal market economy. Political opposition has been very high and the binary distinction behind Tett's comments now reflects the prevailing assertion in the press that there is a clear choice between utility and enterprise business models for banks and that only the latter can deliver growth.

Enterprise and entrepreneurship are relatively recent arrivals in the political lexicon and have been extended across ideological, geographical and professional boundaries with remarkable ease. In this chapter we explain this rise with specific reference to the emergence of regulatory reform and the rise of financialization. Both place a premium on the enterprise as a sign to validate these reforms. We draw on Jessop's (2010) cultural political economy (CPE) approach to demonstrate how enterprise, and its synonyms, have (1) been used to reduce complexity for policy-makers and financial markets alike and (2) contributed to new regulatory and financial imaginaries that have transformed broader societal relations. By demonstrating the common emphasis on the meanings conveyed through the symbol of the entrepreneur we can also then show how the sign of enterprise has both privileged activities and been privileged by them as a symbol of post-industrial capitalism. The sign of the 'entrepreneur' contributes both to imaginaries of governance in the form of the regulatory state, and to financialization in the form of risk finance. Both are at the heart of a neoliberal ideology that has been adopted by both sides of the political spectrum in British politics (Lazzarato 2009). Both of these imaginaries create a hierarchy of meaning that sustain political and financial elites through the entrepreneurial sign. The sign of the entrepreneur both connects and reinforces the two imaginaries that frame regulatory reform and financialization (Kenny and Scriver 2012). Here we further argue that it also acts as an important decoy that detracts from the social and political tensions that have emerged around financialization.

The political consensus surrounding the need for an enterprise culture supports the idea that financial innovation, delivered by financial entrepreneurs, is a good thing. Rather than addressing the highly unpredictable consequences of dismantling major financial institutions, policy-makers have linked financial risk-taking to individuals by stimulating the supply of risk finance from individuals to companies through the sign of the entrepreneur. In this way untrammelled risk-taking in financial markets can be presented as a good thing generating great societal benefits. In the political imaginary, the construct of the entrepreneur explains why liberty and freedom are vital ingredients to the delivery of successful policy. This is because the contracting out of government policy to entrepreneurs, albeit in contracts constrained by good practice obligations, greatly simplifies the complexity of delivering policies and making difficult political choices. The deployment of the entrepreneurial sign has expanded greatly since the 1980s both to describe innovations in public sector reform and to provide simple contract based solutions for new or previously intractable policy problems. By examining the hegemonic construction of the entrepreneur in the UK (as a good thing, as a way of organizing society, as a measure of competitiveness and positive behaviour) we can begin to understand why the simple policy choice is to reach for enterprise policy.

Engineering enterprise

Cultural political economy examines 'the social production of inter-subjective meaning' through the study of signs (Jessop and Sum 2010). The automobile, for example, has the form of a vehicle and is signified by the word 'car'. But as a sign it was iconic because it 'combined forces of technocratic state modernization, misguided industrialization and thoughtless consumerism of Fordism' (Inglis 2004: 206). As a sign the car expressed much more than a mode of transport. It gave meaning to a wide range of behaviours and social institutions that helped people to organize the complexities of social relations relevant to the

Fordist regime of accumulation. The organization of symbols into meaning is a universal characteristic of human existence (Lévi-Strauss 1966). But there are differences in how a collection of symbols can be interpreted to order the chaos of nature. The *bricoleur* takes the symbols as they currently exist and through trial-and-error constructs a practical solution to the problems faced. The scientist would be selective of symbols with a view to creating a hierarchy based on the creation of a new order or one associated with other universal truths that could be communicated externally.

> The elements which the 'bricoleur' collects and uses are 'pre-constrained' like the constitutive units of myth, the possible combinations of which are restricted by the fact that they are drawn from the language where they already possess a sense which sets a limit on their freedom of manoeuvre.
>
> (Lévi-Strauss 1966: 19)

> The engineer is always trying to make his way out of and go beyond the constraints imposed by a particular state of civilisation while the 'bricoleur' by inclination or necessity always remains within them.
>
> (Lévi-Strauss 1966: 19)

Symbolic orders need not be functional but can normalize and sustain the societal conformity and inequality required to sustain capitalist accumulation regimes (Bourdieu and Nice 1980), gendered hierarchies (Kerfoot and Korczynski 2005; Pettinger 2005), cultures of consumption (Hilton 2000; Richey and Ponte 2008) and currencies (Goux 1990).

Reducing uncertainty through sense- and meaning-making can be achieved in very different ways. Even if the symbols are the same, their meanings are proposed by those assembling them into semiotic orders (Elder-Vass 2007). For example there are many meanings of the entrepreneur (Ireland and Webb 2007), so there is no single 'enterprise imaginary' but many. Yet one of the most potent symbols associated with the entrepreneur is that of the individual that has persisted in both academic and policy discourses (Drakopoulou Dodd and Andersen 2007). This heroic, saviour-like entrepreneurial imaginary has sustained market-oriented responses to the economic crisis by equating entrepreneurial success and the Irish national identity (Kenny and Scriver 2012). This national imaginary links the subject to a neoliberal ideology that in turn sustains the idea of the entrepreneur.

Saussure explains how these imaginaries exist by splitting the sign into the signified and the signifier. This highlights the arbitrary connection between the two and shows how language and linguistic conventions structure the ways in which the signifier 'entrepreneur' can be used (de Saussure 1959) (Figure 5.1). The polyvalence of the 'entrepreneur' leads to it becoming a floating signifier (Hall 1996; Lévi-Strauss 1987; Mehlman 1972) with no intrinsic relation between these conventions and the economic behaviour signified as entrepreneurial (Figure 5.1) (Jones and Spicer 2005; Perren and Dannreuther 2012; Richie 1991).

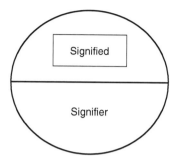

Figure 5.1 Signified and signifier (de Saussure 1959: 114).

We need to differentiate between the signifier (the word, 'entrepreneur') and the signified (the ensemble of concepts related *prima facie* to a person) (de Saussure 1959). A large literature in management science now critically examines the sign of the entrepreneur showing how it is sustained through a wide range of arbitrary associations between unrelated events and unconnected people (e.g. du Gay 1994; Jones and Spicer 2005). The symbol of the entrepreneur is therefore not solid or coherent nor is it structurally determined by a hegemonic ideology. Rather it is a weak, ghost-like construct (Jones and Spicer 2005) that needs reinforcing and sustenance to retain its power (Marttila 2013). Given the wide range of activities needed to support such a symbolic order they are clearly fragile and not, as sometimes suggested, determinant. Constantly fading, imaginaries require reaffirmation through governmental technologies if they are to come to coordinate everyday life (Hall 1985; Jessop 2010). This reflective element to the maintenance of the imaginary informs the evolutionary dynamic of the imaginary.

One characteristic of how public and academic discourses construct the entrepreneur is that an entrepreneur is recognized by what she has done rather than any innate characteristic: entrepreneurs create institutions (Steyaert 2007) or speculate on uncertainty (Blaug 1997) or release 'creative social energy' (Hjorth 2007: 713). Conceptualizing the entrepreneur in this heroic fashion makes it difficult to separate what she is from what she does (Gartner 1988 although see Cromie 2000).[1] This is what gives the entrepreneur its universal and democratic appeal: anyone can be an entrepreneur and anything can be done in an entrepreneurial way. Entrepreneurs are therefore able to administer ever increasing areas of once public activity such as 'new' managerial style depicted by Boltanski and Chiapello (2005; Budgen 2000). The entrepreneurial construct has varied across a wide range of policy arenas and investment contexts because of this very emptiness (Dannreuther and Perren 2013). Individuals can become the flexible, risk-taking, self-responsible individual of advanced liberalism by performing the activities associated with the entrepreneur (Rose and Miller 2010). The sign of the entrepreneur therefore allows neoliberal arguments to take hold because they assert the equivalence of the entrepreneur to a wide range of other, especially public sector, actors.

Decision-makers have been greatly empowered in exercising judgement under complex conditions because they can pass on the administration of challenging policy goals to entrepreneurs. Providing these entrepreneurs comply with terms of contracts they can be almost anyone from anywhere. The diversity of behaviours attributed to entrepreneurs allows decision-makers to justify their decisions by calling on the sign of the entrepreneur. Because it is assumed that entrepreneurs innovate it is also assumed that they can provide dramatic savings in public services and new solutions to long-standing problems. The potential for symbols that value entrepreneurial practice (such as achieving value for money or promoting reform) can be transferred to new areas, allowing entrepreneurs to practice in policy areas once the purview of the state alone.

Drawing on a longitudinal study of meanings associated with the entrepreneurial sign in British Parliament the following section reviews how the denotation and connotations of the entrepreneur changed over time (Perren and Dannreuther 2012). This study is used to place the meaning of the entrepreneur within broader shifts in the UK's political economy that generated tensions in political and economic relations. As the signified behaviours attributed to the entrepreneur change over time the relationship between the state and society also changes. These attributes change from actions that have meaning independent of the state, to conduct that is helpful to the state's operations, to behaviour that is promoted by government policies. While we can see that the initial construct is connected to reality, implying a potential link to a constituency and the characteristic of the debate is like that of the *bricoleur*, constrained by meanings generated externally to parliamentary debates. In subsequent decades the entrepreneurial figure is increasingly captured and engineered to help financial actors 'go beyond the constraints' imposed by traditional banking and expand to new areas of activity. For the state, the figure of the entrepreneur signified individual sufficiency and flexibility that could support new active labour market policies, for example. These symbols allowed a more centralized hierarchy of the state to emerge, based on new truths of globalization and 'no alternatives' and the need to support market competitiveness through a vibrant enterprise culture.

These different meanings showed how the sign of the entrepreneur provided a decoy that would divert political attentions from social conflicts and towards a new discipline that would sustain society as it underwent financialization. Subsequent sections demonstrate these patterns through the powerful governmental narratives that have drawn heavily on the construal of the entrepreneur: regulatory reform and financialization.

The entrepreneurial imaginary and the simplification of policy complexity

In a survey of the use of the word entrepreneur and its derivatives in British Parliamentary debate, Perren and Dannreuther identify a dramatic increase in the use of the term entrepreneur from the mid-1970s that accompanied the emergence of the regulatory state (Perren and Dannreuther 2012). Over time entrepreneur was used more frequently and in increasingly differentiated contexts as the idea of the entrepreneur attracted new meanings:

> During the 1980s the portrayal of the entrepreneur is still emerging, the balance is towards their personal agency; portrayal of their actions outweigh actions on them by the State; the stem entrepreneur is prevalent denoting ontological connection to the sentient form, that is a common sense realist portrayal of the entrepreneur....
>
> (Perren and Dannreuther 2012: 619)

At this early stage the entrepreneur represented a symbolic order that was explicitly free from the influence of the state representing liberty and individualism as an alternative to the corporatism of the 1970s. The key words associated with the entrepreneur included 'freedom' and 'ingenuity'. Representing entrepreneurs as separate from the state created a 'real' constituency that could be called on not only to offer political support but also to provide new economic growth at a time of economic decline (Wiener 1981). Presenting the entrepreneur as the natural constituency of the Conservative administration was also an expression of Parliamentary sovereignty. Thatcher explicitly used Parliament, and her majority within it, to challenge and undermine the forms of corporatist representation that informed economic policies in previous decades and to speak instead to entrepreneurs and enterprise (Bonnett *et al.* 1985).

But in addition to this party political agenda for decreasing the role of the state, there was another practical one. Smaller government was easier to govern and this appealed to both sides of the political spectrum:

> During the 1990s the construct of the entrepreneur becomes active. The portrayal of actions by them has lost the dialectic of negative exploitation and is now solely positive. Actions on them by the State have grown and the portrayal of support and measurement of them has emerged as a central construct. During this period abstracted portrayal increases to bring the reified form entrepreneur-[ship] to prominence in political discourse. There is still, as in the 1980s, the depiction of entrepreneurial need that sits alongside support. Entrepreneurial attributes are amplified to link them to other political discourses of flexibility and innovation.
>
> (Perren and Dannreuther 2012: 619)

Within a decade the entrepreneur had become an important recipient of state support and references to the entrepreneur were scattered across a wide range of issues and areas. During this period the idea that the state could govern by regulating markets through kite marks and correcting market failures, became entrenched. John Major's administration (1990–1996) aggressively privatized a wide range of public services, promoted regulatory standards as a technique that would ensure quality, and also focused heavily on deregulation and regulatory reform. Promoting enterprise and entrepreneurship became associated with the UK's national interest in domestic and international negotiations.

> By the 2000s the construct of the entrepreneur has been subsumed into political discourse. Portrayal of action by them has diminished at the expense of their personal agency and actions on them by the state has grown still further and now focuses on support and measurement; the rhetorical battle to justify the need for them presumably having been won.
>
> (Perren and Dannreuther 2012: 619)

Between the decades the shifting meaning of the entrepreneur implied that entrepreneur was a floating signifier, plastic enough to be constructed in relation to the wide variety of debates of the time. In two decades construals of the entrepreneur had shifted from representing the radical alternative to collective statism advocated by the free market liberals of the New Right, to constructs used to implement a wide range of government policy.

Through the sign of the entrepreneur government policy shifted from delivering social rights through state institutions to enabling individuals to realize their social and economic rights through the market. Policies designed to promote social inclusion and economic development were not delivered by public authorities but thorough social entrepreneurs established to support women into work, or to help people with disabilities to become entrepreneurs. These were radical changes that transformed the political relationship between governed and government in the UK. Yet it was not ideology alone that drove enterprise into the heart of the political system. In addition to the semiotic construction of the entrepreneur as a Swiss-army knife that could solve the complex demands of policy-making, a wide range of extra constraints selected, adapted and reinforced the concept of enterprise across the state. In the following section we explore the material changes in the power structure of the UK state and its relationship to the semiosis of enterprise.

Technologies of power and the regulatory state

As an economic imaginary was assembled around the entrepreneur, new forms of political relationship structured the relationship between the state and its subjects. The focus on regulation, and specifically the reduction of regulatory burdens on entrepreneurs, was explicitly linked to the liberation of entrepreneurs and the extension of individual sovereignty as a political right. But in practice it led to the radical centralization of political power in the British state.

In the 1970s this was a key argument of the modernizing section of the Conservative Party. The free market agenda agreed by Ted Heath explicitly sought to promote the interests of the individual as an entrepreneur and to capture the votes of these people. Keith Joseph and Margaret Thatcher became animated champions of the entrepreneur, promoting the alternative to the state interventionism of the crisis-torn mid-1970s. The introduction of the 'Building

Business not Barriers' White Paper in 1985 set in place a powerful association between reducing regulatory burdens and helping small business and entrepreneurs (Dept of Employment 1985).

For the first time a wide range of consultative mechanisms were put in place that would discipline the operation of policy analysis to consider the costs on enterprise before the benefits of the legislation on society. These technologies evolved in different forms – from Compliance Cost Assessment (CCA) to Regulatory Impact Assessment (RIA) to Small Firms Impact Test (SFIT). Each technology was introduced to reinforce enterprise in policy and each technology was reinforced through its association with enterprise. By the mid-2000s, the state department for regulating the economy was finally named as the Department for Business and Enterprise and Regulatory Reform (BERR). Enterprise was now a mandatory part of a legislative process that was highly centralized and privileged a quasi-scientific form of consultation. As well as creating a bias in favour of an abstract market, the technologies of regulatory reform had begun to construct an entrepreneurial interest that was now 'real' because it had been generated in accordance with official consultation processes and supported by executive orders.

As well as privileging a particular constituency, the focus on due process and the market also attributed rationality to the regulatory process that could be translated to other political environments (Froud and Ogus 1996; Froud *et al.* 1994). The UK government vociferously pursued similar regulatory reforms at the EU level. The third and longest section of Margaret Thatcher's famous 1988 Bruges Speech was on 'Europe Open to Enterprise'. In it she asserted that the 'Treaty of Rome itself was intended as a Charter for Economic Liberty' (Thatcher 1988). In fact, liberty was mentioned only once – in the opening preamble – and then not in relation to economic liberty (Treaty of Rome 1957: 2). But the speech was an opportunity for Thatcher to reassert her opposition to the European Social Model advocated by Jacques Delors (explicitly referred to in Article 51 of the Treaty Thatcher lobbied for in the 1975 Referendum).[2]

Such a technocratic form of regulatory reform would contribute to a political environment in which decisions were rendered depoliticized, became remote from political debate and fomented a growing distrust of politics and politicians (Hay 2006). Rather than increasing the legitimacy of the government, constant demands to reduce red tape and cut back on government played to the populist audiences and would serve to undermine the credibility of government in the run up to the financial crisis. From reducing regulations that applied universally, government policy evolved into targeting actors most likely to cause harm. This risk based form of protection confirmed that the state was inherently undesirable in the delivery of rights (Taylor 2009). The redefinition of the representation of society through the various compliance cost technologies also negated the voice of organised labour for over a decade. Democratic trade unions, long seen as representing society in tripartite discussions, were replaced by accounting technologies that presented society as individuals. This shift was propelled on the back of the myth that deregulation would lead to more entrepreneurial behaviour and assist entrepreneurs (Drakopoulou Dodd and Anderson 2007). The individual would be free from the tyranny of the state.

But in fact the use of the entrepreneur as a symbol does not tell us a story of reduced state involvement but rather the opposite. Accompanying the attack on regulation has been a shift in political power to the core executive made in the name of reducing the regulatory burdens felt by enterprises. For the first time since the reign of Henry VIII, the 1994 *Deregulation and Contracting Out Act* 1994 gave statutory powers to executive orders. A now wide network of Deregulation Units was set up to report to the centre of government. From here the Cabinet Office was able to make orders that could remove or reduce a burden. This had huge constitutional significance because 'unusually, it enables primary legislation to be amended by secondary legislation, which raises questions of parliamentary and constitutional significance' (Walker 2001).

While these powers were introduced under the Conservatives they were extended and amplified under the New Labour administration (1997–2010) which enthusiastically embraced the attack on red tape in the name of promoting an enterprise culture (Smith and Morton 2001). For almost 30 years, political technologies dedicated to the elevation of the sign of enterprise have disciplined civil servants at all stages of the policy process. While initially used to promote liberty, regulatory reform later brought authoritarian policy-making not seen before in modern Britain.

Financialization, enterprise and the limits of popular sovereignty

In the previous section the construction of the entrepreneur created a system of symbols that political elites could exploit. In this section we show how the introduction of the entrepreneurial sign helped change the way investment in the economy was made. The public service of the bank – as a utility for which it was given privileged status in the economy – became increasingly marginalized as new technologies of lending reinforced risk based modelling in banks. This would put pressure on the provision of financial services to the real economy in favour of investments in abstract financial products. In society at large the meaning of capital investment was redefined around signs of enterprise that privileged risk capital supply over mundane financial investments.

Entrepreneurship and financialization have grown symbiotically in the UK but this was not inevitable for the UK. It is common to regard the UK as a liberal market economy where the dominance of financial markets and ideologies of enterprise are the norm. But much of the twentieth century was characterized by state intervention in industry, welfare and education. Margaret Thatcher, who dismantled much of the institutional apparatus for industrial dirigisme, also explicitly attacked the City of London in the early 1980s for its conservatism and lack of entrepreneurial finance (Thatcher 2012). The reasons that the sign of enterprise is so closely associated with financialization is that they were coterminous, with the idea of enterprise supporting financialization and financialization sustaining and supporting the idea of enterprise from the early 1980s to the present day.

Project Merlin, which was the UK government's attempt to stimulate finance to small firms after the 2008 financial crisis, was the product of longstanding structural problems in the relationship between finance and small firms (Macartney 2013). The central problem of small firm finance was defined in 1932 when the Macmillan Committee, established to identify how industry and capital could furnish more productive relations, identified a gap in financial provision between credit from retail banks and equity from the City. The publication of its findings were hidden by the failure of the Reichsbank that signalled the last great depression, but the problem of a small firm finance gap became normalized and cemented as a fact of the modern industrial economy (Dannreuther and Kessler 2005).

During the mid-twentieth century, the issue of small firm finance was lost as the focus of policy moved to economic and industrial concentration. The 'Macmillan Gap' highlighted the lack of supply of finance for firms between credit available from banks and equity finance available from the stock market. From the publication of the Macmillan report in 1932 this was seen as a natural state of affairs. But in the late 1960s pressure emerged for state action to rescue the small firm sector from the forces of modernization and the supply of finance was one part of this. Beginning with the Bolton Committee in 1972 and the Wilson Committee in 1980 a series of reports raised the importance of small firm finance and led to schemes such as the Small Firm Loan Guarantee Scheme. These effectively spread the risk of lending to small firms between the public and the private sectors.

But from the early 1980s onwards, as the entrepreneurial imaginary was in its early ascendance, there was a clear shift towards support for and use of risk capital in UK financial markets. The risk-averse Industrial and Commercial Finance Corporation (IFCF), established in 1945 to lend to companies that had been supplying the war effort, was re-branded as the venture capital fund '3i'. From its rebirth 3i explicitly associated itself with addressing the Macmillan Gap through supplying risk capital to enterprise (3i 2013). Institutional innovations, like AIM, provided small cap markets for investors to exit and realize their gains (NESTA 2009). Common to all of these assertions was that the City of London approach of 'arms' length' regulation should prevail in the financial sector. Government support grew for risk capital into smaller companies through generous tax breaks to investors. The Business Start Up Scheme was one of the first of Thatcher's new administration's initiatives and established in 1981 to encourage investment in small companies. It soon evolved into the Business Expansion Scheme to promote private venture capital supply for unquoted companies and 1994 became the Enterprise Investment Scheme. Since then the supply of risk capital to enterprise has been closely associated with tax breaks.

Both these government policies encouraged the growth in both the scope of activities that financial markets could expect to operate in and the extent of control that they could expect to have. Both were introduced on the basis of their association with the entrepreneurial sign. This would separate the signified from the signifier. No longer were individual small investors only able to put their money into large publically listed companies listed on the stock exchange. Rather government policy explicitly rewarded individuals who invested in local business, hotels and shoe shops (race horses and crates of whisky also became popular) as long as these businesses could conform to the regulations of the scheme.[3] The small investor could claim equivalence to the City investor by quite literally buying into the enterprise sign.

The construction of the entrepreneur around the protection of property rights was evident in other important technologies that would accelerate the process of financialization. These included practical applications such as accounting, statistics and credit scoring. Accounting regimes formed powerful constructions of the entrepreneur because they communicated meaning across space and time in a way respectful of professional, regulatory and statistical conventions (Mennicken and Miller 2012). These conventions then disciplined individuals who sought compliance (Lambert and Pezet 2012). New data sets were collected by a wide range of actors to standardize measures of entrepreneurship and enable the exchange of good practice. International organizations such as the World Bank, OECD and the EU all created their own data sets while other networks such as the Global Entrepreneurship Monitor (GEM) were collated and coordinated by academics under well paid contracts. Through these measures the meaning of the world economy could be broken down into constituent elements of enterprise culture so that governments could demonstrate that they were 'open to business' to international markets. The GEM website claims significant policy impact because 'GEM collects world-class data on entrepreneurship, and uses it to identify policies that can increase the level and quality of entrepreneurial activity' (GEM 2013).

The entrepreneur as signifier could be used to coordinate a wide range of political actions in the hope that the practices that it signified would be reproduced anywhere around the world. These data sets are however contested, not least because the measurement of entrepreneurial behaviour is controversial and often based on casual empiricism (Curran and Blackburn 2001; Nicholas 1999). The World Bank Group Entrepreneurship Survey provides similar sets of data to GEM but produces different results (Acs *et al.* 2008). The success of GEM as a global standard for data used for academic research and policy comparison was closely linked to the focus on competitiveness of academic guru consultants like Michael Porter (GEM 2013) and to the influence of Austrian economics (Levie and Autio 2008). Practical policy decisions to address policy problems are resolved through reference to these benchmarks.

The use of empiricist technologies to capture and to commodify the sign of the entrepreneur has perhaps been most marked in the banking sector. In one of the most significant financial market innovations of the late twentieth century small firm credit scoring emerged as a transformative technique for managing the risks of small business lending. It emerged as an important practice when studies showed that information on the principal business owners' past credit record explained variations in the performance of the small business' credits (Akhavein *et al.* 2001). This allowed larger banks to make offers to small companies and contributed to significant changes in the practice of banking (Berger *et al.* 2011; Burton *et al.* 2004). Driven largely by computing capacity but also influenced by diverse non-technological factors (DeYoung *et al.* 2011), the technology was seen to dramatically change the accessibility of small firms to credit in utility or retail banking and also the banking sector itself. One observer in 1996 suggested that

> if it becomes possible ... to develop easily implemented and cost effective numerical credit-evaluation systems to assess and quantify the risks of small-business borrowers then it becomes possible both to value and to monitor the payment performance of portfolios of these assets so they can be securitized and funded in the open market. When this happens, then the value of the traditional banking charter will decline even more, and the door will rapidly open for non-traditional suppliers of credit to tap this market, not subject to the regulatory and other cost burdens characteristically borne by commercial banks.
>
> (Eisenbeis 1996: 288)

Each of these shifts apparently indicated radical change in the enterprise/financial relationship. The European Investment Bank and its European Investment Fund, for example, provided the mezzanine finance that allowed an SME based Collateral Loan Obligation to be issued as long ago as 2006 (EIB 2006). But the norms of market-mediated exchange were reaffirmed. Banks using credit scoring techniques found the most useful scores to not be those of the small business to which the loan was being made, but the credit history of the business owner information they could only exploit because of their privileged access to private banking accounts (Berger *et al.* 2011). Following the recession, as the nationalization of some banks has made the supply of commercial credit a political issue, credit scoring practices have come under scrutiny and can be appealed against. Approximately one-third of these credit rejections (worth around £30 million) were overturned for reasons that the average credit consumer would not be able to understand. The author of the report acknowledged that 'while many items that you would use to judge a consumer are the same for a business, some are not' (Banking Taskforce 2013: 25). Whatever the quality of information exchange is used to explain bank lending decisions to regulators, the centralization of banking decisions through credit scoring makes it far harder for loan applicants to understand. It is unsurprising therefore that a 2012 survey of UK business found that firms with an above average risk were less likely to understand the credit scoring process or to have a good relationship with their bank than those with a lower risk (BIS 2013: 32).

There have certainly been dramatic changes in the supply of finance for enterprise – propelled in large part by innovation in banking practices. But it is hard to argue that risk capital or retail credit have seen a greater supply of finance to small firms and new enterprises. Recent reports of a dramatic reduction in demand for finance by small firms and enterprises have confirmed that banks are not open for business (Bank of England 2013).

Conclusion – enterprise and the politics of financialization

Enterprise is not a solution to the problems of the financial sector because enterprise has no stable meaning, at least in the UK's political discourse. Throughout the relatively recent period of its ascendance as a sign, the notion of the entrepreneur has been most closely associated with the idea of the individual operating in the free market. But on closer inspection we see that this makes little sense. The symbol of the entrepreneur enabled the creation of meaning and order in financialized Britain but did not deliver freedom or free markets. Rather it led to centralized political control and abuses of privileged information by banks in their lending decisions. A better explanation is that the sign of the entrepreneur allowed policy-makers to make decisions when faced by uncertainty. This helped policy-makers to manage the uncertainties brought about during a period of dramatic change in British society.

The second section showed how the sign 'the entrepreneur' had only an arbitrary connection with the practices signified as entrepreneurial and that this could be exploited to assist in the ordering of capital relations. We showed that the meaning of the entrepreneur changed over time in Parliamentary debate. We then sought to explain these shifts through an examination of the regulatory reforms conducted in the British state in the name of enterprise. The technologies employed by the state to consult enterprise excluded organized labour and replaced that voice with an signifier of the enterprise society that bore very little relation to the signified practices of the entrepreneur. Such elite narratives on enterprise have been typical of how 'governments … draw on knowledge in order to construct policies and practices, especially those that regulate and create subjectivities' (Bevir 2010: 438).

The third section demonstrated how the idea of the entrepreneur enabled the introduction of dramatic reforms in the financial sector. New institutions were created to both expand the supply of short term venture capital investments in the UK economy and to enable these investors to exit easily. This encouraged speculative finance into new areas of activity that had previously been left as unviable. Investments channelled through tax breaks to wealthy individuals made investment in enterprise popular for tax reasons alone. Within banks dramatic changes accompanied credit scoring both in the provision of finance and in the ways they were able to manage these debts. But the use of the enterprise sign was not constrained to national financial markets as new statistics were created that offered 'practical' guidance on how to 'create' entrepreneurial economies. These reports are perhaps the best example of the signification of the entrepreneurial sign and its dissociation with forms of behaviour that could be signified as 'entrepreneurial'.

The implications of this discussion are less pessimistic. If the reforms of the financial system in the 1980s that set off the process of financialization were based on policy-makers managing uncertain times through the thin veil of entrepreneurial symbolism, the mobilization of support through more rigorous and stable signifiers that bear more resilient correspondence to the activities they signify presents real opportunities. It does at least help us to begin (or return to) a debate on how we should understand the world without the emptiness and the obfuscation that terms like enterprise or entrepreneur bring.

Notes

1 Much of this also examines the discursive construction of the entrepreneur (Hjorth and Steyaert 2004, Livesey 2002) highlighting, for example the importance of narrative (O'Connor 2002), aesthetics (Hjorth and Steyaert 2009) and macro culture (Lawrence and Phillips 2004). So entrepreneurship and its synonyms have been present in the formation and interrogation of symbolic orders meaning in the contemporary political economy.

2

> The Council shall, acting unanimously on a proposal from the Commission, adopt such measures in the field of social security as are necessary to provide freedom of movement for workers; to this end, It shall make arrangements to secure for migrant workers and their dependants
>
> (Treaty of Rome 1957: 22)

3 These regulations referred to the rules about the kind of company it is, the amount of money it can raise, how and when that money must be employed for the purposes of the trade, and the trading activities carried on.

References

3i (2013) Our History, retrieved from www.3i.com/about-us/our-history, accessed on 4 November 2013.

Acs, Z.J., Desai, S. and Klapper, L.F. (2008) What does 'Entrepreneurship' Data Really Show?, *Small Business Economics*, 31: 265–81.

Akhavein, J., Frame, W.S. and White, L.J. (2001) The Diffusion of Financial Innovations, available at http://archive.nyu.edu/fda/bitstream/2451/26212/2/1–8.pdf.

Banking Taskforce (2013) *Banking Taskforce Appeals Process Independent External Reviewer Annual Report 2012/2013*, available at www.betterbusinessfinance.co.uk/images/uploads/Annual_Report_Master_2013.pdf.

Bank of England (2013) *Trends in Lending* January, available at www.bankofengland.co.uk/publications/Documents/other/monetary/trendsjanuary13.pdf.

Bevir, M. (2010) Rethinking Governmentality: Towards Genealogies of Governance, *European Journal of Social Theory*, 13(4): 423–41.

Berger, A.N., Cowan, A.M. and Frame, W.S. (2011) The Surprising Use of Credit Scoring in Small Business Lending by Community Banks and the Attendant Effects on Credit Availability, Risk, and Profitability, *Journal of Financial Services Research*, 39(1): 1–17.

BIS (2013) *2012 Small Business Survey – Credit Risk Analysis Special Report*, available at https://www.gov.uk/government/uploads/system/uploads/attachment_data/file/204181/bis-13–881-small-business-survey-2012-credit-risk-analysis.pdf.

Blaug, M. (1997) *Not Only an Economist – Recent Essays by Mark Blaug*, Cheltenham: Edward Elgar.

Boltanski, L. and Chiapello, E. (2005) *The New Spirit of Capitalism*, London: Verso.

Bonnett, K., Bromley, S., Jessop, B. and Ling, T. (1985) Thatcherism and the Politics of Hegemony: A Reply to Stuart Hall, *New Left Review I/153*: 87–10.

Bourdieu, P. and Nice, R. (1980) The Production of Belief: Contribution to an Economy of Symbolic Goods, *Media, Culture & Society*, 2: 261–93.

Budgen, S. (2000) Luc Boltanski and Ève Chiapello, A New Spirit of Capitalism, *New Left Review 1:* 149–56.

Burton, D., Knights, D., Leyshon, A., Alferoff, C. and Signoretta, P. (2004) Making a Market: The UK Retail Financial Services Industry and the Rise of the Complex Sub-Prime Credit Market, *Competition and Change*, 8(1): 3–25.

Cromie, S. (2000) Assessing Entrepreneurial Inclinations: Some Approaches and Empirical Evidence, *European Journal of Work and Organizational Psychology*, 9 (1): 7–30.

Curran, J. and Blackburn, R.A. (2001) *Researching the Small Enterprise*, London: SAGE.

Dannreuther, C. and Kessler, O. (2005) Performativity as Power: Risk, Uncertainty and SME Finance, paper presented to Millennium conference, LSE London.

Dannreuther, C. and Perren, L. (2013) *The Political Economy of the Small Firm*, London: Routledge.

Dept of Employment (1985) Building Businesses not Barriers White Paper Cmnd. 9794 London HMSO.

DeYoung, R., Frame, W.S., Glennon, D. and Nigro, P. (2011) The Information Revolution and Small Business Lending: The Missing Evidence, *Journal Of Financial Services Research*, 39(1): 19–33.

Drakopoulou Dodd, S. and Anderson. A.R. (2007) Mumpsimus and the Mything of the Individualistic Entrepreneur, *International Small Business Journal*, 25(4): 341–60.

du Gay, P. (1994) Making up Managers: Bureaucracy, Enterprise and the Liberal Art of Separation, *British Journal of Sociology*, 45(4): 655–74.

EIB (2006) EIB and EIF Support the First Securitisation of SME Loans by BES in Portugal, press release retrieved from www.eib.europa.eu/about/press/2006/2006–125eib-and-eif-support-the-first-securitisation-of-sme-loans-by-bes-in-portugal.htm, accessed on 31 October 2013.

Eisenbeis, R.A. (1996) Recent Developments in the Application of Credit-Scoring Techniques to the Evaluation of Commercial Loans, *IMA Journal of Mathematics Applied in Business & Industry*, 7: 271–90.

Elder-Vass, D. (2007) Reconciling Archer and Bourdieu in an Emergentist Theory of Action, *Sociological Theory*, 25(4): 325–46.

Financial Ombudsman Service (2009) *Ombudsman News*, Issue 74 December 2008/January 2009, www.financial-ombudsman.org.uk/publications/ombudsman-news/74/74-small-businesses.html.

Froud, J. and Ogus, A. (1996) 'Rational' Social Regulation and Compliance Cost Assessment, *Public Administration*, 74(2): 221–37.

Froud, J., Boden, R. and Ogus, A. (1994) Toeing the Line – Compliance Cost Assessment in Britain, *Policy & Politics*, 22(4): 313–22.

Gartner, W.B. (1988) 'Who is an entrepreneur?' Is the Wrong Question, *American Journal of Small Business*, 12(4): 11–32.

GEM (2013) Policy impact, retrieved from www.gemconsortium.org/policy-impact, accessed on 31 October 2013.

Goux, J.-J. (1990) *Symbolic Economies: After Marx and Freud*, Ithaca, NY: Cornell University Press.

Hall, S. (1985) Signification, Representating Ideology: Althusser and Post Structuralist Debates, *Critical Studies in Mass Communication*, 2(2): 91–114.

Hall, S. (1996) Race the Floating Signifier. The Sage Anniversary lecture and the Harvard lecture. Goldsmiths College/Lewisham Council, transcript available at www.mediaed.org/assets/products/407/transcript_407.pdf.

Hay, C. (2006) *Why We Hate Politics*, Cambridge: Polity.

Hilton, M. (2000) Review Article Class, Consumption and the Public Sphere, *Journal of Contemporary History*, 35(4): 655–66.

Hjorth, D. (2007) Lessons from Iago: Narrating the Event of Entrepreneurship, *Journal of Business Venturing*, 22: 712–32.

Hjorth, D. and Steyaert, C. (eds) (2004) *Narrative and Discursive Approaches in Entrepreneurship*, Cheltenham, UK and Northampton, MA: Edward Elgar.

Hjorth, D. and Steyaert, C. (eds) (2009) *The Politics and Aesthetics of Entrepreneurship: A Fourth Movements in Entrepreneurship Book*, Cheltenham: Edward Elgar.

Inglis, D. (2004) Auto Couture Thinking the Car in Post-war France, *Theory, Culture & Society*, 21(4/5): 197–219.

Ireland, R.D. and Webb, J.W. (2007) A Cross-Disciplinary Exploration of Entrepreneurship Research, *Journal of Management*, 33: 891–927.

Jessop, B. (2010) Cultural Political Economy and Critical Policy Studies, *Critical Policy Studies*, 3(3–4): 336–56.

Jessop, B. and Sum, N.L. (2010) Cultural Political Economy: Logics of Discovery, Epistemic Fallacies, the Complexity of Emergence, and the Potential of the Cultural Turn, *New Political Economy*, 15(3): 445–51.

Jones, C. and Spicer, A. (2005) The Sublime Object of Entrepreneurship, *Organization*, 12(2): 223–46.

Kenny, K. and Scriver, S. (2012) Dangerously Empty? Hegemony and the Construction of the Irish Entrepreneur, *Organization*, 19: 615–33.

Kerfoot, D. and Korczynski, M. (2005) New Directions for the Study of 'Front-Line' Service Work, *Gender, Work and Organization*, 12(5): 387–99.

Lambert, C. and Pezet, E. (2012) Accounting and the Making of *Homo Liberalis*, *Foucault Studies*, 13: 67–81.

Lawrence, T. B. and Phillips, N. (2004) From Moby Dick to Free Willy: Macro-cultural Discourse and Institutional Entrepreneurship in Emerging Institutional Fields, *Organization*, 11(5): 689–711.

Lazzarato, M. (2009) Neoliberalism in Action Inequality, Insecurity and the Reconstitution of the Social, *Theory, Culture & Society*, 26(6): 109–33.

Levie, J. and Autio, E. (2008) A Theoretical Grounding and Test of the GEM Model, *Small Business Economics*, 31: 235–63.

Lévi-Strauss, C. (1966) *The Savage Mind*, London: Weidenfeld & Nicolson.

Lévi-Strauss, C. (1987) *Introduction to the Work of Marcel Mauss*, London: Routledge.

Livesey, S.M. (2002) New Vistas in Qualitative Research in Business, *Journal of Business Communication*, 39(1). 6–12.

Marttila, T. (2013) Whither Governmentality Research? A Case Study of the Governmentalization of the Entrepreneur in the French Epistemological Tradition *Forum: Qualitative Social Research Sozialforschung*, 14(3), Art. 10, retrieved from www.qualitative-research.net/, accessed on 4 November 2013.

Macartney, H. (2013) From Merlin to Oz: The Strange Case of Failed SME Lending Targets in the UK, *Review of International Political Economy*, 21(4): 820–46.

Mehlman, J. (1972) The 'Floating Signifier': From Lévi-Strauss to Lacan, *Yale French Studies*, 48: 10–37.

Mennicken, A. and Miller, P. (2012) Accounting, Territorialization and Power, *Foucault Studies*, 13: 4–24.

NESTA (2009) From Funding Gaps to Thin Markets UK Government Support for Early-Stage Venture Capital, Research Report: September, available at www.nesta.org.uk/library/documents/Thin-Markets-v9.pdf.

Nicholas, T. (1999) Clogs to Clogs in Three Generations? Explaining Entrepreneurial Performance in Britain Since 1850, *The Journal of Economic History*, 59(3): 688–713.

O'Connor, E. (2002) Storied Business: Typology, Intertextuality, and Traffic in Entrepreneurial Narrative, *Journal of Business Communication*, 39(1): 36–54.

Perren, L. and Dannreuther, C. (2012) Political Signification of the Entrepreneur: Temporal Analysis of Constructs, Agency and Reification, *International Small Business Journal*, 31(6): 603–628.

Pettinger, L. (2005) Gendered Work Meets Gendered Goods: Selling and Service in Clothing Retail, *Gender, Work and Organization*, 12(5): 460–78.

Richey, L.A. and Ponte, S. (2008) Better (Red)TM than Dead? Celebrities, Consumption and International Aid, *Third World Quarterly*, 29(4): 711–29.

Richie, J. (1991) Enterprise Cultures: A Frame Analysis, in R. Burrows (ed.), *Deciphering the Enterprise Culture: Entrepreneurship, Petty Capitalism and the Restructuring of Britain*, London: Routledge.

Rose, N. and Miller, P. (2010) Political Power Beyond the State: Problematics of Government, *The British Journal of Sociology*, 61(s1): 271–303.

Saussure, F. de (1959) *Course In General Linguistics*, New York: Philosophical Library.

Smith, P. and Morton, G. (2001) New Labour's Reform of Britain's Employment Law: The Devil Is Not Only in the Detail but in the Values and Policy Too, *British Journal of Industrial Relations*, 39(1): 119–38.

Steyaert, C. (2007) 'Entrepreneuring' as a Conceptual Attractor? A Review of Process Theories in 20 Years of Entrepreneurship Studies, *Entrepreneurship and Regional Development*, 19: 453–77.

Taylor, J. (2009) Systemic Risk and the Role of Government Keynote Speech. *Conference on Financial Innovation and Crises Federal Reserve Bank of Atlanta*, available at www.stanford.edu/~johntayl/Systemic_Risk_and_the_Role_of_Government-May_12_2009.pdf.

Tett, G. (2013) *Fixing the System*, BBC Broadcast 21.00 Wed 22 May, 2013.

Thatcher, M. (1988) Speech to the College of Europe 1988 Sep 20 Bruges, retrieved from www.margaretthatcher.org/document/107332, accessed on 10 May 2013.

Thatcher, M. (2012) *The Downing Street Years*, London: Harper Press.

Treaty of Rome 25 March 1957, available at http://ec.europa.eu/economy_finance/emu_history/documents/treaties/rometreaty2.pdf.

Walker, A. (2001) *The Regulatory Reform Bill [HL]*: order-making power and parliamentary aspects (Revised edition) Bill 51 of 2000–2001 *House of Commons Library research paper* 01/27, available at www.parliament.uk/briefing-papers/RP01–27.pdf.

Wiener, M. (1981) *English Culture and the Decline of Industrial Spirit, 1850–1980*, Cambridge: Cambridge University Press.

6 Booms, busts and the culture of risk

Raphaële Chappe, Edward Nell and Willi Semmler

In the early years of Wall Street, the age of the Robber Barons, the main image of the banker or financier was that of the 'trustee', the prudent and scrupulous manager of other people's money. The trustee exhibited the virtues of thrift and good judgement, of careful and conservative planning for the future. We could expect such a person to be politically conservative, but this would be a traditional conservative in the old-fashioned sense, someone who celebrated the staid and quiet values of community and hierarchy – 'a place for everything and everything in its place' – not the disruptive uproar of radical individualism. Even with the rise of consumerism that led to the 1929 crash, the financial culture on Wall Street was still dominated by family dynasties and conservative values. This culture, which we call the 'culture of trust', espoused the values of prudence and thrift, along with hard work, careful foresight and good judgement. Going into debt should not be undertaken lightly; debts should be paid on time, promises should be kept, and one's reputation must be protected and preserved. In the culture of trust, you see your banker as the person to whom you entrust your money, your savings. Banks can be trusted.

These conservative values seem to have been displaced, and today a reckless attitude to risk-taking prevails on Wall Street. There are different aspects and manifestations of this shift, such as overconfidence, a sense of entitlement to excessive compensation, a tendency to focus on short-term profits at the cost of long-term stability, excessive leverage, the growing reliance on proprietary trading as a source of revenue for investment banks, a reluctance to acknowledge conflicts of interest as long as profits are made, and reliance on flawed models to manage risk. In this chapter, we explore the rise and nature of what we label the culture of risk, where short-termism, speculation and reckless risk-taking has come to dominate Wall Street and replace the culture of trust. We argue that the culture of risk is partly responsible for the 2008 credit crisis and the near collapse of financial markets.

The existence of cyclical financial crises has been explained in terms of diverse factors, including the macroeconomic environment (low interest rates, external imbalances, and so on), deregulated markets, leverage cycles and credit expansion, asymmetric information, 'animal spirits', 'irrational exuberance' and other psychological and behavioural explanations. Indeed, boom-bust cycles have existed for centuries, and most exhibit similar features,[1] suggesting that they are driven by recurrent observable mechanisms that lead to synchronized behaviour of economic agents. In this chapter, we argue that the cultural environment in US financial firms and markets played a critical role in the recent crisis and, more specifically, that the emerging culture of risk exacerbated the mechanisms of boom-bust cycles, such as overleveraging and the underestimation of risk. Our hypothesis is that there were significant micro-macro links that accelerated both the boom as well as the bust, due to the introduction of securitized products and other complex securities, and that the cultural environment played a critical role in enabling the formation of these links.

Some of the decision-making processes evidenced in the recent financial crisis can be analysed strictly from the perspective of a microeconomic framework, for instance financial executives optimizing behaviour in response to existing incentives, with compensation structures and other principal-agent type issues playing a key role in encouraging executives to place their companies at risk. However, this is a limited perspective in that it fails to address the exact formation of preferences underlying decision-making on the part of key financial executives and market participants. Decision-making in finance can be understood at the meso level in terms of the context and structures that predetermine the way choices are made, rather than from a microeconomic or macroeconomic perspective. The culture of financial firms and markets frames the decisions of market participants by shaping the environment in which such decisions are made, providing a model for how work should be conducted and what values should be used to assess employees.

In this chapter we first outline typical mechanisms of boom-bust cycles in so far as they are relevant to understanding the 2007–2008 financial crisis. Then we outline the rise of the culture of risk and its role in accentuating the traditional mechanisms of boom-bust cycles leading to the 2007 financial crisis. We examine the recent Dodd-Frank legislation and assess perspectives given the current environment on Wall Street. We then draw some basic conclusions.

The mechanisms of boom-bust cycles

The macroeconomic environment

The origins of the 2007–2008 financial crisis lie in a macroeconomic environment marked by low interest rates, rising levels of household debt and inflated housing values. The housing bubble was accelerated by the outsourcing of risk due to the securitization of mortgages. Liquidity in the housing sector (and financial markets) was pumped up by capital inflows that lowered the interest rate on the long end of the yield curve. A context of low interest rates and low default rates led investors to expect higher and higher returns, furthering the growth of the securitization industry.

The burst of the bubble was triggered by Bear Stearns' internal 'hedge funds' failure, accelerated through the bankruptcy of Lehman Brothers in September

2008, leading to a tightening of credit in the entire banking sector. Suddenly default risks and risk premia began shooting up, resulting in a credit crunch (as in all beginning cycles of financial downturns). Often a stock market crash triggers the downturn. Yet, this time, the stock market reaction came somewhat late, in response to the credit crunch. As the credit crisis worsened, it spread to Europe and other parts of the world. The feedback to the real sector caused a decline in the growth rate of GDP, with further feedback effects from the real to the financial side.

There are clear links between the financial crisis and macroeconomic trends. For instance, the long-run downward trend of interest rates, low mortgage rates and upward trends in housing prices are correlated. Another related factor in the housing boom was the rising level of consumer debt. According to Hudson (2006), American households are now deeper in debt than ever. In fact, mortgage loans now constitute close to 90 per cent of the increase in debt since the 1990s and make up 50 per cent of bank loans in general, with $13.4 trillion at year-end 2011.[2] This trend is driven by a combination of factors, including record low interest rates, which increase the borrowing capability of home buyers, favourable tax treatment of mortgage interest, and the 'wealth effect', that is, the increased spending caused by the recognition of the value of one's home (cf. Montgomery and Young 2009). There were other trends, ostensibly, independent of interest rates, such as the rapid growth of Collateralized Debt Obligations (CDOs) during the same period.

The housing boom and securitized products

In the recent meltdown, the usual boom-bust mechanism was reinforced by new financial innovations; specifically, the housing boom was financed with credit derivatives and securitized products, resulting in a huge issuing of CDOs and Mortgage Backed Securities (MBSs) that helped to outsource risk. The securitization process allows for the creation of securities backed by a pool of risky mortgages and loans, whereby each security (or 'tranche') entitles investors to a share of the cash flow produced by the underlying assets, mortgages or loans (both interest and principal).[3] In short, MBSs derive their values from the underlying mortgages but, in so far as risky mortgages are pooled, investors are exposed to the risk profile of the total pool rather than to that of individual assets and the risk of default is thereby diluted. Different tranches carry different priorities of repayment, thus re-assigning the risks into different classes, and are priced accordingly. Securitization thus allowed for fairly illiquid high-risk assets to be packaged together and converted into securities with different risk profiles, including securities that obtained very good ratings (AAA) from the rating agencies. Financial institutions derived fees from the engineering and marketing of such products, with the possibility of earning low risk profits, rather than retaining the products on their balance sheets and putting their own capital at risk. This has been described as the shift from an 'originate and hold' to an 'originate and sell' business model.

Under this business model, volume is of the essence: banks had every incentive to create and market as many securities as possible and had little incentive to monitor and fully disclose the risk profile of these complex securities. Specifically, the possibility was overlooked that the different underlying bundled assets might not, in fact, be independent of each other (in other words, one asset defaulting makes the chances of others defaulting more or less likely). This phenomenon is called default correlation and, along with default risk, is an important driver of the overall structure. Further complications can be introduced by mixing risky assets of different types, taking more complex positions within the tranches, and by investing in multiple products. All of this is usually simulated with computers, which can keep track of the details. However, once mortgage delinquency rates rose, senior tranches of securities lost value much quicker than anticipated. Original pricing did not correspond to the true risk profile, leading to sudden and unanticipated losses in value. The sophisticated computer models failed.

The alarming rise in mortgage delinquencies started in 2006, with default correlation becoming a critical component in the bursting of the bubble. This mechanism can be simulated in a model. Semmler and Bernard (2009) show how underlying financial market instruments can influence prices and macro-phenomena in extreme ways and can produce such a collapse of housing prices. Simulations show the extreme sensitivity of SPV profits and home prices. This holds for complex securities and housing prices to mortgage delinquency rates, to time varying interest rates, to default correlation and to mortgage recovery rates.

The complex securities, which were supposed to outsource and diversify idiosyncratic risk, actually accelerated the boom and subsequent collapse, providing the underlying financial intermediation mechanism through which the asset price boom and busts were fuelled. The recent crisis can be analysed in terms of the combination of two leverage cycles, both in the housing sector and in the market for these complex securities.[4] Liquidity spirals emerged as a result of underlying self-reinforcing feedback mechanisms between the two. The tightening of margins led to lower security prices, which slowed the issuance of new mortgages and adversely impacted homeowners' ability to refinance. This in turn increased default risk, thereby making down-payment requirements more stringent. This led to a reduction in demand for housing, which made housing prices fall and increased security margins, prompting the whole sequence to repeat.

The links between leverage and asset pricing

As was very apparent in the recent meltdown, boom-bust cycles are often interrelated with financial cycles. The established view is that such cycles are mostly driven by the linkage of credit and asset prices. Recent studies focus on the mechanism of credit extension, its amplifying effect on ups and downs of the real sector, and the extent to which the leverage cycle is a contributing factor to economic booms and busts. In contrast to the traditional economic theory that asset prices are driven by fundamentals, recent analyses of booms and busts show that the leverage cycle plays a critical role in determining market fluctuations. Many economic analyses relate asset prices and debt dynamics.[5] Leverage cycles are a recurring phenomenon: in a boom period competition drives leverage higher and asset prices increase, while the crash is accompanied by a sharp decrease in prices and de-leveraging.[6] Other studies attempt to model the links between funding liquidity (the ability to raise cash at short notice) and overall market liquidity (the difference between market price and the asset's fundamental value).[7]

This interconnectedness is very apparent in the context of collateralized borrowing. For example, the tightening of funding standards lowers market liquidity, leading to higher margin requirements,[8] which in turn reinforces the tightening of credit. This self-reinforcing mechanism results in liquidity spirals, leading to sudden liquidity dry-ups. Bernanke develops the concept of a 'financial accelerator' effect to explain the amplitude of cyclical fluctuations and the procyclical movement of the cost and volume of credit (cf. Bernanke *et al.* 1999). Because the cost of debt finance and the strength of a borrower's financial position are inversely related, any increase in productivity that improves the cash flows and balance sheet positions of firms lowers their cost of borrowing, allowing firms to continue expanding long after the initial productivity shock.

Psychological mechanisms

Some studies attribute the recent US housing boom to overshooting mechanisms and excess volatility in the equity market and in the real estate sector. Shiller (2007) notes that inaccurate popular economic valuation models that investors and the general public rely on are important factors driving asset prices. For example, investors might base their decisions on nominal interest rates when real rates would be more appropriate, a behavioural bias called the 'money illusion'. Further, as opposed to standard economic theory where the world can be analysed with a stable framework of 'rational expectations', public thinking is inconsistent and popular models and beliefs change over time. Shiller argues that such biases can explain bubbles even more than macroeconomic variables such as a low interest rate environment. In equity markets, this phenomenon is also visible when price-to-dividend ratios can significantly overshoot their mean values.

This line of reasoning is consistent with Keynes' view on the role of 'animal spirit' in booms and busts. Many studies of financially driven boom-bust cycles in the Keynesian tradition are influenced by such psychological insights, see for example Minsky (1975, 1982, 1986), Tobin (1980) and Kindleberger and Aliber (2005). Another important insight into this interaction is found in Robert Shiller's (1991, 2001) overreaction hypothesis as well as in his notion of 'irrational exuberance' (2001). Another non-neoclassical tradition originating with Stiglitz and Weiss (1981) draws upon recent developments in information economics, wherein systematic attempts have been made to describe how actual financial markets operate by referring to the concepts of asymmetric information, adverse selection and moral hazard.

The culture of risk

The changing landscape

The structure of US and global markets changed significantly due to several factors and trends, including the repeal of Glass-Steagall, the explosion of derivatives markets, the unprecedented bonuses for top managers on Wall Street, the rise of proprietary trading desks within banking institutions, the rise of alternative investment vehicles and, more generally, higher levels of financial innovation. We outline these trends below. Overall, they led to an increase in the risk profile of financial institution with high leverage, volatile returns and increased responsiveness to market swings.

In the 1980s, the financial sector became fast-paced, globalized and competitive, with increasing competition from foreign firms and unregulated alternative investment vehicles such as private equity firms and hedge funds. This led to a higher degree of concentration of the large players in the financial sector, as consolidation through mergers and acquisitions increased firms' chance of survival and overall profitability. This ultimately led to the end of the partnership model for most Wall Street firms, as all major firms had to be taken public in order to continue to grow in size and remain competitive. The consolidation continued throughout the 1990s and 2000s, which saw the rise of very large financial conglomerates. As discussed by Kaufman (2009), the share of financial assets held by the ten largest financial institutions rose from 10 to 50 per cent between 1990 and 2008. There was an overall increase of risk in the system and it was also concentrated on a just a few balance sheets.

Financial markets became increasingly complex. Trading volume was inexorably increasing. Derivatives markets exploded following the development of the Black-Scholes option-pricing model in the 1970s – this extraordinary growth continued in the 1980s and 1990s, accentuated by the fact that many derivatives could be privately negotiated outside of any regulated trading platform.[9] Options became an essential tool in modern portfolio management. The Black-Scholes model enabled the development and pricing of a host of other derivatives. Wall Street firms started to rely more heavily on programmed trading to handle the mathematical complexity of these instruments as well as the large volume of trading.

Investment banking had traditionally been relationship driven. Yet, starting in the 1980s, the existence of long-term relationships became less important than the ability to deliver a deal efficiently, as corporate clients became more transaction-driven, shopping around for the best securities firm. At the same time, investment banks started deriving a larger fraction of their revenue from proprietary trading, due to the increased pressure on profitability.[10] This practice intensified in the 1990s and 2000s, and with the repeal of Glass-Steagall in 1999, proprietary desks also developed within commercial banks. These desks are often considered internal hedge funds; and their risk profile is indeed as complex as that of hedge funds or private equity funds. Proprietary trading is more volatile than the traditional investment banking fee-based activities.[11] Lacking a wide deposit base, investment banks turned to high leverage to finance proprietary trading, which requires intense use of the firm's own capital. The US Securities and Exchange Commission (SEC), which is the regulatory agency in charge of monitoring investment banks and securities firms, allowed leverage as high as 30–35 times or more of capital for the major investment banks. This business profile was inherently risky in that investment banks continually borrowed with short maturities, but held risky and potentially illiquid positions – its weakness became all too apparent when credit markets (including repo markets) dried up in 2008, and investment banks like Goldman Sachs and Morgan Stanley had to resort to a change in regulatory status (electing to convert to Bank Holding Company status) to access the Federal Reserve emergency lending facilities (lender of last resort).[12]

With the end of the partnership-type organizational structure, where the business model was based on trust and loyalty and where there was also little employee mobility between firms, employee retention – and motivation – became a key issue. This explains why, while high compensation had always been the norm on Wall Street, the size of bonuses and stock options for top traders and bankers reached unprecedented levels. The incentives for financial institutions to seek to increase leverage in order to enhance profitability are strong. Wall Street bonuses are assessed on the basis of short-term profits rather than the long-term profitability of an investment. A large portion of total compensation comes in the form of a bonus linked to the profitability of the firm (or a division of the firm), such as company stock or stock options. Thus the performance of the employee is economically tied with the short-term earnings of the firm.

These changes occurred during a period when deregulation was gaining momentum under the influence of the Chicago School of Economics and neoliberal thinkers such as Friedrich von Hayek and Milton Friedman. We identify three major deregulatory initiatives. First, the Gramm-Leach-Bliley Financial Modernization Act repealed Glass-Steagall in November 1999 and created a new regulatory status, the Financial Holding Company banks, which allowed commercial banks, securities firms and insurance companies to affiliate under common ownership. All the main commercial banks (Citigroup, JP Morgan Chase, Bank of America) converted with a view to offering a complete range of financial services. Financial Holding Companies were under the regulatory supervision of the Federal Reserve, while the SEC had supervision over securities firms and investment banks. The second major deregulation initiative was the Commodity Futures Modernization Act of 2000 (CFMA), initiated at the request of Treasury Secretary Robert Rubin, Federal Reserve Board Chair Alan Greenspan and SEC Chair Arthur Levitt.[13] It ensured that over-the-counter derivatives (privately negotiated instruments traded outside of an exchange platform) would continue to be substantially unregulated. And, third, until the recent Dodd-Frank regulatory overhaul, alternative investment vehicles operated with little regulatory supervision. Hedge funds were not obliged to disclose balance sheets and income statements and typically remained secretive about their positions and strategies, even to their own investors.[14] Kaufman (2009) stressed the role of defective regulation in causing the 2007–2008 crisis.

The rise of the culture of risk

In a broad sense, the notion of culture in a sociological or anthropological framework describes a set of commonly shared attitudes. Culture can be thought of as a process or as a state (Jackson 2009).[15] In this chapter, we advance the notion of culture as a process whereby social behaviour on Wall Street has evolved over time from a relatively risk-averse environment into a very aggressive environment where speculative and reckless risk-taking has become the norm. By culture of risk, we refer to the reckless attitude towards risk-taking that is prevalent on Wall Street, and which manifests itself through overconfidence, a sense of entitlement to excessive compensation, a tendency to focus on short-term profitability at the cost of long-term stability, excessive leverage, the increasing reliance on proprietary trading as a source of revenue for investment banks, a reluctance to acknowledge conflicts of interest as long as profits are made, and a reliance on flawed models for risk management. While the term itself is used in a number of articles in the press,[16] these themes have been developed in a number of non-academic books and publications, including Michael Lewis's *Liar's Poker* (1990), Charles Geisst's *Wall Street: a History* (2004) and Nomi Prins's *Other People's Money* (2004).

Technically speaking, many aspects of this culture of risk could be analysed strictly from a microeconomic perspective in terms of the incentive structures in place and principal-agent type issues, such as executives having incentives to take large risks when their pay is linked to short-term profit and when shareholders, not managers, suffer the major economic loss in the event of bankruptcy; or, again, when banks have incentives to create and market as many securities as possible under the 'originate and sell' business model (and less incentive to monitor and disclose the risk profile to investors). However, collectively these trends have gone unchallenged for 30 years and have been accepted as normal business practices on Wall Street. As such, they lend themselves to a meso level of analysis, in terms of the context and structures that frame decisions.

With the rise of mass production and a global interconnected economy, success came to depend on the ability to assume new forms of risk. In a global world with new opportunities that hinged on the willingness to take on new risks, the claim that risk could be managed privately by the market offered a whole new field of enterprise for financial firms. There was plenty of money to be made (...and lost, too, though few in the financial world admitted that at the time) through the pricing and selling off of risks (financial engineering). The business of finance developed to provide large corporations products and solutions to hedge against these new forms of risks. Yet it was no longer a matter of avoiding or minimizing risk. Taking risks had become the route to high rewards; risks were not to be avoided, they had to be actively managed. The response to the emergence of new risks was to try to solve real problems by financial means – buying fire insurance instead of rewiring the house. In recent decades the financial sector has become fast growing and large, seeing a lot of increased productivity and financial innovation, as financial engineering developed these new products. Financing hedging may be useful, but it is easy to see that a real solution would be better, although it might be out of reach as a practical matter in the here and now.

The new breed of financiers and financial advisors are not concerned to show themselves as trustworthy and prudent, careful stewards of our wealth. On the contrary they are guides who know the secret roads and paths to wealth, who will lead us along the way to riches. They can manage the risks, show us how to outsource them, and take advantage of the opportunities to cash in. They are gamblers, not stewards, they are speculators, not conservators, daring, not prudent, smart rather than wise. And this leads to, or helps to support, a completely different set of outcomes. First, it supports the tendency to adopt the maximization of shareholder value as the criterion for good performance, leading to short-termism, with the target as maximum present value. And, second, managing risk and maximizing shareholder value deserves high pay, very high pay. So this approach tends to justify enormous salaries and earnings, especially in the form of stock options.

With the end of the partnership culture, spreading from big investment firms, a con-artist behaviour towards investors became very common, where big returns were promised without risk. This encouraged huge speculation on excessive returns and huge risk-taking, using large borrowed funds from capital markets. Take the cases of Merrill Lynch, where the risk managers who warned against excess risk-taking were fired, and Goldman Sachs, where credit risk was packaged in such a way that securitized products were actually failing and doing so with high probability. These cases illustrate that big investment banks have developed an institutionalized sense of entitlement to huge profits and are unable (or 'unable') to see conflicts of interest as long as profits are made. This is not surprising given that the importance of long-term client relationships, key to a firm's success in the partnership culture, declined in the fast-paced globalized and competitive environment that emerged in the 1980s. Goldman Sachs pocketed huge profits by marketing securities (CDOs) to investors, while betting against those very products (see *New York Times* 2009). Goldman Sachs saw no conflict of interest or ethical issues, viewing its own bets as prudent hedging management and their marketing of CDOs as simply a response to client demand. The SEC charged Goldman Sachs with fraud related to the structuring and marketing of subprime mortgage CDOs.[17] The case was ultimately settled for $550 million on 15 July, 2010.

Finally, there was not only over-optimism, undervaluation of risk and over-leveraging, but also pure Ponzi finance such as came out in the Madoff scandal. The case of Bernie Madoff perfectly illustrates a situation where a hedge fund adopted a Ponzi financing scheme. In a Ponzi scheme, a con-artist promises very attractive high returns at a seemingly low risk from a business model that is purely fictional. The con-artist pays earlier investors their promised high return from the money handed over by later investors. The scheme collapses when there are insufficient new investors. The collapse of Bear Stearns' internal hedge funds in 2007 illustrates that investment activities conducted by hedge funds have the ability to destabilize the economy and increase systemic risk.[18] As Minsky well understood and articulated with his concepts of speculative finance and Ponzi finance, today many financial firms borrow heavily to fund speculative investments (for example, securities that are heavily dependent on a continued rise in housing prices) rather than assets with solid fundamentals or actual productive activities undertaken by the real sector.

As we have discussed, there are strong incentives for financial institutions to seek to increase leverage in order to enhance profitability. In a classic moral hazard problem, banking executives have a lot to gain from risk-taking, but little economic penalty. The culture of bonuses linked to short-term profits has created incentives for excessive risk-taking. The opportunity for short-term gains has led management to take on new unregulated risk (increasing leverage to boost profitability, off balance sheet trading, and so on) with no guarantee that long-term results would remain positive. There was more to gain from high volatility (allowing banking executives to cash-in their bonus) than from slow but steady appreciation in value with lower underlying risk levels. The compensation structure in the hedge fund industry, typically a 2 per cent management fee based on assets under management, and a 20 per cent performance fee on total return, also gives managers an incentive for volatility in returns (Cochrane 2005).

Shareholders, not managers, suffer the major economic loss in the event of bankruptcy. Further, with the rise of large investment firms that were sufficiently large to present a threat to the economy, basking in the dominant view that they were 'too big to fail', these firms found that, when on the brink of bankruptcy, they could rely on state institutions for safety nets – as we saw with the bailout of huge firms such as AIG. As Stiglitz points out in a recent book, the effort to rescue the banking system was inherently flawed (2010). Firms used the threat of systemic risk to shift all risk to the government, reduced to the role of 'garbage disposal' (the expression is Stiglitz's) for toxic assets created by financial institutions. The implementation of the multi-trillion dollar bailout for the banks orchestrated by the Bush and Obama administrations was inconsistent – some institutions were rescued, others not, without clear guidelines underlying the decisions. Goldman Sachs received billions from AIG (funded by the AIG bailout) as settlement of credit default swaps, while other market participants received only 13 cents on the dollar in settlement of credit default swaps. The expectation that banks are entitled to a socialized take-over of losses while privately pocketing gains is obscene. For these reasons, Stiglitz refers to the bailout as the 'Great American Robbery'.

There are no or few outsiders on the Boards, a sense of the legitimacy of risk-taking and a reckless belief that the business cycle has been conquered so that the only way forward is up. Asked in an interview with the *Financial Times* about the prospects of a liquidity crisis, the then CEO of Citigroup, Charles Prince, infamously said:

When the music stops, in terms of liquidity, things will get complicated. But as long as the music is still playing, you've got to get up and dance. We're still dancing.

The new breed of bankers welcomes innovation and dances to the global music.

To make matters worse, all of this can operate strictly within the existing legal framework. As regards the failing investment banks, it does not appear that there were violations of clear corporate accounting standards nor, in general, were there improper balance sheet reports or violation of capital requirements. So, overall, in a legal sense, the banks did not fraudulently mislead investors regarding the excessive leverage and insolvency.[19] The entities that failed remained compliant with the SEC's Consolidated Supervised Entity regime's rules at all relevant times. Further, many accounting rules (FASB standards, and so on.) require judgement calls from management (for example regarding discount rates, fair value estimates for assets that are not regularly traded, reserves associated with accounts receivable). Accountants, who are not trained in risk assessment, do not have the expertise to challenge these estimates. The extent to which financial statements are subject to interpretation, management policies and judgement calls is not something that can be fully appreciated by investors short of disclosing the nature and rationale of the decisions that were made. Financial statements simply do not provide that level of detail. An added issue is that current accounting rules do not properly take into account 'off balance sheet' risk. Assets and financing not appearing on the balance sheet include loan commitments and derivatives. This accounting treatment may result in situations where consolidated financials do not accurately reflect the firm's economic situation.[20] Unfortunately, legal and accounting rules are not sophisticated enough to allow for the proper disclosure of risk in the financial sector, let alone its monitoring.

A final characteristic of the culture of risk involves, in our opinion, an epistemic fallacy, namely, the idea that all forms of risk can be managed in a probabilistic framework. During the financial crisis, it became apparent that many firms took very large risks they did not fully understand. Many in-house risk management controls and models failed spectacularly. There are various issues. First, risk management has become homogenous. Professionals tend to use the same models learned at the same schools. The models are based on the same information (historical data) and methodology, essentially reflecting the same view of the world. In the mid-2000s credit rating agencies started disclosing their rating models to banks, leading to further homogenization as financial products were designed with those specific guidelines in mind (so as to secure targeted ratings) rather than on the basis of an independent risk assessment. There are also serious limitations to the current theoretical approaches to risk management. Value at Risk (VaR), in particular, has been denounced as inherently flawed – it is based on a historical simulation of past risks and returns, conveniently assumes a normal distribution of returns, and neglects to disclose the magnitude of losses in 'black swan' type rare events (for example 5 per cent or 1 per cent probability of occurrence). Other tools of modern finance, such as CAPM, the Efficient Market Theory and the Black-Scholes model are also based on this normalcy assumption. The mathematician, Benoit Mandelbrot, and others are working to develop more robust foundations, incorporating the possibility of fat tails and developing a comprehensive theory of market behaviour based on fractal mathematics, which is no easy task.

We argue that the culture of risk accentuated the traditional mechanisms of boom-bust cycles and played a key role in the 2007 financial crisis. Boom-bust cycles are driven by self-reinforcing linkages between leverage and asset prices. The role of the macroeconomic environment of low interest rates has been high-lighted. However, with Wall Street bonuses assessed on the basis of short-term profits, aggressive risk-taking became the norm and significantly contributed to increased leverage levels. Boom-bust cycles are fuelled by rising asset prices and inflated values, furthering the leverage cycle. The 'originate and sell' business model, and the limited incentives for banks to monitor and disclose risk, led to a huge issuing of complex financial securities, fuelling the housing boom. Animal spirits and other psychological mechanisms also typically play a role in boom-bust cycles. Regarding the recent crisis, the culture of risk helped create false perceptions of risk. The claim that financial innovation delivers value is based on the belief that market-based mechanisms help price and outsource new forms of risks in our modern global economy. Yet there are serious limitations to current theoretical approaches to understanding and modelling risk. The culture of risk brushed aside these limitations as long as profits could be made.

Financial reform and the culture of risk

Prudential regulation in Dodd-Frank

The Obama administration passed in 2010 the Dodd-Frank Act, a major legisla-tion designed to reform the financial sector and prevent future bailouts.[21] Dodd-Frank explicitly provides that taxpayers should not be expected to save a failing financial company or to cover the cost of its liquidation. In addition to measures that specifically target the mortgage industry, there are many key provisions designed to prevent a meltdown of the sort that recently occurred in 2007–2008, including monitoring systemic risk, reducing excessive growth and complexity, and creating more transparency with respect to hedge funds and derivatives.

One prevalent focus is prudential regulation and preventive measures designed to allow for a better monitoring of systemic risk. Dodd-Frank has created a regulatory agency designed to look after the stability of the financial system as a whole, the Financial Services Oversight Council (hereafter FSOC). For this purpose, there are data-gathering measures designed to allow the regu-lator to aggregate information across institutions to develop systemic scenario analyses. For instance, the SEC is empowered to collect systemic risk data with respect to the hedge fund industry.[22] There are also data collection and publica-tion requirements for derivatives markets, through clearing houses.[23] The FSOC is empowered to require that financial institutions creating risks to the financial system be regulated by the Federal Reserve, and to make recommendations to the Federal Reserve regarding capital, leverage, liquidity and risk management requirements. These enhanced prudential standards automatically apply to any large bank holding company (assets of $50 billion or more). However, Dodd-Frank provides limited substantive guidance as to what these enhanced prudential standards should consist of, and specific development and implementation of enhanced standards rests with the Federal Reserve, which recently published a proposed rule on 5 January, 2012. The proposed rule outlines risk-based capital and leverage requirements, liquidity standards, requirements for overall risk management, single-counterparty credit limits, stress test requirements, and a debt-to-equity limit for systemically relevant companies. Dodd-Frank also provides for an orderly liquidation mechanism whereby Treasury, the FDIC and the Federal Reserve would agree to unwind failing financial institutions that are systemically relevant, at the cost of shareholders and unsecured creditors.

Another key provision designed to stabilize financial markets and institutions is the Volcker rule. The Volcker rule restricts proprietary operations undertaken by commercial banks.[24] This falls short of a complete ban on proprietary desks, and there are various exceptions to the ban. There is a list of permitted activities, including investments in US government securities, transactions made in connection with underwriting or market-making related activities, transactions on behalf of customers, and 'risk-mitigating hedging activities' in connection with individual or aggregated holdings of the banking entity. The market-making exception is somewhat controversial. There are many challenges to implementation in that it is very difficult to distinguish proprietary trading from market-making activities. A market-making position is booked as inventory and is typically entered into with the intent of meeting reasonably expected near term customer demands. Yet with illiquid markets, with higher risk levels, there might not be a ready counterpart on the other side of the transaction. When the market maker commits capital and takes on more risk, the distinction from proprietary trading is not so clear-cut. The other exceptions to the Volcker rule are also somewhat broad and ambiguous. Will investments in funds that mostly trade government securities (for example fixed income arbitrage funds) be allowed? Will activities conducted to facilitate customer relationships qualify as activities done 'on behalf of customers'? What types of activities will constitute 'risk-mitigating hedging activities'? There is enough ambiguity to allow banks to get away with a lot, if they can successfully interpret the rules as they see fit.

Systemic risk and the culture of risk

Many individual financial institutions have failed to properly manage their risk profile, as was evidenced during the 2007–2008 financial crisis. Individual institutions also have no incentive to monitor systemic risk. Hence, it would seem that the FSOC has been given sole responsibility to prevent future market collapses. Yet its ability to do so is unclear, untested. The FSOC comprises representatives of existing regulatory agencies, which were not particularly successful in controlling systemic risk in the past. There is also some question as to how exactly the FSOC is to evaluate systemic risk. Practically, there is the issue of developing systems to aggregate information across financial institutions in order to prepare systemic scenario analyses for the financial sector as a whole. The data-collection process will have to be streamlined, leveraging existing data sources and technologies. But the real challenge is the ability to formulate new formal measures of systemic risk. What criteria are to be used by the regulator to determine whether an entity is too big to fail, or too interconnected to fail?

There are currently some attempts to develop a methodology for this purpose. For example, Adrian and Brunnermeier (2009) develop the concept of CoVaR as an indicator capturing the marginal contribution of a particular firm to the whole systemic risk. CoVaR is calculated as the VaR of the whole financial system conditional on an individual firm being in distress. The approach attempts to overcome the shortcomings of the VaR method (such as fat tails) by using historical data over a long period of time. However, the robustness of this methodology remains to be tested. Further, given the complexity of the global financial system, it is unlikely that one single measure will suffice. And, as pointed out by Andrew Lo in his testimony to Congress (Lo 2009), the increased complexity and connectedness of financial markets requires new approaches in risk management – a fundamental shift in our linear mode of thinking, to better understand chaotic behaviour and complex systems. This new paradigm remains to be developed. Meanwhile, the regulator lacks clear guidelines for decision-making and for monitoring systemic risk.

The current environment presents new forms of increasing systemic risk. For example, even though hedge funds played no significant role in the 2008 financial crisis, there is the potential for hedge fund failures to contribute to destabilize the economy because of the size of the industry. The risk profile of hedge funds and other new products (for example structured and securitized products, credit derivatives) is also not well understood, and in dire need of some new risk metrics.[25] There is also no reason to believe that private sector actors such as lawyers, accountants, banks' internal risk management and rating agencies can on their own ensure the reliability of the system and well-functioning markets. They have already failed to do that.

In this context, we argue that it is more important than ever to address the dangers posed by the culture of risk. Unless the financial culture on Wall Street embraces more conservative values and the incentives for short-termism and reckless risk-taking are eliminated, there is unlikely that a stable financial system will emerge. The risk is for a meltdown of the same magnitude, or worse, to happen in the near future. Hence, whether the Dodd-Frank reform will succeed in fundamentally reforming mentalities on Wall Street is a critical issue.

Unfortunately, Dodd-Frank did not really change the incentives for short-termism. Specifically, regarding corporate governance and executive compensation, Dodd-Frank merely includes measures to *encourage* management to shift focus from short-term profits to long-term growth, rather than strict guidelines.

All directors on compensation committees of publicly traded companies are required to be independent from executives whose compensation they are supervising. In addition, the committees will have the authority to hire independent compensation consultants. The strengthened independence of compensation committees is unlikely to impact the size of Wall Street bonuses and the fact that Wall Street executives operate like a guild system of insiders who have acquired the power to pay themselves (and each other) with no effective input from shareholders. Dodd-Frank also requires the disclosure of executive compensation as compared with the company's stock performance over a five-year period, so as to strengthen executive accountability. This might alert shareholders to the issue of a discrepancy between executive compensation and stock performance, but may not be sufficient to prevent the issue altogether. Unless bonuses are reduced, or at least assessed on the basis of long-term profits rather than short-term (yearly) results, incentives for risk-taking and stock volatility will still exist, and it will be business as usual. The fact that 2010, 2011 and 2012 were record years in terms of Wall Street bonuses while economic recovery in the US is still fragile, to put it mildly, bears no good sign for the future.

Finally, it is unclear whether the SEC has the resources to properly monitor the activities of hedge funds and private equity fund managers, given the massive amount of filings it will have to review and process. The Madoff case illustrates that, unless the SEC is properly equipped (and staffed) to monitor the activities of all investment managers, its ability to detect fraudulent activities may be limited.[26] More generally, there is the issue of lack of funding and resources of government agencies compared with the financial industry. The fact that the SEC settled the Goldman Sachs investigation on fraud charges related to the structuring and marketing of subprime mortgage CDOs for a mere $550 million (barely 14 days' worth of earnings) illustrates the power dynamics at play. The settlement will likely result in new disclosure standards in the mortgage and securitization industry (Goldman Sachs is required to increase training for employees who structure or market mortgage securities), and possibly a more scrutinized internal approval process. However, the firm did not take the opportunity to reflect upon the appropriateness of the conflict of interest associated with the marketing of the CDOs. In fact, it admitted no legal wrongdoing, and merely acknowledged that it had made a simple mistake in that marketing materials contained 'incomplete information'. The settlement sent the firm's shares up 4.4 per cent.

Conclusion

The current environment on Wall Street encourages risk-taking, short-termism and profit making without taking into account the external effects (and systemic risk implications) of short-term profit seeking. Instead of fulfilling a socially desirable purpose of reducing the costs of doing business on the real side of the economy, the financial sector grew because there was a lot of money to be made by offering market solutions to risk management. In doing do, it gave rise to a new breed of financiers and financial advisors. Yet this cultural shift was accompanied by increased risk on a widespread scale. The culture of bonuses linked to short-term profits has created incentives for excessive risk-taking. In a classic moral hazard problem, managers had (and still have) strong incentives to increase the risk profile of financial institutions in order to enhance profitability. The regulatory framework did discourage this mentality, allowing excessive leverage ratios for the major investment banks, and encouraging banks to rely on their own internal risk management models for regulatory capital purposes. But this approach failed. Structurally, the system and its private sector actors were incapable of preventing a major breakdown.

What are the perspectives in light of the new financial regulatory overhaul in the US? There are specific provisions that are welcome developments, such as the increased transparency with respect to hedge funds and derivatives, the attempt to limit proprietary trading and the focus on systemic risk. However, there is still much risk in the system – neither the risk profile of new investment vehicles and products nor systemic risk is well understood. In this context, we argue that a reform of the current financial culture is as important as solving specific problems that led to the 2007 crisis, such as practices in the mortgage or securitization industries. Unless a more conservative framework for decision-making replaces the culture of risk, it is unclear that Dodd-Frank in itself can safeguard the stability of the financial sector. It is far from certain that Dodd-Frank will succeed in fundamentally reforming mentalities on Wall Street. What is needed is a collective debate around the values that dominate Wall Street, and an acknowledgement that enormous risk-taking cannot continue to be the norm. A financial sector that feels entitled to excessive compensation at all costs is not sustainable in the long run. Ultimately, a sense of accountability and social purpose must be restored. After all, the financial sector is designed to facilitate intermediation with respect to payments and exchanges, and serve the real sector of the economy – not the other way around.

Notes

1 In a boom, the market is driven by overconfidence, asset overvaluation, overleveraging and underestimation of risk. The transition from boom to bust is sudden and usually triggered by a specific event. The market mood turns pessimistic and is characterized by undervaluation of asset prices, tightening of credit and deleveraging. There are many historical examples, for example, the Tulip mania in Holland (1630s), the South Sea bubble (1720s), the Wall Street crash of 1929, the emerging market crises of the 1990s (in Mexico, South-East Asia, Russia and Argentina) and the information technology 'dot-com' bubble in the 1990s.

2 Per Federal Reserve statistics (Economic Research & Data) for mortgage debt outstanding, as compared with $6.9 trillion of commercial bank loans.

3 For more detail, see Coval *et al.* (2009a, 2009b) and Semmler and Bernard (2009, 2012). In an MBS, the underlying assets are mortgages. The regular interest payments from those mortgages are income to a Special Purpose Vehicle (SPV), an entity designed to hold the pool of mortgages. Different tranches are assigned with appropriate attachment points. If the number of defaults remains below the lower attachment

point, the investors in that level simply collect the pre-arranged premium. However, once the percentage exceeds the lower attachment point, defaults are paid out of the capital posted by the investors of that tranche. Once the upper attachment point is reached, the next tranche takes over since the lower tranche is effectively exhausted. Investors in the MBS will demand compensatory interest commensurate with the assumed default risks and recovery values. These are paid with the interest income from the mortgages. The difference between the two cash flows is profit to the SPV investors. As long as it is profitable to construct these instruments, liquidity in the mortgage market will only be limited by the default probabilities, the recovery values and the rates obtainable elsewhere.

4 Geanakoplos and Farmer (2009) develop models to explain the double leverage cycle, in the housing and securities sectors, and conclude that the introduction of CDS contracts into the mortgage market in late 2005 was an important trigger for the collapse of 2007–2008. Semmler and Bernard (2009, 2012) propose a baseline model that replicates financial market boom-bust cycles and demonstrates the magnifying effects arising from the pricing of the new financial market instruments.

5 See Semmler and Sieveking (2000), Grüne et al. (2004, 2007, 2008). A more behavioural foundation of the involved asset pricing theory is given in Grüne and Semmler (2008), who study asset pricing with loss aversion.

6 Geanakoplos and Farmer (2009) find that a single supply-equals-demand equation for a loan can determine both the interest rate and the leverage ratio.

7 Brunnermeier and Pedersen (2009) provide a model that links an asset's market liquidity with traders' funding liquidity. The model shows that a mechanism of mutual reinforcement between market liquidity and funding liquidity may result in liquidity spirals.

8 Margins are the difference between the security's price and collateral value, and must be financed by the investor's own capital.

9 First developed in 1973 by Fischer Black and Myron Scholes, the Black-Scholes mathematical model calculates the price of an option. While options had always been traded, the existence of a mathematical model ensured some level of consistency and rigorousness that allowed for a higher degree of precision.

10 Proprietary trading refers to the use of the firm's own capital to actively trade financial assets, as opposed to traditional investment banking fee-based activities, such as underwriting and consulting.

11 For example, in 2007 the Trading and Principal Investments division of Goldman Sachs accounted for $13.3 billion of the $17.6 billion of the firm's pre-tax earnings. Yet in 2008, the division generated a loss of $2.75 billion (when the firm generated pre-tax earnings of $2.34 billion). Proprietary trading is also more capital intensive.

12 The stand-alone large investment bank is now a thing of the past. By late autumn of 2008, the five major US investment banks (Merrill Lynch, Goldman Sachs, Morgan Stanley, Lehman Brothers and Bear Stearns) had either failed or abandoned their status as independent investment banks. Goldman Sachs and Morgan Stanley decided to convert to Bank Holding Companies and thus become regulated by the Federal Reserve instead of the SEC. This was in great part motivated by the need to ensure that they would have access to a loan facility from the Federal Reserve, since the Federal Reserve acts as a lender of last resort (but only for bank members of the Federal Reserve System). In future, these two firms will have to adhere to stricter requirements regarding regulatory capital, which may affect the extent and nature of their proprietary trading desks. The banks might increase the level of deposit taking on their balance sheet, although the extent to which they will engage in retail banking is yet to be determined. In line with the repeal of Glass-Steagall, Wall Street might well reorganize to form even larger financial institutions offering a complete range of financial services, including commercial banking, broker-dealer services and insurance.

13 Rubin, Greenspan and Levitt had issued a letter asking Congress to prevent the Commodity Futures Trading Commission (CFTC), the regulator of commodity exchanges, from bringing swaps and other OTC derivatives within its regulatory oversight.

14 Unlike their mutual fund counterparts, most hedge funds fell outside the scope of the Investment Company Act of 1940 by availing themselves of applicable exemptions, such as having one hundred or fewer beneficial owners and not offering securities in a public offering, or because investors were all 'qualified' high net-worth individuals or institutions. This explains why hedge funds have deliberately chosen not to raise capital on public markets. Hedge fund advisers have also been exempt from regulation under the Investment Advisers Act of 1940, in spite of the SEC's unsuccessful attempt to impose mandatory registration.

15 As a process, culture can help explain the evolution and reproduction of social behaviour and institutions. As a state (way of life, the arts), it focuses on the final products of cultivation at the social level. When conceived as a process, culture is more significant for economic and other social analysis to the extent it can shed light on the relations between individuals and society (Jackson 2009: 22).

16 See for instance *Business Week* (2006), *The Economic Times* (2008), *Financial Times* (2009).

17 The accusation was that Goldman Sachs omitted to disclose key facts to the investors, including the role played by a major hedge fund (Paulson & Co.) in the selection of the underlying mortgages, and the fact that the bank had taken short positions against the CDOs.

18 'Systemic risk' refers to the possibility that the failure of one financial institution can disrupt the entire financial system through a series of correlated defaults, if there is enough interconnectedness between financial institutions. The Bear Stearns funds had heavily invested in CDOs and hoped to make big returns from the flourishing housing sector. As mortgage default rates increased, top-tranche mortgage backed securities suddenly declined in marketable value to become 'toxic' assets.

19 Note that there were some instances of questionable accounting practices. For example, Lehman used an accounting trick known as REPO 105 to improve its balance sheet.

20 The Sarbanes-Oxley Act amended Form 8-K to capture material off-balance-sheet obligations, such as the creation of a direct financial obligation under an off-balance sheet arrangement. However, this is only a small step in ensuring that investors can understand the risk implications of off-balance-sheet companies and activities.

21 The Dodd-Frank Act passed the House of Representatives on 30 June, 2010, and was approved by the Senate on 15 July, 2010.

22 There are now registration requirements for investment advisers to private funds with assets under management of $150 million or more. Hedge funds must register with the SEC and disclose assets under management, use of leverage (including off-balance-sheet leverage) and other information regarding trading practices. Other information to be disclosed includes counterparty credit risk exposures, trading practices, valuation policies and practices of the fund, types of assets held, and side arrangements or side letters (whereby certain investors in a fund obtain more favourable rights or entitlements than other investors). Hedge funds must also have assets audited by public accountants.

23 Dodd-Frank gave the SEC and the Commodity Futures Trading Commission the authority to regulate over-the-counter derivatives, and requires central clearing and exchange trading for derivatives that can be cleared, including credit default swaps.

24 Banks can place up to 3 per cent of their Tier 1 capital in hedge fund and proprietary trading investments. Banks are also prohibited from holding more than 3 per cent of the total ownership interest of any private equity investment or hedge fund.

25 Lo (2001) stressed the need for a new set of risk analytics designed to address the unique features of hedge funds and go beyond traditional Value at Risk analysis. Lo

(2008) proposed new measures of hedge fund performance that capture both static and dynamic aspects of decision-making on the part of the hedge fund manager.

26 Madoff registered voluntarily with the SEC in September 2006. Many hedge fund managers had voluntarily registered with the SEC to give the market a higher level of confidence and potentially minimize the amount of due diligence performed by new investors. In spite of some red flags (for instance, the fund relied on a small unknown auditing firm, and the returns were too high to match the proclaimed low-risk trading strategy), the SEC failed to detect irregularities. The SEC did not have the resources to review all funds, and tended to focus on funds with high-risk trading strategies. Because he claimed to engage in very low-risk 'plain vanilla' option trading, Madoff attracted no specific scrutiny.

References

Adrian, T. and Brunnermeier, M. (2009) CoVaR, FRB of New York Staff Report No. 348, http://ssrn.com/abstract=1269446.

Bernanke, B., Gertler, M. and Gilchrist, S. (1999) The Financial Accelerator in a Quantitative Business Cycle Framework, in J.B. Taylor and M. Woodford (eds), *Handbook of Macroeconomics, vol. 1*, Amsterdam: North-Holland.

Brunnermeier, M. and Pedersen, L. (2009) Market Liquidity and Funding Liquidity, *Review of Financial Studies*, 22(6): 2201–38.

Business Week (2006) Inside Wall Street's Culture of Risk, 12 June, www.businessweek.com/magazine/content/06_24/b3988004.htm.

Cochrane, J. (2005) Betas, Options, and Portfolios of Hedge Funds, www.slidefinder.net/B/Betas_Options_Portfolios_Hedge_Funds/2799231.

Coval, J., Jurek, J. and Stafford, E. (2009a) Economic Catastrophe Bonds, *American Economic Review*, 99(3): 628–66.

Coval, J., Jurek, J. and Stafford, E. (2009b) The Economics of Structured Finance, *Journal of Economic Perspectives*, 23(1): 3–25.

Financial Times (2009) Wall Street to Re-price Culture of Risk and Rewards, Francisco Guerrera, 4 February, www.ft.com/cms/s/0/1b69c1d0-f2e9–11dd-abe6–0000779fd2ac.html#axzz1HS9226Up.

Geanakoplos, J. and Farmer, J. (2009) The Virtues and Vices of Equilibrium and the Future of Financial Economics, *Complexity*, 14(3): 11–38.

Geisst, C. (2004) *Wall Street: A History: From Its Beginnings to the Fall of Enron*, New York: Oxford University Press.

Grüne, L. and Semmler, W. (2008) Asset Pricing with Loss Aversion, *Journal of Economic Dynamics and Control*, 32(10): 3253–74.

Grüne, L., Semmler, W. and Sieveking, M. (2004) Creditworthiness and Threshold in a Credit Market Model with Multiple Equilibria, *Economic Theory*, 25(2): 287–315.

Grüne, L., Semmler, W. and Bernard, L. (2007) Firm Value, Diversified Capital Assets and Credit Risk, *Journal of Credit Risk*, 3(4): 81–113.

Grüne, L., Chen, P. and Semmler, W. (2008) Boom Bust Cycles, Default Premia and Asset Pricing, www.newschool.edu/nssr/cem.

Hudson, M. (2006) The New Road to Serfdom, *Harpers Magazine*, May.

Jackson, W. (2009) *Economics, Culture and Social Theory*, Cheltenham and Northampton: Edward Elgar.

Kaufman, H. (2009) *The Road to Financial Reformation: Warnings, Consequences, Reforms*, New York: Wiley.

Kindleberger, C. and Aliber, R. (2005) *Manias, Panics, and Crashes: A History of Financial Crises*, 5th edn, New York: Wiley.

Lewis, M. (1990) *Liar's Poker: Rising through the Wreckage on Wall Street*, New York: Penguin Books.

Lo, A. (2001) Risk Management for Hedge Funds: Introduction and Overview, *Financial Analysts Journal*, 57(6): 16–33.

Lo, A. (2008) Where do Alphas Come From? A New Measure of the Value of Active Investment Management, *Journal of Investment Management*, 6(3): 6–34.

Lo, A. (2009) The Feasibility of Systemic Risk Measurement, written testimony for the US House of Representatives, Financial Services Committee, Washington DC.

Minsky, H.P. (1975) *John Maynard Keynes*, New York: Columbia University Press.

Minsky, H.P. (1982) *Can it Happen Again?* Armonk: ME Sharpe.

Minsky, H.P. (1986) *Stabilizing an Unstable Economy*, New Haven, CT: Yale University Press.

Montgomery, J. and Young, B. (2009) Home Is Where the Hardship Is: Gender Dimension of Indebtedness and Homeownership, CRESC Working Paper Series, WP 79, www.cresc.ac.uk/publications/documents/wp79.pdf.

New York Times (2009) Banks Bundled Bad Debt, Bet Against it and Won, G. Morgenson and L. Story, 23 December.

Prins, N. (2004) *Other People's Money: The Corporate Mugging of America*, New York: New Press.

Semmler, W. and Bernard, L. (2009) Banking, Complex Securities, and the Credit Crisis, *Economic and Political Weekly*, 64(13): 137–43.

Semmler, W. and Bernard, L. (2012) Boom–bust Cycles: Leveraging, Complex Securities, and Asset Prices, *Journal of Economic Behavior & Organization*, 81(2): 442–65.

Semmler, W. and Sieveking, M. (2000) Critical Debt and Debt Dynamics, *Journal of Economic Dynamics and Control*, 24(5–7): 1–24.

Shiller, R.J. (1991) *Market Volatility*, Cambridge, MA: MIT Press.

Shiller, R.J. (2001) *Irrational Exuberance*, New York: Random House.

Shiller, R.J. (2007) Low Interest Rates and High Asset Prices: An Interpretation in Terms of Changing Popular Models, Cowles Foundation for Research in Economics, Yale University, http://cowles.econ.yale.edu/P/cd/d16a/d1632.pdf.

Stiglitz, J. (2010) *Freefall: America, Free Markets, and the Sinking of the World Economy*, New York: W.W. Norton.

Stiglitz, J. and Weiss, A. (1981) Credit Rationing in Markets with Imperfect Information, *American Economic Review*, 71(3): 393–410.

The Economic Times (2008) Culture of Risk on Wall Street Not Seen Changing, 22 March, http://articles.economictimes.indiatimes.com/2008–03–22/news/27695513_1_credit-crisis-bankers-risk.

Tobin, J. (1980) *Asset Accumulation and Economic Activity*, Oxford: Blackwell.

Part III

Cultural factors in financial crisis generation

7 Financial stability and technological fixes as imaginaries across phases of capitalism[1]

Brigitte Young

Setting the stage

The financial crisis first became apparent to most observers as a subprime crisis in the United States (2007), turned into the Great Recession and then crossed the Atlantic to engulf the Eurozone in 2010, leaving in its wake a serious sovereign debt crisis with drastic declines in economic growth and high unemployment rates in the peripheral countries of the Eurozone. Mainstream financial academics, chief economists at central banks and the International Monetary Fund as well as national finance ministers were quick to construct a narrative of the financial and debt crisis. They tried to circumvent any discussion about systemic instabilities of finance, and instead focused on market failure as the culprit for financial instabilities. Focusing on a narrative of market failure had the advantage that financial actors, the financial sector and the political elite could avoid dealing with the contradictions, tensions, incoherence and tacit assumptions inherent in the perfect capital market paradigm. Namely, the literature on Capital Market Liberalization (CML) has concentrated on constructing a story of the benefits of financial market liberalization over the last decade. Champions of the benefits of financial globalization are found among the American business and financial community, and also the Council on Foreign Relations (Council on Foreign Relations 2002). New technological innovations such as Value at Risk (VaR) models, new complex securities, new types of rating models, structured investment vehicles (SIV) and computer algorithms provided the tools to liberalize capital markets. Such technologies were seen as diversifying risks across markets and sectors, increasing allocative efficiency and ensuring financial stability (IMF 2006). Alan Greenspan, the Governor of the Federal Reserve, added that globalization of capital markets would ensure financial competition across the globe. Owing to the break-up of the Soviet Union, the establishment of global markets for products and financial services was on the horizon (Greenspan 2008).

Such a depiction of stable global markets is very different from the more realistic narrative of imperfect capital markets. Financial intermediation is usually undertaken by imperfect markets and this often leads to failures, disintermediation and market meltdowns. These market imperfections are frequently observed as financial instabilities in terms of boom-bust cycles (Semmler and Young 2010). Inherent in these finance-led models, in which finance, insurance and real estate (so called FIRE sectors) play a key role (Deutschmann 2014; Heires and Nölke 2014; Stockhammer 2010), the emphasis is on rent-extracting activities at the expense of production in the real economy.

The role of technological innovations and technological fixes

What is most interesting in the crisis narrative is the role played by technological innovations and technological fixes in ensuring financial stability such as securitized credit, structured debt and credit derivatives. Relying on such technological fixes, financial actors continued to conceptualize and construct a world that may be interrupted by short-term financial aberrations in the markets, but they were of the opinion that these markets would eventually return to an original steady-state (Mittnik and Semmler 2012). The proponents of the CML generally disregarded the imperfectly working of capital markets and attributed too much of a self-correcting mechanism to the capital markets.

In constructing narratives of capital markets as perfect and stable markets while neglecting the negative aspects of CML (Stiglitz *et al.* 2006), new macroeconomic models provided the theoretical justification for financial market liberalization. Ben Bernanke, as Chair of the Federal Reserve, announced in 2004 a new age of *Great Moderation* implying that financial volatility was history (Bernanke 2004). Equally confident, E.F. Fama (1998) promulgated the *Efficient Market Hypothesis* that suggests that any long-term return anomalies in stock prices are fragile. They can be the result of methodology, and thus the 'long-term return anomalies tend to disappear with reasonable changes in the technique' (1998: 283). In other words, market efficiency as a powerful imaginary of market liberalization came to represent the norm during the pre-crisis stage.

Focusing on the benefits of perfect markets is a strategy for actors trying to make sense of their experiences and 'engage in a selective sense- and meaning making based on discursively-selective *imaginaries*' (Sum and Jessop, Ch. 1). These imaginaries help to reduce the complexity that financial actors face in times of great uncertainties. Thus the imaginary of perfect markets and financial stability helps financial actors to relate to their environment and provide a roadmap for political leaders to engage in strategic actions. According to Sum and Jessop, imaginary is a meaning system 'that frames individual subjects' lived experience of an inordinately complex world and/or guides collective calculation about that world' (Sum and Jessop, Ch. 1). That a particular imaginary becomes dominant out of a universe of different imaginaries has much to do with specific historical conjunctures, the existing hegemonies within and across financial networks, and the availability of technology. Without the emergence of the information technology (IT) boom in the 1990s, imaginaries of complex derivatives and computer algorithm innovations could not have emerged to change financial intermediaries from traditional deposit banking institutions to global investment firms. Thus we witness at particular historical conjunctures specific imaginaries that emerge to construct finance's new role in capitalist accumulation and at the same time constitute new economic interests, activities, organizations, institutions and economic subjectivities (Jessop and Oosterlynck 2008). As such, they provide a road-map to guide business and politics, and at the same time form new subjects that are more closely adapted to these new challenges.

The imaginary of market efficiency and the trust in stable markets of the last three decades was not just geared to empower the financial sector and promote the material interests of finance. The symbolism these financial actors invoked was also an appeal to the hearts and minds of citizens around the world that they could trust in the stability of the financial sector despite the 'irrational exuberance' already visible on the horizon in 2004. In other words, the theoretical construction of *Great Moderation* and the *Efficient Market Hypotheses* were intended to create a new collective social reality for a finance-led capitalism.

Economic imaginary across four different phases of capitalist crisis

The intent of this chapter is to focus on the effects of a given economic imaginary in specific crisis situation and the efforts to transcend these economic crises by constructing new imaginaries while at the same time preserving and protecting the interests associated with that specific imaginary. Key is the narrative of *stable economic markets* in finance that actors construct and re-construct through specific discourses, practices and new technological innovations across various phases of capitalist development. If we take money and credit as a structural form of finance and focus on the emerging contradictions and destabilizing effects in the pursuit of stable markets which accompany each phase, we can identify four different regimes. The first is the gold standard of the nineteenth century constructed as a mechanism to balance the current account positions and thereby create a social order for international trade and monetary stability. But we know from the accounts of Polanyi (1957) and others that the discourse and the technical modes of calculation to achieve this stability functioned as a disciplinary tool over wage relations and workers' rights. Not only did the commodification of labour with its tacit reduction of humans to tradable factors of production lead to the 'double movement' (Polanyi 1957), it also destroyed the idea that the gold standard could achieve international economic stability. Influenced by this experience, the political elites of the western world (particularly in the United States and United Kingdom) with the support of large industrial firms and agricultural enterprises in the US-Midwest sought a new social imaginary in Atlantic Fordism after the Second World War. It was based on a capital-labour compromise to guarantee full employment with states enjoying capital controls, fixed but adjustable exchange rates, and a Keynesian welfare national state that temporarily secured the link between Fordist mass production and mass consumption (Jessop 2013).

Contradictions between the power of labour unions on the one side and business profits on the other were initially resolved through rising productivity and, as this was gradually exhausted, through a lenient monetary policy that led to higher inflation rates and rising welfare demands which in turn led to public deficits in the 1970s. The subsequent instability on the capital markets which impacted the profit margins of business was used by neoclassical economists in the Hayekian tradition and their political supporters such as Margaret Thatcher in Great Britain and Ronald Reagan in the United States to shift to new economic imaginaries. Reagan's much repeated election slogan of the late 1970s 'Get the state off our back' exploited and reinforced the subjectivities which had already begun to emerge to prioritize a more individualistic risk-taking culture that encouraged private debt as an economic demand engine in place of the old 'bad' Keynesianism with its reliance on public debt. The new privatized Keynesianism (Crouch 2009; Young 2009) put the market risks on wage-earners who were perceived by supply-siders as tipping the balance of power 'dangerously' towards labour. At the same time, banks and bank-like institutions developed new narratives of supposedly risk-free products through slicing and dicing securitized assets and bundling them into mortgage-backed securities (MBS), collateralized debt obligations (CDOs) and credit default swaps (CDS), thus leveraging their asset balances at ever higher levels. Unsurprisingly, but to the surprise of many financial analysts, the house of cards came crashing down with the collapse of the subprime market, leaving the banks exposed to toxic securitized loans.

The power of the imaginary of a world with stable capital markets institutionally embedded in formally deregulated and highly innovative financial markets created a specific mode of finance-led capital accumulation, what has become known as financialization (Heires and Nölke 2014; Stockhammer 2010). This process also shaped new subjectivities of individual against collective (social) risk-taking and agents' preferences to interpret and adapt to this new environment benefitting mostly asset owners. When the crisis hit and governments bailed out the banks and financial structures, the political and financial elites relied on anxiety-ridden discourses to convince the frightened citizenry to support the bail-out at the cost of higher public deficits and national debt. The new narrative which invoked once again the view that financial stability was possible in the post-crisis era was constructed by the very same experts who had been at the helm before and during the financial crisis. While the political rhetoric focused on bailing out the banks in order to avoid a depression-style meltdown, the question as to who was going to pay for the financial clean-up was largely ignored by the political and financial elites.

That average citizens bear the brunt of financial repression and witness their savings dwindle in light of low interest rates is not altogether surprising. Low interest rates have surely advantages for taxpayers to get cheap loans or to buy assets, but they generally have a negative impact on small savers who rely on returns of pension funds and life-insurances to provide retirement security. While many citizens in the Eurozone countries, particularly those in the peripheral member states, feel that they have shouldered the major burden of the financial crisis, economists and political leaders try to persuade the public that despite low economic growth rates the financial crisis has been tamed. As a sign of recovery, Ireland is cited as having exited the EU-IMF-ECB's bail-out programme in December 2013, followed by Spain in January 2014. But this narrative about a new economic stability is based on a slippery foundation. This was evident in some of the rhetoric at the World Economic Forum in Davos at the end of January 2014. Many participants addressed the increasing inequalities across and within countries as a phenomenon that, to most of the Davos elites, had little to do with the dominance of the finance-led capitalism that they have constructed over the last three decades and from which they continue to appropriate most of the benefits. Despite the positive news that Ireland and Spain returned to the capital markets, the narrative that the financial crisis has been resolved may be true at the aggregate level of economic growth rates, however insignificant these figures may in fact be. The picture is quite different if the focus is on the micro- and meso-levels of continuing high household indebtedness and high unemployment rates in many Eurozone countries. These economic asymmetries spell also political instabilities in that political right-wing fringe-groups have gathered momentum in Greece with the Golden Dawn, in France with Marine Le Pen, in Austria with Heinz-Christian Strache of the FPÖ (Freiheitliche Partei Österreich), the United Kingdom Independent Party (UKIP) with Nigel Farage, and among others the Dutch Party for Freedom with Geert Wilders to promise a populist return to an idyllic world of closed nation-states.

The next section will deal with the narrative of *financial stability* and the different technological innovations used to construct these market stabilities across four phases of capitalist accumulation. My focus will be less on which forces developed these imaginaries, how they are promoted, how they are articulated to earlier and concurrent imaginaries, what channels are used to promote and institutionalize them and how they are translated into politics and policies. Instead, I will focus on the effects of a given economic imaginary and how financial actors and political elites responded to specific crisis and their efforts to overcome these with new technological fixes while preserving the institutional foundations of finance and protecting its interests associated with that imaginary. Such an approach also includes the way different imaginaries seek to reconcile the tensions, dilemmas or contractions in a given monetary and financial regime, and how objectives and subjects are formed and get modified across these phases to create different forms of capital accumulation.

The gold standard and its deflationary contradictions 1871–1930s

In *The Great Transformation* (1957) Karl Polanyi gave a vivid account of the contradictions of the international gold standard in the nineteenth century and the subsequent calamitous social consequences of adhering to it, which led not only to the Great Depression but also to the collapse of the edifice of the self-regulating market doctrine. The gold standard, as the financial imaginary of imperial Great Britain to finance the construction of its global empire beginning in the eighteenth century, became an international monetary system in 1871 when Germany adopted the gold standard. Countries adhering to this standard committed themselves to the prompt and direct convertibility of their currencies into gold, thus giving rise to a system of fixed exchange rates. The rationale for introducing the gold standard was the need for a reliable exchange rate system in times of growing trade liberalization and demand for foreign investment. Gold was constituted as world money to ensure economic stability across international borders, and it had the 'function of unit of measure, means of payment and *international reserve*' (Amato and Fantacci 2012: 157).

A major drawback of the gold standard was the limited supply of gold, both in total and in terms of annual production. Since the supply of gold was inelastic, so was the supply of money. This had invariably a deflationary impact on the international system, since any disequilibrium in international trade (surplus and deficits) had to be compensated by a transfer of gold. When imports exceeded exports, the deficit country was faced with automatic stabilizing mechanism to re-create an international equilibrium. Gold had to 'leave the country' (or its ownership in bullion vaults be transferred), decreasing the domestic supply of money, thus decreasing prices, and in the process increase competitiveness of the deficit country. Adjustment meant that businesses were forced to exit the market, thereby increasing unemployment. According to Polanyi, the problem for deficit countries 'was not low prices, but falling prices' (Polanyi 1957: 214).

The gold standard was only able to stabilize the international current account imbalances temporarily because the contradictions were externalized to other parts of the economy, creating tremendous social hardship for those in the labour market and their families. But there is another story to the gold standard. In order to mask the contradictions created by the gold standard,

> the international gold standard was *at the same time* a 'sterling standard', in other words a system in which all countries were, of course, obliged to ensure convertibility of their currencies into gold, but provisions was made for different ways of doing it depending on whether their currency was the sterling or not
>
> (Amato and Fantacci 2012: 160)

Rather than interpreting the gold standard as a depoliticized technical system with automatic equilibrium mechanisms, it was foremost a geopolitical and global economic system for British interests of empire building. The Bank of England played the role of 'the conductor of the orchestra' (Keynes, cited in Amato and Fantacci: 2012: 162) in a game that had different rules for different actors but had all the trappings of a stable rule-based system.

In actuality,

> what was taking shape on the basis of the United Kingdom's hegemonic position was the possibility of securing a global sustainability of the British structural trade deficits through their financing by means of credit

instruments, hence by avoiding payment in gold, as the rules would have officially required

(Amato and Fantacci 2012: 164)

Great Britain thus did not transfer gold to pay for its trade deficits, but used sterling deposited in the City. But the sterling only maintained a credible convertibility as long as the trade credits issued in sterling were not converted into gold. 'Thus sterling convertibility was structurally based on its non-conversion' (Amato and Fantacci 2012: 165). The Bank of England provided a structural form for a money regime that temporarily stabilized capitalist relations only as long as it had enjoyed hegemony in the international economy. Once the United States started to become an international creditor and challenged the position of Great Britain in hoarding gold, Britain's only remaining gambit was to exploit economically its colonies and turn India's trade surpluses into gold, which was deposited in the City (Strange 1971). Only by including its colonies into the gold system could Great Britain circumvent the reality that sterling was not convertible into gold. Already the financial crisis of 1907 was a foreboding of the instability of the gold standard with its incessant shortage of liquidity, which finally caused the loss of trust in the convertibility of currencies into gold prior to the outbreak of the First World War (Kindleberger 1989). While European countries had to suspend the gold standard during the war so that they could print money to finance the war effort, the newly created Federal Reserve (1913) stabilized the gold standard in the United States. In the interwar period, most countries returned to a modified gold standard which was a system based on gold and foreign exchange, but the capital movements needed for post-war construction flowed mostly from the USA to Europe. The short-term interwar period of the gold standard, hailed as the 'roaring twenties' in the United States and the 'goldenen Zwanziger' in Germany, was possible only due to the supply of unlimited and unconditional US credit. Finally, the contraction of American short-term credit in 1928 brought the house of cards down ushering in the Great Depression and by 1932 all countries that had subscribed to the gold standard in the interwar period had to abandon it (Amato and Fantacci 2012: 156).

Despite efforts of internationalists and imperial powers to construct a solid institutional foundation to stabilize international trade and finance, these forces were never able to fully overcome the contradiction between the national and international dimensions of the world market and, in particular, of money as national currency and world money. Only by externalizing through extra-economic hegemonic colonial means could the gold standard temporarily provide the basis for an international monetary system. But

the international gold standard could not be borne by the nations whom it was supposed to serve, unless they were secured against the dangers with which it threatened the communities adhering to it.... '[Namely,] devastating effects as to its welfare, whether in terms of production, income, or employment.... [Bankers believed the gold standard could guarantee] sound

domestic finance and external stability of currency. That is why when both
had lost their meaning bankers as a class were the last to notice it'

(Polanyi 1957: 207 and 208)

This is a good example of how economic imaginaries have the power to block
perceptions. To return once again to Polanyi, he mocks that despite the emerging
contradictions bankers as professional guardians of the gold standard continued
to regard the metal as the guarantor of stability and prosperity. It was bankers
after 1929 that did not understand that the gold standard could no longer provide
both sound domestic finance and external stability of the currency. Internal equilibrium had consequently to be sacrificed for external equilibrium. As such, the
quest for economic stability failed as a result of the changing balance of forces
which transformed the state system and its strategic selectivities so that the state
no longer could bear the costs for the 'required social repair work' (Jessop and
Oosterlynck 2008: 1157) for the reproduction of the gold system.

State Keynesianism and its inflationary contradictions (1950s–1973)

A period of new social forces emerged after the Second World War which
rejected the self-regulating market doctrine and the gold standard after the
Second World War to create new social imaginaries to obtain financial stability
after the collective experience of the Depression of the 1930s. Of primary
importance was the theoretical work of John Maynard Keynes, *The General
Theory of Employment, Interest, and Money* (1936). The purpose of Keynes was
to refute the neoclassical imaginary of the gold standard and demonstrate instead
that money and financial arrangements affect the economy. In rejecting the
previous imaginary that money was separate from the general theory of supply
and demand, the new narrative of money was linked to the fundamental theory
of value. At Bretton Woods, John Maynard Keynes was the British negotiator
and Harry Dexter White his American counterpart. They agreed to reverse the
liberal order and create a post-war international system that explicitly gave
national states the right to control capital movements. The shift to state intervention meant to create the precondition for national economic imaginaries and new
technologies such as capital controls, intervening in the currency markets and
countercyclical tools to manage the economy. State intervention along these
lines meant a radical rejection of the gold standard and its supposedly automatic
equilibrium mechanism that existed prior to 1933, which as pointed out previously depended on colonial support. The turn to a new cultural political economy
was expressed best by Keynes when he said: 'What used to be a heresy is now
endorsed as orthodoxy' (Keynes, cited in Helleiner 1994: 25).

The four pillars, which became the new imaginary, of the Bretton Woods
System comprised: 1) the adoption of a fixed exchange rate in which the value of
the dollar tied to gold and that of other currencies was tied to the dollar; 2) progressive liberalization of trade through the General Agreement of Trade and

Tariffs; 3) the creation of the International Monetary Fund to provide counter-cyclical measures for countries with liquidity problems so that domestic problems would not spill over into the international arena; and 4) the International Bank for Reconstruction and Development to provide funds for reconstruction after the Second World War, and later (as the World Bank) to provide financial investment for developing countries. The restrictive money form that shaped the post-Second World War period was based on the Keynesian insight that a liberal financial system cannot coexist with both stable exchange rates and a liberal international trading system. In this configuration that became known as the 'impossible trinity' the liberal financial system was sacrificed to achieve free trade and stable exchange rates (Helleiner 1994).

The new national imaginary of state intervention to achieve financial stability was celebrated as the answer to economic disequilibria. Andrew Shonfield, in *Modern Capitalism*, published in 1965, confidently extolled the superiority of public intervention for economic growth as against countries that practiced a hands-off approach (such as the United Kingdom and the US) and left the market to private actors. State intervention did not develop spontaneously: it required the creation of new subjectivities and their embedding in the broader networks of social networks and institutional ensembles. Only then did the national conditions exist for a new economic stability based on the *will of governments* to manage the economy, an issue which Shonfield closely tied to the construction of democratic legitimacy (1965). This change to a new structural institutional arrangement of the money form transformed the dynamic of accumulation to a regime which became known as Fordism. Its characteristics were fixed exchange rates, collective wage bargaining tied to productivity increases, Keynesian demand management, mass production and mass consumption, and an extensive social welfare system. The Keynesian welfare state temporarily stabilized capitalist relations, but it had two contradictory fault-lines. First, the accumulation regime was based on Keynesian macroeconomic intervention based on monetary, budgetary and fiscal policy to provide the link between supply-side mass production and the demand-driven mass consumption. Money played a dual and contradictory role in that it was both a national currency and international money. As national currency, it was linked to the control of national sovereign states; in its guise as international money, it was traded on international currency markets. A temporary stability was possible since the dollar became the hegemonic international currency, but at the cost of balance of payment deficits for the United States (Strange 1986). Keynes had opposed the dual status of the dollar as a national currency and international money at Bretton Woods and suggested the introduction of an artificial money, the *bancor*, for international trade as a unit of account backed by gold. The insistence of the United States to have the dollar play the dual role caused a permanent international shortage of dollar liquidity. Only via the creation of the Eurodollar market in the 1960s could the international dollar demand be met and stabilize the monetary system temporarily.

Domestically the constructed and tenuous class compromise between industrial capital and organized labour, with its economic foundation in collective bargaining and full employment guarantee, built up an inflationary momentum, which led to permanent pressure towards a spiral of inflation and subsequent higher wages (Streeck 2011) countered by bouts of higher interest rates, austerity and deflation. This process could only be provisionally accommodated through an expanding monetary policy. The resulting stagflation of the 1970s demonstrated that the pressures build up in the monetary system and the wage relations could no longer be externalized to other forms of capitalist relations. In the process the inflationary build-up in the American economy reinforced the inflationary pressures in Europe, especially in Britain, but also Japan and eventually led to the collapse of the Bretton Woods System in 1973 (Amato and Fantacci 2012; Helleiner 1994). Thus the hegemonic post-war social imaginary of economic and financial stability through the strategic selectivity of national states to empower unequally capital and labour to guarantee economic and financial stability failed as a result of the increasing internationalization of money and trade. The answer to these experiences of instabilities on the national monetary and credit front was now a shift to new discourses and imaginaries based on Hayekian-Friedman monetarist and supply-side solutions championed by political leaders such as Margaret Thatcher in the United Kingdom and Ronald Reagan in the United States, economic think-tanks, and chief economists in the International Monetary Fund and the World Bank.

A new economic imaginary of monetarism and public indebtedness (1970s–1980s)

Both the gold standard and the Bretton Woods system tried to construct regulatory systems for stable capitalist relations. While the gold standard accommodated an external equilibrium through domestic deflationary adjustments, the Bretton Woods system was able to accommodate the goals of collective bargaining, full employment and free trade only at the expense of unsustainable inflation rates. The answer to this inflation conundrum was to be found in the imaginary of monetarism based on a mechanical quantitative theory of money. Against the Keynesian view of monetary arrangements setting limits to the level of economic activity, Milton Friedman argued that the money supply causes increases in the price level. For monetarists, inflation is always and everywhere a monetary phenomenon (Friedman 1956). The antidote to inflation was to control a country's economy by limiting the money supply. Hence Paul Volcker, who was appointed by President Carter as Chair of the US Federal Reserve in the late 1970s, drastically increased the interest rate at the end of the 1970s that reduced inflation at the cost of exorbitant increases in unemployment (Helleiner 1994).

The shift to supply-side economics and the initial turn to monetarism under the Reagan and Thatcher regimes involved more than an economic antidote to inflation. The new ideological doctrine of disciplinary neoliberalism (Gill 2003), which was used as a control measure to break the power of unions and move away from social citizen rights was accompanied by changes of norms and values targeting the state as the problem and forming new subjectivities which emphasized personal responsibility, autonomy and self-reliance. Forming such economic subjects was underpinned by the mechanic application of a quant-itative theory of money that failed to take into account the complex interaction between costs, prices and the money supply. While it provided a temporary tech-nocratic fix it led to new contradictions and dilemmas in a largely debt-driven economy. Since inflation was no longer available as a safety valve to accom-modate the pressures of wage demands (Streeck 2011), it was the state via public deficits that compensated for the fiscal squeeze (Grunberg 1998). The 'retreat of the state' in economic affairs meant that tax revenues as percentage of GDP declined, which symbolized a general fiscal retrenchment. As public spending increased as a result of the dislocation of workers due to globalization, their capacity to raise revenue also weakened. The option for states was rather limited to deal with the fiscal squeeze. They could either borrow on the capital market and increase their public debt or cut spending and thus risk the social peace. Once again the regulatory structures of largely national-oriented financial markets could no longer accommodate the emerging instabilities in the glo-balized world economy. Out of these rather bankrupt ideas of monetarism emerged new economic imaginaries of deregulation, privatization and liberaliza-tion which spread globally through discourses, financial incentives, new techno-logical financial innovations and network-based expert think tanks, US-American elite business schools and international organizations who were able to transform the state system and consolidate the dominance of private power over state inter-vention globally.

Privatized Keynesianism and private debt (1990s–2007)

While Francis Fukuyama (1992) theorized that economic liberalism with its emphasis on the legitimacy of private property and free enterprise was the only game left in town after the collapse of communism, it became increas-ingly clear that a new meaning system and ideology of private market power that rested on very different normative premises was transforming capitalist relations. Market fundamentalism reshaped subjectivities into individual atoms and integrated them into a market citizenship at the expense of social citizen-ship. Margaret Thatcher had, even before attempting to break the National Union of Miners in 1984–1985, started to deregulate the City with the intent to make London the epicentre of global finance. The Big Bang eventually occurred in 1986 but was prepared earlier. In the United States it was Bill Clinton eager to ensure his re-election in 1996 who presided over the most extensive deregulation programme of the financial markets, which resulted in both a stock market and information-technology boom in the 1990s. As a further step, Clinton reversed the New Deal compromise of 'welfare as we have come to know it' in *The Personal Responsibility and Work Opportunity Reconciliation Act* of 1996. This finance-led capitalist period benefitted mostly the wealthy (lenders) who profited from the high-interest environment of the 1980s and 1990s. James Galbraith argues that, as Wall Street rose to dominance under Bill Clinton as reflected in a finance-driven technology boom that concentrated incomes in just five states the rest of the country suffered from unprecedented inequalities in income. This happened because rising inequality is closely associated with the act of earning capital gains from global financial investment (Galbraith 2012; Reich 2011).

Constructing this new meaning system was based on the irrational praise of technological innovations that would reduce risks and thus ensure financial stability (Chappe *et al.* 2013). Innovations such as collateralized debt obligations, mortgage-backed securities, credit default swaps, credit derivatives, special purpose vehicles and structured investment vehicles were tools used by financial institutions to create the US subprime mortgage markets and in the process institutionalize a home-owner society championed by Presidents Bill Clinton and G.W. Bush alike. As Crouch pointed out,

> two things came together to rescue the neo-liberal model from the instability that would otherwise have been its fate: the growth of credit markets (which includes credit cards, bank cards, bank and students loans, BY) for poor and middle income people, and of derivatives and futures markets among the very wealthy
>
> (Crouch 2009: 390)

The model of *Privatized Keynesianism* (Crouch 2009; Young 2009) no longer relied on governments taking on debt to stimulate the economy; individuals were encouraged to take on private debts in order to finance their consumption needs. Extending cheap credits via bank loans and the housing market coincided with the conservative agenda started already under Margaret Thatcher in the United Kingdom to encourage private home-ownership. As President George W. Bush explained, 'if you own something, you have a vital stake in the future of our country' (Bush 2004). To integrate the poor and middle class into the expanding highly leveraged housing market, easy access to relatively cheap refinance, the possibility to 'cash-out' the accumulated home equity as well as the securitization of mortgage loans was essential to free up purchasing power for consumption. In other words,

> [A]s nominal interest rates fell, homeowners refinanced mortgages, shifting considerable purchasing power away from rentier interests towards individuals with a higher propensity to consume goods, services, and housing. This consumption in turn generated new employment through standard Keynesian multiplier effects, sustaining the expansion by helping shift the US federal budget into surplus and thus enabling the Federal Reserve to continue lowering interest rates
>
> (Schwartz 2008: 268)

The regime of *Privatized Keynesianism* required more than just low interest rates to recycle housing equity into additional purchasing power.[2] In fact, the global recycling of current account surpluses played the essential role in providing the United States with the money to finance the housing bubble. Since the US had a notoriously high current account deficit since the 1990s, which amounted to 739 billion USD or 6 per cent of US GDP (Reinhart and Rogoff 2009), they had to rely on capital imports from current account surplus countries such as Asia and the oil exporting countries.[3] The total global current account surpluses amounted to 1,700 billion USD in 2007, of which the US alone imported 44 per cent (IMF 2008). This international asymmetry between surplus and deficit countries produced a situation in which the US dollars of the surplus countries flowed back into the United States as foreign direct investment, investment in assets, bonds, or as credit for mortgage-backed securities. As a result, the emerging markets not only subsidized corporate America, more important for our discussion is that 'fifty-nine percent of foreign investment in US bonds as of December 2005 occurred as purchases of US government and government-guaranteed agency debt' (Schwartz 2008: 265). Agency debt is defined as investments in mortgage-backed security obligations (MBOs), which the two quasi-public Federal Mortgage Agencies, *Fannie Mae and Freddie Mac*, securitized and resold on the global financial markets. These two agencies connected international credit markets to the domestic US housing market via the sale of securitized mortgages (Schwartz 2008).

The global recycling strategy starting in the 1990s has parallels to the petro-dollar recycling strategy of the 1970s and the subsequent debt crisis of many Latin American countries in the 1980s. The US banking system also acted as an intermediary between the oil exporting countries and the debtors in Latin American countries. The difference from today is that, although large sums of money are flowing into the United States, the relations between debtor and creditor have been reversed. Some emerging markets had become current account surplus countries and were on the side of the creditors. The new twist is that the majority of foreign inflows of capital from the emerging markets were recycled in an underdeveloped part of the US economy. In this way billions of dollars were utilized to buy US Treasury Bills and mortgage backed securities, which provided the incentive for banks and mortgage companies to market ever more risky loans (Young 2009). Instabilities in finance worsened as inflationary real estate prices acted as a *financial accelerator* (Minsky 2008) which made borrowers feel that they in fact possessed equivalent (real) values. The new subjects with new economic and financial subjectivities no longer judged their personal financial security according to the income they earned, instead they 'felt richer' because the nominal value of their homes increased substantially. This reinforced a procyclical effect on the upward spiral of the real estate prices. The final downward spiral as credits turned to debts, with the resulting deleveraging effects, demonstrates the same mechanism but the other way around. These complex and contradictory forces finally led to the worst financial crash since the Great Depression starting in 2007.

Conclusion: the reconfiguration of finance and the green economy

As we have seen, each phase of capitalist accumulation was based on the narrative to ensure economic and financial stability. The different imaginaries used represented a variety of meaning systems that had the task to signal future economic shifts to guide business and political leaders and to create subjects to fit the new logic of capitalist accumulation. While the technocratic innovations varied across the stages of capitalist development, they had in common the unshakable belief among political and economic agents that technological innovations can provide the conditions for financial stability. It is only a matter of finding the right tools and mechanisms to shape agents' preferences. Yet the regimes of deflation, inflation, public debt, private debt and finally the triple debts since 2008 (sovereign debts, banking debts and household debts) provided only temporary stability. Each new technological innovation accompanying these phases of capitalist development relied on externalizing the tensions to other forms of regulation such as the state, the international system, wage relations, or extra-economic means such as putting the burden of adjustment on the household, consumers, workers, non-financial businesses and on tax payers. But the moral of the story is that the different technological innovations across periods of capitalist development were socially constructed imaginaries in and for the interests of capital to ensure the reproduction of capitalist relations (Jessop 2013; Sum and Jessop 2013).

To regain financial and economic stability in the post-crisis era the imaginary of the 'green economy' has been suggested as a possible technological fix (Fücks 2013; UNEP 2009). However this shift cannot occur within the present state structures of methodological nationalism which put domestic factors ahead of global issues. In other words, while the Westphalian state system with its structural and strategic selectivities based on the sovereignty principle established by the United Nations in its Preamble in 1948 served the interests of national capitalist forces, the future struggle is to transform the state system and its selectivities to a Post-Westphalian system, based on responsible sovereignty, which takes into account the responsibility of states to cooperate with other states to control such global problems as diseases, terrorism, financial crisis, ecological and environmental crisis, energy, food and water shortages and wars (Kaul 2006, 2011).

UNEP (2009) has advocated as part of a new 'Global Green New Deal' (GGND) that fiscal stimulus packages should move from supporting the 'brown economy' to the 'greening' of such financial products to reinvigorate the global economy. These suggestions are tied intrinsically to creating a post-recession economy which would stimulate the present stagnant world economic growth rates, create jobs, reduce poverty and at the same time invest in future sustainability. UNEP argues that an investment of 1 per cent of global GDP over the next two years could provide the critical mass of green infrastructure needed to seed a significant greening of the global economy (UNEP 2009: 1). Similarly,

Ralf Fücks from the Heinrich Böll Foundation in Germany sees the European Union as a strong partner with business to spearhead the innovations necessary for a 'Green New Deal' (Fücks 2013). Once again, despite the fuzziness of the meaning of the 'Green New Deal', the danger is that it is an imaginary, albeit attractive to many different audiences, that is steeped in technological fixes which can easily be accommodated within the existing finance-dominated accumulation. The danger is, as Bob Jessop has pointed out, '[T]his provides one basis for recuperating and normalizing the GND and, indeed, re-contextualising and re-appropriating it on neoliberal lines (e.g., cap and trade) so that it no longer challenges the economic logic that created the triple crisis' (Jessop 2013: 20). How difficult it is to think outside the 'capitalist box' (Jessop 2013: 21) has been amply demonstrated by economic and financial agents hunting for the magic of economic stability but have remained within the narrow confines of capital relations.

Notes

1 I wish to thank Bob Jessop for his careful reading of the text and for his extensive written and personal comments and suggestions.
2 Between 2001 and 2004, The Federal Reserve Chair, Alan Greenspan, pursued a policy of low interest rates (1 per cent) in order to provide liquidity after the dot.com bubble in 2000.
3 The ten most important surplus countries are China, Japan, Germany, Saudi Arabia, Russia, Switzerland, Norway, Kuwait, the Netherlands and the United Arab Emirate (IMF 2008).

References

Amato, M. and Fantacci, L. (2012) *The End of Finance*, Cambridge: Polity.
Bernanke, B. (2004) The Great Moderation, Remarks by Governor B.S. Bernanke, at the Meeting of the Eastern Economic Association, 20 February. Washington, D.C., www.federalreserve.gov/Boarddocs/Speeches/2004/20040220/.
Bush, G.W. (2004) President Bush's Policies to Promote the Ownership Society, Washington, D.C.: White House, Office of the Press Secretary, 17 June.
Chappe, R., Semmler, W. and Nell, E. (2013) The US Financial Culture of Risk, *Constellations*, 20(3): 422–41.
Council on Foreign Relations (2002) Building a Transatlantic Security Market. Authored by B. Steil, www.cfr.org/publication/8282/building_a_transatlantic_securities_market.html.
Crouch, C. (2009) Privatised Keynesianism: An Unacknowledged Policy Regime, *British Journal of Politics and International Relations*, 11(3): 382–99.
Deutschmann, C. (2014) Vorwort. In M. Heires and A. Nölke (eds), *Politische Ökonomie der Finanzialisierung*, Wiesbaden: Springer VS.
Fama, E.F. (1998) Market Efficiency, Long-term Returns, and Behavioral Finance, *Journal of Financial Economics*, 49: 283–306.
Friedman, M. (1956) The Quantity Theory of Money – A Restatement, in *idem*, *Studies in the Quantitative Theory of Money*, Chicago: University of Chicago Press.
Fücks, R. (2013) *Intelligent Wachsen. Die grüne Revolution*, München: Hanser.

Fukuyama, F. (1992) *The End of History and the Last Man*, London: Hamish Hamilton.

Galbraith, J.K. (2012) *Inequality and Instability: A Study of the World Economy Just Before the Great Crisis*, London: Oxford University Press.

Gill, S. (2003) *Power, Resistance in the New World Order*, Basingstoke: Palgrave Macmillan.

Greenspan, A. (2008) *The Age of Turbulence.* 2nd edn, Harmondsworth: Penguin.

Grunberg, I. (1998) Double Jeopardy: Globalization, Liberalization and the Fiscal Squeeze, *World Development*, 26(4): 591–605.

Heires, M. and Nölke, A. (2014) Die Politische Ökonomie der Finanzialisierung. Einleitung, In M. Heires and A. Nölke (eds), *Politische Ökonomie der Finanzialisierung*, Wiesbaden: Springer VS.

Helleiner, E. (1994) *States and the Reemergence of Global Finance. From Bretton Woods to the 1990s*, Ithaca, NY: Cornell University Press.

International Monetary Fund (2006) *Global Financial Stability Report of April 2006.* Washington, D.C.: IMF.

International Monetary Fund (2008) *World Economic Outlook of October 2008: Financial Stress, Downturns, and Recoveries*, Washington, D.C.: IMF.

Jessop, B. (2013) Revisiting the Regulation Approach: Critical Reflections on the Contradictions, Dilemmas, Fixes and Crisis Dynamics of Growth Regimes, *Capital & Class*, 37(1): 5–24.

Jessop, B. and Oosterlynck, S. (2008) Cultural Political Economy: On Making the Cultural Turn without Falling into Soft Economic Sociology, *Geoforum*, 39: 1155–69.

Kaul, I. (2006) Blending External and Domestic Policy Demands. The Rise of the Intermediary State, in I. Kaul and P. Conceição (eds), *The New Public Finance Responding to Global Challenges*, New York: Oxford University Press.

Kaul, I. (2011) Kapitalismus 4.0: Ein Weg zu nachhaltiger Entwicklung, Discussion Paper 'Fortschrittsforum' of the Friedrich Ebert Foundation, Berlin, 15 November.

Keynes, J.M. (1936) *The General Theory of Employment, and Money*, London: Macmillan.

Kindleberger, C.P. (1989) *Manias, Panics, and Crashes. A History of Financial Crisis*, New York: Basic Books.

Minsky, H.P. (2008) *John Maynard Keynes*, New York: McGraw-Hill.

Mittnik, S. and Semmler, W. (2012) Regime Dependence of the Multiplier, *Journal of Economic Behavior and Organization*, 83(3): 502–22.

Polanyi, K. ([1944] 1957) *The Great Transformation: The Political and Economic Origins of Our Time*, Boston, MA: Beacon Press.

Reich, R.B. (2011) *AFTERSHOCK. The Next Economy & America's Future*, New York: Vintage Books.

Reinhart, C.M. and Rogoff, K.S. (2009) *This Time is Different. Eight Centuries of Financial Folly*, Princeton, NJ: Princeton University Press.

Schwartz, H. (2008) Housing, Global Finance, and American Hegemony: Building Conservative Politics One Brick at a Time, *Comparative European Politics*, 6(3): 262–84.

Semmler, W. and Young, B. (2010) Lost in Temptation of Risk: Financial Market Liberalization, Financial Market Meltdown and Regulatory Reforms, *Comparative European Politics*, 8(3): 327–53.

Shonfield, A. (1965) *Modern Capitalism. The Changing Balance of Public and Private Power*, London: Oxford University Press.

Stiglitz, J., Ocampo, J.A., Spiegel, S., Ffrench-Davis, R. and Nayyar, D. (2006) *Stability with Growth*, Oxford: Oxford University Press.

Stockhammer, E. (2010) Financialization and the Global Economy. Political Economy Research Institute (PERI), University of Massachusetts Amherst, Working Paper Series, 240, November, 1–16.

Strange, S. (1971) *Sterling and British Policy: A Political Study of a Currency in Decline*, London: Oxford University Press.

Strange, S. (1986) *Casino Capitalism*, Oxford: Basil Blackwell.

Streeck, W. (2011) Die Krisen des Demokratischen Kapitalismus, *Lettre International*, Winter: 7–13.

Sum, N.L. and Jessop, B. (2013) *Towards a Cultural Political Economy*, Cheltenham: Edward Elgar.

Sum, N.L. and Jessop, B. (2014) Sense- and Meaning-Making in the Critique of Political Economy, Ch. 1 (this volume).

UNEP (2009) *Global Green New Deal. Policy Brief.* New York: United Nations Environment Programme.

Young, B. (2009) Vom Staatlichen zum Privatisierten Keynesianismus. Der globale Makroökonomische Kontext der Finanzkrise und der Privatverschuldung, *Zeitschrift für Internationale Beziehungen*, 1: 141–59.

8 Varieties of Capitalism

Beyond simple dichotomies

Stefan Beck and Christoph Scherrer

Peter A. Hall's and David Soskice's edited volume, *Varieties of Capitalism* (2001), remains popular in comparative political economy (e.g. Jackson and Deeg 2006; Schneider and Soskice 2009; Kalinowski 2013). This approach belongs to the political economy tradition of categorizing in a comparative manner national variants of capitalism. It sets itself apart from this tradition in so far as it places firms at the centre of its analysis and reduces the many variants of capitalism to two: coordinated and liberal market economies (CME and LME). Its great strength lies in making visible the compatibility between these two different forms of capitalism. Despite the alleged homogenizing force of globalization, the two forms can coexist because their institutional settings reflect their historically evolved specialization in the product and service markets.

The concept of Varieties of Capitalism (VoC) has challenged mainstream economics by a differentiated view of capitalist economies. It has become an integral part of the debate about the coherence, convergence or divergence of national, regional and sectoral institutional settings. However, from a cultural political economy perspective the approach comes with some fundamental limitations that are mainly the result of its reductionist way of making sense of the complex, dynamic interactions among territorially defined economic spaces. Its dichotomous ideal types are a-historic, static and, especially in the case of the liberal market economies modelled according to their self-representation but not to real-life practices. VoC is not explicitly concerned with the issue of how sense- and meaning-making takes place in and across the respective national settings. Indeed, its reliance on the rational actor model reveals a very narrow view of sense- and meaning-making which basically follows a functional logic of institutional specializations and complementarities identified *ex post*.

This chapter will explore these limitations by focusing on how the financial system has been treated by the Hall-Soskice inspired Varieties of Capitalism approach. It turns out that the financial crisis did not only challenge neoclassical economics but also this variant of comparative political economy. Emphasizing the strategic role of the financial sector in the USA and the UK, Soskice himself implicitly confirmed this by trying to take account of the financial sector and factors of demand (Iversen and Soskice 2012). We will argue first that its typology does not take sufficient account of the evolution of these two (plus hybrid) variants of capitalism with the result that it over-emphasizes differences between the banking systems of the coordinated and the liberal market economies. Second, the VoC approach, despite its own functionalism, prioritizes theoretically form over function and thereby overlooks functional equivalencies in the respective financial systems. Third, we will challenge the common claim in the Hall-Soskice literature that the financialization emanated from the liberal market economies. We will show that the financialization of the liberal market economies was brought about not least by the strong competition of companies from the coordinated market economies. Fourth, we will highlight the discrepancy between the characteristics of the actually practiced financial system in the liberal market economies and what the VoC literature imagines it to be. Fifth, we will criticize the dominant view of the financial system as an intermediator, service provider and risk-manager for non-financial companies for overlooking the decisive quality of the financial system as a profit-driven sector that pursues its own goals and has increasingly been engaged in financial speculation and risk-taking. Sixth and last, this will lead to noting the insufficient conception of macroeconomic dynamics within the VoC approach. We will illustrate how financialization and its crisis has been depicted in the Varieties of Capitalism approach, based on the model economies of the USA and Germany which are frequently chosen as examples in the VoC literature. We will start with an introductory outline of the VoC approach and its conceptualization of the financial sector.

Key elements of the Varieties of Capitalism approach

The Varieties of Capitalism debate rests on a long tradition within the field of political economy of categorization and comparison of national varieties of capitalism (cf. Streeck 2010). One of the first post-war works on comparative capitalism, the modernization-theoretical work of Andrew Shonfield (1965), dealt primarily with questions of national development in the era of post-war reconstruction and in the process highlighted the economic governance and allocation functions of state and non-state actors. Shonfield worked with a contrast between state (or public) power and private (or market) power. His understanding of other forms of coordination was limited. In the 1970s attention turned to the role of business-union relations in crisis-management, with an emphasis on the benefits of (neo-)corporatism in dealing with problems of stagflation. With the rise of the neoliberal agenda, the focus moved from macroeconomic to a broader set of factors bearing on the competitiveness of nations (Porter 1990), of production models (Piore and Sabel 1984), business or national production systems (Hollingsworth and Boyer 1997; Whitley 1999). In addition, collective actors, such as the state (e.g. Schmidt 2002) or trade unions and business associations in neo-corporatism research (e.g. Schmitter and Lehmbruch 1979), and societal goals beyond competitiveness (cf. Becker 2007), played a role in various works. The frequent juxtaposition of state and market (Boyer and Drache 1996) was resolved in favour of a multitude of essentially contextually based institutional forms and modes of governance summarized under the heading of 'variegated capitalism' (cf. Peck and Theodore 2007; Jessop 2012).

Hall and Soskice took the methodological step of introducing a historically oriented approach to a rational (actors) and functional model, which – analogous to neoclassical thinking – tends toward an institutional equilibrium (cf. Deeg 2005: 17; Streeck 2010: 21). Indeed, the authors themselves consider their approach within the tradition of Shonfield, neo-corporatist studies and the concept of Social Systems of Production influenced by the French regulation theory[1] (Hollingsworth and Boyer 1997). Yet they seek – corresponding to the social and scientific zeitgeist – to transcend these traditions, by establishing the firm as a strategic-rational actor in the conceptual centre. For the two authors the firm's behaviour provides a microeconomic basis that allows the application of game and transaction cost theories. Firms are identified by an array of different coordination requirements – in the areas of *industrial relations*, *corporate governance* and *finance*, *intercompany relations* and *vocational training* – which they (must) meet in the context of specific institutional arrangements.

The character of the institutional assemblages in the various areas has an influence on the form of interaction and strategic behaviour of a firm. The different institutions across the various areas may imply coherent, divergent or even contradictory incentives or sanctions. Hall and Soskice tie this to the concept of institutional complementarity, developed particularly by Aoki (1994), according to which similarly operating, i.e. coherent, institutions mutually reinforce their efficiency and promote a coherent and efficient coordination across various areas and bestow specifically competitive advantages. Hall and Soskice distinguish between the ideal forms of Liberal Market Economies (LME) and Coordinated Market Economies (CME) by their respectively high degrees of complementarities depending on whether they are predominantly affected by market-based or non-market coordination (see Table 8.1). The former category is exemplified by the United States, and the latter by Germany (Hall and Soskice 2001:17ff.).

The financial sector in Varieties of Capitalism

Due to the central role accorded to firms, Hall and Soskice also examine the financial sector in terms of how it relates to individual (manufacturing or other industrial or profit-producing) enterprises with regard to corporate financing, corporate governance and – in the context of complementarity – innovation capacity, product strategy, vocational education and also industrial relations. Tying in the work of Sigurt Vitols (2001), the authors differentiate between the bank-based financial systems in CME and market-based systems in LME within VoC. In the following we present their depiction of the role of the financial sector in these two types of capitalism.

Within *bank-based* systems there are relatively close connections between firms and banks. Banks enjoy privileged access to firm-specific information and as a result are more prepared to advance, when necessary, long-term credit (patient capital). Conversely, firms are less dependent on short-term profits or

Table 8.1 Complementarities of *Liberal Market Economies* (LME) and *Coordinated Market Economies* (CME) according to Hall and Soskice

Institutional area	LME	CME
Industrial relations	Largely limited to wage–profit distribution One-directional control by management	Important for strategic interaction and negotiations Participation of those involved, employee participation
Corporate governance	Focus on the capital market; short-term orientation	Focus/dependence on bank loans; long-term orientation
Intercompany relations	Competitive; price determines supplier relationships	Network relationships, cross-ownership; strategic interaction
Vocational education	Preference for general skills; limited vocational training	Preference for specialized skills; apprentice system, etc.
Social security	Residual social protections; few restrictions or obstacles to hiring/firing	Relatively 'generous' social security; employment protection
Product market regulation	Few limits on competition; *laissez faire* principle	Level of competition dependent on additional, e.g. social, objectives

Source: Becker (2007: 267).

stock price increases (shareholder value) and are therefore less exposed to the volatility of capital and retail markets. Long-term oriented financing through bank loans and retained profits allows not only for a longer-term investment horizon, but also promotes cooperative intercompany and industrial relations. Voice-oriented industrial relations, including job protection, collective bargaining and co-determination, together with the mutual interdependence with banks protect firms in turn from hostile takeovers by financial market actors. These institutional complementarities were allegedly strengthened in the long run, as in the case of Germany, through legal regulation of financial markets, e.g. regulation of the sale of corporate shares or rules for voting rights, and through a large public banking sector. Finally, coordinated market economies gain competitive advantages primarily by incremental innovations of diversified, skill- and R&D-intensive products (cf. Hall and Soskice 2001: 22ff.).

In *market-based* financial systems firms are financed in contrast more through capital markets and a comparatively broad ownership of freely tradable shares. Due to the relatively low level of close institutionalized relations between investors and firms, disclosure obligations for firms are an essential requirement. Access to capital as well as performance-based compensation for upper management depend to a great extent on current profitability. A low share price not only hinders access to capital, but also increases the risk of a hostile takeover. Dependence on short-term success can conflict with long-term investment plans and cooperative relationships, which is why, for example, fluctuations in demand directly impact labour markets. The comparative advantages of liberal market economies are seen correspondingly in either mass production without high skill requirements or in innovative cutting-edge technologies funded by venture capital. In LME, economic policy support is less aligned with industrial policy, and instead relies on a comparatively strict set of laws enforcing competition, weak regulation of product and labour markets, and short-term (attempted) stimulation of consumer demand (cf. Hall and Soskice 2001: 27ff; Soskice 2007).

Simple conceptualization of the financial sector

Static view underestimates the dynamics of globalization

The dichotomous conception of the financial sector by Hall and Soskice is based on a limited time frame, approximately beginning in the mid-1980s. The fact that the US financial system was subject to a high degree of governmental oversight up to the beginning of the 1980s is rarely mentioned. The government even determined the interest rates for deposits (Kroos and Blyn 1971: 186). In this phase, capital markets played a secondary role for industrial enterprises, as their oligopolistic dominance gave them a relatively steady above-average return on capital. This allowed them to self-finance in most cases. Firms capitalized through the stock market, and the long-term debt financing was conducted through the issuance of bonds. Credit banks met short-term financial needs

(Scherrer 1992: 127–9). Only in a few cases did banks hold significant blocks of shares in industrial companies. Nevertheless, there were close relationships between companies and particularly the most important banks of New York. Representatives of these New Yorker banks sat on the supervisory boards (Mizruchi 1982). In normal times, these banks allowed internal management to make decisions autonomously (Herman 1981: 134). This balance of power, however, was reversed in the case of liquidity constraints. In this event, banks would make the decision whether to release further funds necessary for the company's survival. To secure these loans, banks repeatedly demonstrated their readiness to directly intervene in company policy (Scherrer 1992: 129).Thus, the difference from the German banking system was less pronounced than presented in the VoC literature.

Furthermore, the focus of the VoC on institutional differentiation leads to a prioritization of the form over the function of an institution, and in doing so overlooks the possibility of functional equivalents, i.e. similar functions shared by different institutional forms. Adam Dixon demonstrated that although no publicly regulated banking sector exists in the USA, a number of institutions perform similar corrective actions in the market (Dixon 2012: 594). Even though market share by asset size of the biggest commercial banks (>1$ trillion) increased to more than 50 per cent, mostly at the expense of the number of smallest banks, strong regional (>10$ billion) and community banks still exist (FDIC 2012; Lynch 2012). The latter hold the major part of small loans to farms and businesses. Other instruments making loans available to local development and specific segments of the population (students, homeowners, low income neighbourhoods, etc.) are loan guarantees or the Community Reinvestment Act (CRA). CRA-covered banks' market share of all loans was in 2006 above 20 per cent and nearly 40 per cent of home mortgage loans to low- and moderate-income individuals. The latter increased 2007 even to 50 per cent (Traiger & Hinckley 2008, 2009).

Overall, the relationship between financial institutions and industrial corporations in the USA can be described as interdependent but distanced up to the 1970s. Managers of industrial enterprises were for the most part not forced to comply with instructions from financial institutions, major shareholders or other industrial groups. There was no market for corporate control. This changed as industrial groups increasingly lost their oligopolistic market power from the 1970s onwards due to increasing foreign competition. Conglomerates initially took over the less competitive capital-intensive firms. They 'milked' the high cash flow resulting from fixed capital; thereby depleting the capital stock. The invention of junk bonds in the 1980s allowed hostile takeovers through private equity firms, which mostly focused on restructuring or dividing up of the acquired firm. By the 1990s, in the course of the gradual deregulation of the financial system, the market for corporate control was established as an enduring feature of the financial system (Krippner 2005). However, fixed investment continued to be financed almost exclusively from reserves. Stock issuance did not contribute to financing investments. In fact, the stock market absorbed corporate finances. It was a net user of finance in the USA, suggesting an active market for corporate takeover (Corbett and Jenkinson 1997).

As the VoC literature regards the end result of this process as the essence of Anglo-Saxon capitalism, it is not able to recognize the dynamic resulting from changed world market constellations. Contrary to the invocation of Anglo-Saxon capitalism as the source of financialization in the VoC approach, the above historical digression shows that it is precisely the competitive success of firms from the CME-area (including Japan) which in recent decades were conducive for the turn to market-based finance in the LMEs. As mentioned above, this success undermined the oligopoly of industrial corporations in the Anglo-Saxon world and, thereby, subjugated them to gradually liberalized financial markets. In the CME, the successful corporations largely emancipated themselves from domestic banks which had earlier supported them. These enterprises, for example the electronics company Siemens, moreover wanted direct access to markets in foreign countries and were therefore reciprocally open to demands for more transparence and protection of the rights of outsiders, i.e. international investors, in their home domain, the CME regions (Dixon 2012: 585). In Germany, these demands were accordingly met in the late 1990s in a quick succession of four deregulating laws on financial markets (Kellermann 2005). Shortly afterwards, the public state banks and savings banks, due to pressure from the EU Commission, lost their state guarantees ('Anstaltslast' and 'Gewährträgerhaftung'; Grossmann 2006).

One of the consequences of these laws was that the large German banks reduced their industrial holdings. By 2005, they were no longer significantly better represented on the boards of non-financial companies than US banks, where they likewise used their supervisory mandate less to control the management as they did to solicit their own services as lender or advisor for mergers and takeovers (Dittmann *et al.* 2010). Thus, a dynamic adjustment of the American and German financial systems in the direction of deregulation and liberalization has taken place. Not only has the German system adapted, but also the US financial landscape, as universal banks and multi-state bank branch networks emerged. However, these deregulations were embedded in different growth models. In the US financialization drove growth by expanding consumption through loans and asset appreciations. In Germany financialization was supportive of an export-oriented growth strategy which moved from a classical trade mercantilism to an asset mercantilism as a result of increased currency competition after the end of the fixed currency regime of Bretton Woods (Spahn 1990; Herr 1994). As a consequence, financialization in Germany did neither lead to the supremacy of finance nor to an expansion of credit. Instead, it served mostly to ease access to investment opportunities abroad for the income arising from trade surpluses.

In contrast to VoC lore, the shift to more market-based finance has certainly left the majority of firms largely untouched, as these companies lack access to stock markets for issuing stocks and bonds. Small and medium-sized enterprises (SME) with fewer than 500 employees employed almost 80 per cent of all those engaged in the private sector in the USA in 2007, and more than 70 per cent in Germany (Dixon 2012: 587). These figures qualify the assertions of the VoC literature on the effects of the different financial systems in LME and CME.

Limited view on finance

The previously mentioned centrality of firms to the VoC approach can be further substantiated: VoC is focused on firms in manufacturing and service industries, and the financial system only enters the picture when discussing its function in allocating credit for these firms. This shows its proximity to neoclassicism, which sees money only as a convenient form of exchange. Yet the financial system in a profit-based economy has not only a serving function, but rather is in itself committed to the maximization of profits (Heinrich 2010). Before the crisis, trade in debt and similar claims had proven to be more profitable than the traditional savings and loan business of banks.

Just before the crisis this profit-seeking characterized the accumulation regime. The creation of credit based on securitization led to rising prices in asset markets, where the ownership can be traded for goods whose supply cannot (e.g. property or gold) or should not (e.g. stocks) be increased to conform to rising demand. This asset price inflation raised household wealth and thereby encouraged higher spending (and higher debt), which boosted the overall demand. Under President Clinton technology stocks played this role; under President Bush real estate. In these phases the growth rate of the US economy was clearly above those of the continental European economies, and so the financialization of the economy was cast in a good light. The downside to this model of accumulation, however, is that the asset price increases are not permanent and thus the (fictitious) credit chains built on these increases collapse like a house of cards if asset prices no longer increase, as in 2000 for technology stocks and 2006 for real estate (Herr 2010).

The role of the banking sector for overall economic growth remains thus largely ignored in the VoC approach. In a paper published after the outbreak of the financial crisis, Peter Hall and Daniel Gingerich compare the growth dynamics of LME and CME in terms of GDP per capita, but without considering among the explanatory variables for growth the rising indebtedness of private households as well as companies (Hall and Gingerich 2009: 481–2). In a recent article on the Euro-Crisis, Hall points to debt-driven growth dynamics, however just for Southern Europe, not known as a classic LME region (Hall 2012). The distinction between financialized and export-driven economies made by Thomas Kalinowski (2013) seems to be closer to the mark.

Finally, they overlook the fact that the larger enterprises within the manufacturing sector are themselves central actors in financial markets (Krippner 2005).

The distorted view of the LME financial system

The argument by Iain Hardie and Sylvia Maxfield (2011) that the VoC literature is based on an ideal market-based financial system which doesn't correspond to reality is particularly serious. In 2009, after the outbreak of the financial market crisis in the USA, Peter Hall, one of the major representatives of the VoC approach, described the financial system of a LME by stating that

> the United States is a typical LME. Here, firms face large equity markets marked by high levels of transparency and dispersed shareholding, where firms' access to external finance depends heavily on publicly assessable criteria such as market valuation. Regulatory regimes allow hostile takeovers that depend on share price, rendering managers sensitive to current profitability.
>
> (Hall and Gingerich 2009: 453)

The financial crisis demonstrated, however, that the market-based financial systems of the USA and Great Britain in their real-world forms fail to exhibit the characteristics of this LME ideal on three accounts: the nature of transactions, the institutional location of risk and the degree of liquidity risk (Hardie and Maxfield 2011).

Market-based transactions are conducted without the presumed transparency. They resemble to a large extent the relational banking of the bank-based systems, i.e. transactions were not among ever-changing, widely dispersed market participants, but rather with repetitive intensity between a few financial firms, well-known to one another. The lack of transparency stems from the fact that most derivatives are not traded on exchange platforms but rather between individual financial firms and investors *over the counter* (OTC). The financial institutions which conduct these transactions, especially, before the crisis, the investment banks, refinance on the inter-bank market usually short term. In most cases, these unsecured loans, due to a lack of transparency, require a high degree of trust. This trust can be produced through a high level of transactions, which only a few financial institutions are capable of maintaining. The close relationship between bank and borrower, characteristic of bank-based systems in real, not idealized, market-based systems shifts into the financial system itself, in the inter-bank market. Accordingly, the risk becomes concentrated there. In case trust is lost among banks, as in the case of JP Morgan acting as a clearing house for Lehman Brothers (Sorkin 2009: 281), then, due to the close relationship between the few central actors, the whole system will be affected. Refinancing by making collateral available can even intensify the crisis. Since the collateral is also a financial product, if sold by the creditor it could trigger panic among other market actors. The much sought after insurance against default (Credit Default Swaps) at the beginning of the crisis only offered the illusion of safety, as only a few providers were involved, who in the course of the crisis became unable to meet their payment obligations and had to be rescued by the government (the most prominent case being American International Group, AIG).

In other words: the risk of a banking crisis for depositors (bank run) in a bank-based system mutated into a banking crisis among banks. Refinancing through the trust-based inter-bank market as well as trading with complex financial products developed primarily by major financial institutions led to an extreme concentration of financial transactions between a handful of financial actors and thus, contrary to expectations concerning market-based financial systems, to a higher concentration of risk. This, in a climate of fading trust, led to a liquidity squeeze, actually more typical for bank-based systems (Hardie and Maxfield 2011).

Campbell (2011) provides a further contribution to the explanation of the financial crisis in the USA, turning to a sophisticated concept of institutional complementary. Specifically, he distinguishes between forms of mutual reinforcement of institutional incentives and forms of mutual compensation for (negative, far-reaching, dysfunctional) effects or incentives. Following this, the crisis can be understood as the consequence of mutually reinforcing institutional forms. While risky financial innovations were made institutionally possible, compensatory institutions that could balance such behaviour were dismantled. The consequence of this was an increased willingness to undergo risks to such a degree that system failure resulted (Campbell 2011: 212f.; cf. also Boyer 2013).

A few conclusions can be drawn from Campbell's study relating to the VoC approach. First, a functionalist or rational-intentional understanding of institutional complementarities is extremely problematic. The variety of incremental changes is hardly traceable to an overall strategy. Reinforcing complementarities can also lead to crisis-provoking developments (cf. Campbell 2011: 224ff.) which elude the methodological and conceptual grasp of Varieties of Capitalism. The latter criticism can also be asserted in regards to the Campbell study, which is essentially based on an empirical-descriptive ex post analysis and created no implicit criteria to assess the quality of institutional complementarities.

Macroeconomic blind spots

The virtual absence of a macroeconomic basis contributes to biased conclusions about the performance of national models. Competitiveness alone cannot serve as an indicator of performance. Indicators such as growth dynamics or income distribution have to be considered as well. Although empirical studies occasionally include macroeconomic variables (e.g. Hall and Gingerich 2004), the performed correlations with selected macroeconomic variables lack theoretical foundations. In light of the already complex concept of institutional complementarities, such correlations display significant explanatory uncertainty. This is primarily due to a failure to capture the debt dynamics of the analysed countries.

The lack of a clear macroeconomic conceptualization is especially clear in the study of financialization trends, when, for example, institutional developments are used as an explanation for economic performance without considering macroeconomic dynamics, restrictions or inherent instability. From the perspective of heterodox macroeconomics, the crisis of the US growth model, which rested upon the real estate bubble, the excessive use of debt-financed consumption, the steady import of foreign savings and financial profits coupled with declining productive investment, was entirely foreseeable (Bluestone 1999; Minsky 1992; Epstein 2005; Palley 2005).

Explanatory weaknesses and limits of Varieties of Capitalism

Not only the centrality of firms, but also the narrow focus on non-financial enterprises in the VoC literature led to the neglect of the dynamics of the financial system and its macroeconomic effects. The financial system is seen only in its intermediary function with regards to industrial and service companies, not as a profit-maximizing economic sector with its own interests. The significance of debt for growth dynamics of a national economy, even after the crisis, remains partly unrecognized.

The static vision of the VoC approach overlooks the interdependence of LME and CME in processes of globalization and especially financialization. By not taking account of evolutionary developments it attributes these processes exclusively to LME. Pressure from CME exporters is thereby ignored. Likewise, VoC's characteristic ideal types of national specialization are not sufficiently questioned regarding their correspondence to existing real-world practices. Within the VoC literature, even after the financial crisis, the financial system of LME was ascribed attributes such as transparency and the diversification of risk, which are not empirically recognizable. Market-based systems exhibit a distinct lack of transparence, a high concentration of risk and liquidity squeezes due to the oligopolization of markets.

The failure to include social norms, as well as political power and power relations finally points to other problems of the VoC approach: an 'institutional reductionism' (Bruff 2011: 482) and the lack of a basis in social theory to accompany any basic comprehension of the capitalist economy (Bieling 2011: 6). The operationalization indicates a tendency towards a contradictory understanding of institutions. Institutions are sometimes functionally conceptualized (virtually as dependent variables) from a rational actor perspective, and sometimes presented as a reductionist basis (and independent variable) of social relations. In all this, the contradictions, lines of conflict and power relations disappear from sight, and with the reduction of capitalism largely to a market economy, such a firm-centred approach can better be described as Varieties in Capitalism.

The VoC approach won its merits by introducing to a larger audience the idea that specialization in product markets comes along with specific institutional settings. However, the broader reach came at the expense of a misleading reductionism. The reduction of global capitalism to two ideal types, centring social strategies on production firms, assuming a one-dimensional rationality and taking national boundaries for granted, fails not only to capture the dynamics of these allegedly ideal types but also the interplay of more or less universal dynamics resulting from prevalent basic capitalist relations and the variety in not always nation-centred business and political cultures.

Note

1 We are explicitly not covering the regulationist work on national production systems (e.g. Amable *et al.* 1997; Boyer and Saillard 2001) in this chapter. This tradition deserves its own assessment.

References

Amable, B., Barré, R. and Boyer, R. (1997) *Les systèmes d'innovation à l'ère de la globalisation*, Paris: Economica.

Aoki, M. (1994) The contingent governance of teams: analysis of institutional complementary, *International Economic Review*, 35(3): 657–76.

Becker, U. (2007) Open systemness and contested reference frames and change: a reformulation of the varieties of capitalism theory, *Socio-Economic Review*, 5(2): 261–86.

Bieling, H.-J. (2011) Varieties of Capitalism, Regulationstheorie und neogramscianische IPÖ – komplementäre oder gegensätzliche Perspektiven des globalisierten Kapitalismus?, *Discussion Paper*, ISSN 1868-4947/23, Universität Hamburg.

Bluestone, B. (1999) Wall Street contra Main Street: Das US-amerikanische Wachstumsmodell, in S. Lang, M. Mayer and C. Scherrer (eds), *Jobwunder USA – Modell für Deutschland*, Münster: Westfälisches Dampfboot, 22–43.

Boyer, R. (2013) The present crisis: a trump for a renewed political economy, *Review of Political Economy*, 25(1): 1–38.

Boyer, R. and Drache, D. (1996) *States against Markets: The Limits of Globalization*, London and New York: Routledge.

Boyer, R. and Saillard, Y. (eds) (2001) *Régulation Theory: The State of the Art*, London: Routledge.

Bruff, I. (2011) What about the elephant in the room? Varieties of capitalism, varieties in capitalism, *New Political Economy*, 16(4): 481–500.

Campbell, J. L. (2011) The US financial crisis: lessons for theories of institutional complementary, *Socio-Economic Review*, 9(2): 211–34.

Corbett, J. and Jenkinson, T. (1997) How is investment financed? A study of Germany, Japan, the United Kingdom and the United States, *The Manchester School*, 65, Issue S, 69–93.

Deeg, R. (2005) Complementarity and institutional change: How useful a concept?, WZB *Discussion Paper*, SP II 2005–21, Wissenschaftszentrum Berlin für Sozialforschung, http://skylla.wzb.eu/pdf/2005/ii05–21.pdf, accessed on 10 September 2012.

Dittmann, I., Maug, E. G. and Schneider, C. (2010) Bankers on the boards of German firms: what they do, what they are worth, and why they are (still) there, *Review of Finance*, 14(1): 35–71.

Dixon, A. (2012) Function before form: macro-institutional comparison and the geography of finance, *Journal of Economic Geography*, 12(3): 579–600.

Epstein, G. A. (ed.) (2005) *Financialization and the World Economy*, Northampton, MA: Edward Elgar.

FDIC (2012) FDIC Community Banking Study, December 2012, Federal Deposit Insurance Cooperation, www.fdic.gov.

Grossman, E. (2006) Europeanization as an interactive process: German public banks meet EU state aid policy, *Journal of Common Market Studies*, 44(2): 325–48.

Hall, P. A. (2012) The economics and politics of the Euro crisis, *German Politics*, 21(4): 355–71.

Hall, P. A. and Gingerich, D. W. (2004) Varieties of capitalism and institutional complementarities in the macroeconomy: an empirical analysis, *MPIfG Discussion Paper*, 04/5.

Hall, P. A. and Gingerich, D. W. (2009) Varieties of capitalism and institutional complementarities in the political economy: an empirical analysis, *British Journal of Political Science*, 39(3): 449–82.

Hall, P. A. and Soskice, D. (eds) (2001) *Varieties of Capitalism – The Institutional Foundations of Comparative Advantage*, Oxford: Oxford University Press.

Hardie, I. and Maxfield, S. (2011) What does the global financial crisis tell us about Anglo-Saxon financial capitalism?, University of Edinburgh, Working Paper, www.pol.ed.ac.uk/__data/assets/pdf_file/0005/64562/HardieMaxfieldUSUKCrisis32011.pdf, accessed on 10 September 2012.

Heinrich, M. (2010) Das analytische Potential der Marxschen Theorie angesichts der Krise. In C. Scherrer, B. Overwien and T. Dürmeier (eds), *Perspektiven auf die Finanzkrise*, Leverkusen: Barbara Budrich.

Herman, E. S. (1981) *Corporate Control, Corporate Power*, Cambridge: Cambridge University Press.

Herr, H. (1994) Der Merkantilismus der Bundesrepublik in der Weltwirtschaft. In K. Voy, W. Polster and C. Thomasberger (eds), *Marktwirtschaft und politische Regulierung*, Marburg: Metropolis Verlag.

Herr, H. (2010) Die Mechanismen der Vermögensmarktblasen. In C. Scherrer, B. Overwien and T. Dürmeier (eds), *Perspektiven auf die Finanzkrise*, Leverkusen: Barbara Budrich.

Hollingsworth, J. R. and Boyer, R. (eds) (1997) *Contemporary Capitalism: The Embeddedness of Institutions*, Cambridge: Cambridge University Press.

Iversen, T. and Soskice, D. (2012) Modern capitalism and the advanced nation state: understanding the causes of the crisis. In N. Bermeo and J. Pontusson (eds), *Coping with Crisis*, New York: Russell Sage Foundation.

Jackson, G. and Deeg, R. (2006) How many varieties of capitalism? Comparing the comparative institutional analyses of capitalist diversity, *MPIfG Discussion Paper*, 06/02.

Jessop, B. (2012) The world market, variegated capitalism, and the crisis of European integration. In P. Nousios, H. Overbeek and A. Tsolakis (eds), *Globalisation and European Integration: Critical Approaches to Regional Order and International Relations*, London: Routledge.

Kalinowski, T. (2013) Regulating international finance and the diversity of capitalism, *Socio-Economic Review*, 11(3): 471–96.

Kellermann, C. (2005) Disentangling Deutschland AG. In S. Beck, F. Klobes and C. Scherrer (eds), *Surviving Globalization? Perspectives for the German Economic Model*, Dordrecht: Springer.

Krippner, G. R. (2005) The financialization of the American economy, *Socio-Economic Review*, 3(2): 173–208.

Kroos, H. E. and Blyn, M. R. (1971) *A History of Financial Intermediaries*, New York: Chelsea House.

Lynch, D. J. (2012) Big banks: Now even too bigger to fail, *Bloomberg Businessweek*, 19 April, www.businessweek.com, accessed on 10 September 2012.

Minsky, H. P. (1992) The financial instability hypothesis, *Working Paper* no. 74, Levy Economics Institute of Bard College, http://levyinstitute.org/pubs/wp74.pdf, accessed on 10 September 2012.

Mizruchi, M. S. (1982) *The American Corporate Network 1904–1974*, Beverly Hills, CA: Sage.

Palley, T. (2005) The questionable legacy of Alan Greenspan, *Challenge*, 48(6): 17–31.

Peck, J. and Theodore, N. (2007) Variegated capitalism, *Progress in Human Geography*, 31(6): 731–72.

Piore, M. J. and Sabel, C. (1984) *The Second Industrial Divide*, New York: Basic Books.

Porter, M. E. (1990) *The Competitive Advantage of Nations*, New York: Free Press.

Scherrer, C. (1992) *Im Bann des Fordismus. Die Auto- und Stahlindustrie der USA im internationalen Konkurrenzkampf*, Berlin: Ed. Sigma.

Schmidt, V. A. (2002) *The Futures of European Capitalism*, New York: Oxford University Press.

Schmitter, P. C. and Lehmbruch, G. (eds) (1979) *Trends Toward Corporatist Intermediation*, Beverly Hills, CA: Sage.

Schneider, B. R. and Soskice, D. (2009) Inequality in developed countries and Latin America: coordinated, liberal and hierarchical systems, *Economy and Society*, 30(1): 17–52.

Shonfield, A. (1965) *Modern Capitalism. The Changing Balance of Public and Private Power*, Oxford: Oxford University Press.

Sorkin, A. R. (2009) *Too Big To Fail*, London: Allen Lane.

Soskice, D. (2007) Macroeconomics and Varieties of Capitalism, In B. Hancké, M. Rhodes and M. Thatcher (eds), *Beyond Varieties of Capitalism. Conflict, Contradictions, and Complementarities in the European Economy*, New York: Oxford University Press.

Spahn, H.-P. (1990) Währungssicherung und außenwirtschaftliches Gleichgewicht – Prinzipien der 'Geschäftspolitik' der Bundesbank und volkswirtschaftliche Aufgaben der Geldpolitik. In H. Riese and H.-P. Spahn (eds), *Geldpolitik und ökonomische Entwicklung – Ein Symposion*, Regensburg: Transfer-Verlag.

Streeck, W. (2010) E pluribus unum? Varieties and commonalities of capitalism, *MPIfG Discussion Paper*, 10/12.

Traiger & Hinckley (2008) The Community Reinvestment Act: a welcome anomaly in the foreclosure crisis, 7 January, http://traigerlaw.com, accessed on 20 February 2014.

Traiger & Hinckley (2009) The Community Reinvestment Act of 1977: not guilty, 26 January 26, http://traigerlaw.com, accessed on 20 February 2014.

Vitols, S. (2001) The origins of bank-based and market-based financial systems: Germany, Japan, and the United States, *WZB Discussion Paper*, FS I 01–302.

Whitley, R. (1999) *Divergent Capitalisms: The Social Structuring and Change of Business Systems*, Oxford: Oxford University Press.

9   Competitive concerns and imaginaries in the liberalization of European finance

Daniel Mügge

Introduction

Financial systems stand at the heart of developed economies. They channel credit from savers to investors, allow the storage of purchasing power, provide tools for stimulating or dampening economic activity and redistribute wealth between socio-economic groups and over time. Financial systems have developed differently around the world, however, for example by putting more or less emphasis on relationship banking or capital markets or by being more or less open to the rest of the world. These financial systems, in turn, have been embedded in wider ensembles of economic institutions, which have most prominently been labelled 'Varieties of Capitalism' (VoC; Hall and Soskice 2001).[1]

In the decades leading up to the financial crisis that erupted in 2007, economic globalization was argued to exert pressure on the traditional positive coordination between domestic institutions (cf. Zysman 1983) and to enforce convergence towards more 'Anglo-Saxon' models of capitalism (Jayasuriya 2001). In this perspective, financial systems changed because domestic coordination of institutions had become incompatible with economic and in particular financial openness. The regulatory reforms institutionalizing such change resulted from pressure at the 'systemic' level.

The chapter argues that such a depiction of how capitalism evolves is unduly mechanistic and deterministic (cf. Becker 2009 for a critical perspective). Its focus on institutional complementarities underplays the importance of economic agents who translate perceived threats and opportunities in their environment into pressure for institutional adaptation. Financial reforms, which have altered the role of finance in contemporary capitalism, have in key respects been shaped by competitive struggles between financial firms seeking to bend regulation to their advantage.

Explicit attention to competitive struggles between financial firms stresses the importance of two central insights of cultural political economy. First, the variegation of capitalism (cf. Macartney 2009) invalidates a stark dichotomy between national institutions on the one hand and external constraints on the other. Economic actors operate on different scales. Small savings banks may do business in a single town. German Landesbanken have traditionally operated at the

Länder-level, as have regional German stock exchanges. Many wholesale financial institutions compete at the national level, some have branched out through Europe. A small subset of financial firms operate globally. The relevant competitive arenas of firms thus vary from single towns to truly global markets. The outlines of these arenas, demarcated by regulatory barriers, are the outcome not of a single competitive clash – national incumbents versus foreign firms – but of a range of variegated competitive struggles. The perspective embraced here thus breaks with the methodological nationalism of many comparative institutionalist analyses, which pit national institutions against 'systemic' pressures.

Second, what cultural political economy calls 'imaginaries' permeate these competitive struggles and hence the dynamics of regulatory and institutional change (cf. the introduction to this volume). Under conditions of high uncertainty, firms' regulatory preferences are strongly inspired by these commonly shared narratives about what the future will hold. They offer guidance about the most relevant trends to which business and political strategies should be adapted. Examples of such narratives are an 'inevitable rise' of investment banking throughout the EU or 'the dissolution of national financial markets' in a single European one – both of which were powerful ideas guiding regulatory politics, but have turned out to be wrong, certainly in a strong form.

Appreciating these points exposes a rational-institutionalist perspective as unduly reductionist, even when it is married to insights from historical institutionalism (cf. Katznelson and Weingast 2005). How actors make sense of their situation, individually or collectively, affects their willingness to support or undermine extant institutions. The motivations of actors to effect change cannot be explained without reference to the imaginaries that order their experiences.

The first half of this chapter spells out its theoretical arguments in more detail. Its second half shows how these shed light on financial market reforms in Europe over the past two decades, concentrating on key domestic reforms in Germany and France. Both countries used to count as exemplars of coordinated market economies and both saw sweeping changes in their financial systems starting in the mid-1980s. Liberal, capital-markets focused financial integration in the EU as we have witnessed it in the 1990s has crucially relied on German and French support and concomitant domestic liberalization (Mügge 2010; Quaglia 2010; Story and Walter 1997). Focusing on these countries' early reforms allows us not only to understand the ignition of financial liberalization on the European Continent but also to study national policy responses to economic openness that are not yet mediated by active policy coordination through the European Community.

Financial regulation and varieties of capitalism revisited

The varieties of capitalism approach to comparative political economy, understood broadly, has portrayed economic institutions as elements of encompassing institutional ensembles. In its strong, functionalist version Hall and Soskice (2001) have emphasized institutions' complementarity with financial systems as an integral part of national institutional ensembles. In his classic treatment of different national adjustment politics Zysman (1983) accorded financial systems a central place in how 'national economies' operate. In France, government control over credit allocation became a key plank of industrial policy (Coleman 1997; Loriaux 1991; Schmidt 1996). In Germany, patient bank capital, buttressed by extensive cross-shareholdings, facilitated a high degree of inter-firm coordination (Deeg 1999).

The financial facets of national institutional ensembles have been underpinned and stabilized through financial regulation, broadly understood, as it codifies which financial institutions can provide which financial services to whom under which conditions. Regulation directs the evolution of financial systems in one direction or the other, with enormous consequences for the economy at large. In debates about continuity and change in contemporary capitalism (Crouch and Streek 1997; Kitschelt *et al.* 1999) the motivations of actors to buttress or undermine particular financial rules have received surprisingly little attention, however. Some scholars highlighted economic openness, and capital mobility in particular (Frieden 1991), as the key driver of change towards a 'new embedded financial orthodoxy' (Morin 2000; Streeck 1997). Others emphasized the resilience of national institutions due to path-dependency and the compatibility of very different kinds of institutions with capital mobility (Mosley 2003; Pauly 1995). Also financial systems were found to be surprisingly resilient (Radice 2000). Later writing therefore acknowledged the pitfalls of the 'convergence or divergence'-dichotomy; the rise of 'hybridization' as an answer to questions about institutional change has been the conceptual consequence (Deeg 1999; Lane 2000).

For all its limits, this debate has been instructive for the shared assumptions underlying it: national sets of institutions served as units of analysis. Change in these, so the tenor in this debate would be caused by emerging dysfunctionalities at the level of the set of institutions itself – the systemic level, so to say. Asking whether coordinated market economies – 'Rhenish capitalism' – were still viable in the age of 'globalization' implied that its viability *as an institutional set* would decide its fate.

Coordinative and competitive imperatives in financial market reform

This chapter raises three arguments against the view outlined in the preceding section. First, while shaping how financial markets operate within capitalism at large, financial reform can be driven by dynamics that swing free of the macrovariables and institutional complementarities described above. In particular, financial firms themselves selectively buttress or undermine market orders based on their perceived business interests. This argument chimes with actor-centred institutionalism (Scharpf 1997), in which agents translate structural conditions into institutional change in complex but essentially predictable ways based on their own interests (cf. Katznelson and Weingast 2005). For example, employers could assess whether it was in their self-interest to support collective bargaining or not (Martin and Swank 2012). By the same token, financial firms might identify the opportunities presented by contemporary technology and financial openness and hence 'opt out' of national coordinated arrangements.

Financial policy communities tend to be fairly circumscribed (Coleman 1996). They typically include the finance ministry, the central bank, financial firms themselves and regulatory agencies. Non-financial corporations are rarely involved. An institutionalist perspective had implicitly assigned an important role to public actors, who combined an awareness of institutional complementarities with an eagerness to optimize policy and gain political advantage. Scholarship on regulatory politics, in contrast, gave private interests pride of place. Stigler (1971) famously argued that producers would systematically beat other stakeholders at influencing regulation, leading to 'regulatory capture'. From the perspective of financial firms regulation fulfils a very different function than from the viewpoint of public actors: its most important aspect is its impact on the competitive landscape. Financial firms therefore not only adapt to their regulatory environment (for example in their business model and regional dispersion) but try to influence that regulatory environment at the same time. In that way, financial firms as key stakeholders in regulation can change 'national financial systems' from within (cf. Lütz 2002).

Second, to the degree that markets are organized at sub- or supranational levels, political struggles over financial regulation, which may reverberate throughout the political economy at large, will not necessarily play out at the national level or between a 'domestic' financial industry and foreign firms. Local savings banks, for example, may well be indifferent to the intrusion of foreign firms into trading services on the domestic bourse. And internationally oriented banks may actually welcome such intrusion if it entails market access for them abroad. An analysis of how and why financial rules change therefore has to be attentive to the multi-scalar nature of financial markets.

If producers perceive serious threats to their market positions or see new opportunities appearing on the horizon, they may push for regulatory change to address those threats or exploit those opportunities. Studying domestic markets, Sobel (1994) has shown how commercial banks in Japan, the US and the UK have pushed for the decompartmentalization of financial markets in the face of falling interest rate spreads and rapidly growing securities markets from which they had hitherto been excluded. Kroszner and Strahan (1999) have demonstrated that the dilution of the 1927 McFadden Act prohibiting bank interstate branching in the US was best explained by private interests and regulatory capture.

Third, a key contribution from cultural political economy to our understanding of institutions lies in its emphasis on imaginaries that shape agents' preferences. As laid out in the introduction to this volume, agents need to reduce the complexity they confront, and for financial firms this includes ideas about the impact of technology or market regulation abroad on their own business models. The rise of derivatives trading and its (temporary) ability to generate profits may suggest that 'derivatives trading is the future' of investment banking. Other such narratives include 'the need for a global presence' to survive in global financial markets or the need for 'pan-European strategies in the wake of the single currency'.

An emphasis on imaginaries breaks the direct link between macro-developments – for example increasing global capital flows or technological innovations – and changes in financial regulation and hence finance's role in contemporary capitalism. That does not mean that agent-driven change is haphazard, but that we need to study how key agents (often collectively) interpret the developments around them with an eye to their own ambitions. As the following two section show, firms' variegated competitive concerns and the imaginaries guiding them are key to understanding the launch of financial market liberalization in Continental Europe's two largest economies.

The launch of financial reform in France

French financial policy in the 1980s shows how competitive considerations of financial firms were central to reforms and how important specific narratives about what the future would hold were for their specific direction. The first set of reforms had been devised as a comprehensive package initiated by Jacques Delors as finance minister and fully developed under Pierre Bérégovoy (cf. Coleman 2001; Loriaux 1991; Morin 2000; Schmidt 1996; Story and Walter 1997). In the first half of the decade, the main initiative still rested with the Trésor and its top officials. The 1984 Banking Act aimed at tearing down barriers between different banking segments and introducing a modicum of competition between financial institutions ranging from the local *Caisse d'epargne* to commercial giants such as the Banque National de Paris. But this competition was still state-controlled and a means to a policy end (a more flexible allocation of credit), and competitive imperatives were still fully subordinated to coordinative ones.

In the 1988 *petit* Big Bang, as French stock market reforms became known, competitive imperatives became distinct from coordinative ones, but the two were still successfully reconciled. The Stock Exchange Reform Act was meant to create a French investment banking industry that could mirror Britain's – with the difference that it was intended to support an industrial structure more reminiscent of the German one. Eventually, these reform steps were to create a dynamic that transformed French finance much more than had been originally envisaged.

These reforms, and many that followed later, were not in any narrow sense 'rational' reactions to objective political and economic circumstances. Instead, they took their cue from prevalent imaginaries at the time. Two stand out in particular: first, as Abdelal (2006) has detailed, after Mitterrand's *grand tournant* in 1983 leading French politicians and policymakers became convinced that financial innovation and openness were not enemies of French economic advancement but essential preconditions. In contrast to reforms in the UK or the USA this modernizing force of finance was not to be unleashed completely but to be harnessed by the government. Even if greed was not necessarily good in French eyes, 'modern' finance definitely was.

This line of thinking matters to the reform of French capitalism because it fails to appreciate one of the key effects that financialization has on economies: it boosts credit-provision and thereby hides problems elsewhere in the economy, for example a shortfall in domestic demand or inefficiencies in domestic production. It also overestimates the financial sector as a source of growth, because it mistakes profits that accrue at financial firms for an indication of the value of the services that they provide to the economy (rather than seeing them as the appropriation of surplus that has been created elsewhere, cf. Krippner 2005). The idea of deregulated finance as an engine of growth seems highly dubious in hindsight, but it was an important driver of reforms in France and Continental Europe more broadly.

The second imaginary that energized financial reforms was the belief among big French banks that they might in time rival big American or British firms in London, in particular in the lucrative investment banking business (Mügge 2010). As detailed below, several large French banks increasingly felt that they had outgrown French financial markets; the City was beckoning. To be sure, none of them ever made a serious attempt to compete on the truly global level – they never challenged the competitive pecking order on Wall Street. But they did want to join a 'Champions League' of European financial institutions. The policy preference flowing from that ambition was not only an increasing, if carefully managed, financial openness, but also an emphasis on *European* integration of financial markets – essentially preparing the ground for a European financial services industry to emerge, of which large French banks would be a part.

This second imaginary was forceful in garnering private support for financial liberalization coupled with a growing emphasis on European financial integration and a European regulatory framework. Just as the unqualified benefits of financial innovation turned out to be an illusion, so did the idea that French firms could become leading investment banks on the European level. More generally, in light of shrinking margins in traditional credit intermediation, investment banking was seen as the future of the financial sector (and its profitability). As we know today, however, stock market capitalizations in France, as well as Germany, never reached the British or American levels, and enthusiasm waned markedly after the dot.com bubble burst in early 2000. By then, however, the idea that investment banking was the future had already triggered a wide array of reforms that were to encourage the financialization of France and buttress financial liberalization and integration in the European Union.

French stock market reform came only *after* the 1986–1988 stock market boom that had been fuelled by privatizations of the conservative government. Before reforms, stock broking had been the reserve of *agents de change* who officially were no broking firms but government-appointed officials. As in many other countries, commercial banks in France were eager to secure a piece of the growing securities business (Fidler 1987; cf. Sobel 1994). When *agents de change* were turned into commercial *sociétés de bourse*, the new law allowed other financial firms to progressively buy them. What had happened elsewhere was to be repeated in Paris: large financial firms could buy themselves into the stock market through the acquisition of smaller ones (Graham 1987a). By the end of 1990, close to 80 per cent of them had effectively been taken over. The removal of bond trading from the stock exchange monopoly in 1987 equally served banks' business interests: the market share of large financial firms surged to 73 per cent in the first half of the following year (Graham 1988a).

Developments around French derivatives trading show how competitive imperatives increasingly followed their own rationale. MATIF – the French derivatives exchange introduced in 1986 – had been the brainchild of the Trésor and became an instant success. Soaring trading volumes, however, generated rising profits for the *agents de change* and sparked the jealousy of the banks cut out from the action. The latter wanted to make markets in futures contracts themselves instead of trading through the *agents de change*. The conflict got out of hand, and the banks referred it to the Treasury. Considering the weight of state patronage at the time, this escalation was remarkable. When the banks finally prevailed, the head of the stock exchange, Xavier Dupont, spoke of a 'civil war' that the authorities had put to an end (Graham 1987b).

The struggle continued, however, as the reform initiative passed more and more to the private sector. A mere two years after the settlement, a consortium of French banks and a Swedish specialist set up a rival exchange, dubbed OMF, much to the chagrin of the MATIF and its official sponsors (Graham 1989). The sponsoring banks, coincidently, were the two who had already broken ranks by setting up their capital market operations in London – BNP and Paribas – plus Crédit Commercial de France, which had been privatized in 1987 (Graham 1988b). With growing independence, financial institutions more and more opted out of cosy public-private arrangements and became pace makers of French financial reform.

Many of the reforms eventually transformed not only French financial market institutions themselves but also economic practices at large – what Morin has called the shift from the 'financial network economy' around 1990 towards the 'financial market economy' a decade later (Morin 2000). Much of the regulatory groundwork for this shift was pushed by individual firms with an agenda that had little to do with the viability of a French 'model of capitalism' per se. Coordinative imperatives – the interest of public actors in embedding financial markets in economic policy at large – played a much smaller role than is commonly assumed. Instead, the commercial opportunities that financial firms identified – at the national, European or global level – motivated them to push for reforms. Guided as they were by specific narratives about the future of finance and the attendant opportunities and threats, they turned out to be champions of transformations that in the end benefitted them much less than anticipated.

Competitive imperatives in German financial reform

In the case of German financial reform, we also find competitive considerations of financial firms as an important driver (Lütz 2003; Story 1997). Just as in France, in early reforms they were still easily reconciled with public policy imperatives. German monetary policy is a case in point: when a wave of new financial instruments started to appear on global financial markets, for example floating rate notes and zero coupon bonds, the Bundesbank introduced them only cautiously, fearing that they might obstruct monetary policy. For example, it resisted calls for Certificates of Deposit (CDs) which would function much like time deposits for lenders but in contrast to those would be tradable.[2] The Bundesbank had used banks' reserve requirements against time deposits as a preferred instrument to expand or contract credit. CDs, it had initially found, would not fall under reserve requirements (Carr 1985a). Thus, if time deposits would be replaced by CDs, the Bundesbank would lose one of its favourite instruments.

At the same time, the private sector called for their introduction because their attractiveness to borrowers meant that business was lost to players in the Euromarkets where they were readily available. When the Bundesbank finally did introduce CDs in Germany, it did not fully give up its hesitations – and against its earlier intentions introduced reserve requirements also for CDs (Carr 1985b). However, it compensated national banks by lowering the overall level of reserves these had been required to deposit with the central bank, freeing up DM8bn of capital. Competitive interests of firms and public policy imperatives had been reconciled in the reform package.

Such squaring of the circle became more difficult in the introduction of a futures and options exchange some years later. The Deutsche Terminbörse (DTB) was launched in 1990 (Campbell and Hargreaves 1990). In tune with many German reforms, it came relatively late. The City's LIFFE had been opened in 1982, France's MATIF in 1986 and the Swiss Soffex in 1988. This German exceptionalism had done little to worry the Bundesbank or the finance ministry or, for that matter, German banks. Indeed, the Bundesbank had been decidedly cool on the matter because it feared that Bund futures in particular might disrupt its way of managing government debt and conducting its monetary policy.

Once other countries started to introduce their derivatives exchanges, German banks grew anxious. Unless Germany established its own exchange, the worry was that foreign competitors might start offering products referring to German securities such as equity options or bond futures (Simonian 1987a). More importantly, they feared that cash markets might follow the derivatives trading, deserting the Frankfurt markets they controlled. The top firms – Deutsche Bank, Dresdner Bank, Commerzbank and Deutsche Girozentrale – set up a committee to study the matter. It soon encountered legal obstacles to setting up a German derivatives market. Dresdner's chairman used its position as head of the German Federation of Private Bankers to send an official wish-list with necessary regulatory changes to the government in the federation's name. Despite some hesitations, the government eventually complied. A year later, most of the required legal changes were underway while the banks themselves worked out regulatory details (Simonian 1988). The competitive concerns of firms overruled the public policy imperatives embodied in the Bundesbank's hesitation.

On closer inspection, other aspects of regulatory reform resembled trade politics much more than 'adjustments to global pressures'. In securities underwriting, for example, the Bundesbank kept a tight lid on foreign competition, even if rules were eased over time. Traditionally, a 25 per cent coupon tax on foreign holdings of German bonds had deterred such holdings and kept German government debt in German hands. In October 1984 the Kohl-government abolished it as high US interest rates and a high dollar put German primary markets under pressure (Cornwell and Housego 1984). For once, capital mobility that normally rewarded German investors with higher returns turned back on the government. As hoped, the measure more than tripled foreign holdings of Bunds over the following two years (Carr 1986a). In 1986, after consultation with German banks and the Bundesbank, the government for the first time invited foreign banks to participate in the Federal Bond Consortium through which the government placed its debt in the market (Carr 1986b). The aim was not so much to let foreigners in on financial business, but to increase demand for German government securities and thereby drive down financing costs. Almost a third of the new players came from Japan, easing access to that country's huge savings pool. With the foreign players' share fixed at 20 per cent of the total, however, there remained clear limits to serious competition and a foreign challenge to domestic dominance of the market. Coordinative imperatives had pushed for adaptation, but competitive imperatives had salvaged regulatory protectionism.

The trade politics-like aspect of regulatory reform was even more obvious in the case of corporate bonds: in 1985 the Bundesbank had allowed foreign firms to lead-manage foreign issues of DM-denominated bonds in Frankfurt – another step in the internationalization of hitherto relatively closed financial markets (Davies 1985).[3] The move was primarily intended to increase the standing of Frankfurt as a financial centre opposed to the City's Euromarkets where D-Marks were also readily available. More than anything business going through Frankfurt promised a cut of these fees for German banks. Foreign corporations in need of German currency would probably approach their national firms first; attracting foreign issues to Germany therefore meant allowing foreign banks to lead-manage the issues and take part of the associated fees. German banks had such rights in most other important countries – apart from Japan. Thus, when the Bundesbank discussed its ideas with foreign banks in Frankfurt, it scheduled an extra meeting with representatives of Japanese banks and announced that in effect, they would be excluded from the new privileges until Japanese authorities would make concessions to German firms (Carr 1985c).[4] Again liberalization stood in the sign of 'updating Frankfurt', but not to the detriment of the large German players. Indeed, German institutions continued to dominate the Frankfurt market; instead of introducing stiff competition, one senior US banker found foreign lead managers in Frankfurt rather 'like gnats buzzing around German heads' (Carr 1985d).

As Lütz (2003) has found, the large commercial banks were an important driving force behind the 'Finanzplatz Deutschland' initiative seeking to promote securities markets and Frankfurt as a financial centre. The latter broke a long tradition of spreading share trading over eight exchanges, including four larger ones. It sparked the ire of smaller players as well as regional authorities but the coalition behind the initiative prevailed. Again, however, it would be misleading to think of this move as part of a unilateral adjustment to pressures to make national financial systems more attractive for mobile capital. Instead, the struggle was one between different regional financial centres against a national one – Frankfurt – on the ascendance.

Growing capital market importance, we had argued above, had not happened 'naturally' or been owed only to external pressure – agency from financial institutions had played a crucial role. Reforms that were at least intended to move the financial system from an emphasis on relationship banking in the direction of capital markets financing were in large measure driven by competitive imperatives. They in turn set in motion a dynamic of financial system change that was central to disembedding a part of German financial markets from its traditional positive coordination with national economic policy (cf. Zysman 1983). Because of the three-pillar system of the German banking sector, however, only one part of the financial system – the private banking sector – was fully exposed to the liberalizing effects of the reforms. Throughout the 1990s, local Sparkassen continued to go their own ways, and only towards the very end of the decade did some Landesbanken leave their traditional turf and (very unsuccessfully) try their hand at investment banking in London. They too had briefly been swayed by the idea, much more deeply entrenched among second-tier private banks like Dresdner Bank and Commerzbank, that they could make it big in the City. In the end, only Deutsche Bank really established itself as a European and indeed global bank. But the intermittent belief of German financial institutions in the blessings of 'modern' investment banking had in the meantime provided political support to the reforms that would liberalize European financial markets for good.

Conclusion

A common line of argument in comparative political economy holds that the German and French models of capitalism were seriously challenged by increasing globalization since the 1980s and adapted in response. In particular, the active coordination of various economic institutions, including financial markets policy, was rendered ineffective as trade and investment flows were liberalized.

As this chapter has shown, that view needs to be nuanced. It has examined central moments of financial reform in the mid-1980s in both countries. The picture that emerges is one in which liberalization is not driven by dysfunctionalities of a 'national model of capitalism', but by identifiable stakeholders with clear interests. Most importantly for this chapter, financial reform has been championed by financial firms themselves who perceived tempting business opportunities either abroad – most importantly in the City of London – or in other domains of national financial markets.

Because these competitive incentives for reform fully depend on the specific position of a firm, there is nothing per se 'national' about the resulting dynamics.

In Germany, for example, the Frankfurt stock exchange modernized at the expense of other, regional ones, mainly in an attempt to play a bigger European, rather than global, role. An attentiveness to such variegation leaves much more room for a nuanced understanding of institutional reforms and also for the contradictions and frictions between them.

Most noteworthy about the specific interests that have driven financial reform, however, is how strongly they have been imbued with imaginaries that were later exposed as such when real-world developments turned out very different than firms themselves had anticipated. Even second-tier European banks for a long time cherished the vision of a global future in European investment banking once financial markets would be liberalized. With hindsight we know not only that the likes of Commerzbank and Société Générale had it wrong, but that even the temporary winners in the game, like Barclays, were eventually caught in the maelstrom caused by excessive financial liberalization. In the panoply of powerful but also toxic imaginaries, 'the economic promises of modern finance' surely deserve a special place.

Notes

1 The term 'varieties of capitalism' is used here in the broad sense and interchangeable with other concepts aiming at institutional complementarities (models of capitalism, social systems of production, etc.). It is not intended as a specific endorsement of Hall and Soskice's full model and its implications.
2 The idea of a CD is to earn the interest of a longer-time deposit while giving the lender full flexibility to get the loan back at any time – by simply selling the CD to someone else.
3 A foreign issue in this case refers to selling bonds of non-German corporations denominated in DM to a German audience.
4 The rules for Japanese firms were only eased more than two years later, in October 1987 (Simonian 1987b).

References

Abdelal, R. (2006) Writing the rule of global finance: France, Europe, and capital liberalization, *Review of International Political Economy*, 13(1): 1–27.

Becker, U. (2009) *Open Varieties of Capitalism. Continuity, Change and Performances*, New York: Palgrave Macmillan.

Campbell, K. and Hargreaves, D. (1990) Frankfurt fights to regain bunds, *Financial Times*, 26 November.

Carr, J. (1985a) Challenge on several fronts, *Financial Times*, 13 May.

Carr, J. (1985b) Bundesbank to allow issue of D-Mark CDs, *Financial Times*, 20 December.

Carr, J. (1985c) Bundesbank presses for greater deregulation, *Financial Times*, 10 April.

Carr, J. (1985d) Germans see no profit in novelty, *Financial Times*, 2 August.

Carr, J. (1986a) Foreigners may join DM bond consortium, *Financial Times*, 12 June.

Carr, J. (1986b) Foreign banks drawn into German bonds net, *Financial Times*, 14 July.

Coleman, W. (1996) *Financial Services, Globalization, and Domestic Policy Change*, Basingstoke: Macmillan.

Coleman, W. (1997) The French state, dirigisme, and the changing global financial environment. In G. Underhill (ed.), *The New World Order in International Finance*, Houndmills: Macmillan.

Coleman, W. (2001) Governing French banking: regulatory reform and the Crédit Lyonnais fiasco, in M. Bovens, P. 't Hart and G. Peters (eds), *Success and Failure in Public Governance: A Comparative Analysis*, Cheltenham: Edward Elgar.

Cornwell, R. and Housego, D. (1984) Paris joins Bonn in plan to abolish withholding tax, *Financial Times*, 4 October.

Crouch, C. and Streek, W. (eds) (1997) *Political Economy of Modern Capitalism: Mapping Convergence and Diversity*, London: Sage.

Davies, J. (1985) West Germans open bond sector to foreign managers, *Financial Times*, 13 April.

Deeg, R. (1999) *Finance Capitalism Unveiled: Banks and the German Political Economy*, Ann Arbor, MI: University of Michigan Press.

Fidler, S. (1987) Deregulate or risk being left behind, *Financial Times*, 21 October.

Frieden, J. (1991) Invested interests: the politics of national economic policies in a world of global finance, *International Organization*, 45(4): 425–52.

Graham, G. (1987a) French bourse flourishes after years of evolution, *Financial Times*, 11 March.

Graham, G. (1987b) A late run for the winning post, *Financial Times*, 7 April.

Graham, G. (1988a) Major reforms under way, *Financial Times*, 29 September.

Graham, G. (1988b) After the scandal, the real trouble starts, *Financial Times*, 4 July.

Graham, G. (1989) Taste for regulation revived, *Financial Times*, 2 November.

Hall, P. and Soskice, D. (eds) (2001) *Varieties of Capitalism: The Institutional Foundations of Comparative Advantage*, Oxford: Oxford University Press.

Jayasuriya, J. (2001) Globalization and the changing architecture of the state: the regulatory state and the politics of negative coordination, *Journal of European Public Policy*, 8(1): 101–23.

Katznelson, I. and Weingast, B. (eds) (2005) *Preferences and Situations. Points of Intersection between Rational Choice and Historical Institutionalism*, New York: Russell Sage.

Kitschelt, H., Lange, P., Marks, G. and Stephens, J. (eds) (1999) *Continuity and Change in Contemporary Capitalism*, Cambridge: Cambridge University Press.

Krippner, G. (2005) The financialization of the American economy, *Socio-Economic Review*, 3(2): 173–208.

Kroszner, R. and Strahan, P. (1999) What drives deregulation? Economics and politics of the relaxation of bank branching restrictions, *Quarterly Journal of Economics*, 114(4): 1437–67.

Lane, C. (2000) Globalization and the German model of capitalism – erosion or survival?, *British Journal of Sociology*, 51(2): 207–34.

Loriaux, M. (1991) *France after Hegemony: International Change and Financial Reform*, Ithaca, NY: Cornell University Press.

Lütz, S. (2002) *Der Staat und die Globalisierung von Finanzmärkten*, Frankfurt am Main: Campus.

Lütz, S. (2003) Finanzmarktregulierung: Globalisierung und der regulative Umbau des 'Modell Deutschland', in R. Czada, S. Lütz and S. Mette (eds), *Regulative Politik: Zähmung von Markt und Technik*, Opladen: Leske + Budrich.

Macartney, H. (2009) Variegated neoliberalism: transnationally oriented fractions of capital in EU financial market integration, *Review of International Studies*, 35(2): 451–80.

Martin, C. and Swank, D. (2012) *The Political Construction of Corporate Interests: Cooperation and the Evolution of the Good Society*, New York: Cambridge University Press.

Morin, F. (2000) A transformation in the French model of shareholding and management, *Economy and Society*, 29(1): 36–53.

Mosley, L. (2003) *Global Capital and National Governments*, Cambridge: Cambridge University Press.

Mügge, D. (2010) *Widen the Market, Narrow the Competition. Banker Interests in the Making of a European Capital Market*, Colchester: ECPR Press.

Pauly, L. (1995) Capital mobility, state autonomy and political legitimacy, *International Affairs*, 48(2): 369–88.

Quaglia, L. (2010) *Governing Financial Services in the European Union*, London: Routledge.

Radice, H. (2000) Globalization and national capitalisms: theorizing convergence and differentiation, *Review of International Political Economy*, 7(4): 719–42.

Scharpf, F. (1997) *Games Real Actors Play: Actor-Centered Institutionalism in Policy Research*, Boulder, CO: Westview Press.

Schmidt, V. (1996) *From State to Market? The Transformation of French Business and Government*, Cambridge: Cambridge University Press.

Simonian, H. (1987a) Frankfurt studies the options game, *Financial Times*, 10 June.

Simonian, H. (1987b) Japanese bring D-Mark issues, *Financial Times*, 2 October.

Simonian, H. (1988) Swiss influence plan for new exchange, *Financial Times*, 13 July.

Sobel, A. (1994) *Domestic Choices, International Markets: Dismantling National Barriers and Liberalizing Securities Markets*, Ann Arbor, MI: University of Michigan Press.

Stigler, G. (1971) The theory of economic regulation, *Bell Journal of Economics*, 2(1): 113–21.

Story, J. (1997) Globalisation, the European Union and German financial reform: the political economy of 'Finanzplatz Deutschland'. In G. Underhill (ed.), *The New World Order in International Finance*, Basingstoke: Macmillan.

Story, J. and Walter, I. (1997) *The Political Economy of Financial Integration in Europe: The Battle of the Systems*, Cambridge, MA: MIT Press.

Streeck, W. (1997) German capitalism: does it exist? Can it survive? In C. Crouch and W. Streeck (eds), *Political Economy of Modern Capitalism*, London: Sage.

Zysman, J. (1983) *Governments, Markets, and Growth*, Ithaca, NY: Cornell University Press.

Part IV

Economic imaginaries, financial calculation, and crisis dynamics

10 Hedge funds and the limits of market efficiency as a regulatory concept

Horacio Ortiz

Hedge funds occupy a particularly symbolic place in the conceptual framework of market efficiency that pervades regulation, orthodox academic analysis and relevant professional practices. Although they are an integral element of the financial industry, they are consistently singled out as representing extreme positions within it, which either pose a danger to the whole system or, on the contrary, are fundamental to its correct functioning. In this chapter, I would like to explore this position, not because hedge funds per se deserve to be singled out but, on the contrary, because of what they say about the broader regulatory framework for the financial industry. Although fragmented along national borders, relevant regulations share a common conceptual apparatus, according to which the financial industry is the social space in which 'investors' meet through 'free' exchanges that occur in 'efficient markets' and lead to an 'optimal' allocation of social resources (Lee 1998).[1] This frame both defines the technical rules and procedures within the industry and provides the moral and political justification for the social role of the financial industry in the distribution of resources (Ortiz 2011). Regulation distinguishes 'qualified' or 'sophisticated' investors, defined by their high net wealth or, more importantly, by their knowledge of financial theory and their capacity to evaluate investments, a quality concretely only found in the financial industry itself. Although hedge funds are heterogeneous, they are supposed to use methods of investment that are very sophisticated and, as such, can only be offered to 'qualified' investors, whose number is usually limited.

Yet there is a specific point of tension in this respect that shapes an important part of regulatory and academic debates in general: for markets to be efficient, there need to be actors who consider them inefficient and carry out the valuation and arbitrages necessary for efficiency to be obtained; yet, if too many actors consider markets to be inefficient, they may engage in speculative activities that may distort the adequacy of prices as signals for an optimal allocation of resources, a tension that is often superficially evoked and left unresolved in manuals of financial analysis. In this debate, as an almost always recurrent theme, hedge funds occupy an ambivalent position: they are either portrayed as the arbitrageurs necessary to correct market inefficiencies or, on the contrary, as disruptive actors preventing markets and the financial industry from performing the optimal allocation that justifies its current regulation. This even holds when their role is assessed critically (for example, this view structures the title of Aglietta *et al.* 2010).

My chapter draws on fieldwork conducted through a four-month internship with a team of hedge fund managers in 2003 and broader participant observation in the financial industry and interviews with professionals between 2002 and 2005. This was a transition period during which hedge funds were becoming 'alternative investments' as they increasingly became just another product sold by and within the financial industry, as they remain today. In the first section of the chapter, I analyse the place of hedge funds in the financial industry today and give an account of how this process of 'institutionalization', which I observed in my fieldwork at the beginning of the 2000s, was understood by the employees of the financial industry in terms of a debate about 'market efficiency'. In the second section, I analyse the uses of this frame by hedge funds in a specific case. I describe the investment and commercial strategy of a long/short global equities hedge fund observed in 2003, as it tried to position itself within the growing market of institutional investors developing 'alternative investment' products. Their activities could only function in a social network within the financial industry, in which institutional investors give hedge funds the capacity to pursue certain investment strategies, problematized with the terms of the tension I described above concerning market efficiency.

The chapter shows that hedge funds are an integral part of commercial strategies of the financial industry, countering the idea that they might be 'independent', a quality that informs part of the regulatory discussion about them. It also shows that the concept of 'market efficiency' is fundamental to the meaning that hedge funds have in the financial industry but that this concept is used in complex, multifarious and sometimes contradictory ways by employees, as they try to make sense and justify their everyday standardized practices. Thus the example of hedge funds highlights the distance between (1) the liberal utopias that ground the concept of 'market efficiency' and are used to justify financial regulation and professional financial practice and (2) the use of these concepts in everyday practice.

From 'hedge funds' to 'alternative investments': the institutionalization of hedge funds as a matter of market efficiency

Hedge funds as we know them today are one of the many investment vehicles of the financial industry and, in particular, of its biggest players, namely, pension and mutual funds and insurance companies, either as direct holders of the hedge funds shares or through funds of funds. The share of traditionally recognized investors, such as big personal fortunes and university endowments, is relatively small – at least since the mid-2000s. Data are hard to collect, and subject to several objections, but different sources point in the same direction. The 'institutional investors' of the financial industry constitute at least 75 per cent of the sources of the funds (see Figure 10.1) and, in the list of biggest hedge funds, we find many that directly belong to some of the biggest players in the financial industry, such as Goldman Sachs (Holmes 2009).

The financial industry's crucial role in the capacity of hedge funds to exist at all commercially explains why the biggest lobbies in the 1990s influencing the regulation of hedge funds in the USA were led by the main financial companies (Justin Miller, personal communication, 2011) and also, for instance, in the early 2000s in France, as I observed during my fieldwork. Yet, the theoretical framework in which the lobbying was done and which still organizes the regulation of hedge funds is linked to a more or less mythological image related to their origins, which corresponds little to their current place in the global organization of financial flows.

According to the history ritually repeated in every presentation about hedge funds, including critical ones, the concept was 'invented' by a fund manager in the late 1940s, who took 'long' positions on certain stocks and sold others 'short', thereby supposedly obtaining a hedge against market volatility, his whole investment yielding positive results whether the 'market' went up or down. Hedge funds could therefore provide an 'absolute' return, 'de-correlated' from market movements. Hedge funds were associated with free global capital, established in offshore sites, uncontrolled by most regulation and arbitraging and speculating in ways that often went against professional standards of diversification and even moral standards that would wish the prices of stock to rise.

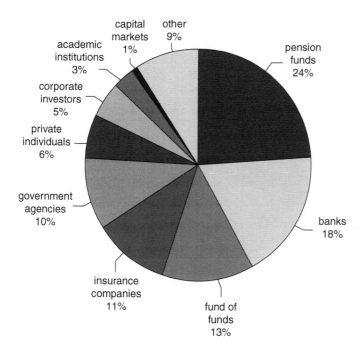

Figure 10.1 Origins of investments in hedge funds (source: Rigot 2010).

Especially in the USA, the funds were considered acceptable since they had only a limited amount of clients, all wealthy and who were therefore supposed to know the risks they were facing: in regulatory parlance, they were 'qualified'. The small size of the funds also meant that they were not deemed to pose systemic problems that demanded more control. Finally, the figure of the manager was central: he was supposed to design the original strategy that allowed constantly positive and high returns. This explained why his fees were much higher than in the rest of the financial industry, and were supposed to be justified by the fact that the manager invested an important amount of his own money in the fund.

It is against this background that hedge funds such as that of Georg Soros, or LTCM, became more visible as actors in the 1990s. Soros was considered to be a main cause for the destruction of the European Monetary System in 1992, shorting the pound and forcing it out of the EMS. Soros, who studied philosophy, publishes books, has an immense fortune and a very active (and visible) foundation, seems to have carefully cultivated this image of an independent mind who can go against established norms to achieve the kind of success everybody desires, a mixture of genius and pirate. LTCM presented a more decent image, run by Nobel laureates in economics and renowned traders coming from some of the most successful investment banks. Its investment techniques were backed by supposedly scientific thinking and decent morality. Its collapse in 1998 sparked fears of a global crisis, which was averted by a private bail-out brokered by the Fed. In these two cases, the story told was one of some genius fund manager or management team who were able to exploit market inefficiencies and make money (or not!) in the process.

The regulatory debate concerning these cases, as well as hedge funds in general, was the one I highlighted at the beginning of this chapter: either Soros and LTCM were exploiting market inefficiencies and helping the market to become more efficient (as the pound was devalued, or as the initial gains of LTCM proved there were arbitrage opportunities) or, on the contrary, these geniuses created part of the volatility that they exploited, thereby extracting a profit from their disruptive activity against market efficiency (if Soros had not shorted the pound and created a buzz about it, it would have stayed within the EMS, if LTCM did not have so much leverage, its initial profits would have been meagre, and not proportional to the risks it was taking). But in both cases, this way of addressing the issue hides the crucial role played by the major financial institutions. To achieve his attack against the pound, Soros obtained the phenomenal amount of 15 billion dollars in loans from big investment banks, who must have been aware of his strategy, decided to support it and probably benefited from it too (Aglietta et al. 2010: 36ff). He was not 'alone'. LTCM was explicitly built with the backing and the investment of major global banks, which came to its rescue when it needed bailing out. It operated in a network where the lenders that allowed it to have its considerable leverage knew its bets. These brokers supported LTCM's strategy and it is when they decided to stop doing so that the company was driven towards bankruptcy (MacKenzie 2003).

As some authors have shown, this image of an isolated fund manager opposed to 'markets' that would be more or less efficient is too distant from reality. Hedge funds gather information and develop investment techniques within a network of financial professionals with which they interact and communicate (Hardie and MacKenzie 2007). To locate the 'source' of the investment techniques and knowledge in the hands or head of the manager is a mystification of his 'personality', which veils the social organization in which it happens. But, more crucially, the 'decision' to invest in one way or another is also not just that of a 'free will' that needs to be preserved (for the sake of market efficiency) or controlled (because of its antisocial individualism). Whether hedge funds were ever the mythical 'free' enterprises conveyed by the mythology still needs to be seriously researched. But, in their current form, with around 75 per cent of their funds coming from institutional investors, they are bound by a series of contracts in which they do not 'decide freely' about their investment techniques. On the contrary, they apply previously negotiated investment processes, with regular controls concerning their compliance. It is therefore not really accurate to state that hedge funds are in themselves 'obscure' or 'not transparent', in particular if this lack of transparency refers to their relation to major clients. It may be more accurate to say that they are an element of the global financial industry that the major companies prefer to leave outside of the regulatory focus. The observations I did in my fieldwork at the beginning of the 2000s shed light on how institutional investors were indeed quite close to the activity of the hedge funds, whose existence they allowed for in the first place.

The fieldwork I conducted between 2002 and 2005 concerned hedge funds, funds of funds and institutional investors based in the jurisdictions of the US, the UK and France, the latter constituting most of my sources. I did three four-to-five months internships, with stock brokers in New York, 'Brokers Inc.', in 2002, with hedge fund managers and consultants in Paris, 'Alpha Consulting', in 2003, and with a team of fund managers investing in asset backed securities for a major French multinational of asset management, 'Acme', in 2004.[2] I also conducted 70 interviews with other financial professionals. Many of them spoke about hedge funds and their increasing presence and institutionalization. Concerning the hedge fund sector itself I did interviews with four hedge fund managers, six managers of funds of funds, two sales people in alternative investment (one in a fund of funds, one in a major global investment bank), one regulator and two high rank employees concerned with integrating hedge funds in asset allocation in big financial companies.[3]

My observations occurred when the wave of 'institutionalization' was well under way but still considered something 'new'. I could therefore observe the financial professionals involved in it as they attempted to make sense of it. To do this, they mobilized two main bodies of meaning or imaginaries: on the one hand, the mythology of the independent hedge fund and, on the other, the 'classical' approaches to financial investment defined by diversification and the hypothesis of market efficiency, such as developed in Modern Portfolio Theory (MPT) and Capital Asset Pricing Model (CAPM) (see MacKenzie 2006). MPT and CAPM are part of the basic curriculum of any finance programme. To synthesize the main elements that interest us here, they state that financial markets are 'efficient', implying that prices, as the result of the interactions of all the 'investors', reflect the 'true', 'fundamental' or 'intrinsic value' of the assets. Since prices vary 'randomly', and since no single investor can evaluate them 'better' than the market, market efficiency implies that investors buy 'the whole market' and keep it, without speculating. This diversification will statistically 'dilute' the volatility of a single asset in that of the 'whole', which, by construction, is lower. If 'investors' only buy one asset, or buy just a fraction of the market, they can calculate the deviation between overall price movements in the market and movements in their own investment. This statistical relation is often described by the mathematical variable 'beta'. Thus, if beta=1, then the investment moves in exactly the same way as the market and, when beta=0, there is no relation between them. These theories are at the basis of the expanded use of indexes today, which otherwise could be probably considered as a form of 'gambling' (cf. de Goede 2005; Preda 2009).

In Paris in 2003, there were only a handful of funds of funds investing in hedge funds. Some were based in big asset management firms, such as Acme. Others were 'independent' structures, which had developed since the 1970s catering for wealthy families and some institutional investors. Institutional investors were developing the use of hedge funds in two complementary ways: by creating departments composed solely of hedge funds, and by developing funds of funds who would invest in hedge funds outside of the company. Their strategies were directed to sell these funds as investment services to the general clients of the companies, charging higher fees for what were expected to be higher returns. The team Alpha Consulting had first developed in one of such departments in the 'Compagnie Universelle', a major French investment bank. In Acme, a similar department, with around 1.5 billion euros under management in 2004, had developed since the early 2000s. A fund of funds invested in turn 400 million euros in external hedge funds, aiming to reach around 1 billion euros under management. These products occupied a small part of the 300 billion euros under management of the company, and were supposed to keep up with the new commercial offers in the industry.

At the time, these projects were in their inception, and the firms only invested their own funds in them. The goal of this strategy was to let the employees refine their investment techniques and obtain presentable track records. Once lobbying in the regulatory bodies reached its aim, the hedge funds would be sold to a larger public as just another financial product: not the index-tracking 'classical' buy-and-hold investment vehicles, but 'alternative investment'. The 'independent' funds of funds complained of this process, saying that the lobbying consisted in particular in negotiating with the regulatory bodies that, for hedge funds to be sold, they could only be proposed through funds of funds that could show they had well-developed risk-control techniques. The definition of the resources necessary for these risk-control techniques meant that only investment banks could afford them, thereby forcing traditional funds of funds out of the business.

In their critique of the process of 'institutionalization', the heads of the funds of funds that did not belong to big institutional investors, whom I will call 'traditional', each with around a billion euros under management, developed an almost identical discourse. They denounced a 'democratization' of the industry, which meant that more hedge funds would arise, attracted by the important volume of funds available in the financial industry, a multiplication that 'necessarily' meant a decrease of the average 'quality' of the managers. The heads of the funds of funds developed at length the mythology of the fund manager as an isolated individual who needed to be left free to choose her investment strategy and to change it if she considered it suited the moment. The role of the fund of funds was only to minimize entry costs and to provide access to often already closed hedge funds.[4] They also provided liquidity as they could smooth the effects of the lock-up period.[5] But they had to preserve the original and hard to find qualities of the hedge fund managers, whom they met at cocktails, golf courses and other such socially restricted and sophisticated venues, generally by word-of-mouth and introduction through third parties. The traditional funds of funds did develop a diversification approach, trying not to concentrate on a single strategy of hedge funds, but without a systematic discourse about it, such as that of MPT, in particular because the main rationale was that good hedge fund managers are hard to find, and cannot be discarded on the basis of diversification: they provide absolute return and need not be diluted, on the contrary.

The discourse of the institutional funds of funds was almost identical but involved a redefinition of the hedge fund. While the traditional managers of funds of funds insisted on the primordial importance of the person of the hedge fund manager, institutional funds of funds were bound to the classic theories of portfolio diversification, MPT and CAPM, that I described above. In the institutional approach, hedge funds were considered just another asset class, along stocks, bonds and the like. This implied that one could calculate their average returns, their volatility and that one could create indexes, in order to compare them to 'the whole market' of which they were now part. The radical break was that each hedge fund was no longer an incomparable single manager, but an object of investment that needed to be overseen and of which some stability was expected. Concretely, since the hedge fund depended on its manager or managing team, the hedge fund managers were more closely monitored than most other employees in the financial industry. The managers of the funds of funds asked data research companies to collect all public information concerning them (which could include the juridical procedures of a divorce, judgements for fraud, newspaper articles and so on), and hired private detectives when their personality seemed strange to the fund of fund manager's intuition. If a hedge fund manager was proven to have problems with alcohol, or a distressing family life that may render his professional activity unstable, his fund was not retained, or the fund of funds sought to terminate the contract, with more ease than it would be to fire an employee for similar reasons.

But, even more crucial for the issue of financial regulation, there was close monitoring of the investment techniques of the funds. Contrary to the understanding of the 'traditional' managers of funds of funds, in 'institutional' funds of funds, hedge fund managers were not allowed to change their investment technique during the contract with the fund of funds, for instance going towards distressed companies instead of doing long-short or M&A. Only 'Global Macro' funds were allowed to do it, but not many were retained as objects of investment. On top of this, the funds of funds demanded a monthly reporting of the positions of the hedge fund. Even if this did not mean a control of the rationales for each trade, or a knowledge of the logarithms if there were any, it did mean the establishment of patterns in the investment techniques, and the fact that if there was a change, the hedge fund manager had to justify it or else the contract could be considered to be breached.

Integrating hedge funds as just another asset, within an approach that followed officially the theories of MPT and CAPM and the standard procedures inspired in them, meant that hedge funds themselves had now betas, average returns and volatilities, with subclasses of hedge funds (just like there are subclasses of stocks and bonds) that were expected to be stable in time. This strategy of funds of funds and major companies of asset management was due to several reasons. On the one hand, for regulatory reasons that are similar across jurisdictions, these major players needed to comply with standard approaches of risk management in the financial industry, in order to remain within the limits of what could be proposed to a general public of non-qualified or non-sophisticated investors. On the other hand, these were also the approaches with which the managers of the fund of funds and their institutional clients or owners were most acquainted with and most respected. They did not really need to justify their use but, on the contrary, not doing so would have necessitated lengthy explanations which they were unable to provide, and for which the sole mystique of the fund manager was insufficient in the bureaucratic environments in which they operated. In contrast with the traditional managers of funds of funds, for whom having the right social network to find the unknown geniuses was a major expertise, the manager of 'Logos', a fund of funds with which Alpha Consulting tried to work, invoked his PhD in financial mathematics and was adamant that his marketing pitch to institutional investors was the statistical treatment of the data of each of the hedge funds in which he invested his clients' money. If a hedge fund's performances did not correspond to what was expected for his class of comparable hedge funds, it was simply not included in the investment.

The managers of the institutional funds of funds, as well as the person responsible for the hedge fund department at Acme, all considered that there was a 'risk' of losing that which made hedge funds attractive in the first place, that is the original personality of the hedge fund manager. But they considered that the time for this approach was past. Hedge funds were now to be compared to the 'free interest rate' in terms of spread, and hence to any other asset class, in line with the mode of reasoning of MPT and CAPM. According to the manager of the fund of hedge funds in Acme:

> alternative [investment], it won't yield 15% a year, it will yield 7–8% a year, but hey! That's not so bad! But one has to stop aiming for flabbergasting stuff.

I would even say, I think it's going to be like this, it's going to be 'Cash +', alternative [investment], 'Cash ++', but, overall, Libor +4%, and that you'll very hardly get more than Libor+4%, with the funds we are receiving. But institutional [investors], they're pretty happy with Libor+4%, that suits them very well! Today, what is it that yields Libor+4? Bonds? Don't even talk about it! You could hope, stocks, but that's much, much more volatile. So, in sum, you can hope for the performance of bonds, without the risk on capital, or maybe a little more, but that's all ... It is illusory to believe that there are markets that are going to yield 15% a year every year, it's physically, financially not possible. So there will be good years, and there will be bad years and, on average, the average, it won't be 15, it will be 7, half! ... Where you will have a lot of disillusion, is with those who are stuck on the dream: 'alternative [investment] is totally decorrelated, it yields 1% every month whether markets go up or down'. Those, they'll see quite quickly that that's not the case, and there is a risk that they simply leave. Those who understood that it is an investment management method that presents a certain interest, for certain periods, for certain market conditions, well, they will stay.

These examples show the type of thinking and the movement that led to the volume of investments described at the beginning of this section, that is the fact that hedge funds are today an integral part of the financial industry, in which they operate as a specific financial product managed by the main players of the industry. It remains to be studied how much the idealized 'independent' hedge was ever a widespread occurrence, although some such cases do exist today. But they do not correspond to the vehicles where the majority of funds are channelled, and that are supposed to be the target of the regulatory framework. Yet, the symbol of the hedge fund as an independent and somewhat uncontrolled operator remains strong in the marketing and in the widespread talk of hedge funds. This may have much to do with the fact that as such, hedge funds seem to radicalize a fundamental element of the current theoretical and regulatory framework that legitimizes the social role of the financial industry, that is the existence of 'free investors' who orient their capital according to their 'own' valuations and utilities. While today, most investment management is the deed of employees of bureaucracies managing their client's money for payment, hedge funds still appear as the 'real' investor depicted by the liberal utopia,[6] a perception that I hope to have shown here to be misguided. In the following section, I would like to show, through a detailed case, how this comprehension of hedge funds is not just external to the industry, but also constitutes part of the narrative with which employees in the industry make sense of them, even if it is with a plasticity that is quite distant from the liberal framework from which these concepts stem.

Alpha Consulting: exploring the possibilities of the new conditions of 'market efficiency'

In the mid-2000s, although the hedge fund mythology of the independent manager still pervaded regulatory discourse and helped to make sense of them, hedge funds were starting to take another place in the discourse on market efficiency: not just subjects that enhance or disrupt market efficiency, but also objects that can be treated as investment targets within an approach of market efficiency. The incorporation of hedge funds within MPT and CAPM as another asset class found its limit in the fact that, by definition, as a class, hedge funds were 'undefinable', that is, they were absolute singularities that challenged any characterization. Within this tension, the different actors I could observe between 2002 and 2005 attempted to make sense of the procedures and career strategies that they developed in their everyday, in order to justify their own doings and the field in which they operated. This led to multiple manipulations and explorations of the imaginaries of the individual hedge fund manager and of market efficiency as developed by financial theory and the regulatory framework. Like in many moments of transition, this created a certain cacophony and multiplicity of ways to make sense in a more or less contradictory or unwarranted way. There was of course no empirical justification to expect a spread of 4 per cent out of a diversified pool of hedge funds, nor was it warranted that these investment vehicles would provide lower volatility, unless the mythology of the hedging genius manager was somewhat upheld. These were all ways to try to define the growing market for 'alternative investments', within which the Alpha Consulting team attempted to insert itself to exist commercially.

The Alpha Consulting team was composed of three members, four counting myself during the few months of my internship.[7] The contradictions and possibilities offered by the process of institutionalization of hedge funds framed the way in which the members understood their own personal and professional trajectories, the way in which they defined their own activity as consultants, and the way in which they designed and marketed the investment techniques of the long/short global equities fund that they managed and tried to sell. In their commercial practices and discussion, they explored the plasticity of the concept of market efficiency to make sense of their own endeavour. This allows us to see the limits of the concept as a consistent descriptive and normative tool, but its potential as a discourse of legitimization.

The team members met during the establishment of the alternative investment department in a big French investment bank, the Compagnie Universelle in the early 2000s. Julie was a 27-year-old engineer trained in one of the most prestigious Parisian engineering schools (*grandes écoles*). She explained to me that, like many of her fellow students, she was more interested in making money in the financial district in Paris, La Défense, than spending her life at an industrial site in the suburbs of some second-tier city. She therefore obtained the diploma of the Société Française des Analystes Financiers, which, as she claimed, allowed her to learn all the valuation models, well within her skills in the use of statistical tools. She then entered the Compagnie Universelle, where she participated in the development of a systematized approach of risk exposure for all the fund managers of the company, in the risk management department. This meant drawing statistical series for all the positions, their averages, volatilities and possible correlations, across assets, fund managers and time. It was aimed at reducing volatility, creating alerts and generating a general picture of the bank's exposures.

After doing this, she met Charles, in his fifties, who had been vice-president of an important French investment bank in the 1980s, where he had developed hedging techniques with the bank's traders, profiting from the newly created and booming derivatives and monetary markets in Paris. He explained to me that he left the bank when he was told that he would not advance in his career if he did not become a *franc-maçon* (freemason), something that conflicted with his aristocratic upbringing. He only came back to finance at the end of the 1990s, to develop the hedge fund activities at the Compagnie Universelle, the alternative investments department being directed by one of the traders he had trained and helped in the 1980s.

When I met Julie and Charles, Julie had 30 million euros under management at the Compagnie Universelle. Yet, a month into the internship, a violent latent conflict erupted with the head of the department. Charles encouraged Julie to leave the company and join him in an independent endeavour. At this stage in their careers, both presented themselves as somewhat outsiders to the financial industry. Julie claimed that she was harassed because her fund had better performances than her co-workers' and, in particular, the one personally managed by the head of the department. She also claimed that, as her management procedures were completely automated in logarithms and, following the results of statistical tools, she could demonstrate the reasons for her good results, something that the other funds, which looked more like unreliable traders making personal bets without systematic warrant, could not provide. Charles explained to me that the bureaucratic infighting at the Compagnie Universelle prevented original minds like Julie from developing.

The two members therefore positioned themselves as outsiders to a bureaucratic institutionalized financial industry, whose inertia they often mocked. Their personalities and their rejection of the hierarchies of the industry had therefore pushed them to seek an independent organizational position, in line with the mythology of the independent hedge fund manager. At the same time, Julie's defence of her hedge fund was fully marked by the risk management approach of the big bank in which she worked, which was oriented towards creating an overview of the banks' exposure by comparing the volatilities and returns of all its investments, a methodology deployed as an application of MPT and CAPM. Julie also took from this professional environment the imperative of being completely 'transparent' about her investment strategy, which she had had to justify to her superiors within the bank's hedge fund department. In her marketing material, she put forward mathematical justifications for each of her calculations, for each of the chosen variables, and for the results of the investment.

For all its members' claims about disengaging from their former employers, the team's 'independence' was a specific legal and organizational role within the web of institutional investors in which they evolved. Having lost the 30 million euros under management, and the fees that came with it, the team was now searching for new 'investors', which it invariably looked for within the connections of Charles, that is within insurance companies, pension funds and the like, contacts that he had established in his former important position in an investment bank. To do this, the team explored the multiple commercial possibilities offered by the increasing presence of hedge funds and alternative investment talk within the milieu of Parisian institutional investors.

I was hired in this context. Charles and Julie expected me to help them in their commercial strategy. I had to do a survey of the 'hedge funds market' in Paris and internationally, in order to understand who the main actors were and what were their types of activities. Also, I was to help them write an introductory book synthesizing our findings, giving a view of the market and a technical description of all the hedge fund techniques. This aimed at establishing Alpha Consulting as the main expert in the place, and to sell its expertise as counselling when it came to establish funds of funds and alternative investments departments, the activity that Charles had done at the Compagnie Universelle. The team was replicating what was being done by other consultants at the time, in France and elsewhere (see for instance the books published in France by Bengel 2001 and in the USA by Jaeger 2003). The commercial targets were not the big banks, which were already launching the hedge fund activities, but smaller players that, according to Charles, were interested but 'scared'. In order to do this, we carried out interviews with major players in the field, and explored extensive documentation online and in specialized publications.

In their attempts to narrate a consistent overall view of hedge funds, to sell their own hedge fund and to make sense of their difficult professional situations, which they considered also a phenomenal opportunity, Charles and Julie tried to come to grips with the tension I described at the beginning of this chapter. They had to insist on the fact that hedge funds proposed new investment techniques, which allow for a different pattern of performance than the classic one based on MPT and CAPM. Yet, they considered that it was a taboo to claim that markets were never efficient, or that hedge fund managers allowed for a constant positive return. This latter point was impossible, Charles claimed, because he had never come across such a thing in his long experience. Julie, in turn, put forth a mathematical reason, following a precept of MPT: since prices move randomly, there is no systematic way to profit from them forever. Yet, these arguments had to be finely monitored. Julie had left the Compagnie Universelle with the software she developed as a hedge fund manager there, which she considered her 'own'.[8] The team was trying to find investors for it, based on its constant positive performance, which contrasted with the volatile result of the stock markets on which it invested.

The investment technique of long/short global equities fund created by Charles and Julie at the Compagnie Universelle was fully based on statistics. The fund had three equally weighted baskets invested in the USA, Europe and Japan. Currency exposure was hedged with swaps. Each basket was defined by 25 long positions and 25 short positions. The stocks were picked from the biggest indexes, and were all very liquid, based on large capitalizations. Julie explained that the large capitalizations composed 'a material' on which to operate; there was no individual stock picking by doing a personal analysis of the company's 'fundamental value'. The software would project onto the biggest capitalizations several methods of fundamental analysis, the variables for which were taken from the analyst consensus published by Bloomberg. The team explained that these numbers represented the compounded view of 7000 analysts which, in a rationale close to that of market efficiency theory, were less likely to be 'wrong' than a single analyst. This data, concerning expected returns, expected inflation, expected cash flow and so on, was plotted into different valuation models (discounted cash flow, book-to-value and so forth.). The result would indicate which method 'the market' was actually using in pricing the asset. It also indicated the future possible valuation of the asset according to analysts' expectations. The software then defined patterns of price variation for the stock in consideration, which gave it its position either as a long or a short, or as out of the investment.

In terms of CAPM and MPT, the model was both in and out of the theory. It used all the techniques of fundamental valuation in order to consider the reasons behind the current price of the asset. It diversified the investment along 50 securities, using short positions in a way that would not be disavowed by the financial theorists of market efficiency. Yet, it also attempted to find trends in pricing and to make bets on future price movements, something which, according to market efficiency hypothesis, leads nowhere.

The team also used the typical variables of CAPM to position itself. Each stock was defined in relation to its beta, that is its relation to 'the whole market'. This allowed the investment to be 'beta neutral', that is to have a beta=0 position, as the positive and negative betas of each stock cancelled each other out. This latter point was supposed to explain the independence of the fund's performance in relation to market price variations since, by construction, there could be no correlation with them. Yet, it puzzled the members of the team when they had to present the model. There were lengthy discussions within the team exploring several possible meanings of these concepts within MPT and CAPM. Since the beta was 0, the fund could be said to be independent of market variations, it was not 'market driven'. Yet, the construction of such a position used the betas of each stock. Another alternative approach would have been to study each stock, decide whether it is a long or a short, and end up with a beta=0 position. But this was not the team's approach. Betas were part of the investment process, that is the fund positioned itself in relation to 'the market', and was therefore not 'market neutral'. If the formulas and their mathematical interpretation (beta=0 means no relation to market variations, by construction) seemed clear, its positioning in relation to the imaginaries of hedge funds in the process of institutionalization was not. Either the fund claimed that markets were not efficient, and that there was a way to play against them: this was implied by the bets with the long and short positions and the capacity to change the stocks of the baskets along time; it was also implied by the idea that the fund would produce results that would tend to be positive most of the time, and less volatile than the market itself. Or the fund claimed that markets were efficient and that it was therefore justified to use CAPM and MPT and their related formulas. The first position appealed to Julie, who saw herself as a different kind of manager, but she rejected it in the name of random price movement. The second position seemed to defeat the whole purpose of the hedge fund: why go through such a lengthy process if, after all, CAPM and MPT taught that the best investment was to buy the whole market and keep it? The name of the fund, like that of many hedge funds, included the word alpha, which, within CAPM itself, means obtaining a return that is above that of the 'market' (cf. Holmes 2009). It is impossible to detail here all the tensions in the fund's position, not only because it would be too lengthy, but also because their most interesting aspect is that they were hard to grasp even the team members themselves.

This conundrum occupied several hours of the team's discussions, sometimes interrupted by Charles, claiming: 'we don't care about the real real truth of the markets! We just want to make money!' Yet, the seemingly existential or philosophical debate about 'market efficiency' was crucial exactly in order to reach the more worldly objectives. The team needed to position itself in relation to the hypothesis of efficient markets, and any position would entail commercial risks and opportunities.

We went to London to meet the sales representative of one of the major global investment banks, the Stainless Corporation. Julie made a half hour presentation of the models, the kind of logarithms used, making it clear that the investment process was both original and completely transparent. After 30 minutes, the sales representative told us that this would not open the doors to his institutional clients. At the moment, they were rejecting any quantitative approach. For the category of long/short global equities, they were only interested in fund managers doing the fundamental analysis of each of the stocks picked for the investment. We left the office with a sense of crushing defeat. Charles, with a humour not unrelated to a carefully designed aristocratic aesthetics, said in a detached and calmed voice: 'OK, we lost this client but now we know they don't want quantitative approaches. So next time we will say that our approach is essentially based on fundamental analysis ... after all, that is what we do.' Indeed, as I explained, the investment process involved exploring all the models of fundamental analysis to detect one which would correspond to the current price, and which would be considered as being the one 'used by the market'. This change of marketing strategy, nevertheless, implied again to reposition the place of the hypothesis of market efficiency in the definition of the fund, within a limited set of possibilities.

I left the team a little after that, without following their immediate evolutions, and only kept in casual contact with them over the years. They eventually secured a small investment of a few million euros from a major French broker. The broker invested its own money and attempted to be legally the owner of the hedge fund, as it was at the time of the Compagnie Universelle. Julie and Charles managed to resist this move, and kept looking for new sources of funding. Thus, without ever clarifying their position in relation to 'market efficiency', the team kept presenting the image of the individual hedge fund manager as a way to make sense of, and to market, their financial services within the network of the financial industry, on which their livelihood depended, and in which they first developed their investment strategies.

This example, like the discourses of the managers of funds of funds, shows that, within the financial industry, the concepts of the 'free investor' and of 'market efficiency' play a crucial role to make sense of the everyday operations of valuation and investment, and to justify personal careers and companies' strategies. But this does not happen as it is expected in the liberal theories from which these concepts stem, where 'investors' engage in 'efficient markets' producing 'representative prices' that can orient 'optimally' the allocation of social resources. In a context of transition and uncertainty, the actors mobilize all the available concepts and combine them in particular ways, which, in spite of sometimes quite visible contradictions, inconsistencies, or ambivalences, are workable enough to keep up with their operations and their career advancements.

Conclusion: market efficiency and the limits of financial imagination

The case of Alpha Consulting is interesting not because it is somehow representative of the financial industry but because of the way in which it reveals the plasticity of the theoretical, descriptive, and normative concept of market efficiency. According to this concept, the 'market' is composed of 'free investors' who maximize return by integrating information. Yet, the legal owners of the funds who entrust their money to the financial industry often have little knowledge of the technicalities of the investment and may even lack the legal entitlement to influence it (Clark 2000; Montagne 2006). They are 'investors' only insofar as they are represented by the employees to whom they entrust their money. And the latter are 'investors' insofar as they represent their clients' interests. The figure of the 'investor' is thus only realized in the act of its representation, in the use of financial formulas, in the everyday talk and self-comprehension of financial professionals, and in regulatory activity (Ortiz 2011). The mythology of independent hedge fund managers seems to embody this figure, since the fund manager is supposed to invest his own money and develop his own valuation approach. This partly accounts for the fascination and respect that hedge funds inspire within the financial industry, and for their image as something that is somewhat external to it. Yet, as we have seen, the majority of the structures labelled 'hedge funds' today are mainly investment vehicles, part of a new financial product called 'alternative investments', within this industry.

This by itself would cast doubt on the idea that financial flows constitute the 'markets' defined in liberal theory, that is, open arenas for free political subjects to interact. They are more like bureaucratic commercial networks (Clark and Thrift 2005), where employees attempt to advance their careers by playing with the margins left to them within the procedural norms which they have to follow (Zaloom 2006; Godechot 2007). Yet this is the frame in which most financial regulation occurs. It is also the frame that gives hedge funds an ambivalent role, which attracts so much attention. Hedge funds' role in generating 'financial crises' makes sense in terms of their role in disrupting 'market efficiency' (Ortiz 2012). Legal differences account for the concentration of hedge funds in certain jurisdictions, of course, and the history of economic and financial development accounts for the concentration of financial networks in specific hubs. But as the simple example of Alpha Consulting highlights, this frame is not specifically linked to a jurisdiction or 'national' tradition. MPT, CAPM and the mythology of the individual hedge fund expand across jurisdictions and financial constellations, within the multiple forms of the financial industry, in a commercial network that spans the whole world.

This case reveals that the theory of market efficiency, which frames most regulatory practices and even some critiques of hedge funds, does not really grasp their investment techniques. What is more, it does not provide for a consistent account of the role of hedge funds within the financial industry, which is more akin to that of an investment vehicle. By focusing the attention on hedge funds as independent and ambivalent 'investors', it thereby impedes addressing the ways in which the broader financial industry is responsible for their existence and their effects.

Notes

1 This process has been extensively documented; see, for instance, Abdelal (2007) for Europe, Kripner (2011) for the USA, Zhu (2009) for China, Reddy (2009) for India, and Amyx (2004) for Japan.
2 All of these company names are fictitious, to protect their identity.
3 This fieldwork was furthered by obtaining a diploma of financial analyst in 2010 and teaching courses of finance in business schools in Paris and Shanghai between 2008 and 2012. In agreement with the people I observed, and to preserve their anonymity, all names have been changed.
4 Some hedge funds do not accept more clients after reaching a certain funding limit.
5 The contract between the hedge fund and its clients may imply that they cannot disengage from the investment without heavy penalties.
6 An extreme example of this imaginary is an apologetic book, co-authored by Theys and Young (1999), that advocates dissolving states in favour of global financial markets composed of single individuals investing their own money. It treats hedge funds in a chapter entitled 'Power to the People' (1999: 114–47).
7 One of them did not participate systematically in these endeavours and I will not talk about him here.
8 Godechot (2007) has thoroughly analysed this kind of behaviour for traders.

References

Abdelal, R. (2007) *Capital Rules: The Construction of Global Finance*, Cambridge, MA: Harvard University Press.

Aglietta, M., Khanniche, S. and Rigot, S. (2010) *Les HEDGE FUNDS. Entrepreneurs ou requins de la finance?*, Paris: Perrin.

Amyx, J.A. (2004) *Japan's Financial Crisis: Institutional Rigidity and Reluctant Change*, Princeton: Princeton University Press.

Bengel, E. (2001) *La gestion alternative. Objectif: performance absolue*, Paris: Editions de Verneuils.

Clark, G.L. (2000) *Pension Fund Capitalism*, Oxford: Oxford University Press.

Clark, G.L. and Thrift, N. (2005) The Return of Bureaucracy: Managing Dispersed Knowledge in Global Finance, in K. Knorr Cetina and A. Preda (eds) *The Sociology of Financial Markets*, Oxford: Oxford University Press.

de Goede, M. (2005) *Virtue, Fortune and Faith: A Genealogy of Finance*, Minneapolis: University of Minnesota Press.

Godechot, O. (2007) *Working rich: salaires, bonus et appropriation du profit dans l'industrie financière*, Paris: La Découverte.

Hardie, I. and MacKenzie, D. (2007) Assembling an Economic Actor: the Agencement of a Hedge Fund, *Sociological Review*, 55(1): 57–80.

Holmes, C. (2009) Seeking Alpha or Creating Beta? Charting the Rise of Hedge Fund-Based Financial Ecosystems, *New Political Economy*, 14(4), 431–50.

Jaeger, R.A. (2003) *All About Hedge Funds: The Easy Way to Get Started*, New York: McGraw-Hill.

Krippner, G.R. (2011) *Capitalizing on Crisis: The Political Origins of the Rise of Finance*, Cambridge, MA: Harvard University Press.

Lee, R. (1998) *What is an Exchange? The Automation, Management, and Regulation of Financial Markets*, Oxford: Oxford University Press.

MacKenzie, D. (2003) Long-Term Capital Management and the Sociology of Arbitrage, *Economy and Society*, 32(3), 349–80.

MacKenzie, D. (2006) *An Engine not a Camera: How Financial Models Shape Markets*, Cambridge, MA: MIT Press.

Montagne, S. (2006) *Les fonds de pension. Entre protection sociale et spéculation financière*, Paris: Odile Jacob.

Ortiz, H. (2011) Marchés efficients, investisseurs libres et Etats garants: trames du politique dans les pratiques financières professionnelles, *Politix*, 2011/3: 155–80.

Ortiz, H. (2012) Anthropology – of the Financial Crisis, in J. Carrier (ed.), *Handbook of Economic Anthropology*, Cheltenham, UK and Northampton, MA: Edward Elgar.

Preda, A. (2009) *Framing Finance: The Boundaries of Markets and Modern Capitalism*, Chicago: University of Chicago Press.

Reddy, Y.V. (2009) *India and the Global Financial Crisis: Managing Money and Finance*, London: Anthem Press.

Rigot, S. (2010) La proposition de directive AIFM et les *hedge funds*: une analyse critique, paper presented at the seminar of the Association des Etudes Sociales de la Finance, preliminary version.

Theys, T. and Young, P. (1999) *Capital Market Revolution: The Future of Markets in an Online World*, Harlow: Pearson Education.

Zaloom, C. (2006) *Out of the Pits: Traders and Technology from Chicago to London*, Chicago: University of Chicago Press.

Zhu, M. (2009) China's Emerging Financial Industries and Implications, in M. Zhu, J. Cai and M. Avery (eds), *China's Emerging Financial Markets: Challenges and Global Impact*, Singapore: John Wiley & Sons (Asia).

11 Derivatives as weapons of mass deception and elite contestation

The case of FIAT

Andrea Lagna

Critical scholars on finance – especially those who contribute to the interdisciplinary debate on *financialization* – have advanced fascinating insights into the complex world of derivatives.[1] In so doing, they have questioned orthodox perspectives on derivatives according to which these instruments reflect the true essence of modern finance in its pursuit of market efficiency (Greenspan 2002). In contrast, critical researchers have shown how derivatives are inherently linked to capitalist exploitation and unstable financial cultures. The debate has taken two directions. On the one hand, some studies have explored how derivatives affect the present-day financialized capitalism. For instance, Bryan and Rafferty (2006) argue that derivatives represent a third degree of separation in the ownership of capital after the joint-stock form. If we take the case of a stock option, this instrument entitles the holder only to the price change in the underlying shares but not to the actual shares. This implies that derivatives holders become less concerned with events occurring in the field of production. Building on such argument, Wigan (2009) has shown that derivatives are like artifices of indifference because they make financialization disengage from the 'real' productive economy. On the other hand, scholars in the social studies of finance (SSF) field have uncovered the socio-cultural embeddedness of derivatives markets, agents and devices. For example, in a remarkable study, MacKenzie and Millo (2003) have captured the performativity of the Black-Scholes-Merton formula for pricing options through an ethnographic study of the Chicago Board Options Exchange. They have shown that the empirical success of this theory was due to the fact that traders used it in their activities on the pits. In short, options theory shaped the market in a performative manner.

Thus, critical scholars have proposed alternative views on derivatives that innovatively challenge the assumption that these contracts can produce a complete market in the sense given by Arrow and Debreu (1954).[2] This is certainly a laudable achievement. However, despite their original insights, *critical studies fall short of providing the appropriate analytical tools to explore the specificities of derivatives excesses in distinct contexts such as the Italian political economy.* This is the case for two main reasons. First, analyses that contextualize derivatives within the abstract contours of modern capitalism are geared towards explaining how these instruments expand the frontiers of global capital accumulation. Yet, they focus too much on the abstract features of finance-dominated growth and ultimately ignore what Nölke *et al.* (2013) define as the *politics* of financialization, namely: the actual actors and power struggles constructing financial developments on the ground. Thus this literature glosses over how *the global expansion of derivatives – or, more generally, financialization – essentially depends on the distinct conflicts in which key social forces are involved.* Second, the politics of financial innovation could be addressed through the heuristic framework of SSF. After all, scholars in this specialism seek to show how financial markets and models – far from being efficient and objective – are inherently driven by changing socio-cultural norms and conventions. Hence, at a first glance, this perspective could provide a useful understanding of financial agents and their pragmatic initiatives. However, SSF conflate actors and technologies within small-scale networks, often relying on the notion of performativity to explain how markets – together with the subjects involved – are produced through discursive reiteration. Consequently, this approach fails to appreciate the wider political-economic environment in which actors are situated and how key social forces might deploy derivatives for *strategic* purposes.

Against the shortcomings of the critical literature on derivatives, this chapter focuses particularly on the cultural-performative perspective and argues that the latter exemplifies a 'cultural turn' in political economy that does not account for the tactical scenario constraining – or enabling – the realization of any given performance (Sum and Jessop 2013). Pushed to its logical conclusion – a path which, as we will see, Foucauldian-inspired studies have taken (Aitken 2007; de Goede 2005; Langley 2009) – performativity implies that differences amongst agents are mostly irrelevant since it is through their *combined action* that financialized norms are performed and reproduced. The paradox is that, although the role of agency is recognized, the latter nonetheless lacks differential political-economic and socio-cultural leverage. In such analytical context, it is difficult to capture 'who', 'how' and 'why' adopts financialized practices – such as derivatives – differentially and tactically.

Premised on this critique, my chapter re-introduces *active* agency to the analytical picture in order to uncover the power struggles underpinning the growth of derivatives in the Italian context. By drawing on insights from Political Marxism (Knafo 2002, 2010, 2013) and Critical Institutionalism (Konings 2008, 2010b, 2011), this work conceives social construction as a fluid phenomenon in which historical agents interact with each other through the mediation of continuously renegotiated practices. In this historicized framework, people are seen as exerting power by exploiting extant materialities and meanings in the attempt to enhance their positions over others. However, far from structurally reifying human reality, contested praxis opens up opportunities to further transform existing inter-subjective rules.

Through these lenses, the study focuses on how Italian neoliberal-minded technocrats and centre-left politicians (henceforth neoliberal reformists) attempted to challenge the country's old political and business elites over the course of the 1990s.[3] They did so by implementing a market-oriented modernization of Italian capitalism, a crucial component of which was the shareholder-oriented transformation of the country's financial system – that is banking, securities markets and corporate governance (Cioffi and Hopner 2006; Deeg 2005). The work focuses particularly on the 'enabling' (Konings 2010b) character of these pro-market reforms and how they provided opportunities for the Agnellis – the founding family and historical blockholders of the car-manufacturer FIAT – to do exactly the opposite of what neoliberal reformists hoped for: to secure ownership over their business empire through the strategic use of equity swaps.

The chapter proceeds in six steps. First, it advances a critique of cultural-performative approaches in critical research on finance. Second, it comments briefly on derivatives as essential tools of tactical accounting deception. Third, it explores the political-economic and socio-cultural context in which neoliberal reformists emerged and began to put forward the necessity to modernize the domestic financial system from the mid-1990s onwards. Fourth, it focuses on the specificities of the corporate governance reform. Fifth, it examines the FIAT case and how the Agnelli family avoided diluting their ownership and control by using equity swaps. Finally, the chapter concludes in support of undertaking a cultural turn in the financialization debate that elucidates the political-strategic environment in which financial innovation thrives.

Underperforming cultures of finance

Critical research on finance is currently experiencing a cultural revival. Rather than focusing on the material and quantitative reality – as in the case of Régulation School (Boyer 2000), Post-Keynesian economics (Stockhammer 2008) and Marxist political economy (Lapavitsas 2009) – culture-oriented studies explore financial markets as domains constituted by conventional habits and discourses. In this regard, SSF scholars are doing much to uncover the construction of modern finance as experienced by practitioners in their daily activities (Beunza and Stark 2012; MacKenzie 2006; Preda 2009; Zaloom 2006). Far from depicting financial developments as abstract entities, they examine the microcosm of actors, technologies, no-nonsense practices and bricolage-like innovation producing such phenomena. For instance, MacKenzie and Millo (2003) deploy the notion of performativity to examine the extent to which options pricing theory was an empirical success not because it discovered pre-existing patterns, but because it performed – that is, moulded – markets in a way that increasingly fitted the model.[4]

Expanding on this notion of performing discourses and practices, other culture-oriented scholars such as Aitken (2007), De Goede (2005) and Langley (2009) draw on Butler (1997) and Foucault (1977) to explore how actors collectively create the dominant discourse of modern finance by performing it – that is, carrying it out – in their daily habits. This is obviously a more dense and pervasive understanding of performativity that incorporates society at a macro-level rather than being confined within the small-scale boundaries of trading floors, as is the case with SSF. For instance, Langley (2009) examines how people choose to invest in the stock market as a rational form of saving compared to using more traditional accounts at thrift institutions. Hence, by becoming a normal and largely unquestioned ensemble of everyday practices, present-day finance – with its complex and highly marketized activities – turns into an overarching apparatus that spreads its *disciplinary power* deep inside subjective identities. Following a similar understanding of discursive production in everyday life, de Goede (2005) examines the events concerning the enactment of the 2000 Hedge Fund Disclosure Act in the USA, following the collapse of the hedge fund Long-Term Capital Management in 1998. She argues that this regulatory framework did not represent a ban on hedge funds, but a *depoliticization* and *normalization* of their operations. In other words, authorities created a legitimate discursive environment for hedge funds to operate. Furthermore, the philosophy behind – such as the assumptions of derivatives trading as an efficient risk-management practice – represents the major contemporary discourse that legitimizes contemporary finance as a highly profitable business.

Thus, as these studies show, cultural-performative approaches are on the rise. This is a much-needed development in critical scholarship on finance for at least two reasons. First, it shows the importance of focusing on human agency as the architect and interpreter of hegemonic discourses (Amoore *et al.* 2000: 62–3). Second, it strongly asserts the significance of discursive phenomena in a field overly dominated by a materialist bent. However, as this chapter claims, such growing interest for the inter-subjective processes of meaning creation tends to obscure the strategic environment in which actors experience their existence. In fact, as Konings (2010b: 63) notes, culture-focused studies properly explore the semiotic constitution of subjectivities. Yet, what they fail to deploy is an understanding of discursive not only as shaping actors' identities but also as *enabling* their action. In particular, the extensive use of performativity analysis has the unfortunate effect of flattening social relations by transferring power from historically specific forces to the general discursive space the features of which constrain everyone in similar ways.[5] As a result of this – when applied to the Italian case or elsewhere – cultural-performative studies end up disregarding the fact that key actors do not merely adopt derivatives because the dominant financialized discourse condition them. On the contrary, *they often do so to advance their objectives against other agents in a tactical manner*. In other words, people aim at achieving context-specific aims by managing ever-present unintended events and by attempting to influence commonly shared norms.

To rectify such limitations in cultural studies of finance, this chapter calls for a more historicized approach to financial innovation and – in our specific case – derivatives. It advances a critical method that aims at capturing the tactical and conflictual character of people's discursive and material interaction.[6] Significantly, this perspective does not conceptualize power as structured in and through the discourses of financialization. On the contrary, power is introduced at the level of agency once discursive structures are recast as *mediating* social relations amongst actors (Knafo 2010: 504). In other words, actors interact with each other by negotiating complex discourses and materialities, continuously exploiting – or more simply, relating to – these interconnecting architectures. This radically alters our understanding of power, which becomes the agential ability to construct discursive norms and gain leverage in a particular scenario. In other words, power is interpreted at a pragmatic level where some agents experiment with extant institutions whilst others abandon their search for empowering themselves and live reality according to existing norms. Yet, far from reifying human reality, the process of structuration is constantly open to conflictual relations and transformation.

The following sections deploy this method to investigate first how Italian neoliberal-minded reformists attempted to challenge the country's old political and business elites by implementing a market-oriented modernization of Italian capitalism and, in particular, a shareholder-oriented transformation of the country's financial system. Next, the study focuses on the Agnelli family and their tactical use of derivatives. First, however, I reconsider derivatives as instruments of accounting dissimulation.

A brief excursus: financial derivatives as weapons of mass deception

Derivatives-like contracts existed for a long time (Swan 1999). Yet, it is only in the late-nineteenth-century USA that contracts on the future shipment of wheat were standardized into so-called *futures* and systematically disconnected from the final delivery of the underlying commodity. This innovation generated a surge in speculative activities that clashed with the interests of farmers and the rising populist movements (Geisst 2002: 4; Goodwyn 1976). At this point, facing agrarian forces, representatives of commodity exchanges recast derivatives trading and its speculative activities as essential resources for the management of business risk. In the end, this idea was institutionalized in such terms and the modern practices of derivatives-based risk management were eventually consolidated (Levy 2006).

Still, as long as the majority of derivatives were traded on organized commodity exchanges, derivatives-based techniques did not reveal their full potential. It was only in the early 1970s – once American power relations were turning in favour of finance (Gowan 1999; Panitch and Gindin 2008) – that Chicago exchanges successfully lobbied for the introduction of financial derivatives on their trading pits (MacKenzie 2006; MacKenzie and Millo 2003). In this regard, the discipline of financial economics provided scientific legitimacy by describing derivatives as tools that protect investors from the risk of financial market volatility (Wigan 2009).

During the 1970s, derivatives trading expanded but several regulatory uncertainties between the Commodity Futures Trading Commission (CFTC) and the Securities and Exchange Commission (SEC) still remained (Markham 2002: 88–9). Once these issues were solved in the early 1980s, derivatives grew in size and rate of innovation, becoming essential components of American financial power in the global economy (Konings 2006: 508–9). Three markets were particularly remarkable: index derivatives, asset-backed securities and, above all, swaps. According to the mainstream narrative, swaps emerged as useful instruments through which investors hedged their risk exposures to interest rates and exchange rates (Markham 2002: 192). That was true to a certain extent. But, at a non-rhetorical level, swaps became also *the perfect tools that companies, financial actors and governments can use to avoid regulation and to window-dress their books*. As Partnoy (2009: 46) explains in reference to the case of the historic investment bank Bankers Trust:

> Merton Miller's insight implied that companies would do swaps not necessarily because swaps allocated risk more efficiently, but rather because they were unregulated. They could do swaps in the dark, without the powerful sunlight that securities regulation shined on other financial instruments. And here was the crucial point: to the extent companies and their financial officers could use custom-tailored swaps to avoid regulation or to hide risks, Bankers Trust's profits from selling swaps to those companies might not disappear so quickly. Corporate treasurers hoping to benefit from such swaps would pay a premium – it wasn't their money, after all – if the swaps were structured in a way that created more opportunity for profit, but hid the risks from their bosses.

Over the course of the 1980s, as derivatives trading expanded, other societies also began to adopt these very useful 'weapons of mass deception' (Dunbar 2006; Norris 2013).[7] How and why were they used in the Italian context? Let us look particularly at the case study of FIAT and equity swaps.[8]

Modernizing Italian capitalism

In the early 1930s, Adolf Berle and Gardiner Means (1968: 8) famously described the most crucial development of American capitalism as 'the dissolution of the old atom of ownership into its component parts, control and beneficial ownership'. They argued that the consolidation of the joint-stock company implied a separation of corporate ownership and control such that a myriad of dispersed owners – the shareholders – emerged. Whilst diversifying their investment portfolios across several firms listed on the stock exchange, these shareholders exerted almost no control over the managers who ran day-to-day operations. The condition was such that the latter were potentially able to form a 'technostructure' through which they could consolidate their power over other social groups (Galbraith 2007). The research by Berle and Means became very influential and many studies focused on the various practices – such as independent boards of directors and the market for corporate control – that could make managers more accountable to shareholders (Grossman and Hart 1988; Jensen and Meckling 1976).

Contrary to the American case but like other European countries, Italian business was historically characterized by a relatively limited separation of ownership and control. In fact, Italy's economic history evolved through an ownership liaison between private business oligarchies and the expanding public enterprise (Segreto 1998). So the Italian story was not one in which dispersed shareholders should develop mechanisms to make strong managers accountable (Roe 1994). Rather, the problem concerned instead the presence of strong block-holders – state and oligarchs – influencing the activities of weak managers against the interests of unprotected minority shareholders (Melis 2000: 354).

Particularly from the late 1950s onwards, two intense forces – public and private capitalism – marked with their respective logics and points of friction the Italian political-economic arena. On the one hand, governing political parties – the alliance between Christian Democrats and Socialists – were concerned with controlling and driving the expansion of public enterprise as a way to guarantee their 'self-reproduction' (Bianchi 1987). In so doing, the dynamics of so-called *Partitocrazia* came into being, a condition in which the ruling parties eliminated any possibility for alternation in power and consolidated their clout over the state and society at large (Pasquino 1995). They politicized appointments in nearly every state-owned institution – from industry to banks, via schools, hospitals and post offices – through widespread networks of patronage and factional loyalty (Ginsborg 2001: 139–42). On the other hand, private business oligarchs necessitated of adequate solutions to protect their ownership structures against the expansion of the state-owned apparatus. As Barca (2001: 44–6) shows, the architectures of ownership in the private industry were so complex that they secured control even when the ownership quotas of blockholders decreased as a result of business expansion. Two mechanisms were indispensable for such condition to be achieved. The first one was the pyramidal group, in which two or more companies were legally separated but controlled by a holding through ownership chains. For instance, at the top of the pyramid sat the family-owned holding, whilst all the other companies had a mere subsidiary role. Of course, the voting rights of minority shareholders were dispersed over a large number of these subsidiary firms. The blockholders' shares were instead concentrated in the holding at the top of the pyramid. Second, besides these pyramidal constructions, cross-shareholding alliances were cultivated to further secure a narrow separation of ownership and control. In addition to these two mechanisms, several other artifices were adopted such as: including insurance companies as part of the pyramidal group in order to inject liquidity whenever it was needed; proxy votes with no obligations by the proxies to the principals; or the possibility for the management to refuse new shareholders as a protective measure against takeovers. Of course, the inefficient stock exchange and the absence of a transparent corporate governance regime completely sealed the power of blockholders over minority shareholders.

It was the imperative to hold such high degrees of ownership concentration in the hands of few actors – whilst at the same time maintaining open channels for external funding and corporate growth – that encouraged blockholders to gather around several gravitational centres of Italian capitalism (Segreto 1997: 649). Such meeting places were also crucial to cultivate the equilibria between private and state ownership. The most important hub was the Milan-based investment bank Mediobanca that – due to the peculiar public-private nature of its share-holding syndicate – mediated the conflictual dynamics between the oligarchies and the expanding state-owned enterprises. Above all, Mediobanca became the financial engineer for large private companies by providing funding strategies that also guaranteed the oligarchic structures of ownership and control (Batti-lossi 1991; Segreto 2008). As authoritative journalists labelled it, Mediobanca was the so-called *salotto buono* of Italy: the exclusive saloon where a clutch of business and political echelons managed tacitly the existing shareholding alliances (*Economist* 2010).

This private-public liaison reached its most collusive and corrupt essence during the 1980s. It is at this point that a pro-market technocratic elite – based primarily at the Bank of Italy and the Ministry of Treasury (Deeg 2005: 528) – launched a critique of the Italian political economy that exalted the benefits of reducing public debt (Giavazzi and Spaventa 1988), privatizing the state-owned sector (Goldstein 2003; Scognamiglio 1990) and, a few years later, modernizing the domestic financial system in favour of shareholder value (Amatori and Colli 2000; Associazione Disiano-Preite 1997; Lazonick and O'Sullivan 2000). Through their neoliberal critique of the Italian 'mixed' economy, technocrats aimed at undermining the foundations upholding conservative politics-cum-business affairs. To begin with, downsizing and privatizing the public enterprise implied hindering the normal reproduction of *Partitocrazia* that, as already mentioned, depended on the clientelistic exploitation of the state-owned apparatus. In addition, the objective of reducing public debt entailed removing government expenditure as an essential tool of mass consensus. In fact, especially during the Craxi administration (1983–1987), public spending was instrumental to creating an atmosphere of *enrichissez-vous* amongst large strata of privileged groups (Pasquino 2000: 79).

Regarding instead private capitalist oligarchies, the shareholder-oriented transformation of the financial system implied an attack on their concentrated structure of ownership and control. Especially during the 1980s, companies had turned towards equity finance after comprehensive strategies of industrial and financial restructuring (Amatori and Colli 2000; Graziani 1998). However, the stock-market expansion did not signal concrete transformation in the traditional strategies of ownership concentration. Indeed, it was the result of the long-established practice of pyramid-building through which major groups increased the number of related spin-offs listed on the stock exchange (Deeg 2005: 528). Hence, more transparent rules of corporate governance, as well as an efficient and liquid equity markets, would have ensured equality of rights amongst share-holders and less opportunities to weave cross-shareholding alliances. In a word, a growing call for meritocracy in corporate ownership and control endangered the traditional practices of private capitalism in Italy (McCann 2000: 49–50).

The neoliberal ideas put forward by technocrats became influential in the late 1980s and early 1990s, when the process of European integration revealed a new impetus with the launch of the single market and the project of monetary union.

In a context where the political-economic establishment and the popular discourse were supportive of Europe in a general sense (Quaglia 2011), crucial reforms were introduced such as the removal of capital controls, the transformation of public banks into joint-stock companies and the independence of the central bank.[9] Above all, technocrats gained considerable power over the policy contents during the intergovernmental conference (IGC) on EMU. In February 1992, by adhering to the convergence criteria for joining EMU, they imposed an external discipline on the country's vested interests and their reproductive capacities (Dyson and Featherstone 1996). Of course, technocrats gradually advanced practices that disturbed the reproduction of the status quo in Italian capitalism. Yet, these tactics were insufficient to dismantle long-established power structures, both in their political and business dimension. In reality, it was only when the bribery scandals of *Tangentopoli* exploded in February 1992 that the traditional political system – with most part of its business connections – began to collapse.[10] From this moment onwards, technocrats together with the centre-left coalition of the Olive Tree – who got to power in 1996 – captured the executive power and embarked on an extensive season of liberalizing reforms with the objective of joining EMU in 1999 (Cioffi and Hopner 2006; Deeg 2005). In particular, they normalized labour relations in order to curb inflation and cut down government expenditure to stabilize public finance (Sbragia 2001: 81). Furthermore, they undertook a far-reaching privatization programme (Goldstein 2003) and – more importantly for our purposes – they attempted to transform Italian finance in line with the ideology of shareholder value. This was done in order to eradicate the oligarchic structure of Italian business. Let us now focus on the main traits of this financial modernization.

The shareholder-oriented transformation of Italian corporate governance

The shareholder-oriented transformation of Italian finance entailed constructing a regime of corporate governance that favoured the dispersion of ownership as well as the development of a liquid and efficient stock market. In other words, this strategy was coherent with the objective of diluting the long-lasting oligarchic nature of Italian business in the attempt to render it more reactive to global market inputs and innovation. As Massimo D'Alema – a leading figure of the centre-left – explained, 'we still have not done enough to create a proper financial market ... We do not have guarantees for small shareholders, no rules for public companies' (Betts and Blitz 1997).

As Lazonick and O'Sullivan (2000) show, the ideology of shareholder value originated in the historical evolution of American corporate capitalism, particularly once the latter fully unleashed the dynamics of financialization after the 1970s crisis. At its core stands a large and transparent stock market that functions as a source of business investment and corporate control for public companies. In a given company, dispersed and legally protected shareholders – primarily institutional investors – are the ultimate owners. These actors delegate to the board of directors the task of monitoring the managers who are in charge of directing the company's day-to-day activities – e.g. investment, production, pricing, marketing and so on. In other words, managers are accountable to the board of directors and, ultimately, to the shareholders who have the voting power to select the board. The crucial point of this shareholder-oriented regime of corporate governance is the following: once the management fails to deliver profits and dividends, shareholders exercise their power at the general meeting and vote for a new board of directors and management. However, in reality, shareholders are too fragmented to exercise this control vis-à-vis the management and the passive board of directors. In this case, the market for corporate control enters the picture. Shareholders could show their dissatisfaction by selling the company's shares and, in turn, depressing the share price accordingly. At this point, the company turns into an attractive target for takeover strategies. Potential bidders buy up shares of the target company in order to take control of the board and replace the top management. In this sense, the market for corporate control disciplines the managers by pushing them to maximize shareholder value, otherwise they would succumb to hostile takeovers (Clarke 2007: 130–1).

Applied to Italy, this simple story concerning shareholder value promised a profound impact on the national business establishment. To be exact, as already seen, the historical rationale of Italian capitalism was rather different than the Anglo-American experience. In Italy, strong blockholders – such as the oligarchs and the state – influenced the activities of collusive managers against the interests of unprotected minority shareholders. Yet, as McCann (2000: 49–50) clearly explains:

> A properly functioning capital market with strong institutional investors would ensure a greater equality of rights between shareholders, thus undermining the capacity of [blockholders] to gain a dominant control of firms despite possessing only minority holdings. The marginalization of cross-shareholding alliances would greatly increase the feasibility of successful takeover bids and thus intensify the pressure on management to deliver higher profitability and larger dividends ... This would serve to enhance economic efficiency and contribute to a growing meritocracy of ownership and control.

Italian liberal intellectuals had for a long time advanced the importance of reforming Italian company law to prevent the formation of blockholders (Marchetti 2001). Yet, despite these influential opinions, it was particularly during the 1990s that the political-economic and cultural climate turned conducive to introducing the institutions and discourses of shareholder value. The major push to corporate governance reforms came from the process of privatization. Indeed, the 1994 privatization law was important in two respects.[11] First, by introducing norms that protected minority shareholders in the soon-to-be privatized companies, neoliberal reformists were free to experiment without any particular resistance from the blockholders of existing private companies. Second, it created a contrast between privatized companies and other listed firms that did not conform with a transparent governance structure (Enriques 2009: 7).

Concrete action towards a comprehensive reform of corporate governance was taken in 1996, when the Parliament delegated to the executive the power to transfer several EU directives into the Italian legislation.[12] Besides importing the European Capital Adequacy Directive and the Investment Services Directive, the Parliament gave the government also the task to consolidate financial market regulation into a single law.[13] According to the provision, the government had to 'amend the laws on listed corporations with specific regard to the board of internal auditors, minority shareholder rights, shareholder voting agreements and intra-group transactions, with a view to strengthen the protection of savings and minority shareholders' (Enriques 2009: 9). Hence, in order to undertake this task, the Treasury established a technical committee under the leadership of Director-General Mario Draghi. This decision was controversial. In fact, influential voices complained that such an important reform was being implemented behind closed doors and away from a wider political debate (Scalfari 1997). Hence, an enquiry was opened at the lower house of the Parliament in October 1997 (Lonardi 1997). The 'Draghi' reform – as it was soon nicknamed – met the opposition of the centre-right and Confindustria, the major business association. In particular, the issue of mandatory takeover bids was the most controversial point (Puledda 1998a; Repubblica 1998; Scalfari 1998). However, in spite of such resistance, the reform was eventually passed in late February 1998 and came to be known as the consolidated law on finance (*Testo Unico della Finanza*, TUF).[14]

TUF envisioned a new regime of corporate governance in favour of shareholder value. It was an 'omnibus law that aggregated, reformulated and renewed virtually all civil and criminal rules pertaining to capital markets, securities management, institutional investors, brokerage services, public offerings and rules for listed joint stock corporations' (Deeg 2005: 534). Amongst the key points, the following ones were particularly significant.[15] First, the reform increased the protection of minority shareholders through a tighter regulation of shareholder agreements. The latter had to be notified publicly; they could not exceed three years; they were no longer valid in the case of takeover bids (Amatori and Colli 2000: 43). These measures hit the core of those cross-shareholding practices which blockholders traditionally used to consolidate their relations of mutual trust (McCann 2000: 51–2). Furthermore, mandatory takeover bids became compulsory once exceeding 30 per cent of the total capital (Puledda 1998b). Second, minority shareholders – identified according to a minimum ownership ranging from 1 to 10 per cent of the outstanding shares – obtained more governance rights. Third, representation of minority shareholders was mandatory at the audit board, the internal body in charge of auditing activities. Finally, the reform reinforced the power of Commissione Nazionale per la Società e la Borsa (CONSOB), the national stock market authority. CONSOB was put in charge of supervising investor protection, the efficiency and transparency of the stock market, and the effective functioning of the market for corporate control.

CONSOB could now request ad-hoc information and undertake on-site inspections concerning shareholder agreements and blockholding practices.

Needless to say, the Draghi reform emphasized the importance of the stock market in a country where equity finance had traditionally played a marginal role.[16] In fact, whilst the Draghi committee was drafting the reform of corporate governance, the various national stock exchanges merged in the Milan-based Borsa which was then privatized and began to operate as BorsaItaliana in January 1998 (BorsaItaliana 1999). In a context where declining interest rates made government securities a less attractive form of investment for the wider public, people looked at the stock market with enthusiasm (Betts 1997). In particular, the flotation of the recently privatized Telecom Italia mirrored the frenzy for the dot-com bubble in the United States (Rampini 1997).

How to hedge the risk of ownership dilution: FIAT and equity swaps

How far did corporate governance reforms transform Italian capitalism into a shareholder democracy? How did the oligarchies react to such a different regulatory environment? It is now time to look at a unique case of market manipulation that shows how the new corporate governance regime did not simply constrain business oligarchies, but also enabled them to use the new institutions and discourses in a strategic sense. The following case concerns the car-manufacturer FIAT and its founding family: the Agnellis.[17]

In a context of dramatic crisis, FIAT entered a three-year convertible bond of €3 billion with a consortium of eight banks in 2002.[18] As a hybrid of debt and equity, this instrument allowed the holder to convert the bond into the issuing company's stocks – or cash of equal value – at an agreed-upon price. The FIAT's convertible bond had a maturity date that was set for September 2005. More importantly, in the case of insolvency, the bond was to be converted into FIAT shares at a price of €10.3. This conversion implied dramatic consequences for the ownership structure of FIAT. In fact, the 30.6 per cent ownership of the holding Ifil Investments in FIAT – Ifil was controlled by IFI (62 per cent), which was in turn entirely owned by the Agnelli family through the partnership Giovanni Agnelli & Co. S.a.p.az. – would have been diluted of roughly one-third in favour of the banks.

In fact, the worst happened. FIAT announced on 26 April, 2005 – less than five months before maturity – that the convertible bond was going to be converted into shares. In other words, this was a historic event for Italian capitalism: the Agnelli empire was on the verge of collapse after a century of oligarchic control over FIAT. However, the family found an astute strategy to remain in the 'driving seat' (Economist 2005). The very same day when the bond conversion was announced, Exor Group – a Luxembourg-based financial holding which was controlled by the Agnelli family via IFI – entered into an equity swap contract with Merrill Lynch International on €90 million of FIAT ordinary shares.[19] An equity swap would normally be settled in cash. However, the contract between

Exor Group and Merrill Lynch included a clause that allowed also the physical settlement. Neither the investing public nor CONSOB were informed about this operation, except for a communiqué on 24 August, 2005 in which Ifil and Giovanni Agnelli & Co. told CONSOB that no particular manoeuvre on FIAT shares was occurring. In this dispatch, Ifil and Giovanni Agnelli & Co. nonetheless stated that they intended to keep control of FIAT (Boffano and Griseri 2010).

How does an equity swap specifically work? This is a derivative contract in which future cash flows are agreed to be exchanged between two counterparties – respectively known as the equity amount payer and the equity amount receiver – at specific interim dates or in a single maturity date in the future. The equity amount payer transfers to the equity amount receiver the positive difference between i) the spot value of the equity and ii) the initial reference price agreed on the contract. On the contrary, the equity amount receiver pays any potentially negative difference between these two elements. On top of this dimension which is typical of an equity future, the two parties enter into a further reciprocal obligation that is the swap element: the payer transfers to the receiver also the dividends generated by the equities in question, whilst receiving an interest rate (e.g. LIBOR or EURIBOR) on the notional capital equal to the value of equities at the moment of the agreement.

In our case, the equity amount payer Merrill Lynch would have paid the equity amount receiver Exor Group the positive performance in relation to the initial reference price of the underlying equity plus the dividends. Merrill Lynch would have instead received from Exor Group the negative performance together with an interest rate on the notional capital – which is equal to the initial reference price multiplied by the number of underlying shares. After this agreement was signed, Merrill Lynch started to hedge by buying the underlying shares. In line with this hedging strategy, Merrill Lynch bought shares on the stock market from April to June 2005, accounting for the 15 per cent of daily trading and 10 per cent of FIAT's voting capital. Accordingly, FIAT's share price rose from €4.8 to €6. In accordance with the Italian regulation on takeovers, Merrill Lynch communicated that its ownership had reached the 2 per cent threshold but never 5 per cent.[20] How was it possible to hide the remaining share of FIAT's voting capital that Merrill Lynch owned?

The investment bank never exceeded the 5 per cent level by 'swapping out' – that is, entering a reverse contract compared to the one with Exor Group – with two other counterparts, ING bank and Cater Allen International, for a total of 6.5 per cent of FIAT's voting shares. Being in this case the equity amount receiver, Merrill Lynch entered these secondary equity swaps with ING and Cater Allen by transferring to the latter the underlying shares as credit risk collaterals.[21] Hence, both banks also declared they went beyond the 2 per cent threshold. In other words, this is all the market and CONSOB perceived during the period between April and September: three global investment banks merely exceeded the 2 per cent threshold in FIAT's ownership.

In September 2005, when FIAT's convertible bond finally expired, Merrill Lynch had already settled in cash the secondary equity swaps with ING and

Cater Allen. At this point, the investment bank bought back the collaterals that were then transferred to Exor Group. Indeed, as already mentioned, the equity swap contained the clause of physical settlement. Eventually, Exor Group bilaterally sold these shares to Ifil, of which participation in FIAT's ownership went simultaneously down to the 30 per cent threshold – due to the convertible bond's agreement – and up the same level as a result of the shares received by Merrill Lynch and its complex equity-swap strategy.

At that time, few voices denounced the Agnellis' abuse of the most basic rules of shareholder democracy (Bragantini 2005; Penati 2005). In fact, the authorities intervened very late and the case gained momentum only in early 2007, when the Milan court began investigating the affair and CONSOB imposed sanctions on the top management of IFI and Ifil (Repubblica 2007). The main issue at stake concerned the communiqué that Ifil and Giovanni Agnelli & Co. released in late August 2005. Indeed, the latter did not disclose information about the equity swap between Exor Group and Merrill Lynch, therefore constituting an infringement of the current regulation on market communication and market manipulation.[22] In the end, the investigation was transferred to the court of Turin, the city where the Agnelli family is based. Here, the top management of IFI and Ifil was first acquitted in December 2010 and eventually condemned in February 2013 (Boffano and Griseri 2010; Repubblica 2013). In the meantime, the case sparked a debate within CONSOB about how to prevent bidders from accumulating undisclosed equity positions through cash-settled derivatives. These discussions led CONSOB to modify the rules of transparency concerning potential shareholdings with cash settlement. Investors are now obliged to communicate also their positions on cash-settled derivatives.[23]

Conclusions

This chapter has argued that cultural-performative studies on financialization do not take into account the strategic scenario constraining – or enabling – the realization of any given agential performance (Sum and Jessop 2013). Paradoxically, although this approach could provide a prolific conceptualization of financial actors and their tactics, it is still unable to properly capture the power struggles underpinning the global expansion of derivatives and financialization more broadly – an aspect that brings cultural-performative research closer to more abstract-structuralist views on derivatives (Bryan and Rafferty 2006; Wigan 2009). To rectify such limitations, the chapter has aimed at bringing agency back to uncover the conflictual relations shaping the use of derivatives in the Italian context. To do so, it has drawn on insights from Political Marxism (Knafo 2002, 2010, 2013) and Critical Institutionalism (Konings 2008, 2010b, 2011) with the objective of emphasizing how inter-subjective meanings not only influence actors' identities but also enable them to act.

By using this method, the study has examined the shareholder-oriented modernization of Italian finance as a strategy that neoliberal reformists implemented in order to challenge old political and business elites during the 1990s (Cioffi and Hopner 2006; Deeg 2005). After this, the work focused on how these pro-market reforms enabled the Agnelli family to secure ownership over FIAT through the tactical use of equity swaps.

Notes

1 The financialization debate examines 'the increasing role of financial motives, financial markets, financial actors and financial institutions in the operation of the domestic and international economies' (Epstein 2005: 3). Useful introductions to the debate include special issues of: *Economy & Society*, 29(1) 2000; *Competition & Change*, 12(2) 2008 and 13(2) 2009.
2 According to this orthodox view, myriads of derivatives contracts – both plain vanilla and more complex synthetic combinations – enable all possible future states of the world to be captured by being traded on the basis of risk. For a critical examination of this thesis, see Wigan (2008, 2009).
3 The terms 'neoliberal-minded', 'neoliberal' or 'neoliberalism' denote the ideology according to which 'human well-being can best be advanced by liberating individual entrepreneurial freedoms and skills within an institutional framework characterized by strong private property rights, free markets, and free trade' (Harvey 2005: 2). Of course, the emphasis on the free market and the retreat of the state is a rhetorical matter. In reality, neoliberal forces capture state institutions and exploit them to secure their discipline over society (Konings 2010a). 'Technocrat' refers here to experts in specific fields – e.g. economics, law and so on – who apply their knowledge to government affairs either as technical advisers or unelected decision-makers (Silva 2008).
4 Language philosopher John L. Austin (1962) initially developed the concept of performativity. He described as performative those 'self-actualizing' statements that do not simply state facts, but enact what they name in the first place (e.g. a promise). Callon (1998) later explored the performativity of economics and inspired SSF scholars to deal with such notion in their work.
5 Compare Foucault (1977: 176), who sees the latter as a 'multiple, automatic and anonymous' network.
6 This proposition has some similarities with the work of Sum and Jessop (2013; see also this volume). However, whereas they build on a critical-realist ontology and epistemology, this chapter maintains a subjective-constructivist stance that is grounded in Hegelian phenomenology and dialectics. For an entry point on this philosophical position and its significance within historical-materialist studies, see Fraser (1997) and Knafo (2002).
7 Warren Buffett (2003) once defined derivatives as 'financial weapons of mass destruction'. In contrast, this study highlights their potentials for deceiving and concealing accounting rules.
8 This work deals specifically with FIAT. Two other important examples of derivatives excesses in Italy are: (1) the Italian government's use of derivatives markets to comply with the Maastricht criteria; (2) local authorities' adoption of interest rate swaps to circumvent the European Stability and Growth Pact. For a full analysis of these other two case studies, see Dunbar (2000), Lagna (2013) and Piga (2001).
9 About these reforms, cf. respectively ministerial decree 27 April 1990 at www. dt.tesoro.it/export/sites/sitodt/modules/documenti_it/prevenzione_reati_finanziari/ normativa/DM-27-aprile-1990.pdf; law no. 218, 30 July 1990, available at: www.nor-mattiva.it; law no. 82, 7 February 1992, available at: www.normattiva.it (all accessed on 28 February 2014).
10 About these reforms, cf. respectively ministerial decree 27 April 1990 at www. dt.tesoro.it/export/sites/sitodt/modules/documenti_it/prevenzione_reati_finanziari/

normativa/DM-27-aprile-1990.pdf; law no. 218, 30 July 1990, available at: www.nor-mattiva.it; law no. 82, 7 February 1992, available at: www.normattiva.it (all accessed on 28 February 2014).

11 Cf. law no. 474, 30 July 1994, available at www.normattiva.it (accessed on 28 February 2014).

12 Cf. law no. 52, 6 February 1996, available at: www.normattiva.it/ (accessed on 1 March 2014).

13 Cf. *ibid.*, capitolo II, art. 21, 4, available at: www.normattiva.it/. The Capital Adequacy Directive (Directive 93/6/EEC, 15 March 1993) and the Investment Service Directive (Directive 93/22/EEC 10 May 1993) were imported into Italian law through the law decree no. 415, 23 July 1996, available at: www.normattiva.it/ (all accessed on 1 March 2014).

14 Cf. law decree no. 58, 24 February 1998, available at: www.normattiva.it/ (accessed on 1 March 2014).

15 Unless otherwise referenced, the following summary of the 'Draghi' reform is based on Enriques (2009: 9–11).

16 It is important to note that when the 'Draghi' reform was enacted, shareholder value had become a major objective also in Europe. About the market-oriented transformation of European corporate control, see van Appeldoorn and Horn (2007). This dimension was embedded in the wider process of European financial market integration (Bieling 2003; Mügge 2008).

17 For histories of the Agnelli family and FIAT's crucial role in Italian capitalism, see Castronovo (2005) and Clark (2011).

18 Unless otherwise referenced, my analysis of the FIAT-equity swap events is based on de Nova *et al.* (2010: 9–11). This is the transcript of a debate with Italian experts on derivatives, including Giovanni Portioli from the Insider Trading Department of CONSOB.

19 Exor Group merged with Ifil and IFI in February 2009, forming Exor S.p.A. Today, Exor is the key investment holding that controls FIAT S.p.A. and FIAT Industrial. See: www.exor.com/ (accessed on 28 February 2014).

20 Cf. law decree no. 58, 24 February 1998, articles 102–112, available at: www.normattiva.it/ (accessed on 1 March 2014).

21 As explained in de Nova *et al.* (2010: 9–10), each participant in an equity swap is subject to a credit risk exposure to the counterpart. If the underlying share rises in price, the equity payer must make a payment in relation to the increase. Conversely, if the underlying share falls, the equity payer is entitled to a payment. Regarding these secondary equity swaps with ING and Cater Allen, Merrill Lynch was the equity swap receiver rather than the payer, as occurred with the principal swap with Exor Group. Thus, when the stock price fell, there was credit risk to the equity payer (ING and Cater Allen) and vice versa. Hence, both ING and Cater Allen mitigated such credit risk by asking the underlying shares as collateral in line with their price movements. For this reason, Merrill Lynch regularly lodged FIAT shares with ING and Cater Allen.

22 Cf. law decree no. 58, 24 February 1998, articles 114 (par. 7) and 187-ter, available at: www.normattiva.it/ (accessed on 1 March 2014).

23 Cf. regulation no. 17919, 9 September 2011, available at: www.consob.it/main/aree/novita/consultazione_emittenti_20110909_esiti.htm (accessed on 28 February 2014).

References

Aitken, R. (2007) *Performing Capital: Toward a Cultural Economy of Popular and Global Finance*, New York: Palgrave Macmillan.

Amatori, F. and Colli, A. (2000) *Corporate Governance: The Italian Story*, Fontaine-bleau: European Institute of Business Administration (INSEAD).

Amoore, L., Dodgson, R., Germain, R.D., Gills, B.K., Langley, P. and Watson, I. (2000) Paths to a Historicized International Political Economy, *Review of International Political Economy*, 7(1): 53–71.

Arrow, K. and Debreu, G. (1954) Existence of an Equilibrium for a Competitive Economy, *Econometrica*, 22(3): 265–90.

Associazione Disiano-Preite (ed.) (1997) *Rapporto Sulla Società Aperta. Cento Tesi Per La Riforma Del Governo Societario in Italia*, Bologna: Il Mulino.

Austin, J.L. (1962) *How to Do Things with Words*, Oxford: Clarendon Press.

Barca, F. (2001) Compromesso Senza Riforme nel Capitalismo Italiano, in F. Barca (ed.), *Storia del Capitalismo Italiano*, Roma: Donzelli, 3–115.

Battilossi, S. (1991) L'Eredità Della Banca Mista. Sistema Creditizio, Finanziamento Industriale e Ruolo Strategico Di Mediobanca 1946–1956, *Italia Contemporanea*, 185: 627–53.

Berle, A.A. and Means, G.C. (1968) *The Modern Corporation and Private Property*, San Diego, CA: Harcourt.

Betts, P. (1997) The Bourse. Market 'Half the Size It Should Be', *Financial Times*, 10 December.

Betts, P., and Blitz, J. (1997) At the Head of Italy's Table. The FT Interview: Massimo D'Alema, *Financial Times*, 22 December.

Beunza, D. and Stark, D. (2012) From Dissonance to Resonance: Cognitive Interdependence in Quantitative Finance, *Economy & Society*, 41(3): 383–417.

Bianchi, P. (1987) The IRI in Italy: Strategic Role and Political Constraints, *West European Politics*, 10(2): 269–90.

Bieling, H.-J. (2003) Social Forces in the Making of the New European Economy: The Case of Financial Market Integration, *New Political Economy*, 8(2): 203–24.

Boffano, E. and Griseri, P. (2010) Processo Ifil-Exor, Tutti Assolti 'Non C'è Stato *Aggiotaggio'*, *La Repubblica*, 21 December, http://torino.repubblica.it/cronaca/2010/12/21/news/efil-exor_tutti_assolti-10442945/, accessed on 2 March 2014.

BorsaItaliana (1999) *Fatti e Cifre Della Borsa Italiana, 1998.* www.borsaitaliana.it/borsaitaliana/statistiche/tuttelestatistiche/fattiecifre/fattiecifre1998.htm, accessed on 28 February 2014.

Boyer, R. (2000) Is a Finance-led Growth Regime a Viable Alternative to Fordism? A Preliminary Analysis, *Economy & Society*, 29(1): 111–45.

Bragantini, S. (2005) Se l'Equity Swap Dribbla la Comunicazione, *LaVoce.info*, 25 September, http://archivio.lavoce.info/articoli/pagina1756.html, accessed on 1 March 2014.

Bryan, D. and Rafferty, M. (2006) *Capitalism with Derivatives. A Political Economy of Financial Derivatives, Capital and Class*, Basingstoke: Palgrave Macmillan.

Buffett, W.E. (2003) Chairman's Letter, *Berkshire Hathaway Annual Report 2002*, www.berkshirehathaway.com/2002ar/2002ar.pdf, accessed on 8 September 2013.

Butler, J. (1997) *Excitable Speech: A Politics of the Performative*, New York: Routledge.

Callon, M. (ed.) (1998) *The Laws of the Markets*, Oxford: Blackwell.

Castronovo, V. (2005) *FIAT: Una Storia del Capitalismo Italiano*, Milano: Rizzoli.

Cioffi, J. W. and Hopner, M. (2006) The Political Paradox of Finance Capitalism: Interests, Preferences, and Center-Left Party Politics in Corporate Governance Reform, *Politics and Society*, 34(4): 463–502.

Clark, J. (2011) *Mondo Agnelli: Fiat, Chrysler, and the Power of a Dynasty*, Hoboken, NJ: John Wiley & Sons.

Clarke, T. (2007) *International Corporate Governance: A Comparative Approach.* London and New York: Routledge.

Deeg, R. (2005) Remaking Italian Capitalism? The Politics of Corporate Governance Reform, *West European Politics*, 28(3): 521–48.

Dunbar, N. (2000) *Inventing Money: The Story of Long-Term Capital Management and the Legends Behind It*, New York: Wiley.

Dunbar, N. (2006) Risky Finance: Weapons of Mass Deception, *www.nickdunbar.net*, www.nickdunbar.net/articles-and-reviews/risky-finance-weapons-of-mass-deception/, accessed on 1 March 2014.

Dyson, K. and Featherstone, K. (1996) Italy and EMU as a 'Vincolo Esterno': Empowering the Technocrats, Transforming the State, *South European Society and Politics*, 1(2): 272–99.

Economist (2005) Still In the Driving Seat, *The Economist*, 13 October. www.economist.com/node/5026856, accessed on 21 February 2014.

Economist (2010) Ties That Bind Mediobanca's Grip on Generali Shows the Effects of Cross-Shareholdings, *The Economist*, 18 March, www.economist.com/node/15731244, accessed on 21 February 2014.

Enriques, L. (2009) *Modernizing Italy's Corporate Governance Institutions: Mission Accomplished?*, Brussels: European Corporate Governance Institute.

Epstein, G.A. (2005) Introduction: Financialization and the World Economy, in G.A. Epstein (ed.), *Financialization and the World Economy*, Cheltenham: Edward Elgar.

Foucault, M. (1977) *Discipline and Punish. The Birth of the Prison*, New York: Vintage Books.

Fraser, I. (1997) Two of a Kind: Hegel, Marx, Dialectic and Form, *Capital & Class*, 21(1): 81–106.

Galbraith, J.K. (2007) *The New Industrial State*, Princeton, NJ: Princeton University Press.

Geisst, C.R. (2002) *Wheels of Fortune: The History of Speculation from Scandal to Respectability*, Hoboken, NJ: Wiley.

Giavazzi, F. and Spaventa, L. (eds) (1988) *High Public Debt: The Italian Experience*, Cambridge: Cambridge University Press.

Ginsborg, P. (2001) *Italy and Its Discontents, 1980–2001*, London: Penguin Books.

De Goede, M. (2005) *Virtue, Fortune, and Faith: A Genealogy of Finance*, Minneapolis, MN: University of Minnesota Press.

Goldstein, A. (2003) *Privatization in Italy 1993–2002: Goals, Institutions, Outcomes, and Outstanding Issues*, Munich: CESifo Group.

Goodwyn, L. (1976) *Democratic Promise: The Populist Moment in America*, Oxford: Oxford University Press.

Gowan, P. (1999) *The Global Gamble: Washington's Faustian Bid for World Dominance*, London: Verso.

Graziani, A. (1998) *Lo Sviluppo dell'Economia Italiana. Dalla Ricostruzione Alla Moneta Europea*, Torino: Bollati Boringhieri.

Greenspan, A. (2002) International Financial Risk Management, *The Federal Reserve Board. Remarks by Chairman Alan Greenspan before the Council on Foreign Relations, Washington, D.C.* www.federalreserve.gov/boarddocs/speeches/2002/20021119, accessed on 8 September 2013.

Grossman, S.J. and Hart, O.D. (1988) One Share-One Vote and the Market for Corporate Control, *Journal of Financial Economics*, 20: 175–202.

Harvey, D. (2005) *A Brief History of Neoliberalism*, Oxford: Oxford University Press.

Jensen, M.C. and Meckling, W.H. (1976) Theory of the Firm, Managerial Behaviour, Agency Costs and Ownership Structure, *Journal of Financial Economics*, 3(4): 305–60.

Knafo, S. (2002) The Fetishizing Subject in Marx's Capital, *Capital and Class* 76: 145–75.

Knafo, S. (2010) Critical Approaches and the Legacy of the Agent/Structure Debate in International Relations, *Cambridge Review of International Affairs*, 23(3): 493–516.

Knafo, S. (2013) *The Making of Modern Finance: Liberal Governance and the Gold Standard*, London: Routledge.

Konings, M. (2006) The Rise of American Finance. Agency, Institutions and Structural Power from Colonial Times to the Globalization Era, PhD Thesis, Toronto: York University.

Konings, M. (2008) The Institutional Foundations of US Structural Power in International Finance: From the Re-emergence of Global Finance to the Monetarist Turn, *Review of International Political Economy*, 15(1): 35–61.

Konings, M. (2010a) Neoliberalism and the American State, *Critical Sociology*, 36(5): 741–65.

Konings, M. (2010b) The Pragmatic Sources of Modern Power, *European Journal of Sociology*, 51(1): 55–91.

Konings, M. (2011) *The Development of American Finance*, Cambridge: Cambridge University Press.

Lagna, A. (2013) Deriving a Normal Country. Italian Capitalism and the Political Economy of Financial Derivatives, PhD Thesis, Brighton: University of Sussex.

Langley, P. (2009) *The Everyday Life of Global Finance: Saving and Borrowing in Anglo-America*, Oxford: Oxford University Press.

Lapavitsas, C. (2009) Financialised Capitalism: Crisis and Financial Expropriation, *Historical Materialism*, 17: 114–48.

Lazonick, W. and O'Sullivan, M. (2000) Maximizing Shareholder Value: A New Ideology for Corporate Governance, *Economy and Society*, 29(1): 13–35.

Levy, J.I. (2006) Contemplating Delivery: Futures Trading and the Problem of Commodity Exchange, *American Historical Review*, 111(2): 307–35.

Lonardi, G. (1997) La Camera Frena Il Tesoro Sulla Riforma Delle Società, *La Repubblica*, 24 October http://ricerca.repubblica.it/repubblica/archivio/repubblica/1997/10/24/la-camera-frena-il-tesoro-sulla-riforma.html, accessed on 2 March 2014.

MacKenzie, D. (2006) *An Engine, Not a Camera: How Financial Models Shape Markets*, Cambridge, MA: MIT Press.

MacKenzie, D. and Millo, Y. (2003) Constructing a Market, Performing Theory: The Historical Sociology of a Financial Derivatives Exchange, *American Journal of Sociology*, 109(1): 107–45.

Marchetti, P. (2001) Diritto Societario e Disciplina Della Concorrenza, in F. Barca (ed.), *Storia del Capitalismo Italiano*, Roma: Donzelli.

Markham, J.W. (2002) *A Financial History of the United States: From the Age of Derivatives into the New Millennium (1970–2001)*, Armonk, NY: M.E. Sharpe.

McCann, D. (2000) The 'Anglo-American' Model, Privatization and the Transformation of Private Capitalism in Italy, *Modern Italy*, 5(1): 47–61.

Melis, A. (2000) Corporate Governance in Italy, *Corporate Governance*, 8(4): 347–55.

Mügge, D.K. (2008) Widen the Market, Narrow the Competition: The Emergence of Supranational Governance in EU Capital Markets, PhD Thesis. Amsterdam: University of Amsterdam.

Nölke, A., Heires, M. and Bieling, H-J. (2013) Editorial: The Politics of Financialization, *Competition & Change*, 17(3): 209–18.

Norris, F. (2013) Wielding Derivatives as a Tool for Deceit, *New York Times*, 27 June. www.nytimes.com/2013/06/28/business/deception-by-derivative.html, accessed on 1 March 2014.

De Nova, G., Fusco, E., Girino, E., Onado, M., Portale, G.B., Portioli, G., Righi, S. and Rimini, E. (2010) *Quale Futuro Per I Derivati Finanziari?* www.ghidini-associati.it/ Quale%20futuro%20per%20i%20derivati%20finanziari%20-%20Trascrizione%20 Dibattito.pdf, accessed on 1 March 2014.

Panitch, L. and Gindin, S. (2008) Finance and American Empire, in L. Panitch and M. Konings (eds), *American Empire and the Political Economy of Global Finance*, Basingstoke: Palgrave-Macmillan.

Partnoy, F. (2009) *Infectious Greed. How Deceit and Risk Corrupted Financial Markets*, New York: PublicAffairs.

Pasquino, G. (1995) Partitocrazia, in G. Pasquino (ed.), *La Politica Italiana. Dizionario critico 1945–95*, Roma/Bari: Laterza.

Pasquino, G. (2000) Political Development, in P. McCarthy (ed.), *Italy since 1945*, Oxford: Oxford University Press.

Penati, A. (2005) I Furbetti Del Lingotto e Il Dodo Di Piazza Affari, *La Repubblica*, 23 September, http://ricerca.repubblica.it/repubblica/archivio/repubblica/2005/09/23/furbetti-del-lingotto-il-dodo-di.html, accessed on 2 March 2014.

Piga, G. (2001) *Derivatives and Public Debt Management*, Zurich and New York: International Securities Market Association – Council for Foreign Relations.

Preda, A. (2009) *Framing Finance. The Boundaries of Markets and Modern Capitalism*, Chicago: University of Chicago Press.

Puledda, V. (1998a) Da Confindustria e Assonime No Alla Nuova Opa Di Draghi, *La Repubblica*, 28 January. http://ricerca.repubblica.it/repubblica/archivio/repubblica/1998/01/28/da-confindustria-assonime-no-alla-nuova-opa.html, accessed on 2 March 2014.

Puledda, V. (1998b) Rivoluzione in Borsa Piccoli Soci Più Protetti, *La Repubblica*, 21 February. http://ricerca.repubblica.it/repubblica/archivio/repubblica/1998/02/21/rivoluzione-in-borsa-piccoli-soci-piu-protetti.html, accessed on 2 March 2014.

Quaglia, L. (2011) The Ebb and Flow of Euroscepticism in Italy, *South European Society and Politics*, 16(1): 31–50.

Rampini, F. (1997) Il Popolo Telecom, *La Repubblica*, 20 October, http://ricerca.repubblica.it/repubblica/archivio/repubblica/1997/10/29/il-popolo-telecom.html, accessed on 2 March 2014.

La Repubblica (1998) Opa, La Soglia Non Scenderà Sotto Il 30% – La Repubblica.it. *La Repubblica*, 24 November, http://ricerca.repubblica.it/repubblica/archivio/repubblica/1998/02/11/opa-la-soglia-non-scendera-sotto-il.html, accessed on 2 March.

La Repubblica (2007) Consob, Condanne e Multe a Ifil Per l'Equity Swap' Sulla Fiat, *La Repubblica*, 13 February, www.repubblica.it/2006/09/sezioni/economia/fiat-8/consob-ifil/consob-ifil.html, accessed on 1 March 2014.

La Repubblica (2013) Ifil-Exor, Condannati Gabetti e Grande Stevens In Appello un Anno e Quattro Mesi, *La Repubblica*, 21 February, www.repubblica.it/economia/2013/02/21/news/ifil-exor_attesa_la_sentenza_da_torino_gabetti_no_a_onta_di_ una_condanna-53089707/, accessed on 2 March.

Roe, M.J. (1994) *Strong Managers, Weak Owners: The Political Roots of American Corporate Finance*, Princeton, NJ: Princeton University Press.

Sbragia, A. (2001) Italy Pays for Europe: Political Leadership, Political Choice, and Institutional Adaptation, in M. Green Cowles, J. Caporaso and T. Risse (eds), *Transforming Europe: Europeanization and Domestic Change*, Ithaca, NY: Cornell University Press.

Scalfari, E. (1997) Gli Incesti Del Capitale, *La Repubblica.it*, 29 August, http://ricerca.repubblica.it/repubblica/archivio/repubblica/1997/08/29/gli-incesti-del-capitale.html, accessed on 2 March 2014.

Scalfari, E. (1998) Grandi Famiglie e Mercato Globale, *La Repubblica*, http://ricerca. repubblica.it/repubblica/archivio/repubblica/1998/02/08/grandi-famiglie-mercato-globale.html, accessed on 2 March 2014.

Scognamiglio, C. (1990) *Rapporto Al Ministro Del Tesoro. Commissione Per Il Riassetto Del Patrimonio Mobiliare Pubblico e Per Le Privatizzazioni*, Rome: Istituto Poligrafico e Zecca dello Stato.

Segreto, L. (1997) Models of Control in Italian Capitalism from the Mixed Bank to Mediobanca, 1894–1993, *Business and Economic History*, 26(2): 649–61.

Segreto, L. (1998) Italian Capitalism Between the Private and Public Sectors, 1933–1993, *Business and Economic History*, 27(2): 455–68.

Segreto, L. (2008) Il Caso Mediobanca, in C. Bermond, A. Cova, M. Moioli and S. La Francesca (eds), *Storia d'Italia. La Banca, Annali 23*, Torino: Einaudi, 785–823.

Silva, P. (2008) *In the Name of Reason. Technocrats and Politics in Chile*, University Park: Pennsylvania State University Press.

Stockhammer, E. (2008) Some Stylized Facts on the Finance-dominated Accumulation Regime, *Competition and Change*, 12(2): 184–202.

Sum, N.L. and Jessop, B. (2013) *Towards a Cultural Political Economy: Putting Culture in Its Place in Political Economy*, Cheltenham: Edward Elgar.

Swan, E.J. (1999) *Building the Global Market, a 4000 Year History of Derivatives*, London: Kluwer Law International.

Van Appeldoorn, B. and Horn, L. (2007) The Marketisation of European Corporate Control: A Critical Political Economy Perspective, *New Political Economy*, 12(2): 211–35.

Wigan, D. (2008) A Global Political Economy of Derivatives: Risk, Property and the Artifice of Indifference. PhD Thesis, Brighton: University of Sussex.

Wigan, D. (2009) Financialisation and Derivatives: Constructing an Artifice of Indifference, *Competition & Change*, 13(2): 157–72.

Zaloom, C. (2006) *Out of the Pits. Traders and Technology from Chicago to London*, Chicago: University of Chicago Press.

12 A cultural political economy of financial imaginaries

The (re-)making of 'BRIC' and the case of China

Ngai-Ling Sum

'BRIC' is the well-known acronym for Brazil, Russia, India and China. It was coined by Jim O'Neill, at the time Goldman Sachs' Chief Economist, when he watched the television broadcast of the 9/11 attacks on the World Trade Center. He began to imagine a new way of thinking about 'growth' that could transcend national perspectives and look beyond the West. With the onset of the 2007 financial crisis, this imaginary gained fresh popularity and was reinvented through the concerted efforts of diverse national and transnational forces (for example, international investment banks, economic strategists, international organizations, think tanks, national governments and business media corporations). In this light, my chapter explores the development of discourses and practices of BRIC, considering them as economic and financial imaginaries from a CPE perspective. Such imaginaries often involve a search for 'growth', hope' and 'strength' during specific economic conjunctures, especially periods of crisis.

The first section identifies some key questions from a CPE entry-point regarding the construction of economic imaginaries. The second section examines the role of (trans-)national forces in (re-)making the 'BRIC' as a 'growth' and 'hope' object over three overlapping stages. It notes that the national and transnational resonance of the BRIC imaginaries depends not only on developments in the financial and real economies but also on specific discourses, practices and knowledge technologies. The third section examines how the 'BRIC' discourses have been recontextualized in the Sinophone world as 'four golden brick countries' to signify 'strength' and 'greatest at last'. The fourth section investigates how China, as one of the 'golden bricks', was eager to showcase its strength following the 2007 financial crisis. It promoted a vast stimulus package that has posed tremendous fiscal challenges, especially to its regional-local authorities, which increasingly rely on land as collateral for loans and source of revenue. This intensified land-based accumulation, inflating the 'property bubble' and stimulating land clearance/dispossession. In turn this has had very uneven effects on the 'subaltern south', illustrated here through impact on the aspirant middle class and migrant workers' children. Though some measures have been taken to dampen the property market, they have been rather limited and social unrest continues. The final section ends with some general comments on the contribution of the CPE approach to understanding the remaking economic, political and social relations within and across different scales in the world market.

Towards a cultural political economy of imagined recoveries

Cultural political economy (hereafter CPE) is a broad theoretical current that combines the 'cultural-linguistic turn' (namely, a concern with sense- and meaning-making) with critical political economy. It was discussed at length in Chapter 1 and is applied here to the emergence, recontextualization, circulation and sedimentation of the 'BRIC' imaginaries as objects of 'hope'/'strength' from 2001 until 2012. This has involved new discourses and what neo-Foucauldians call knowledging technologies (Dean 1999; Miller and Rose 2008).

CPE recognizes not only the importance of discursive technologies but also how nodal discursive networks of individual and institutional actors (for example, international investment banks) contribute to the (re-)making of social relations. It examines not only 'how' knowledge is constructed but also poses 'where', 'who', 'what' and 'why' questions. Specifically, it asks: (1) where does a particular economic imaginary and its related discursive networks originate; (2) who gets involved in the discursive networks that construct and promote objects of 'hope'/'strength'; (3) what ideas are selected and drawn upon to recontextualize and hybridize the referents of these objects; (4) how are these imaginaries normalized, translated and negotiated; (5) what knowledging technologies are involved in the constitution of subjectivities and identities; (6) how do these ideas enter the policy discourses and everyday practices of the financial and policy worlds; (7) how do they impact unevenly across different sites and scales (for example, the lives of subaltern groups); (8) how are they being negotiated and/or resisted in the rebuilding of social relations; and (9) why do these happen?[1] Answering these complex questions requires inquiry into the relations among discourse, power and structural materialities. My analysis focuses on the BRIC imaginary and its appropriation and recontextualization in China.

The construction of hope/strength: three stages in the turn to 'BRIC'

'BRIC' discourse is grounded in the notion of 'emerging markets', which was coined in 1981 by fund manager Antoine van Agtmael of *Emerging Markets Management*. It maps some 'Third World' and post-socialist economies as sites of 'new growth opportunities' with 'high risks' but potentially high returns. 'BRIC' is a subset of the 'large emerging markets' and was identified as a high-growth investment group after 11 September 2001. The production of the 'BRIC' economic imaginaries has occurred so far in four overlapping stages: (1) investor story, (2) investor-consumer story, (3) investor-consumer-lender story and, most recently, (4) fears that the BRIC are no longer an engine of global growth and/or that China's continued growth threatens US competitiveness and power.[2] As this volume addresses cultures of finance and crisis dynamics, I address only the first three stages here. Each stage is related to nodal actors who are involved in the construction of 'hope'/'strength' via the use of knowledging instruments and technologies (see Table 12.1).

Table 12.1 The production of 'hope'/'strength': three overlapping stages in the production of 'BRIC' knowledge

Stages	Major actors/institutions	Major discourses and knowledge instruments	Knowledging technology
Stage 1 2001–present 'BRIC' as an investor story	International investment banks (e.g. Goldman Sachs) Chief Economist (e.g. Jim O'Neill) & colleagues; fund managers, sales teams, financial journalists, rating agency, etc.	2001 Invented the category in the report on *Building Better Global Economic BRICs* 2003 Research report on *Dreaming with BRICs: The Path to 2050* Other reports, books, webtours, indexes, etc. (see Table 12.2)	Technology of identification Technology of investability
Stage 2 2004–present 'BRIC' as an investor-consumer story	Economists, investment consultants, business media (Bloomberg, The Economist, CNN, blogs, etc.), international organizations (e.g. World Bank, IMF)	Decoupling theses The trans-Atlantic economies are in recession due to the subprime crisis and its fallout. Other regions, especially the BRIC, continue to grow during this downturn – strong consumption '*Decoupling 2.0*' article (*The Economist*)	Technology of identification
Stage 3 Late 2008–present 'BRIC' as an investor-consumer-lender story	International organizations (WB, IMF, G20, BRIC Summit, etc.), national leaders, foreign policy analysts and mass media	BRIC IMF Bond Programme Buying IMF Special Drawing Rights (e.g. USD 50 bn by China on 04/09/09) Shifting global economic balance of power (e.g. from G8 to G20 or even G2)	Technology of agency

Source: Author's own compilation.

First stage of the BRIC construction 2001–present: investor story

Contrary to the vague origin of most discourses, the BRIC idea has a clear date-line. It began with the imagination of the 'BRIC' quartet by Goldman Sachs' Chief Economist, Jim O'Neill, following the attack on the World Trade Center on 11 September 2001. He reckoned that further progress in globalization would need to go beyond Americanization and the northern-western world (Tett 2010). This diagnosis allowed O'Neill and his Goldman Sachs team to imagine new sources of growth based on identifying and bundling some useful 'non-western others' with high growth potentials. By 30 November 2001, these 'others' were presented as the 'BRIC' in Goldman Sachs Global Economic Paper No. 66, which was titled *Building Better Global Economic Brics*. Based on models of GDP growth rates until 2050, this economic quartet was constructed as the new object of 'hope', with 'each set to grow again by more than the G7' (2001: S.03). Whereas China and India were predicted to become dominant global suppliers of manufactured/technological goods and services, Brazil and Russia would grow as suppliers of energy and raw materials.

The creation of BRIC as a new 'growth' and 'hope' object for investors initially met mixed responses. While Goldman Sachs' corporate clients, who were looking for new markets, were supportive of this construction, banks and investors were more sceptical at first because the BRICs were seen to be prone to 'shocks' from political upheavals and changing commodity prices. Nonetheless, O'Neill's team continued to supply their clients with 'hope' based on expected growth and financial returns. For example, *Dreaming with BRICs: The Path to 2050* (2003), argued that:

> The relative importance of the BRICs as an engine of new demand growth and spending power may shift more dramatically and quickly than expected. Higher growth in these economies could offset the impact of greying populations and slower growth in the advanced economies.
>
> Higher growth may lead to higher returns and increased demand for capital. The weight of the BRICs in investment portfolios could rise sharply. Capital flows might move further in their favour, prompting major currency realignments...
>
> (Wilson and Purushothaman 2003: 2)

On the discursive level, this construction of hope/strength was achieved through metaphors such as 'engine of growth' that could provide 'higher returns' and attract 'favourable capital flows'. The growth path was extrapolated up to 2050. By then, for example, China's RMB gross domestic product could be 30 per cent larger than US GDP, India's could be four times Japan's; and Brazil and Russia could be at least 50 per cent bigger than the UK economy. References to economic attributes like size and rates of growth can be seen, in neo-Foucauldian terms, as a technology of identification in which the BRIC are singled out, made knowable, and visibilized as the largest, high growth and potentially lucrative 'emerging economies'. This identification technology, once deployed, was circulated by the Goldman team and other actors such as fund managers and financial sales teams. With the continuing consolidation of neoliberal globalization and China's entry into the WTO since 2001, more and more corporations and financial organizations were looking for new markets and profitable investment sites beyond the core advanced economies. New discursive networks, which included corporate executives, investment bankers, fund managers, and so on, began to appropriate and disseminate the BRIC imaginary as their own object of investment and strategic actions. Moreover, as Tett (2010) records, after the 2003 paper, Goldman economists entered 'briclife' with growing interest from leading clients in this new object of hope and speculative returns.

Goldman sustained this interest by churning out more knowledge products. Between 2001 and 2010, it created 20 such products, ranging from reports, new forecasts, a book, videos and webtours (in different languages) to keep 'briclife' going[3] (see Table 12.2). This Goldman story was occasionally challenged by other economists and investment consultants, who asked why some emerging economies were excluded (for example, South Korea and Turkey) and others included (for example, Russia and Brazil). New acronyms were put forward (for example, BRICK and CRIB) to negotiate its meanings and appeals.

Nonetheless, despite these challenges, with one wag later suggesting that BRIC stood for 'bloody ridiculous investment concept' and another proposing CEMENT to describe 'countries in emerging markets excluded by new terminology', the Goldman Sachs construction of the BRICs as objects of 'hope'/'strength' continued to circulate among economic strategists, investment consultants and sales teams and attracted continuing media attention. Its resonance derived not only from the projection of strength of the individual BRIC group members but also from the purported complementarity and coherence of BRIC as an asset/investment form. Major international banks such as HSBC and other investment banks/hedge funds were bundling stocks/shares/bonds and inventing funds marketed under the BRIC brand. Starting initially with a few funds and index funds, the market has since grown in terms of offers and funds invested (for details, see Sum and Jessop 2013). Great emphasis was placed on their attractiveness as investments because of the spread of risks, asset allocation and portfolio management, prospective profits, and the involvement of legendary stock pickers and fund management by gurus. In neo-Foucauldian terms, this discourse and technology of investability: (1) constructs strength, profitability and confidence of these funds and narrated them as asset choices; (2) directs investor subjects to put their money in these economies; and (3) normalizes BRIC as investment sites.

Armed with these investment products, financial sales teams and other intermediaries marketed them to potential clients, contacting them through advertisements, glossy brochures, financial journalism, phone-calls, home visits, and so on. Knowledging technology and related investment practices of this kind normalize BRIC as a good source of investment. Coupled with the general search for new investment sites, the inflow of portfolio equity funds to BRIC increased

Table 12.2 Major BRIC knowledge products constructed by Goldman Sachs team

Name of the knowledge products	Nature of product (year/month)	Ways of constructing hope and strength
Building Better Global Economic BRICs	Report November 2001	Invented the BRIC category and forecast combined GDP growth rate of 12% in the next 10 years
Dreaming with BRICs: The Path to 2050	Report October 2003	Mapping out BRIC's GDP growth until 2050 Postulating BRIC economies could be larger than G6 in 40 years' time
How Solid are the BRICs?	Forecast December 2005	Updating the 2003 forecast Arguing that BRIC grow more strongly than projection
Web Tour: The BRICs Dream (in English, Arabic, Chinese and Japanese)	Webtours May 2006	A video on the BRIC Dreaming about BRIC and the changing world after 9/11 Contending China would overtake the USA in 2050 Arguing growth of the middle classes in BRIC and major consumers of cars and energies
India's Urbanization: Emerging Opportunities	Report July 2007	Framing boom in city life Identifying investment opportunities in urban infrastructure and fast accumulation of financial assets
BRICS and Beyond	Book November 2007	Updating the 2001 report Postulating increase in value of BRIC's equity markets Moving beyond BRIC to other emerging economies (e.g. N-11)
Interview with Jim O'Neill	Video February 2008	Maintaining BRIC's share of global GDP as 15% Advising individual BRIC countries (e.g. India needs more FDI) Arguing for the sustainability of BRIC Increasing international role of these countries

Title	Type	Date	Description
Building the World: Mapping Infrastructure Demand	Report	April 2008	Identifying increase demand for infrastructure Arguing China will be the source of one-half to three-quarters of incremental demand Intensifying pressure on commodity markets
Ten Things for India to Achieve its 2050 Potential	Report	June 2008	Advising on improvement of governance and the need to control inflation Promoting the liberalization of financial market Supporting improvement for agricultural productivity
BRICs Lead the Global Recovery	Report	May 2009	Arguing BRIC can help to led the stabilization of the world economy Promoting BRIC is one of the driving forces in the export-driven recovery
The BRICs as Drivers of Global Consumption	Report	August 2009	Arguing G3 countries face slow and difficult recovery Maintaining that BRIC can contribute to global domestic demand through higher consumption
The BRICs Nifty 50: The EM & DM winners	Report and stock baskets	November 2009	Stating good consumption and infrastructural demand from BRIC Identifying two BRIC Nifty 50 baskets to help investors to access the BRIC market
BRICs at 8: Strong through the Crisis, Outpacing Forecasts	Video	March 2010	BRIC weathered the global crisis remarkably well On pace to equal the G7 in size by 2032
The Growth Map: Economic Opportunities of BRICs and Beyond	Book	2012	A sole-authored book by O'Neill that reviews the economic opportunities of BRICs and beyond

Source: Author's own compilation based on materials from Goldman Sachs' Idea Website on BRIC.

by almost twelvefold between 2002 and 2007. As for the share of BRIC invest-ment inflow compared with its counterpart in development countries, BRIC's share was about two-thirds of total inflow between 2003 and 2007 (see Table 12.3). Within the BRIC group, China was the biggest gainer in 2006 and India in 2007. With the onset of the financial crisis, the credit crunch led to the sharp slowdown of inflow to the BRIC in 2008 with China as the exception of a positive inflow of USD 3.7 billion.

Second stage of the BRIC construction 2004–present: investor-consumer story

The BRIC as investor story was extended to include a consumption dimension from mid-2004. This again began with a report from the Goldman Sachs team: *The BRICs and Global Markets: Crude, Cars and Capital* (2004). This identified an 'emerging middle class' in these economies, which would lead to increasing demand for commodities, consumer durables and capital services. This BRIC 'dream' was echoed by economic strategists such as Clyde Prestowitz, whose book, *Three Billion New Capitalists*, projected that, by 2020, 'the annual increase in dollar spending by the BRIC will be twice that of the G6' (Prestowitz 2005: 227).

This BRIC-as-consumer story gained traction after the 2007 collapse in the US sub-prime housing market. The long chains of financial bankruptcy of finan-cial houses, bailouts and credit crunch led policy communities and investors to look for new signs of 'hope' and possible objects of recovery. Among other objects (such as the Green New Deal), the BRIC story was re-articulated to include a consumption dimension (see Table 12.1). Thus stage two attributed a new locomotive role to the BRIC on the grounds that their consumer-led demand would defer recession and create recovery opportunities for recession-ridden advanced economies.

This narrative was enthusiastically circulated/negotiated by economists, busi-ness media (including *Bloomberg*, *Newsweek*, *The Wall Street Journal* and *CNN*) and international bodies such as the IMF under the rubric of the 'decoupling

Table 12.3 Net inflows of portfolio equity to the BRIC economies 2002–2008 (USD billion)

Country	2002	2003	2004	2005	2006	2007	2008
China	2.2	7.7	10.9	20.3	42.9	18.5	3.7
India	1.0	8.2	9.0	12.1	9.5	35.0	−15.0
Brazil	2.0	3.0	2.1	6.5	7.7	26.2	−7.6
Russia	2.6	0.4	0.2	−0.2	6.1	18.7	−15.0
BRIC	**7.8**	**19.3**	**22.2**	**38.7**	**66.2**	**98.4**	**−33.9**
Developing Countries	**5.5**	**24.1**	**40.4**	**68.9**	**104.8**	**135.4**	**−57.1**

Source: Adapted from World Bank, Global Development Finance 2008 and 2010.

thesis'. This asserts that the BRIC economies can still expand on the basis of their own investment and consumption, despite recession in the advanced economies. Jim O'Neill was reported in Bloomberg as saying that 'the BRIC consumer is going to rescue the world' (Marinis 2008) and 'since October 2007, the Chinese shopper alone has been contributing more to global GDP growth than the American consumer' (Mellor and Lim 2008). As in stage one, the technology of identification was deployed and BRIC was reinvented to become such a 'decoupled' object with autonomous consumption power that could operate as the 'saviour' of global recession.

This story was popularized by discursive networks of top investment advisors and fund managers through business, mass and Internet media (Shinnick 2008; Lordabett.com 2009). For example, Peter Schiff, President of Euro-Pacific Capital Inc, was one prominent proponent of this thesis and his position was echoed in many YouTube videos, blogs, articles and news items. For example, in his book, *Little Book of Bull Moves in Bear Markets*, Schiff argued:

> I'm rather fond of the word decoupling, in fact, because it fits two of my favorite analogies. The first is that America is no longer the engine of economic growth but the caboose. [The second is] when China divorces us, the Chinese will keep 100% of their property and their factories, use their products themselves, and enjoy a dramatically improved lifestyle.
>
> (Schiff 2008: 41)

Nonetheless the 'decoupling thesis' is also negotiated in different ways. First, some financial analysts, economists and international/regional organizations, such as the World Bank and Asia Development Bank, were more cautious. They pointed to a contraction of trade rather than decoupling. For example, in April 2008, citing reduced exports, the World Bank lowered its growth forecast for China to 6.5 per cent. Second, a different kind of caution was expressed in June 2008, when the IMF released a study called *Convergence and Decoupling*. This argued that decoupling could co-exist with integration. The globalization that has occurred since 1985 has stimulated greater trade and financial integration and this, in turn, has led to the tighter coupling of business cycles among countries with similar levels of per capita income. But there was also historical evidence that some (groups of) countries have decoupled from the broader global economy at various stages of their development. Third, a different concern was expressed by the UK-based foreign affairs think tank, Chatham House, in the wake of the collapse of Merrill Lynch and Lehman Brothers in September 2008. In one briefing paper, *Synchronized Dive into Recession*, a Chatham House author argued:

> Will a severe OECD recession engulf the rest of the world? Up to mid-2008, the emerging markets remained strong – 'decoupling' did work. Now the crisis has deepened, no region will remain immune to shock waves.
>
> (Rossi 2008)

In spite (or perhaps because) of these different views and the ambiguity of the '(de-) coupling' arguments, the thesis was still circulated. Indeed, Jim O'Neill himself reinforced it in *Newsweek* in March 2009:

> Who said decoupling was dead? The decoupling idea is that, because the BRICs rely increasingly on domestic demand, they can continue to boom even if their most important export market, the United States, slows dramatically. The idea came into disrepute last fall, when the US market collapse started to spread to the BRICs, but there's now lots of evidence that decoupling is alive and well.
>
> (O'Neill 2009)

This claim was echoed by *The Economist* in its issue of 21 May 2009 under the rubric of 'Decoupling 2.0'. This interpreted decoupling as 'a narrower phenomenon, confined to the biggest, and least indebted, emerging economies' such as China, India and Brazil. These had strong domestic markets, prudent macroeconomic policies and growing trade among themselves. In an interview on 'Decoupling is Happening for Real', Michael Buchanan, Goldman Sachs' Asia-Pacific Economist in Hong Kong, explained:

> For the last couple of months, data have revealed a growing divergence between western economies and those in much of Asia, notably China and India...
>
> One reason for this divergence is that the effects of the financial crisis hit Asia much later. While the American economy began slumping in 2007, Asian economies were doing well until the collapse of Lehman Brothers in September. What followed was a rush of stimulus measures – rate cuts and government spending programs. In Asia's case, these came soon after things soured for the region; in the United States, they came much later though on a much bigger scale.
>
> In addition, developing Asian economies were in pretty good financial shape when the crisis struck. The last major crisis to hit the region – the financial turmoil of 1997–98 – forced governments in Asia to introduce overhauls that ultimately left them with lower debt levels, more resilient banking and regulatory systems and often large foreign exchange reserves.
>
> (Buchanan 2009)

This creative argument reinterpreted the BRIC-decoupling thesis by narrowing the focus to two BRIC members: China and, to a lesser extent, India. In highlighting the 'new decoupling' thesis, this latest step construed them as 'useful others' with large foreign exchange reserves, buoyant fiscal positions and financial stimulus packages. In November 2009, the World Bank raised its 2010 economic forecast for China's GDP growth to 8.4 per cent. These economies offer 'hope' in terms of their good investment markets, robust consumption from their rising middle classes and relative large stimulus packages (see Table 12.4). This

Table 12.4 The central-local government's share of the stimulus package and sources of finance in China 2008–2010

Level of government	Amount (in trillion RMB)	Percentage of total	Major sources of finance
Central government	1.2	29.5	Direct grants Interest-rate subsidies
Regional-local governments	2.8	70.5	Loan-based finance Policy loans Local government bonds issued by the central government (around 200 billion RMB) Corporate bonds (130 billion RMB were issued in Q4 2008) Medium-term notes (25 billion RMB were issued in March 2009) Bank loans

Source: Naughton 2009; Window of China 2009.

narrowing of BRIC to China and India was reinforced within the policy circuit by Roger Scher (2009) who wrote for the Foreign Policy Blogs Network. He questioned the strength of Russia and whether the growth of China and India needs to be seen as 'From BRIC to BIC ... or Even IC??' Others constructed the term 'BriC' to highlight the position of China (see next section).

Third stage of the BRIC construction: investor-consumer-lender story

This new version of the decoupling thesis survived into stage three, which began in late 2008 (see Table 12.1). As the crisis in the developed countries deepened and the search for 'hope' or objects of recovery continued, more attention was paid to the geo-political significance of the BRIC quartet. A greater role in this search for 'hope' was now played by policy makers, international organizations, think tanks, foreign policy analysts, and so on. This is illustrated by the UK Prime Minister, Gordon Brown, who was coordinating an IMF rescue package for the global economy in October 2008 and called for the support of countries with large reserves. He stated:

> China ... has very substantial reserves. There are a number of countries that actually can do quite a lot in the immediate future to make sure that the international community has sufficient resources to support countries that get themselves into difficulties.

> (cited in Sanderson 2008)

This plea was reiterated as Brown prepared for the G20 meeting in London in April 2009, when China was expected to contribute USD 40 billion to the rescue package. Accompanying these specific policy initiatives, foreign policy rhetoric emphasized the emergence of a 'multipolar world order' and 'comprehensive interdependence' among countries (Renard 2009). These new geopolitical imaginaries became more credible when Russia held the first BRIC Leaders' Summit in Yekaterinburg in June 2009 and Brazil, China, India and South Africa[4] hosted the second, third and fourth summits in April 2010, April 2011, March 2012 and March 2013 respectively. These summits operated (partly) as arenas for the BRIC(s) leaders to perform and confirm their collective identity as well as to envisage their future (for example, the establishment of the BRIC Development Bank) despite their differences.

Thus, in reaction to Brown's 2009 call for them to support the IMF rescue package, the BRIC governments agreed to contribute towards a more diversified international monetary system. Influenced by Stiglitz's *UN Commission on Reforms of the International and Monetary Systems* and the discussions around the *UN Conference on the Global Financial & Economic Crisis*, it advocated 'Special Drawing Rights' (SDRs) as the new 'global currency' that could increase liquidity. The IMF would issue SDR-denominated bonds that the BRIC economies could purchase for their reserves. This new approach was backed at the G20 Summit in April 2009, when the IMF managing director, Dominique Strauss-Kahn, announced the issuance of USD 250 million SDR-denominated bonds. The IMF Executive Board confirmed this on 1 July 2009, China pledged to buy USD 50 billion, and Russia, Brazil and India would each gradually purchase USD 10 billion.

In contrast to conventional IMF loan facilities, this form of financing involved new kinds of lender and governance relations. As lenders to the IMF, the strength of the BRIC quartet was reconfirmed symbolically via: (1) the developed economies' recognition that they should be part of the solution to the crisis by subscribing to these SDR-denominated bonds; (2) their general unwillingness to commit funds on a long-term basis until the IMF re-allocated the country quotes; and (3) their specific demand for an increase in their voting shares within the IMF governance structure from 5 to 7 per cent of the total.[5] Despite these signs of 'hope'/'strength', some observers commented that the new SDR bonds would only absorb a small proportion of the BRIC's foreign reserves and, therefore, doubted that the SDR system would ever challenge the role of the dollar (Kelly 2009).

This (negotiated) amalgam of 'BRIC' discourses and practices (and their continued reworking and re-articulation over three overlapping stages) has helped to sediment and naturalize BRIC as a complex object of 'hope'/'strength'. It deferred the recession by offering investment opportunities for frustrated investors, consumer demand that can facilitate recovery and growth, and reserves that can finance international lending. Given these alleged strengths, the BRIC economies are deemed to have graduated from being 'emerging markets' to an 'emerging global power'. This discursive shift illustrates what neo-Foucauldians call a technology of agency (Cruikshank 1999) that is based on the coexistence of participation and control in the international arena. On the one hand, there is the encouragement of the BRIC to participate as 'we' in the new so-called multi-polar world order. Using the power shift from G8 to G20 as an example; BRIC's increasing roles in the G20 allow for their participation on one hand; and on the other hand, it also steers the manner of their engagement, for example, as engines of consumption, lenders to the IMF, and so forth. Such participation, coordination and steering of the BRIC economies in arenas such as the G20 enables the emergence of a broader 'discussion forum' to address crisis-related issues as well as producing directives to international organizations (for example, the IMF). One effect is that the BRIC economies are drawn into discussions and actions around crisis-management that facilitate the rebuilding and negotiation of the future neoliberal agendas (for example, the dollar-yuan exchange policy, BRIC as consumers and the dollar's hegemonic role).

BRIC-ing of China and its 2008 stimulus package

The transition of the BRIC imaginary of 'hope'/strength through these stages was not a smooth process. The BRIC identity and its boundary is constantly (re-) negotiated by a mix of (trans-)national actors. On the transnational level, global market strategists and economists asked why some emerging economies were excluded (for example, South Korea) and others included (Russia). Some foreign policy analysts question the coherence of the quartet, leading one to use '*BRIC-à-Brac*' to convey their diverse and toothless nature (Drezner 2009).[6] More pro-saically, others warned of the potential 'BRIC bubble' by arguing that, even if their GDP continued to expand, this might not produce higher stock market returns for investors (Tasker 2010; Evans-Pritchard 2011).

In the Sinophone world, the term 'BRIC' is translated as '*bricks*' and has been recontextualized, initially in Taiwan and then more widely, as '*the four golden brick countries*' (金磚四國). The 'golden bricks' imaginary has been embraced by the financial and official communities within China as a symbol of 'strength' and sign of 'greatness-at-last'. This reinforces China's long-standing construction of 'national strength' under a one-party authoritarian regime. There were plenty of printed headlines in its official newspaper, *The People's Daily*, that adopted BRIC-related discourses such as '*Shining, golden "BRIC"*' (6 September 2006) and '*BRIC set to build golden brick*' (16 June 2009). This 'golden' metaphor helps to signify the strength and pride of the Chinese nation, especially after its long history of foreign invasion and national humiliation. More specifically, this claim to strength is expressed quantitatively in terms of a 'shining BRIC' that can 'protect 8% GDP growth rate'.

With the onset of the 2007 North Atlantic Financial Crisis, there was a sharp fall in Chinese exports and growing unemployment. The Chinese central government proactively used the crisis for profiling purpose both nationally and internationally. It reiterated its 'protection of 8% GDP growth rate' to project strength as well as a justification for putting together a vast stimulus package of RMB 4 trillion (USD 586 billion) from November 2008. Concurrently, the US Federal Reserve sought to stimulate its domestic economy by quantitative easing in late

November 2008. It 'printed money' to buy USD 600 billion mortgage-backed securities with the effects of increasing lending activities both at home and abroad.

While the Federal Reserve deployed quantitative easing to support banks deemed too big to fail, China stimulated its economy via loan-based programmes that have affected national-local social relations unevenly. In particular, its use of fiscal and monetary stimulus has intensified the fiscal imbalances between the central-local relationships. It was narrated officially as providing support for ten major industrial sectors (for example, steel, shipbuilding, electronics and petro-chemicals), building infrastructural projects (for example, high speed rail, electric grid), boosting consumer spending, developing the rural economy and encouraging education and housing (for details, see Tong and Zhang 2009). However, based on fiscal practice since the late 1990s, this vast sum was financed by around one-third from central government funding; the rest was expected to come from regional-local governments, governmental ministries and state-owned enterprises (SOEs). To enable these loans, the central government introduced policies such as loosening of credit policies, and abolishing credit ceiling for commercial banks.

China's stimulus package, 'property bubble' and the 'subaltern' South

When these stimulus measures were communicated to the ministries and local governments, they were eager to seize this opportunity and get their pet projects (for example, high-speed trains, industrial upgrading projects) approved (Naughton 2009). Given the central-local fiscal arrangements since the 1990s, local governments are required to provide matching funds. They find this hard because (1) they are expected to channel 60 per cent of their revenue to Beijing; (2) the economic downturn reduced revenue from business taxes; and (3) they have no formal mandate to borrow money. This inevitably resulted in a funding gap. Thus a 2009 National Audit Office survey reported that local governments in 18 provinces were failing to provide the expected level 'matching funds', with the poorest performing province sending only 48 per cent of the amount due (Xi et al. 2009).

In planning terms, this shortfall can be filled by financial resources coming from a mix of local government bonds issued by the central government, corporate bonds, medium-term notes and bank loans (see Table 12.4). However, as China's bond market is not well-developed, local governments seek their own sources of finance. This chapter concentrates on the intensification of the use of land as a means to generate income. This is possible as China's land leasehold market was formally established in the late 1970s under Deng Xiao-Ping. Urban land is state-owned but the separation of ownership and land-use rights mean that public and private actors can shape its disposition and utilization. Urban land-use rights could be leased for fixed periods (for example, 70 years for residential housing) at a fee and land-right leases are tradable by auctions (Hsing

2010: 36). This development encourages local officials to convert rural land, which still belongs to rural 'collectives', into urban land by compensating (at least in principle) village communities.

With these socio-economic changes, local governments can commodify land in two main ways: as an instrument for leveraging loans and source of revenue. First, local governments have accumulated land, licences and equity investments. However, such assets cannot be translated into cash because the Budget Law prohibits these authorities from raising funds directly. Local governments therefore set up related investment companies to raise loans from state-owned banks (for example, Bank of China, China Construction Bank). Land-use rights are used as collateral for these loans. With the easy availability of credit and the close relationship between local governments and state-owned banks, local government debt rose five times between 2008 and 2009 from 1 trillion RMB (USD 146 billion) to an estimate of 5 trillion RMB (USD 730 billion) by the end of 2009 (Zhang 2010). Concurrently, Bank of China and China Construction Bank reported profit rose 26 and 15 per cent respectively for 2009 (*Business Week* 2010).

Second, land-right leases and auctions are used to generate government revenue and stimulate economic growth. These rights are sold to private and state-owned developers (for example, China Poly Group, China Resource Group and China Merchant Group) for property projects. In 2009, the Ministry of Land and Resources reported local governments generated 1.6 trillion RMB (USD 233 billion), which was a 60 per cent increase compared with 2008. Of these land sale revenues in 2009, 84 per cent came from property development (*China Daily* 2010). In this regard, real estate development provides two benefits: first, it is a major source of fiscal revenues for local governments and this provides strong incentives for them to support these endeavours; and, second, state-owned and private property developers (and their partners in local governments) can earn high profit from selling housing units, especially when easy credits is available from state-controlled banks.

This land-based development and its perceived benefits have strengthened the emerging social attitude that property ownership is a source of economic security, hedge against inflation, social status, family safety net and personal pride. The business press, ordinary media and peer pressures help to reinforce these views in everyday life. Given the limited outlets to invest savings, continuously rising property values over the last decade suggested that real estate offers higher returns; indeed, with low interest rates and no national property tax, it was possible to buy and hold speculative property relatively cheaply. Thus real estate increasingly became an object of investment, ownership and/or speculation. This has been articulated with the central government's focus on high growth rates, dependency of local governments upon land/real estate for revenue, the drive of real-estate developers for profit, and the inflow of funds from quantitative easing in the US. All these factors contributed towards real estate inflation as well as fears of a 'property bubble'. According to Colliers International, residential prices in 70 large- and medium-sized cities across China rose in 2009, with 50–60 per cent increases in Beijing and Shanghai. Such increases reduce housing affordability with the conventionally calculated income-to-price ratio in Beijing at 1 to 22 (FlorCruz 2009; Smith 2010; Powell 2010). This ratio means that housing prices for a standard property in 2010 were 22 times the average annual income of families.

This inflationary rise added a political dimension to the housing question. This was acknowledged by the Premier Wen Jiabao when he remarked on 27 February 2010 that 'property prices have risen too fast' and this 'wild horse' must be tamed. Central government leaders took measures to dampen the market (for example, tightening of credit, raising deposits for purchase of new land to 50 per cent; arranging for the exit from this sector of state-owned developers whose core business is not property, imposing a property tax on residential housing, and so on.). However, such measures merely encouraged banks to find other ways to increase their credit (for example, selling off loans to state-owned trusts and asset-management companies and turning loans into investment products and selling them to private investors). These practices were backed by those with vested interests in the property boom, such as jobs and perks for officials, income and growth statistics for ministries and local governments, profit/investment for state-owned banks and related investment vehicles as well as state-owned/private property developers and, of course, gains for property owners (on the real estate coalition, see Sum 2011).

Such apparent advantages to (inter-)national-regional-local elites come at a price. Over-investment in real estate and projects destabilizes the economy and weakens the socio-economic positions of ordinary citizens and the 'subaltern south'. While many issues and sites could be discussed (for example, land seizures, peasant protests, nail houses, and so on), two social issues will be briefly explored here: the affordability of housing and plight of migrant workers in rural towns.

First, the rise of property prices is based on and reinforces the view that property ownership offers a profitable investment and personal security. This underpins the stimulus-loan-property boom and its socio-economic base. Rising property prices, wealth accumulation and regular land auctions co-exist with social unrest related to resettlement compensation, land clearance, affordability of housing/schooling, conditions of migrant workers, inflationary pressures and petty and major corruption. These socio-economic issues have been reflected and popularized in TV sitcoms such as *Dwelling Narrowness* (*Snail House*) about struggles to acquire property and corruption among officials and have also supplied material for countless newspaper columns, policy speeches and appeals for action. A major theme is the plight of white-collar workers who are virtual 'house slaves' (房奴). These are salaried employees who, in the midst of soaring property prices propelled by an easy-credit and over-investment stimulus package, slave to save the deposit for flats and pay their mortgage, and then struggle to balance domestic budgets. It seems as if workers do not own their flats or houses but, rather, their houses and flats own them and dictate their working lives and family relationship.

Second, uneven development is reflected in the plight of the migrant workers in rural towns on the periphery of cities. These workers constitute a significant part of the reserve army of labour and the bedrock of Chinese export-led growth. While they have no opportunity to become 'house slaves', they (and their children) risk displacement by the same property boom dynamic. For this accelerates land clearance in rural towns to make way for real estate projects and therefore displaces workers and raises their rents. Such cases are so rampant that there is rising social unrest related to land appropriation, under-compensation for land/property seizure, corruption, rising prices, and so on. In October 2010, a blogger called '*Blood Map*' used *Google Map* to chart the distribution of sites where there have been land conflicts, use of violence against residents, and people's resistance to illegal land grab and property demolitions in China.[7]

Land appropriation and clearance also affect migrant workers especially their children. Migrant families have no *hukou* (long-term residency)[8] in urban areas and they go to privately run schools set up in slums in these rural towns. These schools provide inexpensive schooling. Urban clearance means that this kind of affordable education may vanish due to school closures. Some schools are now categorized as 'illegal' (and hence receive no compensation for closure) by the local authorities. These 'schools' and authorities are locked in compensation battles as well as faced with the fate of closing down (Li 2010). Some children are locked out from schools, some are rehoused in makeshift schools, and some are sent back to home villages. In the last case, social issues arise around 'left-behind children' living with grandparents (or other relatives).

There are some 20 million 'left-behind children' in China. This also raises more general issues concerning the 'rights of migrant workers' and a *hukou* system that creates second-class citizens. In response to these challenges, 13 newspapers throughout China issued a joint call for the abolition of the 'outdated' *hukou* system[9] on 2 March 2010, but this was soon silenced in a matter of days. The authorities continuously talk of reorienting policies and putting more resources into the social agenda (for example, housing, education and health care). However, as the stimulus package is largely land-led, the injection of funds into health care and social housing tends to grow more slowly than economic expansion, especially where the latter is fuelled by easy credit, land sales and real estate development. These are tied very closely to the vested interests of regional-local governments, the property-owning elite, state-owned banks, state-owned/private property developers, infrastructure-related departments and organizations, and so on. There have been recent calls to tighten credit by suspending home loans to buyers purchasing a third housing unit; rebalance the economy towards greater financial liberalization, reform central-local fiscal relationship and embark on social development. These measures are likely to be counteracted by different groups with vested interests in a particular mode of accumulation. These struggles will continue and tensions are expressed on different levels. On the social level, there is the rise in social unrest (for example, the Wukan peasant riot) and the demand for the return of land. On the economic level, the central government's push for rebalancing towards financial liberalization has stimulated resistance from state-owned and export-oriented sectors.

Concluding remarks

This chapter used a CPE approach to examine the changing discursive-material bases of the BRIC imaginary since 2001. Taking the 'cultural-linguistic turn' seriously in critical political economy, it identifies three overlapping stages in the construction of the BRIC as a (trans-)national object of 'growth'/'hope'/'strength'. These stages were not arbitrary but related to new conjunctures – the 9/11 attack on the World Trade Center and the financial crisis that has been unfolding since 2007. A CPE approach examines how actors experiment with discourses and practices to make sense of changed structural circumstances and reorient their actions in the light of these efforts at (re-) interpretation. It also examines how: (1) sense- and meaning-making is mediated by discursive networks that include, in the present case, international investment banks, economic strategists, business media, think tanks, international organizations and foreign policy-makers; and (2) governmental knowledging technologies of power, such as identification, investability and agency, are deployed to privilege and naturalize the BRIC economies as objects of 'hope'/'strength' relevant for the imagined recovery of the global political economy.

This imaginary is negotiated and appropriated in quite diverse ways. Within the BRIC discourses, China has increasingly been singled out as unique and, within the Sinophone world, it is recontextualized as *'the four golden brick countries'* that symbolizes China's 'strength' and sign of 'greatness-at-last' through its capacity to 'protect 8% GDP growth rate'. After the 2007 financial crisis emerged, China continued its investment-led strategy by marshalling a vast economic stimulus package that has intensified some deep-rooted national-local tensions. The stimulus package signifies a central-government 'green light' for bringing forward 'pet projects' of regional and local governments. Land is increasingly used to leverage loans, raise revenue for sub-national authorities, and fuel investment and speculation in property development. Yet this brings costs such as forced displacement from land, state terror, dispossession of the already vulnerable (for example, migrant children) and increasing inequality. The resulting social tensions represent a 'dark side' of the stimulus package, which is narrated in the (trans-)national arena in 'hope'/'strength' terms. The CPE approach provides tools to critique these hegemonic constructions and to highlight some local subaltern social sites (such as slum schools), everyday resistance (for example, 'Blood Map') and peasant riots that are often neglected or glossed over in mainstream narratives about the prospects of the BRIC economies.

On the global level, some of the worries about the validity of the BRIC imaginary became stronger after 2010, prompting an initially gradual and then accelerating retreat in BRIC portfolio investments. Indeed, in 2013–2014, anticipation of and then the first steps in tapering US quantitative easing and indications of US and European recovery have unsettled investors and governments in the BRIC economies and other emerging markets. There were panics and selling of South African rand, Indian rupee and Brazilian real. For example, the Brazilian real devalued by 20 per cent coupled with inflation and social unrest in August 2013. Lord coined the term *'Fragile Five'* (Brazil, Indonesia, India, Turkey and South Africa) in August 2013 to denote their vulnerabilities (Lord 2013). Åslund of the Peterson Institute for

International Economics even announced that 'the BRICs party is over' (2013). O'Neill himself was reported in saying that 'If I were to change it, I would just leave the "C"' (Magalhaes 2013) and started to promote a new acronym called *MINT* (Mexico, Indonesia, Nigeria and Turkey) as the transnational imaginary. In short, from a CPE perspective, imaginaries must always be related to the underlying extra-discursive context to which they relate. The BRIC imaginary captured for a time key trends in the world economy and even helped to create the potential that it identified, not only economically but also politically. But continuing global trends, including the financial and economic repercussions of crisis-management policies in the advanced economies, have increasingly, as some anticipated, turned the BRIC imaginary sour and prompted the search for new imaginaries of hope and strength.

Notes

1 Sum (2004) outlined six discursive-material moments in the remaking of social relations; see also Sum and Jessop (2013).
2 For example, US Commerce Secretary, Gary Locke, was reported in the *Washington Post* on 9 February 2010 as expressing the US's fear of its 'innovation deficits' in the face of rising 'frugal innovation' in China (and, perhaps, India). See Schmidt (2010).
3 For details of these products, search for BRIC at www.goldmansachs.com/our-thinking/archive, accessed 8 February 2014.
4 South Africa joined the BRIC summit in 2011 at the invitation of China.
5 In the G20 Pittsburgh Meeting (September 2009), the discussion of IMF governance reform was blocked by European governments – notably France and the UK – because of worries about losing influence at the IMF. On 25 April 2010, China's voting power in the World Bank increased from 2.78 to 4.42 per cent.
6 Key differences among the BRIC include diverse political systems, and dissimilar views on key policy issues such as free trade and energy pricing.
7 For details of the 'Blood Map', see 'Elusive "blood map" founder speaks out', http://observers.france24.com/content/20101119-china-evictions-violence-blood-map-google-founder-speaks-out, accessed 8 February 2014.
8 The *Hukou* system refers to residential requirements in Chinese migrants, who do not belong to the *Hukou* system in the urban area, are not entitled to public housing, education for their children or local pension and health care benefits. This system is changing but still favours the educated migrant communities.
9 'Editorial calls for abolition of *hukou* system', *South China Morning Post*, 2 March 2010, www.scmp.com/article/707381/editorial-calls-abolition-hukou-system, accessed on 8 February 2014.

References

Åslund, A. (2013) Now the Brics Party Is Over, They Must Wind Down the State's Role, *Financial Times*, 27 August.
Buchanan, M. (2009) Decoupling Is Happening for Real, 10 July, www.chartwelletfadvisor.com/etf-newsletters/vol. 06-iss096.pdf, accessed on 21 February 2013.
Business Week (2010) China Construction Bank 2009 Profit Up 15 Percent, 28 March, www.businessweek.com/ap/financialnews/D9EO1OQ00.htm, accessed on 8 February 2014.
China Daily (2010) China's Land Sales Revenue Close to $233 bln in 2009, 2 February, www.chinadaily.com.cn/china/2010–02/02/content_9417378.htm, accessed on 1 March 2013.

Cruikshank, B. (1999) *The Will to Empower*, Ithaca, NY: Cornell University Press.

Dean, M. (1999) *Governmentality: Power and Rule in Modern Society*, London: Sage.

Drezner, Daniel J. (2009) BRIC-a-brac, http://drezner.foreignpolicy.com/posts/2009/06/17/bric-a-brac, accessed on 8 February 2014.

Evans-Pritchard, A. (2011) Goldman Sachs Shuns the BRIC for Wall Street, www.telegraph.co.uk/finance/economics/8265175/Goldman-Sachs-shuns-the-BRICs-for-Wall-Street.html, accessed 8 February 2014.

FlorCruz, J. (2009) Will the China Property Bubble Pop?, www.cnn.com/2009/BUSINESS/12/30/china.property.bubble/index.html, accessed 8 February 2014.

Goldman Sachs (2001) *Building Better Global Economic Brics*, Global Economic Paper No. 66.

Goldman Sachs (2010) Idea Website on BRIC, http://www2.goldmansachs.com/ideas/brics/index.html, accessed on 8 February 2014.

Hsing, Y-T. (2010) *The Great Urban Transformation: Politics of Land and Property in China*, Oxford: Oxford University Press.

Kelly, B. (2009) Brazil, Russia, India and China (the BRICs) Throw Down the Gauntlet of the International Monetary System, 28 June, www.eastasiaforum.org/2009/06/28/brazil-russia-india-and-china-the-brics-throw-down-the-gauntlet-on-monetary-system-reform/, accessed on 8 February 2014.

Li, R. (2010) Schools' Demise Forces Migrant Children Home. *South China Morning Post*, 3 February, www.scmp.com/article/705325/schools-demise-forces-migrant-children-home, accessed on 8 February 2014.

Lord, J. (2013) EM Currencies: Fragile Five, *Morgan Stanley Research*, 1 August, p. 15, www.morganstanleyfa.com/public/projectfiles/dce4d168–15f9–4245–9605-e37e-2caf114c.pdf, accessed on 8 February 2014.

Lordabbett.com (2009) Why Decoupling Should Benefit International Investors, https://www.lordabbett.com/articles/wp_why_decoupling_should.pdf, accessed on 3 March 2010.

Magalhaes, L. (2013) China Only BRIC Country Currently Worthy of the Title – O'Neill, *Wall Street Journal*, 23 August, http://blogs.wsj.com/moneybeat/2013/08/23/china-only-bric-country-currently-worthy-of-the-title-oneill/, accessed 8 February 2014.

Marinis, A. (2008) BRIC Consumers Can't Hold Off World Recession, Livemint.com, www.livemint.com/2008/12/18211911/Bric-consumers-can8217t-hol.html, accessed on 8 February 2014.

Mellor, W. and Lim, L-M. (2008) BRIC Shoppers will 'Rescue World', Goldman Sachs Says, www.bloomberg.com/apps/news?pid=newsarchive&sid=a3aTPjYcw8a8, accessed 8 February 2014.

Miller, P. and Rose, N. (2008) *Governing the Present*, Cambridge: Polity.

Naughton, B. (2009) Understanding Chinese Stimulus Package, *Chinese Leadership Monitor No. 28*, Spring, www.hoover.org/publications/clm/issues/44613157.html, accessed on 8 February 2014.

O'Neill, J. (2009) The New Shopping Superpower, www.newsweek.com/2009/03/20/the-new-shopping-superpower.html, accessed on 8 February 2014.

Powell, B. (2010) China's Property: Bubble, Bubble, Toil and Trouble, *Time*, 22 March, www.time.com/time/magazine/article/0,9171,1971284,00.html, accessed on 8 February 2014.

Prestowitz, C. (2005) *The Three Billion Capitalists*, New York: Basic Books.

Renard, T. (2009) A BRIC in the World: Emerging Powers, Europe, and the Coming Order, Royal Institute for International Relations, *Egmont Paper 31*, Brussels: Academia Press.

Rossi, V. (2008) Synchronized Dive into Recession: Focus on Damage Limitation, International Economic Programme, October 2008, IEP BP 08/04, www.chathamhouse.org/sites/default/files/public/Research/International%20Economics/bp1008recession.pdf, on 8 February 2014.

Sanderson, H. (2008) China Wants More Say in Global Financial Bodies, *USA Today*, 29 October, www.usatoday.com/money/economy/2008–10–29–2068576087_x.htm, accessed on 8 February 2014.

Scher, R. (2009) From BRIC to BIC ... or Even to IC??, New York: Foreign Policy Association, http://risingpowers.foreignpolicyblogs.com/2009/06/08/from-bric-to-bic%E2%80%A6or-even-ic/, accessed 8 February 2014.

Schiff, P. (2008) *Little Book of Bull Moves in Bear Markets*, Chichester: Wiley.

Schmidt, G. (2010) Erasing our Innovation Deficit, www.washingtonpost.com/wp-dyn/content/article/2010/02/09/AR2010020901191.html, accessed 8 February 2014.

Shinnick, R. (2008) Decoupling Thesis Intact, Seeking Alpha, 10 February 2008, http://seekingalpha.com/article/63886-decoupling-thesis-intact, accessed on 8 February 2014.

Smith, C. (2010) Global Economy's Next Threat: China's Real Estate Bubble, www.dailyfinance.com/story/global-economys-next-threat-chinas-real-estate-bubble/19302329/#, accessed 8 February 2014.

Sum, N-L. (2004) Discourses, Material Power and (Counter-)hegemony, retrieved from www.lancaster.ac.uk/cperc/docs/Sum%20CPERC%20Working%20Paper%202012–01.pdf.

Sum, N-L. (2011) Financial Crisis, Land-Induced Financialization and the Subalterns in China, in C. Scherrer (ed.) *Social China*, Berlin: Springer-Verlag.

Sum, N-L. and Jessop, B. (2013) *Towards a Cultural Political Economy: Putting Culture in its Place in Political Economy*, Cheltenham: Edward Elgar.

Tasker, P. (2010) Beware the Lure of GDP When Seeking Stocks in Brics, www.ft.com/cms/s/0/18f2c282-ff1b-11de-a677–00144feab49a.html, accessed on 8 February 2014.

Tett, G. (2010) The Story of the Brics, www.ft.com/cms/s/2/112ca932–00ab-11df-ae8d-00144feabdc0.html, accessed on 8 February 2014.

Tong, S. and Zhang, Y. (2009) China's Responses to the Economic Crisis, EAI Background Brief No. 438, National Singapore University, www.eai.nus.edu.sg/BB438.pdf, accessed on 8 February 2014.

Wilson, D. and Purushothaman, R. (2003) Dreaming with the BRICs: The Path to 2050, Goldman Sachs Global Economic Research Website, Global Economic Paper No. 99, www.goldmansachs.com/japan/ideas/brics/book/99-dreaming.pdf, accessed on 8 February 2014.

Window of China (2009) China Updates Details of Stimulus Fund, 21 May, http://news.xinhuanet.com/english/2009-05/21/content_11415559.htm, accessed on 23 June 2014.

Xi, S., Zhang, X.-D. and Cheng, Z.-Y. (2009) Mitigating Debt Bomb for Chinese Local Governments, *Economic Observer*, 1 June, www.eeo.com.cn/ens/2009/0601/138892.shtml, accessed 10 March 2014.

Zhang, M. (2010) CBRC Beefs Up Measures, *Shanghai Daily*, 25 February, www.shanghaidaily.com/Business/finance/CBRC-beefs-up-measures/shdaily.shtml, accessed 8 February 2014.

Part V

Crisis construals and responses to financial crisis in Europe

13 Culture matters

French–German conflicts on European central bank independence and crisis resolution

Eelke de Jong and Femke van Esch

The European sovereign debt crisis has highlighted a fault line between German and French politicians and board members of the ECB. In this chapter we argue that this fault line is rooted in cultural differences between Germany and France. This position is based on previous research on the relation between central bank independence and national culture and the construction of cognitive maps of a French (Jean-Claude Trichet) and German (Axel Weber) member of the ECB's board. Consequently, although a European wide agreement on the ECB's independence has been reached, national cultural differences still play an important role in board members' preferences and the ECB policy. As such, this chapter provides another illustration of how the cultural turn in economics helps to understand financial affairs. Moreover, it develops a new methodological approach to operationalize dimensions of culture in the process.

Introduction

In October 2009, the newly elected Greek Prime Minister, Georgios Papandreou, announced that 'our economy is in intensive care'. The Greek budget deficit and public debt proved to be much higher than had been declared by the previous government. During the months after this announcement, a fierce debate arose among European leaders. On the one hand, we find the then French Prime Minister, Nicolas Sarkozy, and the then President of the European Central Bank, Jean-Claude Trichet, who both pleaded for a European solution. On the other hand, we find the German Chancellor, Angela Merkel, and some Northern member states of the euro-area, who favoured the involvement of the International Monetary Fund (IMF). One of the latter group's arguments was that the Maastricht Treaty explicitly precludes a bail-out of member states, so no European solution could be offered. This dispute dragged on until, in May 2011, the sovereign bond market nearly collapsed. An agreement was then signed in which the IMF, the European Commission and individual members states of the euro-area provided finance. In 2011 two German members of the ECB's board, Axel Weber and Jürgen Stark, resigned. They disagreed with the measures taken, especially with the scheme to purchase sovereign bonds. In their view, this policy contradicts the ECB's mandate, which precludes direct support to governments.

This dispute clearly illustrates that a formal institution, in this case, the Maastricht Treaty, can be interpreted in fundamentally different ways. Bohn and de Jong (2011) have argued that these different interpretations result from systematic differences in culture, where culture is understood as 'the collective programming of the mind' (Hofstede 2001: 9). The central idea is that individuals over their lifetime acquire values, ideas and heuristics, which can be summarized in the term 'mental model'. Since experiences differ among people, no two individuals will have the same mental model. Nevertheless, through communication, individuals will influence each other's mental map. This process will result in similar mental maps for groups of persons, so-called shared mental maps (Denzau and North 1994). These groups can take different forms, for example, those raised in the same region, belonging to the same religion, the same occupation, having had the same education, and so on. Mental maps are particularly important for decision-making in situations of strong uncertainty (Denzau and North 1994: 3; Hogg 2010). The European sovereign debt crisis is certainly characterized by strong (Knightian) uncertainty. We expect that the level of uncertainty was greatest during the first phase of the crisis. In later phases, communication may have led to a more common view and/or those opposed to the solution resigned, as happened regarding the ECB's board.

During the first years of the European sovereign debt crisis, the French and the Germans held opposite positions. The French were often supported by Southern European countries and the Germans by Northern countries, such as the Netherlands, Finland and Austria. Bohn and de Jong (2011) claim that these different positions can be explained by differences in national cultures, especially the extent to which a representative individual accepts differences in power. This argument is based on previous research (de Jong 2002a) on the connection between national cultures and central bank independence. This research is summarized in this chapter's second section. A potential critique of applying these results to the European sovereign debt crisis could be that this research is based on *national* cultures, which refer to the population at large, whereas it is leaders who make decisions in the crisis. The values of these leaders might differ from those of their compatriots. That is why in a more recent paper (van Esch and de Jong 2013) we use a data set for leaders (managers) to check the robustness of our results. The relation appears even more significant for this data set of leaders' culture than the original data set and thus reinforces our claim. Research on leadership also reveals a national component in leadership styles (Hofstede *et al.* 2002; House *et al.* 2004). However, applying the results of these studies to important actors for the European sovereign debt crisis might be criticized on the grounds that these studies are based on surveys held among middle managers of companies, whereas our topic is the value pattern of specific, more political, leaders.

In order to circumvent this critique, in this chapter we construct mental maps of two European leaders who held different economic and political views on how to deal with the crisis during the first period of the crisis, namely, Jean-Claude Trichet and Axel Weber. We suggest that – despite the strong pressure to reach a consensus on the causes of, and solutions to, the crisis – these leaders' mental maps will show distinct national preferences. To test this proposition, their mental maps are compared with the pattern expected from each other's national culture and national scores on Power Distance in particular. We selected two board members of the ECB for several reasons. First, by selecting members of the same institution, the differences in value patterns cannot be ascribed to differences arising from different aims of the organizations to which the selected persons belong. Moreover, their educational and previous occupational background shows much similarity. Both have headed their country's central bank and always worked on issues of international monetary economics. Furthermore, an advantage of selecting members of a European institution instead of national political leaders has the advantage that the views released by the latter might be disturbed by domestic issues, such as regional elections. Nevertheless, we would welcome efforts to construct the mental maps and changes therein of other leaders in future research. In this sense, our study is exploratory.

This chapter is organized as follows. The first section briefly discusses the literature on central bank independence and its relation to culture. The next section describes the method for deriving cognitive maps; and then we present the results for Weber and Trichet. The chapter ends with some concluding remarks. Overall, the chapter aims to contribute to the discussion on the cultural turn in political economy in two ways. First, in ontological terms, we illustrate that semiotic factors like culture and leaders' beliefs are necessary – though not sufficient – factors in understanding policy-making and international policy coordination. Second, in methodological terms, we introduce Comparative Cognitive Mapping as a new technique to study the influence of culture on financial policy-making.

Central bank independence: a survey of trends in the literature

During the negotiations about the EMU, the independence of the future ECB was an important issue. At that time, the 1990s, the literature on central bank independence was inspired by the differences in success of reducing inflation. It was believed that an independent central bank would reduce inflation rates. The Germans, who favour stability and hence also low inflation rates, therefore insisted that the ECB should be at least as independent as the Bundesbank.[1] The French were more used to a dependent central bank but, in the end, they agreed that the ECB would be independent.

The different aspects of central bank independence can be grouped into two notions: functional independence and political independence (Masciandaro and Spinelli 1994). Functional independence refers to the possibility of controlling quantities or prices of money and credit (including the credit to the government). An independent central bank controls these monetary instruments and is not allowed to practice monetary accommodation. Political independence is high if the statutes contain price stability as the bank's main goal: the government may not interfere in the appointment of the members of the board; the board members are appointed for a fixed and long term in office; representatives of the government are not allowed on the bank's board; and there is a set of well-defined rules to settle any conflict between the central bank and the government. All these characteristics refer to formal institutions with respect to the central bank's operation and the appointment procedures of its board members. In both cases the aim of the regulations is to shield the central bank from political forces. The claim that an independent central bank leads to low inflation rates literally means that a low inflation rate is the result of having the right (formal) institutions in place.

One can wonder whether just changing the legislation will have the desired result. Consequently, researchers started to seek other factors that could cause both a high degree of central bank independence and a low inflation rate. Both more material and semiotic factors were suggested, such as government debt and deficit levels (see, for example, de Haan and van 't Hag 1995; de Jong 2002a), checks and balances in the political system (Moser 1999), social cohesion (Prast 1998), preferences (van Lelyveld 2000) and culture (de Jong 2002a; Hayo 1998).

De Jong (2002a) provides the most extensive theoretical and empirical analysis of the relation between culture, central bank independence and inflation. His empirical analysis is based on data for 18 OECD countries and employs the cultural dimensions of Hofstede (2001) (for further discussion, see Chapter 2 in this volume). Two of Hofstede's original four cultural dimensions can theoretically be related to both low inflation and an independent central bank: these are Uncertainty Avoidance and Power Distance. High scores on Uncertainty Avoidance are associated with a preference for strict rules, which corresponds with an independent central bank, and an aversion of uncertainty. Inflation is often associated with uncertainty, so that a high score on Uncertainty Avoidance is expected to correlate with a preference for low levels of inflation. Inhabitants of societies scoring high on Power Distance easily accept differences in power and wealth. High rates of inflation are known to enhance differences in income and wealth because the wealthy have more ways to protect the real value of their wealth. Moreover, high scores on Power Distance are associated with a concentration of power, which implies a high level of political influence on various institutions, including the central bank. Often the latter is part of the Ministry of Finance. The empirical analysis reveals that for a group of Organisation for Economic Development and Co-operation (OECD) countries Uncertainty Avoidance is primarily related to inflation and Power Distance to central bank independence.

Within a group of Western European countries, the scores on Power Distance vary widely, which suggests that these countries show great diversity in attitudes towards concentration of power and central bank independence. In particular, the scores of Germany (low) and France (high) differ considerably. In a series of papers (de Jong 2002b, 2004; van Esch and de Jong 2013), we have used this difference between France and Germany on Power Distance (hereafter PD) to show that this cultural factor provides a more plausible explanation for CB independence than various material factors. This is our starting point for arguing that cooperation between these two countries will not be easy and, in particular, that the divergence in view on central bank independence can easily lead to conflicts about the ECB's operation. The ECB is modelled according to the statutes of the Bundesbank, which implies a high degree of independence. For French politicians, this is hard to accept. It could (and, according to the Germans and Dutch, would) imply that elected officials are subordinate to highly placed civil servants – a position unthinkable to French politicians. This French position is nicely illustrated by President Chirac in May 1998, when Wim Duisenberg refused to announce the date at which he would step down as the first President of the ECB. Chirac expressed his anger with the words: '*Je ne me laisse pas faire chanter par un petit fonctionnaire*' (de Haas and van Lotringen 2003: 25). That is exactly what the ECB President is in French eyes: a little civil servant. Far more than their French colleagues, German politicians are used to sharing power and hold independent organizations in high esteem.

The discussion so far is summarized in the upper part of Figure 13.1, which derives from the framework in de Jong (2009: 57). In the 1990s, the discussion focused on the (formal) institutions as a prerequisite for low inflation. Later on, some stressed the importance of culture as a set of common values for the degree of central bank independence and low inflation (bottom part of Figure 13.1). Based on these results regarding the relation between national cultures and national central banks, the debate on the functioning of the ECB was framed in terms of differences in national cultures. In its first phase the focus was on the attitude of politicians of different countries (in particular France) and the

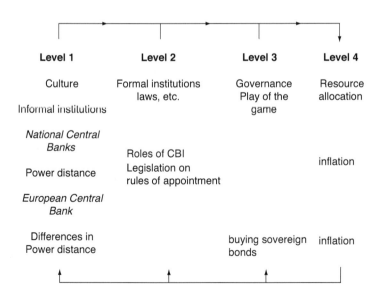

Figure 13.1 Summary of approaches.

independent functioning of the ECB. Bohn and de Jong (2011) use these insights to claim that the differences in political cultures between France and Germany have intensified the Greek and later the European sovereign debt crisis. The cultural difference is manifested in different leadership styles and different views on the best way to solve Greece's debt problem. The French favoured a European solution, whereas the Germans requested IMF involvement; an option dismissed by the French as an Anglo-Saxon invasion. These were discussions between politicians. As could have been expected, the crisis also highlighted differences, however, among several members of the ECB board; in particular between the French (Trichet) and the Germans (Axel Weber and, later, Jürgen Stark). Now the squabble is about the ECB's reaction to the political failure to solve the European debt crisis. Trichet and various South European central bankers favoured buying sovereign debt. This idea was fiercely opposed by the German representatives, who are joined by some central bankers from North-European countries (bottom part of Figure 13.1).

The research summarized above is based on historical events and on the cultural dimensions derived from questionnaires completed by employees of a company (IBM) and participants in an elite seminar. The results based on these data are used to derive hypotheses of the behaviour of individual persons, such as presidents and top civil servants. One can criticize this approach on the grounds that it assumes that individuals behave in accordance to criteria derived from a larger population. This chapter addresses this criticism by investigating the value patterns of two of the individual leaders concerned: the German former President of the Bundesbank, Axel Weber, and the French former President of the ECB, Jean-Claude Trichet. In particular, we conduct a first explorative test into our assumption that in times of crisis these individual leaders show an attitude that corresponds with their nation's value pattern and leadership styles in general and PD scores in particular (see also Hogg 2010: 415).

Method

The technique of Comparative Cognitive Mapping (CCM) is used to establish whether and how far the positions of former Bundesbank President, the German national, Axel Weber, and the French President of the ECB, Jean-Claude Trichet, regarding the role of central banks in the European sovereign debt crisis reflect their nation's value pattern and leadership style.

Cognitive mapping is one of the best developed and systematic methods for studying decision-makers' beliefs and has been successfully applied in political science, social psychology and organizational studies (Axelrod 1976; Bougon *et al.* 1977; Curseu *et al.* 2010; Eden and Ackermann 1998; van Esch 2007, 2013; Young and Schafer 1998). CCM has two further advantages over other methods to study beliefs and belief-change: (1) it enables the systematic qualitative *and* quantitative comparison of leaders' beliefs; and (2) it allows for a more discrete focus on European economic and monetary issues, thereby increasing the construct-validity of the findings (Cursue *et al.* 2010; Laukkannen 2008; van

Esch 2007; Young and Schafer 1998). In order to create a cognitive map, a number of public speeches, statements or writings on the topic of European economic and monetary integration are analysed to derive all the causal relationships alluded to a leader. Subsequently, these relations are transformed into a graphic map as arrows between two concepts using the CM software package, *Worldview* (Axelrod 1976: 3–17; van Esch 2007; Young 1996; Young and Schafer 1998).

Given the general difficulty of obtaining private documents of contemporary events, using public sources to ascertain leaders' views or personal characteristics is a customary practice in political psychological studies of leaders 'at a distance' (Renshon 2009; van Esch 2007: 125). While scholars caution against extrapolating affective reactions from public sources, studies of the validity of public assertions in assessing leaders' beliefs generally conclude that analysis of public sources produce outcomes similar to those of private sources (Renshon 2009). An additional advantage of using public speeches is that one may assume that these speeches reflect the person's opinion in his official role. That is the only position we are interested in. What does this person think and will he (or she) do as member of the ECB's board. One could argue that these public speeches are written by speech writers and thus do not reflect Weber's and Trichet's own views. If that is right, we will find no traces of national culture. In sum, by selecting persons from the same board, with similar educational and occupational backgrounds and using public speeches, we have significantly decreased the probability of finding differences in opinion. Hence, if under such harsh conditions for finding cultural differences, we still find cultural differences, then we can be quite certain that these differences are real.

As an example of this technique, Figure 13.2 displays an excerpt from Axel Weber's cognitive map. This excerpt shows, for example, that, in his speeches, Weber refers to the concepts 'ECB purchasing bonds' as contributing to a 'blurring of fiscal and monetary policies' that, in turn, in his eyes, diminishes the 'credibility' of the ECB. It may also be inferred that the ECB's decision to

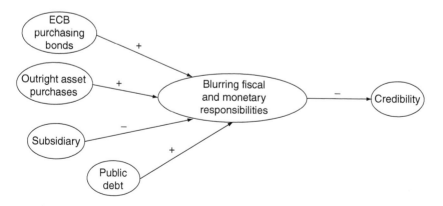

Figure 13.2 Excerpt of Weber's cognitive map.

engage in the purchasing of bonds is not welcomed by the former President, because its 'consequent path' shows that it contributes negatively to the positive goal of 'credibility' of EMU.[2] A cognitive map thus gives a structured overview of a leader's position on a certain topic, shows which concepts are linked in his/ her mind and in what way, and indicates which concepts are valued positively and which negatively.[3] The relative strength of leaders' beliefs is determined by establishing the relative saliency – the frequency with which it is mentioned – and centrality of concepts – the number of dyads to which it belongs. As shown in Figure 13.2, the centrality of the concept 'blurring of fiscal and monetary policies' is 5; saliency is not visualized in a cognitive map. Overall, leaders' policy-preferences, values and causal reasoning may thus be ascertained from the maps by a qualitative analysis of the concepts and relations in the maps.

In addition, the maps are analysed at the level of belief-dimensions, an aggregate of concepts indicating leaders' adherence to an underlying ideal-type policy paradigm or value-construction, like the level to which a leader adheres to Keynesian or Ordoliberal economic ideas (see Tables 13.2–13.8). In order to determine whether a leader adheres (more) to one ideal-type paradigm than another, several calculations are performed: the number of concepts a leader refers to that may be characterized as belonging to a paradigm, the aggregated saliency and centrality of these concepts, their average saliency and centrality, and the amount (in percentage) the aggregated saliency and centrality of the concepts comprise the sum of saliency and centrality of all concepts in a map (see Tables 13.2–13.8; cf. van Esch 2007, 2013). This makes the comparison of cognitive maps possible.

To determine whether Weber and Trichet's views on the financial crisis reflect their nation's scores on Hofstede's PD dimension, a cognitive map was created for each leader based on four public speeches on the Euro-crisis before various national and international audiences from April 2010–April 2011 (Trichet 2010a, 2010b, 2010c, 2011; Weber 2010a, 2010b, 2011a, 2011b). From these speeches, the sections dealing specifically with the functioning of the European Economic and Monetary Union were selected for analysis. These resulting maps (not included here but obtainable from the authors) include up to 94 concepts and 168 causal relationships.

Operationalization

As stated above, the idea of central bank independence is correlated with Hofstede's Power Distance dimension. In a general sense, Power Distance (PD) refers to the extent to which the less powerful members of organizations and the wider society accept and expect that power is distributed unequally. In terms of ideas about the state and politics, PD harbours three interrelated characteristics of interest to our discussion (Hofstede and Hofstede 2005: 67).

First, in terms of the political system, states with high and low PD profiles differ on how power should be distributed. In high PD states, inequalities are accepted as a natural fact and both the people and political elite show a preference and acceptance for centralization of power in the hands of a few. In low PD countries, centralization of power is deemed undesirable, and the fragmentation and dispersion of power over different institutions are preferred (Hofstede and Hofstede 2005: 61). Second, high and low PD states have differing views on the forms of power they deem desirable and legitimate. While high PD countries tend towards traditional, charismatic or political leadership, low PD nations are hesitant simply to accept leadership. Merit-based legitimation of leadership is needed and, to be considered legitimate, authority must be based on expertise. The third relevant aspect of the Power Distance dimension is the attitude towards checks and balances. In high PD countries, might reigns over right, and people feel less need to scrutinize their leaders' authority or to constrain their actions or the decisions by other forms of authority. This is in contrast to low PD states, where people feel right should rule over might and the power and actions of leaders is more often constrained by the rule of law (Hofstede and Hofstede 2005: 61). In combination, these three dimensions reveal a clear picture of the differences in political structure and leadership. High PD states have a relatively high tolerance for centralization of power in the hands of a (small) group of authoritative political leaders whose actions and decisions are less scrutinized and constrained by the rule of law and the power of expertise. In low PD states, people would be highly suspicious of such a political configuration. These states prefer to disperse authority and put their trust in leadership by expertise which is constrained by the rule of law.

In terms of the issue of central bank independence, this distinction translates as follows. Central bank independence would be valued specifically in low PD states due to its reliance on the power of expertise rather than politics. Moreover, the fragmentation of power by separating monetary from general economic policy and delegating these separate tasks to an independent central bank and government respectively corresponds to low PD preferences for dispersion of power. Finally, low PD states would advocate constraining the actions and mandate of political actors and central banks by rooting these firmly into law-like rules. Conversely, in high PD states, people would find far less legitimacy in the power of expertise and see less need for a separation of power or instating a system of regulatory checks and balances. In such states, people find little fault in centralizing monetary and economic policy into the hands of a few authoritarian political leaders (see Table 13.1).

Table 13.1 Power Distance and public policy-making

Power Distance cultural aspects	*High*	*Low*
Division of power & tasks	Centralization Political dependent CB	Fragmentation Independent CB
Legitimate power	Politics (state)	Expertise (central banks)
Checks & balances	Unnecessary or political	Rooted in law

Results

We will analyse and compare the respective maps of Trichet and Weber to ascertain the extent to which their thoughts correspond to their national cultural value-pattern on each of these three aspects.

Division of power and tasks

The first cultural aspect is the division of economic and monetary power and tasks among political actors and central banks. As the issue of central bank independence is rooted in leaders' broader economic views, we start by studying their general view on economic and monetary policy-making in order to contextualize their specific views on the division of power between politics and expertise. Later we will focus on their beliefs of central bank independence in particular.

The idea of separation of power in European economic and monetary policy has a close link to the divide between Ordoliberal versus Keynesian economic thinking. The need for central bank independence is especially pronounced in Ordoliberal economic thought. This view is characterized first and foremost by a belief in the primacy of price stability ('sound money'), which is the guiding principle by which all other policy-measures are assessed. Crucially, in the eyes of the Ordoliberals there is no trade-off between (1) price stability and (2) employment and economic growth (Verdun 2000: 100). To ensure price stability, European economic and monetary unification must meet two requirements. First, it has to ensure that member states adopt stringent budgetary and fiscal policies and denounce monetary financing. Second, Ordoliberals stress the need for CB independence, as only a central bank that is constitutionally, politically and financially autonomous can guarantee sound and credible monetary policy-making based on expert analysis of the economic fundamentals, rather than on political or electoral considerations (Dullien and Guerot 2012; Dyson *et al.* 1999: 276; Verdun 2000: 100). Crucially, they combine these economic ideas concerning European economic and monetary unification with ardent support for the primacy of economic over political or geo-political considerations: 'sound' economic ideas should not be subordinated to political or geo-political interests.

In contrast, more Keynesian-oriented leaders would place less emphasis on the need for CB independence. First, in the Keynesian ideal-type, price-stability is not regarded as the central economic goal and a trade-off is recognized between, on the one hand, economic growth and employment and, on the other hand, price stability. In addition, economic stimulation – as opposed to stringent budgetary policy advocated by politically independent experts – may lead to economic benefits that outweigh possible effects on price-stability in their eyes. Overall, Ordoliberalism and Keynesianism harbour very different beliefs on the separation of power between government and central bank, politics and economics and thereby central bank independence. Adherence to one or the other may thus provide a first indication of a leader's view on division of power.

Tables 13.2 and 13.3 summarize Weber's and Trichet's views on Division of Power and Central Bank Independence. We now discuss Table 13.2 in more detail in order to explain the procedure used and figures listed in the tables. The table lists all the concepts found in Weber's speeches that refer to his economic paradigm. For each view (e.g. Ordoliberal or Keynesian) the table contains four summary statistics. The first two are the number of concepts belonging to this view, and the total score, which is the number of times the concepts are mentioned (Saliency) or form part of a dyad (Centrality). Percentage of total is the number of times concepts belonging to this view (and listed in the table) are mentioned (Saliency-column) or are part of a dyad (Centrality-column) as a percentage of the total number of times concepts in Weber's map are mentioned or form part of a dyad. This percentage is important because it gives us a measure of the relative importance of the concepts listed in the tables. So concepts referring to his economic paradigm make up 32.7 (33.2) per cent of the number of times a concept is listed as Centrality (Saliency) in the entire cognitive map of Weber. Mean score of concepts is the total score divided by the number of concepts (91/25 in column Centrality of Table 13.2).

When we compare the views of Trichet and Weber in terms of Ordoliberal and Keynesian economic thought, a clear pattern emerges (see Tables 13.2 and 13.3). Weber is a clear and univocal supporter of Ordoliberal thought. His reference to ideal-typical Ordoliberal concerns like sound budgetary policy, price-stability and a strong EU Stability and Growth Pact make up a third of his entire map and are almost six times as salient and central to his belief-system than more Keynesian beliefs (see Table 13.2; cf. Young and Semmler 2011).[4] Trichet's views have Ordoliberal tendencies but to a far lesser extent: Ordoliberal concerns make up about a fifth of his entire map and are about three times as salient and central as his Keynesian concepts.

More interesting in the light of the Power Distance score of their respective nation states, however, are the concepts and relations referring directly to central bank independence and their preferred division of power. At first sight, Weber's map reveals a curious pattern: the former President of the Bundesbank does not mention CB independence even once in the speeches under study.[5] Previous studies indicate, however, that prior to the crisis, Weber was an explicit and strong supporter of central bank independence (Boin *et al.* 2012). However, on closer inspection, Weber's map reveals that, with the outbreak of the crisis, Weber shifted his focus from the abstract discussion of aspects of central bank independence to a detailed discussion of the mandate, domain and responsibilities of the ECB and governments respectively. As such, after the crisis erupted, he seems to have become more concerned with the functional than political independence of the ECB.

His views on these matters are clear: In principle, Weber sees some value in the exceptional measures taken by the ECB in response to the crisis as this could lead to solving liquidity problems and serve price stability.[6] However, the former Bundesbank President stresses that these measures should be strictly conditional

Table 13.2 Weber's economic thought

Weber-PD	Ordoliberal	Centrality	Salience	Keynesian	Centrality	Salience
Economic thought	Sound public finances	19	24	ECB liquidity measures	5	5
	Price stability	8	10	Economic growth	2	2
	Sound single monetary policy	7	8	Exceptional measures [E]CB	2	2
	Timely exit from ECB non-standard measures	5	8	German current account surplus	2	2
	Excessive deficits (−)	7	7	Current account deficits in foreign countries (−)	1	1
	Strengthened SGP	5	6	Domestic demand	1	1
	Blurring fiscal and monetary responsibilities (−)	4	5	ECB central player in moneymarket	1	1
	Budgetary deficits (−)	5	5	Economic stimulation	1	1
	ECB asset purchases (−)	4	5	Long-term saviour of banking sector	1	1
	Fiscal discipline	3	4			
	Founding principles of EMU	2	4			
	Incentive for borrowing (−)	3	4			
	ECB standard policy	3	3			
	Public debt (−)	3	3			
	ECB using monetary analysis	2	2			
	German debt brake	2	2			
	Financial stability as ECB goal (−)	1	2			
	Fiscal policy as ECB goal (−)	1	2			
	60% debt ratio	1	1			
	Conditional ECB measures	1	1			
	Convergence criteria	1	1			
	Early warning system	1	1			
	Independent monetary policy	1	1			
	Liquidity growth (−)	1	1			
	Price stability as ECB goal	1	1			
	Number of concepts	25	25	Number of concepts	9	9
	Total score	91	111	Total score	15	16
	Percentage of total in map	32.7	33.2	Percentage of total in map	5.4	4.8
	Mean score of concepts	3.6	4.4	Mean score of concepts	1.7	1.8

Notes

C = Centrality, the number of dyads a concept is part of; S = Saliency, the frequency with which the concept is mentioned; − = negatively valued concepts; 0 = ambiguously valued concepts.

Table 13.3 Trichet's economic thought

Trichet-PD	Ordoliberal	Centrality	Salience	Keynesian	Centrality	Salience
Economic thought	Price stability	13	28	Sustainable economic growth	9	10
	Sound public finances	13	16	ECB increase of interest rate (–)	3	5
	Strengthened SGP	5	6	ECB asset purchases	3	5
	Public debt (–)	3	6	Current account deficits in foreign countries	2	2
	[E]CB independence	2	6	ECB liquidity measures	2	2
	Price stability as ECB goal	5	6	Enlargement of EMU	1	2
	Clear and strong budgetary rules in EMU	4	4	Domestic demand	1	1
	MS responsibility to ensure competitiveness	3	4	Economic growth	1	1
	Rules for competitiveness	3	3	Exceptional measures [E]CB	1	1
	increased fiscal surveillance (SGP)	3	3	Sound public finances alone (–)	1	1
	Budgetary deficits (–)	2	2			
	Austerity programme problem states	2	2			
	Compliance with SGP norms	2	2			
	Conditional financial assistance	2	2			
	Independent monetary policy	2	2			
	Surveillance of competitiveness	2	2			
	Sufficiently strong sanctions	2	2			
	Fiscal discipline	1	1			
	Economic boom	1	1			
	Sound national budgetary procedures	1	1			
	Sound single monetary policy	1	1			
	Acceleration excessive deficit procedure	1	1			
	60% debt ratio	1	1			
	Number of concepts	*23*	*23*	*Number of concepts*	*10*	*10*
	Total score	*74*	*102*	*Total score*	*24*	*30*
	Percentage of total in map	*23.3*	*24.4*	*Percentage of total in map*	*7.6*	*8.2*
	Mean score of concepts	*3.2*	*4.4*	*Mean score of concepts*	*2.4*	*3*

Notes

C = Centrality, the number of dyads a concept is part of; S = Saliency, the frequency with which the concept is mentioned; – = negatively valued concepts; 0 = ambiguously valued concepts.

Table 13.4 Weber's view on the division of power and central bank independence

Weber-PD	Divided	Centrality	Salience	Shared	Centrality	Salience
Central bank independence	Sound single monetary policy	7	8	ECB liquidity measures	5	5
	Timely exit from ECB non-standard measures	5	8	Exceptional measures [E]CB	2	2
	Blurring fiscal and monetary responsibilities (–)	4	5	ECB central player in moneymarket	1	1
	ECB asset purchases (–)	4	5			
	ECB standard policy	3	3			
	ECB using monetary analysis	2	2			
	Financial stability as ECB goal (–)	1	2			
	Fiscal policy as ECB goal (–)	1	2			
	Conditional ECB measures	1	1			
	Independent monetary policy	1	1			
	Price stability as ECB goal	1	1			
	Number of concepts	*11*	*11*	*Number of concepts*	*3*	*3*
	Total score	*30*	*38*	*Total score*	*8*	*8*
	Percentage of total in map	*10.8*	*11.4*	*Percentage of total in map*	*2.9*	*2.4*
	Mean score of concepts	*2.7*	*3.5*	*Mean score of concepts*	*2.7*	*2.7*

Total of all references

	Number of concepts	*14*	*14*
	Total score	*38*	*46*
	Percentage of total in map	*13.7*	*13.8*

Notes

C = Centrality, the number of dyads a concept is part of; S = Saliency, the frequency with which the concept is mentioned; – = negatively valued concepts; 0 = ambiguously valued concepts.

Table 13.5 Trichet's view on the division of power and central bank independence

Trichet-PD	Divided	Centrality	Salience	Shared	Centrality	Salience
Central bank independence	[E]CB independence	2	6	ECB asset purchases	3	5
	Price stability as ECB goal	5	6	ECB liquidity measures	2	2
	Independent monetary policy	2	2	Exceptional measures [E]CB	1	1
	Sound single monetary policy	1	1			
	Number of concepts	*4*	*4*	*Number of concepts*	*3*	*3*
	Total score	*10*	*15*	*Total score*	*6*	*8*
	Percentage of total in map	*3.1*	*3.6*	*Percentage of total in map*	*1.9*	*1.9*
	Mean score of concepts	*2.5*	*3.8*	*Mean score of concepts*	*2.0*	*2.7*
Total of all references						
	Number of concepts	*7*	*7*			
	Total score	*16*	*23*			
	Percentage of total in map	*5.0*	*5.5*			

Notes

C = Centrality, the number of dyads a concept is part of; S = Saliency, the frequency with which the concept is mentioned; – = negatively valued concepts; 0 = ambiguously valued concepts.

and temporary. In addition, Weber discusses the mandate of the ECB at length. Clearly, in his eyes the ECB should not diverge from its formal obligation to focus first and foremost on safeguarding price stability. He fiercely opposes including goals like financial or fiscal stability into the ECB mandate and rejects any blurring of the proper responsibilities of member states and ECB as this would threaten ECB credibility, price stability and sound monetary policy. As such, Weber is clearly a strong supporter of a division of power amongst political actors and central banks as well as central bank independence (overall C and S of 30/38 versus 8/8; see Table 13.4).

Trichet's ideas concerning the need for CB independence reveal that he has a more flexible view on the issue. First, while he refers explicitly to the concept of CB independence in his speeches, he deploys fewer concepts referring to mandate, domain and responsibilities of the ECB and governments than Weber (7 versus 14). Moreover, like Weber he is generally positive about the exceptional measures the ECB engaged in during the crisis which in his eyes have benefited the banking sector and solved liquidity problems. However, in contrast to Weber, he does not explicitly identify the need for these measures to be conditional or temporary. Second, he agrees with Weber that price stability is the ECB's pre-eminent objective but seems less concerned about the topic of the proper ECB mandate: he distinguishes only one concept referring directly to this issue: 'Price stability as ECB policy goal'. The overall saliency and centrality of concepts that point to central bank independence and a division of power is only slightly higher than those indicating a broad and flexible ECB mandate (C and S = 10/15 versus 6/8).

Overall, a comparison of their maps reveals that Weber's concern for the separation of the mandate, domain and responsibilities of the ECB from that of the states is far more salient and central to his mind than it is to Trichet's (see Tables 13.4 and 13.5). This supports our hypothesis that leaders from low PD states have greater concern for division of power and central bank independence.

Legitimate power

A comparison of the cognitive maps of Weber and Trichet also provides some support for our hypothesis about the kind of power people experience as legitimate depending on whether they come from a high or low PD country. As indicated above, in high PD states, people tend to perceive political actors as legitimate policy-makers while people from low PD states feel legitimate power should be merit-based and rests with experts rather than politicians. In the case of European economic and monetary policy-making and the Euro-crisis in particular, this differentiation in politics and expertise is clearly visible in practice, whereby political leadership is located in government officials in the European Council, Council of Ministers and unilateral decision-making by states. Expertise on the other hand is embodied in the national central banks and the ECB. As such, we have studied the references both leaders make to the actions of these actors and their assessment of their performance.

From the analysis it appears that to both Weber and Trichet, governments and central banks are legitimate powers in their own right.[7] However, while Weber refers as much to governmental actions and obligations as to the actions and proper mandate of the ECB, in Trichet's map the saliency and centrality of governmental actions are higher than those of the ECB. Moreover, further analysis reveals that Trichet is more positive about both the political actors as well as his own ECB than Weber: he is fairly positive of governmental action, and – as may be expected – unambiguously enthusiastic about the actions and mandate of the ECB (see bottom part of Table 13.7).[8] In accordance to the image portrayed in the media, we find that Weber is far more critical of the ECB than Trichet, and he is even less positive about the European governments (see Table 13.6).[9]

While the results are less pronounced than they were for the Division of Power and Tasks, they accord with our hypothesis. Reviewing these results, a possible criticism is worth noting. Since Trichet may be regarded as the embodiment of the ECB, his score with respect to the assessment of ECB actions may be distorted by his formal position. The differences in focus on politics and expertise as well as the more critical attitude of Weber regarding governmental actions, however, cannot be explained in this manner. These may thus be taken as valid indications of the thesis that leaders from low PD states are more prone to perceive expertise as more legitimate than politics.

Checks and balances

Finally, we conducted a preliminary test of the third aspect of the Power Dimension relevant to our research topic: leaders' preference for instating checks and balances in the policy-making process. The lower a state's PD, the more its people and leaders are expected to favour binding policy-makers to the mast. Moreover, the lower a nation's PD, the more pronounced its preference for checks and balances in the form of laws, rules and regulations. People and leaders from high PD states see less need for checks and balances and display a preference for political or democratic controls. Since neither Trichet nor Weber mentions political or democratic checks and balances in their assertions, the analysis is focused on their relative concern for more, or more stringent rules and regulations. We will compare the saliency and centrality of such concepts in their minds as well as the value they attach to rules and regulations.

As is evident from Table 13.8, the results of the analysis do not fit our expectations based on Hofstede's dimensions. One would have expected that Weber, as a German (low PD), would be the one to stress the value of regulatory checks and balances. However, Weber identifies fewer concepts referring to (stringent) rules and regulations, and these scores are lower in terms of centrality and saliency as well as portion of his total map than in the case of Trichet. Although the differences are small, one would at least have expected the pattern to be reversed.

Further analysis reveals another interesting pattern in their scores on the checks-and-balances aspect that may call for further research. Both leaders are

Table 13.6 Weber's view on legitimate power

Weber-PD	Politician/government	C	S	Central banks	C	S
Legitimate power	Sound public finances	19	24	Sound single monetary policy	7	8
	Excessive deficits (−)	7	7	Timely exit from ECB non-standard measures	5	8
	Fiscal support package (0)	4	7	Blurring fiscal and monetary responsibilities (−)	4	5
	Member states coping with asymmetric shock	4	7	ECB asset purchases (−)	4	5
	Budgetary deficits (−)	5	5	ECB liquidity measures	5	5
	Fiscal discipline	3	4	[E]CB policy	4	4
	MS problems with refinancing debt (−)	3	3	Low interest rate (0)	4	4
	Public debt (−)	3	3	Tailored [E]CB response	2	4
	Compliance	2	2	ECB standard policy	3	3
	Decision-making by politicians (−)	2	2	ECB using monetary analysis	2	2
	German debt brake	2	2	Exceptional measures [E]CB	2	2
	National policies (−)	2	2	Financial stability as ECB goal (−)	1	2
	Unproductive use of capital	2	2	Fiscal policy as ECB goal (−)	1	2
	Cope with future pension problems	1	1	Conditional ECB measures	1	1

	Positive	Negative
ECB central player in money market	1	1
Independent monetary policy	1	1
Price stability as ECB goal	1	1
Number of concepts	17	17
Total score	48	58
Percentage of total in map	17.3	17.4
Mean score of concepts	2.9	3.4
Central banks	Positive	Negative
Number of concepts	12	4
Total score	40	14
Percentage of total in category	74.1	25.9
Mean score of concepts	3.3	3.5

	Positive	Negative
German policy	1	1
Government investment (0)	1	1
Political commitment	1	1
Procyclical policy (0)	1	1
Number of concepts	18	18
Total score	66	75
Percentage of total in map	23.7	22.5
Mean score of concepts	3.7	4.2
Performance (S) — Politicians/government	Positive	Negative
Number of concepts	8	7
Total score	42	24
Percentage of total in category	63.6	36.4
Mean score of concepts	5.3	3.4

Notes

C = Centrality, the number of dyads a concept is part of; S = Saliency, the frequency with which the concept is mentioned; – = negatively valued concepts; 0 = ambiguously valued concepts.

For 'Performance' only the saliency scores are given.

Table 13.7 Trichet's view on legitimate power

Trichet-PD	Politician/government	C	S	Central banks	C	S
Legitimate power	Sound public finances	13	16	[E]CB policy	4	11
	Public debt (–)	3	6	[E]CB independence	2	6
	Sound national economic and financial policy	5	5	Price stability as ECB goal	5	6
	MS responsibility to ensure competitiveness	3	4	ECB increase of interest rate (–)	3	5
	SGP reform [2004] (0)	3	3	ECB asset purchases	3	5
	Fiscal support package (0)	2	3	ECB liquidity measures	2	2
	Budgetary deficits (–)	2	2	Independent monetary policy	2	2
	Austerity programme problem states	2	2	Exceptional measures [E]CB	1	1
	Compliance with SGP norms	2	2	Sound single monetary policy	1	1
	Economic policy harmonization	2	2			
	Renewal of SGP	2	2			
	Enlargement of EMU	1	1			
	Fiscal discipline	1	1			
	Compliance	1	1			
	Sound national budgetary procedures	1	1			
	Sound public finances alone (–)	1	1			
	Number of concepts	*16*	*16*	*Number of concepts*	*9*	*9*
	Total score	*44*	*53*	*Total score*	*23*	*39*
	Percentage of total in map	*13.8*	*12.7*	*Percentage of total in map*	*7.2*	*9.3*
	Mean score of concepts	*2.8*	*3.3*	*Mean score of concepts*	*2.6*	*4.3*

Performance (S)	Politicians/government	Positive	Negative	Central banks	Positive	Negative
	Number of concepts	*11*	*3*	*Number of concepts*	*8*	*1*
	Total score	*38*	*9*	*Total score*	*34*	*5*
	Percentage of total in category	*80.6*	*19.2*	*Percentage of total in category*	*87.2*	*12.8*
	Mean score of concepts	*3.5*	*3.0*	*Mean score of concepts*	*4.3*	*5.0*

Notes

C = Centrality, the number of dyads a concept is part of; S = Saliency, the frequency with which the concept is mentioned; – = negatively valued concepts; 0 = ambiguously valued concepts.

For 'Performance' only the saliency scores are given.

Table 13.8 Weber's and Trichet's views on regulatory checks and balances

PD	Weber	C	S	Trichet	C	S
Regulatory checks and balances	Strong institutional framework	7	7	Strengthening economic union	10	15
	Macroeconomic surveillance	6	7	Macroeconomic surveillance	7	7
	SGP	6	6	Stronger economic governance of Eurozone	5	7
	Strengthened SGP	5	6	Strengthened SGP	5	6
	Founding principles of EMU	2	4	Clear & strong budgetary rules in EMU	4	4
	ECB standard policy	3	3	Clear & strong multilateral surveillance	3	4
	Subsidiarity	2	2	Increased fiscal surveillance (SGP)	3	3
	German debt brake	2	2	Rules for competitiveness	3	3
	Compliance	2	2	Compliance with SGP norms	2	2
	ECB using monetary analysis	2	2	Conditional financial assistance	2	2
	Sanctions	1	1	Sanctions	2	2
	Crisis management system	1	1	Strong institutional framework	2	2
	Conditional ECB measures	1	1	Sufficiently strong sanctions	2	2
	Convergence criteria	1	1	Surveillance of competitiveness	2	2
	Early warning system	1	1	60% debt ratio	1	1
	60% debt ratio	1	1	Acceleration excessive deficit procedure	1	1
				Compliance	1	1
				Fulfilling conditions	1	1
				Single fiscal authority	1	1
				Sound national budgetary procedures	1	1
	Number of concepts	*16*	*16*	*Number of concepts*	*20*	*20*
	Total score	*43*	*47*	*Total score*	*58*	*67*
	Percentage of total in map	*15.5*	*14.1*	*Percentage of total in map*	*18.2*	*16.0*
	Mean score of concepts	*2.7*	*2.9*	*Mean score of concepts*	*2.9*	*3.4*

Notes

C = Centrality, the number of dyads a concept is part of; S = Saliency, the frequency with which the concept is mentioned; – – = negatively valued concepts; 0 = ambiguously valued concepts.

Weber mentions 'Flexibility' S=1, C=1; Trichet mentions 'Transparency' S=3, C=3 and 'SGP reform [2004]' S=3, C=3 which he values ambiguously.

univocally positive about (more and stronger) regulation of European economic and monetary policy-making. However, apart from Weber's call to bind the ECB to the mast by imposing conditions on the non-standard liquidity measures it took during the crisis, both leaders only refer to checks and balances aimed at curtailing the actions and powers of the European member states. Apart from upholding their formal mandate of guarding price stability, they apparently see no need for checks and balances on the actions and powers of (European) central banks. Extending this study to include political leaders may reveal whether this is a matter of a self-interested role perception rather than culture.

Concluding remarks

The European sovereign debt crisis has highlighted huge differences in opinion. On one side stood the Germans and some Northern European countries who pleaded for IMF involvement. On the other side were French politicians and the French President of the ECB, Jean-Claude Trichet, who supported a European solution that would be independent of the IMF. Disagreement with the solutions provided even led to the resignation of two German members of the ECB's board. In this chapter we argued that cultural differences were at the root of these conflicts. This argument is partly based on previous research that makes use of constructs of national culture. Another piece of our argument consists of constructs of the mental maps of two important European decision-makers Axel Weber and Jean-Claude Trichet. For two of the three concepts we found that the cognitive maps of these two leaders correspond with the hypotheses derived from national culture. This implies that an independent institution such as the ECB is formally (according to its constitution) independent but that its actual behaviour may still reflect national differences. So in spite of an institutional independence, national cultural differences still shape the preferences of the ECB's board members.

We also illustrated the usefulness of the technique of constructing mental maps of public leaders. This technique enables researchers to investigate the views of leaders without having to rely on results of surveys which incorporate respondents from the society at large or subgroups (managers, teachers, and so on) of the society. Since the first results are promising, we would recommend constructing mental maps of more important European leaders in the future. Finally, this chapter has illustrated the increasing importance of soft factors for economic policy. In this manner it illustrates the relevance of Cultural Political Economy.

Notes

1　Historical reasons for the German preference for low inflation are provided in van Esch and de Jong (2013).
2　A decision-maker prefers policies that are linked to a positively evaluated goal by only positive relationships or even an amount of negative relations, or to a negatively evaluated goal by an uneven amount or negative relations. Decision-makers' preferences are

indeterminate when linked to policy by a path containing one or more zero signs or when paths are contradictory.

3 For an elaborate description of the method used, see van Esch (2007, Chapter 4).

4 Keynesian concepts like 'monetary expansionary policy' are listed under Ordoliberal and vice versa in Tables 13.2 and 13.3 when looked upon unfavourably by the respective leader. Similar calculations are conducted for Tables 13.4–13.5. In case of indeterminate concepts, they have been omitted from the calculation.

5 A quick scan through all Weber's post-2009 speeches on the Bundesbank site reveals that this is the case in most of his speeches.

6 He attaches a positive value to the concept of the ECB providing liquidity and the ECB exceptional measures and is ambivalent about the bond purchases by the ECB (see Table 13.2).

7 Governmental action makes up about 13 per cent of Trichet's map with an average centrality and saliency of 2.8 and 3.3. ECB actions and mandate make up approximately 8 per cent with an average centrality and saliency of 2.6 and 4.3. In contrast, they make up about 23 per cent and 17.4 per cent of Weber's map with similar average centrality and saliency values (see Tables 13.6 and 13.7).

8 Trichet identifies only one negative in the actions of the ECB, and his positive references to governmental actions make up about 87 per cent of all concepts in this category against circa 13 per cent for negative references in terms of centrality and saliency (see Table 13.7).

9 Weber identifies four negative aspects versus twelve positives in the actions of the ECB, while he identifies eight negatives and seven positives in governmental actions (see Table 13.6).

References

Axelrod, R. (1976) The Cognitive Mapping Approach to Decision Making, in R. Axelrod (ed.), *Structure of Decision: The Cognitive Maps of Political Elites*, Princeton, NJ: Princeton University Press.

Bohn, F. and de Jong, E. (2011) The 2010 Euro Crisis Stand-Off between France and Germany: Leadership Styles and Political Culture, *International Economics and Economic Policy*, 8(1): 7–14.

Boin, A., 't Hart, P. and van Esch, F.A.W.J. (2012) Political Leadership in Times of Crisis: Comparing Leader Responses to Financial Turbulence, in L. Helms (ed.), *Comparative Political Leadership*, Basingstoke: Palgrave Macmillan.

Bougon, M., Weick, K. and Binkhorst, D. (1977) Cognition in Organizations: An Analysis of the Utrecht Jazz Orchestra, *Administrative Science Quarterly*, 22(4): 606–39.

Curseu, P.L., Schalk, M.J.D. and Schruijer, S.G.L. (2010) The Use of Cognitive Mapping in Eliciting and Evaluating Group Cognitions, *Journal of Applied Social Psychology*, 40(5): 1258–91.

de Haan, J. and van 't Hag, G.J. (1995) Variation in Central Bank Independence across Countries: Some Provisional Empirical Evidence, *Public Choice*, 85(3–4): 335–51.

de Haas, B. and van Lotringen, C. (2003) *Wim Duisenberg: Van Friese volksjongen tot Mr Euro* [Wim Duisenberg: from Frisian People's Boy to Mr Euro], Amsterdam: Uitgeverij Business Contact.

de Jong, E. (2002a) Why are Price Stability and Statutory Independence of Central Banks Negatively Correlated? The Role of Culture, *European Journal of Political Economy*, 18: 675–94.

de Jong, E. (2002b) De ECB onder Vuur: een Botsing van Culturen? [The ECB Subject to Fire: A Clash of Cultures?], *Tijdschrift voor Politieke Economie*, 23(4): 20–40.

de Jong, E. (2004) Differences in Political Culture Hamper European Integration, in F. Astengo and N. Neuwahl (eds), *A Constitution for Europe? Governance and Policy-Making in the European Union*, Montreal: Université de Montréal.

de Jong, E. (2009) *Culture and Economics: On Values, Economics and International Business*, London: Routledge.

Denzau, A.T. and North, D.C. (1994) Shared Mental Models: Ideologies and Institutions, *Kyklos*, 47(1): 3–31.

Dullien, U. and Guerot, S. (2012) The Long Shadow of Ordoliberalism: Germany's Approach to the Euro Crisis, *ECFR/49* February 2012.

Dyson, K.H., Hall, F. and Featherstone, K. (1999) *The Road to Maastricht: Negotiating Economic and Monetary Union*, Oxford: Oxford University Press.

Eden, C. and Ackermann, F. (1998) Analysing and Comparing Ideographic Causal Maps, in C. Eden and J.C. Spender (eds), *Managerial and Organizational Cognition: Theory, Methods and Research*, London: Sage.

Hayo, B. (1998) Inflation Culture, Central Bank Independence and Price Stability, *European Journal of Political Economy*, 14: 241–63.

Hofstede, G. (2001) *Cultures Consequences: Comparing Values, Behaviors, Institutions, and Organizations Across Nations*, London: Sage.

Hofstede, G. and Hofstede, G.J. (2005) *Cultures and Organisations: Software of the Mind*, New York: McGraw-Hill.

Hofstede, G., van Deursen, C.A., Mueller, C.B., Charles, T.A. and the Business Goals Network (2002) What Goals do Business Leaders Pursue? A Study in Fifteen Countries, *Journal of International Business Studies*, 33(4): 785–803.

Hogg, M.A. (2010) Human Groups, Social Categories, and Collective Self: Social Identity and the Management of Self-Uncertainty, in R.M. Arkin, K.C. Oleson and P.J. Caroll (eds), *Handbook of the Uncertain Self*, New York: Psychology Press.

House, R.J., Hanges, P.J., Javidan, M., Dorfman, P.W. and Gupta, V. (eds) (2004) *Culture, Leadership, and Organizations: The GLOBE Study of 62 Societies*, London: Sage.

Laukkanen, M. (2008) Comparative Causal Mapping with CMAP3. A Method Introduction to Comparative Causal Mapping: A User's Manual for CMAP3. *Kuopio University Occasional Reports H. Business and Information Technology* 2.

Masciandaro, D. and Spinelli, F. (1994) Central Bank's Independence: Institutional Determinants, Rankings and Central Bankers' Views, *Scottish Journal of Political Economy*, 41(4): 434–43.

Moser, P. (1999) Checks and Balances, and Supply of Central Bank Independence *European Economic Review*, 43: 1569–93.

Prast, H.M. (1998) Inflation Distortionary Taxation and the Design of Monetary Policy: The Role of Social Cohesion, *Banca Nazionale del Lavoro Quarterly Review*, 204: 37–53.

Renshon, J. (2009) When Public Statements Reveal Private Beliefs: Assessing Operational Codes at a Distance, *Political Psychology*, 30(4): 649–61.

Trichet, J.C. (2010a) *Keynote Speech at the 9th Munich Economic Summit*, 29 April.

Trichet, J.C. (2010b) *European Integration: The Benefits of Acting Collectively*, Speech at the Feri Foundation Award Ceremony Kaisersaal, Frankfurt am Main, 9 June.

Trichet, J.C. (2010c) *Lessons from the Crisis*, Speech at the European American Press Club, Paris, 3 December.

Trichet, J.C. (2011) *The Essence of Economic and Monetary Union*, Speech as the Guest of Honour at the Schaffermahlzeit, Bremen, 11 February.

van Esch, F.A.W.J. (2007) *Mapping the Road to Maastricht. A Comparative Study of German and French Pivotal Decision Makers' Preferences Concerning the Establishment of a European Monetary Union During the early 1970s and Late 1980s*, PhD thesis. Nijmegen: Radboud University Nijmegen.

van Esch, F.A.W.J. (2012) Why Germany wanted EMU. The Role of Helmut Kohl's Belief-System and the Fall of the Berlin Wall, *German Politics*, 21(1): 34–52.

van Esch, F.A.W.J. and de Jong, E. (2013) Institutionalisation without Internalisation: The Cultural Dimension of French-German Conflicts on European Central Bank Independence, *International Economics and Economic Policy*, 10(4): 631–48.

van Lelyveld, I. (2000) *Inflation, Institutions and Preferences*, PhD thesis, Nijmegen: University of Nijmegen.

Verdun, A. (2000) *European Responses to Globalization and Financial Market Integrations: Perceptions of Economic and Monetary Union in Britain, France and Germany*, Basingstoke: Macmillan.

Weber, A.A. (2010a) *Germany and the Financial Crisis: Challenges and Opportunities*, Luncheon Speech at the American Council on Germany in New York, 26 April.

Weber, A.A. (2010b) *Monetary Policy after the Crisis: A European Perspective*, Keynote Speech at the Shadow Open Market Committee (SOMC) Symposium in New York City, 12 October.

Weber, A.A. (2011a) *The Euro: Opportunities and Challenges*, Ragnar Nurkse-Lecture in Tallinn, 7 February.

Weber, A.A. (2011b) *Challenges for Monetary Policy in EMU*, Homer Jones Memorial Lecture hosted by the Federal Reserve Bank of St. Louis in St. Louis, 13 April.

Young, B. and Semmler, W. (2011) The European Sovereign Debt Crisis. Is Germany to Blame? *German Politics and Society*, 29(1): 1–24.

Young, M.D. (1996) Cognitive Mapping Meets Semantic Networks. A Special Issue: Political Psychology and the Work of Alexander L. George, *Journal of Conflict Resolution*, 40(3): 395–414.

Young, M.D. and Schafer, M. (1998) Is There Method in our Madness? Ways of Assessing Cognition in International Relations, *Mershon International Studies Review*, 42(1): 63–96.

14 Interpretations of the EU crisis and their policy implementation[1]

Mathis Heinrich and Bob Jessop

This chapter explores the obvious asymmetries in the capacities of different social forces to interpret the multiple crises affecting the European Union and to translate their construals into national and/or supranational responses to these crises. Drawing on cultural political economy, we relate this to the interaction of meaning-making and structuration in reducing the complexity of the world as a condition for 'going on' in it – specifically, in the following analysis, as a basis for addressing these crises. In this regard we focus on two aspects of the capacities of social forces that, together, shape crisis interpretations as well efforts to manage the crisis in terms of such construals. The first aspect is interpretive power (*Deutungshoheit*), which refers in the present context to differences in the factual ability of social forces to construe the objective character and significance of a crisis and to translate their construals into policies intended to manage and resolve the crisis, whether or not these prove successful. This is not so much a question of having the best scientific analyses and most persuasive arguments as it is a question of having the capacities to act upon a given interpretation, which also involves access to key decision-making structures, the availability of appropriate governmental technologies and the ability to mobilize sufficient support to make a difference in a particular conjuncture. The second aspect is narrower in scope but perhaps more significant in practice, namely, interpretive authority (*Deutungsmacht*). This refers to the legal instance or authority that has the legal right to interpret the law in a given juridico-political framework. This authority is crucial whenever it comes to interpretations that lead to the declaration of a state of economic emergency and authorization of exceptional crisis-management measures. We indicate below how interpretive power and authority have been coupled in shaping economic crisis responses in the European Union since the eruption of the North Atlantic Financial Crisis. Indeed, we show that certain crisis construals are only as good as the means available to authorize their translation into policy and the strategic selectivities and balances of forces that shape this process.

After briefly introducing some relevant aspects of cultural political (cf. Chapters 2 and 4 in this volume), we describe the increasing variegation of the European Union. This is linked to the uneven development and crisis-prone character of the European Economic and Monetary Union (EMU) and helps to explain the growing sovereign debt crisis in the Eurozone within the broader North Atlantic Financial Crisis. We then examine relevant crisis interpretations in different crisis phases and how they got translated into concrete economic strategies and policy initiatives in three areas: (1) the European rescue and guarantee measures for members states with serious payment difficulties; (2) the ECB's increasingly expansionary monetary policy; and (3) reforms of European governance structures concerned with tightening fiscal discipline and boosting global competitiveness. It is striking that, in response to the crisis in Europe, we can observe both a revival of the Lisbon Agenda strategy and a reassertion of discourses of global competitiveness. Finally, we show that the crisis responses, whether due to failures of imagination, structural constraints, technological deficits or agential selectivities, have not contributed to effective crisis management but have (re)produced and intensified a crisis of crisis management.

Cultural political economy

CPE builds on the various cultural turns in the social sciences (on which, see the editors' introduction to this volume). It is less concerned with a simple thematic turn than with the implications of the methodological and ontological turns. It takes sense- and meaning-making as a useful entry point into social analysis; and, above all, it emphasizes that social order always involves meaningful action. This implies that a valid explanation of social phenomena must be adequate at the level of meaning as well as causality. Accordingly, whether or not sense- and meaning-making are the entry point for studying economic and political phenomena, they must sooner or later be included in the analysis to ensure its descriptive and explanatory adequacy.

For CPE the reduction of complexity through *sense- and meaning-making* and *structuration* are equally necessary for social actors to be able to 'go on' in a complex world. Both processes are strategically selective. They entail *asymmetrical configurations of opportunities and constraints on actions* by relevant actors and social forces in so far as they privilege some actors and actions over others. While semiosis is a useful umbrella term for sense- and meaning-making through sign systems, such as language or symbols, structuration usefully identifies the ways in which unstructured complexity is reduced by setting limits to the articulation of different social relations such that not everything that is *possible* when considered individually is *compossible*, that is, can co-exist in specific spatio-temporal contexts. Capacities to establish hegemonic or dominant interpretative orders and/or to order compossible social relations are unequally distributed and exercised and, as we shall see below, have both path-dependent and path-shaping aspects.

CPE also explores the role of technological (governmental) and agential (social forces) selectivities in mediating semiosis and structure (see Kutter and Jessop, this volume; Sum and Jessop 2013). Governmental technologies include various kinds of economic and political calculation (for example, VAR or value-at-risk models), securitization techniques (for example, derivatives), means of governance (for example, macro-prudential regulation) and disciplinary technologies (for example, promoting neoliberal subjectivity) (cf. Amato *et al.* 2010). Further, the field of social action is not only shaped by the underlying balance of forces but also by the ability of particular individual or social agents to read a given conjuncture, identify what potentials for action it contains and to engage in 'the art of the possible' to produce – or prevent – path-shaping changes.

In this sense CPE not only employs Foucauldian concepts of governmentality and analogous concepts drawn from critical governance studies but also builds on neo-Gramscian international political economy with its interest in the differential capacity of social forces to define economic and political imaginaries and establish the hegemony of specific comprehensive concepts of control (see, for example, van Apeldoorn 2002). Nonetheless, while building on their insights and analyses, CPE aims to go beyond Foucauldian and neo-Gramscian approaches because it seeks to understand and explain interpretation and structuration in discourse-analytical terms too. It studies the (re-)production and co-evolution of imaginaries and power coalitions, embedded in specific orders of discourse and economic and political structures and in their concrete articulation as economic, political and ideological practices of power struggles.

Capital groups, world money and variegated capitalism

The Eurozone crisis can be traced to the uneven, divergent development of the EU, which is expressed in structural imbalances among member states. Starting from limited cooperation among six national varieties (models) of coordinated capitalism, the harmonization economic, political and social models through positive integration measures gave way from the mid-1980s onwards to negative integration that was based on removing barriers to the completion of the internal market. This was reinforced through the integration of European economic space into the 'Dollar-Wall Street regime' (Gowan 1999) with its commitment to liberal and, increasingly, neoliberal market forces and policies. Thus, while the Lisbon Strategy still affirmed the European social model, it subordinated this to the imperatives of international competitiveness, which were ambivalently construed along neoliberal as well as Schumpeterian lines. The introduction of Economic and Monetary Union reinforced this trend by imposing monetary and fiscal discipline to facilitate the convergence deemed necessary for Eurozone membership and to attract global capital flows. In this regard, the European Action Plan for Financial Services also promoted the restructuring of European financial markets to advance financial innovations and thereby promoted the financialization of social relations in Europe (Bieling 2010).

This cumulative transformation of Europe was enabled by, and reinforced, a restructuring of the balance of forces between profit-producing and interest-bearing capital. The power of profit-producing capital (which always involves more than traditional industrial capital) is grounded in the dependence of all capital groups, whether productive or parasitic, on the production of the surplus value from which they derive their specific forms of revenue. In contrast, the power and interests of money capital in its various forms[2] have become increasingly tied to the functions of capitalist credit money and, indeed, to the penetration of interest-bearing capital into more areas of economic, political and social life. Banking and financial capital derive their power and interests in the first instance from their control over the allocation of credit to profit-producing capital and/or to other uses that might generate commercial profits and interest payments and, with the rise of finance-dominated accumulation, from the growing autonomy and hyper-mobility of fictitious credit and fictitious capital as the most advanced forms of interest-bearing capital. This is the most fetishistic form of capital because it gives the impression that it is interest and not labour-power that is the source of surplus value. This impression is strengthened as financial innovation leads to ever more rarefied forms of fictitious credit and capital, as evidenced, for example, in the rise of derivatives trading and securitization.

The distinction between profit-producing and interest-bearing capital shapes the divergent development of two interconnected (initially compossible) accumulation strategies in the European Union as well as at a global scale. Thus we can find (1) export-driven strategies based on profit-producing capital and (2) finance-dominated strategies based on fictitious credit and capital (Stockhammer 2009). In the short to medium term these strategies may be complementary, as seen in the pathological co-dependence of China and the USA or, on a European scale, the initial phase of monetary union in which Germany (and other industrial powers) exported goods to the southern periphery thanks to cheap credit enabled by interest rate convergence inside the Eurozone. The global trend towards financialization reinforced this process as it contributed to a massive rise in apparently liquid assets under the management of national and, especially transnational, financial capital (see Lapavitsas 2013).

This said, the ultimate dependence of interest payments on profit-producing capital will sooner or later re-emerge, leading to a forcible re-imposition of the unity of the circuits of capital, as demonstrated in the North Atlantic financial crisis. Thus the displacement and deferral of the contradictions between the strategies of profit-producing and interest-bearing capital finds its limits in growing imbalances due to (1) an explosion of fictitious money, credit and capital; (2) a limited expansion of the always-already monetized 'real' economy, on which these fictitious forms ultimately depend for continuing financial returns; and (3) limited state capacities to absorb 'toxic' debts and securities. These imbalances have shaped the increased power of capital in national, European and supranational policy-making and the displacement of the North Atlantic financial crisis, based mainly on excessive private credit growth, into a crisis of public and government debt that is invoked to justify austerity and further rounds of neo-liberalization. Contributing factors in the case of the EU are the contradictions of the euro considered as a national money and international currency and the attempts to manage or govern the resulting dilemmas and tensions.

Susan Strange (1971) related the circulation of national currencies and their potential role as world money to their different social bases (see Table 14.1).

Table 14.1 Social basis and properties of currency forms

Form	Features
Top currency	Issued in and/or backed by the state that exercises/enjoys world economic leadership, i.e. the dominant state in world market
Master currency	Circulates mostly in geo-political blocs, e.g. thanks to political dominance of issuing state
Negotiated or political currency	Tied to international regimes with emphasis on mutual benefits rather than coercion
Passive or neutral currency	Circulates domestically, minor role in international regimes

Source: Strange (1971).

However, while Strange argued that *market forces* select the top currency, its status is at the same time also ensured by state capacities, in the internal market as well as abroad. Although there is no official world money, the top currency plays the decisive role in the (dis)integration of the world market. This can be seen in the role of the US dollar, which is both the major driving force for the dominant financial accumulation but also currently a leading factor in crises.

Currencies may have features of the first three forms in different mixes, depending on geo-economic and geo-political factors and forces. Thus, while the USD is both a top and master currency, with supplementary elements of threat and negotiation, the euro is a strange mix of master currency and negotiated currency. The outbreak of the crisis in Europe and the difficulties of handling it is also related to the weakness of the euro as the (hoped-for) master currency, which has not (yet) advanced beyond a negotiated currency, and to the disjunction between private credit, Central Bank credit and State credit in the European economy. Whereas EU surplus countries (the so-called Rhine bloc) and European institutions regard the euro as a potential top currency and seek to advance its role in the world monetary system, it represents (at best) a master currency for the Eurozone as a whole that is promoted and sustained by European institutions as a vital part of the economic and monetary system. For a large part of the European periphery, however, the euro is just a negotiated currency that could deliver some reciprocal benefits (for example, convergence of interest rates) but has required strenuous and continuing efforts to prevent a Eurozone breakdown and/or break-up.

The cumulative result of European integration is a heterogeneous, but increasing interdependent, European economy of different, sometimes contradictory, accumulation regimes, regulatory practices and technologies. Indeed, its variegation has increased in response to changes implemented by the European projects in the last two decades. The expansion and deepening of market forces in the EU and their mutual integration into global export-oriented and finance-dominated strategies have reinforced imbalances among three groups of member states that, culminating in the euro crisis, now reveal the pathological nature of European integration and EU governance structures:

EU countries from northern and central Europe (Germany, the Netherlands, Belgium, Austria, Finland, Sweden and Denmark), which all have a substantial current account surplus thanks to export-driven economies with high productivity levels, enforced by strict wage regimes, restrictive and/or corporate forms of labour market regulation and social welfare systems.

The United Kingdom, Ireland (partially) and France, which have weaker and less competitive export sectors and a fragile current account due to the weight of financial capital and (in the case of the UK and Ireland) a massive-financialization of private debt.

The European (inner) periphery, including the new member states from eastern Europe, as well as south and south-east European countries (Portugal, Spain, Greece, and, in part, Italy), which have big current account deficits and relatively high levels of household or private debt, while economic performance and national industrial production are weak. These countries depend heavily on foreign capital inflows or transnational production chains and are thus interlinked with the first two groups via financial and/or trade relations.

(Becker 2011: 13ff; Bellofiore *et al.* 2010: 121ff)

The strategy of competitive deregulation and wage deflation pursued by surplus countries continuously drove expansion of their own exports but, at the same time, undermined the competitiveness of products from other EU economies. The latter states in contrast sought to maintain domestic demand and improve economic efficiency by increasing domestic debt with the help of foreign loans and investments (that is, a dependent financialization) (cf. Becker 2011). Thus EU current-account imbalances involve asymmetrical transnational trade and production relations as well as unequal credit and investment relations between centre and periphery (cf. Bieling 2011). With the collapse of the European interbank market in the wake of the financial and banking crisis (2008), capital inflows into the periphery slackened. The deficit countries fell into a classic, self-escalating cycle of debt-default-deflation dynamics. This could eventually react back on the surplus countries through a collapse of transnational credit relations, production chains and demand impulses, threatening the credit rating of the entire European economic area. However, when we examine the overall effects of European and national crisis management strategies, it seems that the attempts to defend the economic and monetary union, whether through general austerity measures or through the recent crisis-driven constitutionalization of the neoliberal strategy, have intensified imbalances and reinforced core-periphery relations.

This paradoxical outcome results from the ways in which interpretive power and authority have interacted in different phases of the NAFC and the Eurozone crisis and affected the variegated economic dynamic of European economic space as we will show below. The link between factual and legal interpretive power matters in so far as only certain institutions are authorized to declare a state of economic emergency, start or end crisis measures, impose austerity or punish financial misdeeds. Thus, even when more adequate interpretations are available, 'arbitrary, rationalistic and willed' construals may be translated into crisis responses when backed by the requisite interpretive authority. As a result, it matters which interests are reflected and refracted in authoritative crisis construals – those of core states or peripheral ones, dominant fractions of capital or subordinate ones, profit-producing or interest-bearing capital, transnational or domestic forces, and so on. The form and content of crisis construals have always to be seen in the context of the identity, interests and power of those who articulate them as well.

Competing and coordinating interpretations of the euro crisis

The structural imbalances in the EU and the contradictory nature of the euro are reflected in narratives about the nature of the euro crisis and how it should best be managed. At the outset of the crisis, a general disorientation of political elites led to profound debates, not only on the best way out of the crisis, but also concerning its fundamental causes. These conflicts can be traced back to divergences between the national accumulation regimes, modes of regulation, social power constellations and economic imaginaries within the EU as well as to the interests of different fractions of capital within and beyond European economic space.

The deficit countries of European periphery under French political leadership quickly called for a collective mechanism to support states in financial difficulties, to create euro bonds and to practice comprehensive joint EU-management on the basis of the existing treaties. This would also have obliged the export-oriented European countries to reduce their trade surpluses to lessen the macroeconomic imbalances in the EU (see Financial Times 2010a). On the other hand, Germany, speaking on behalf of surplus countries, has endeavoured specifically to prevent collective transfer mechanisms in relying on the 'no bail-out' clause of the Lisbon Treaty and the implied change in the role of the European Central Bank (ECB) (see Young 2011). This group also blamed the crisis on excessive national debt that should be prevented in future through new contracts and, if necessary, by the withdrawal of voting rights from member states that do not comply with strict budget requirements (cf. FAZ 2010a).

In this atmosphere of national conflicts over how to distribute the burden of the crisis and of increasing divergence of national(istic) interpretations, it was the problem-oriented and very technocratically articulated crisis narrative of the EU's economic and political elites that served to synthesize (albeit one-sidedly) these divergent interests. They did so by reviving and reinvigorating EU concepts of austerity and (internal and external) competitiveness. In this regard, the Commission's 'Europe 2020' strategy, announced in March 2010, although not a direct response to the euro crisis, had already defined the decisive framework conditions for a crisis-induced reform of the EMU. In addition to structural adjustments in education and employment policy, a return to fiscal discipline and the expansion of the EU's external economic policy role, the cornerstone of a new European growth strategy has been specified in terms of reducing imbalances in competitiveness and macroeconomic performance through a far-reaching EU-level monitoring of national economic policies (COM 2010a: 24f.). On this basis, in May 2010, the Commission proposed to bring under its control financial and wage policies as well as some aspects of macro – and labour market structure as key policy instruments to overcome the crisis aggravating imbalances in the Eurozone (COM 2010b: 1, 9).

Thus early on in the Eurozone crisis, these elites transcended rival national crisis interpretations by promoting a competitive market-liberal economic imaginary that was already hegemonic at the European level. Thanks to the narrowing down of crisis diagnostics and a rescaling of the principal political battlefield to the European level in earlier stages of the North Atlantic Financial Crisis, they weakened the interpretive authority of alternative policy approaches (for example demand-side policies). Moreover, in focusing on policies of competitiveness to be pursued mainly at the European level, they diverted attention from the structural causes of the crisis. Specifically, discussions on the European level overlooked the excesses of finance-dominated accumulation, the dependent financialization of the European periphery, the asymmetric integration of the European economic area and the role of financial institutions in EU creditor nations.

Instead the way out of crisis was interpreted as depending on overcoming competitiveness differences in the EU as a whole (Barroso in *Financial Times* 2010b), a task to be imposed mainly on deficit countries. Although this approach provoked resistance in the periphery, it did lead to a de-escalation of tensions between the dominant transnational capital fractions (of interest-bearing and profit-producing capital), as well as between the leading member states of the EU. The explicit invocation of crisis interpretations that were already institutionalized in EU structures, previous EU directives and conventions on fiscal, monetary and competition policy not only led to a wide-reaching technocratization of elite discourse and renewed assertion of the competitiveness-oriented imaginaries, but also mobilized the established compromise constellations of the Lisbon Strategy. Indeed, the crisis appeared to be too good an opportunity to waste for further strengthening this strategy through a far-reaching expansion of the EU's executive authority:

> Sometimes crises also do good. Rather than focusing, as in the past, on the pros and cons of stability policy, the discussion is now to strengthen the Pact. The French talk to include limits on public debt in the Constitution. That would have been unimaginable just a few weeks ago. We have now a proposal to strengthen the Stability Pact and for better coordination of economic policy in the euro area presented, which we announced already before the crisis.
>
> (Barroso in FAZ 2010b)

In short, by forcing the initially divergent national interpretations of the crisis into the well-established European competitiveness discourse, the antagonistic interests within the European power bloc could be held together in the face of a crisis that threatened these interests with implosion. And, this was not solely due to the European Commission. The consultation processes on the 'Europe 2020' strategy show rather that it was especially transnationally organized profit-producing capital that pressed unremittingly for the further expansion of the technocratic control function of EU institutions vis-à-vis the economic and fiscal policies of the member states as well as for an expansion of the EU's external role in international economic relations. They succeeded in including these policy aims into a strengthened global competitiveness strategy and in placing it on the EU's agenda well before Greece got into financial difficulties. The consultation processes on the 'Europe 2020' strategy show rather that it was especially transnationally organized profit-producing capital that pressed unremittingly for the further expansion of the technocratic control function of EU institutions vis-à-vis the economic and fiscal policies of the member states as well as for an expansion of the EU's external role in international economic relations. They succeeded in including these policy aims into a strengthened global competitiveness strategy and in placing it on the EU's agenda well before Greece got into financial difficulties. Likewise, whereas member states still disagreed as late as February 2010 about the need to consolidate national budgets and were still inclined to maintain the established EU structures of governing fiscal policy (COM 2010 c: 4, 10), European business networks and think tanks had been calling since 2008 for fiscal consolidation through new and more robust benchmarking instruments on the European level and for deepened economic monitoring and coordination systems regarding compliance with the Stability and Growth Pact to be supervised by EU institutions (ibid. 16, 20, 28). In this regard, the *European Roundtable of Industrialists* played a central role (2009; 2010: 9), calling – in addition to the full implementation of the internal market and the expansion of the European free trade agreement – for an increase of industrial productivity and for far-reaching EU reforms to ensure sustainable public finances through spending cuts and the restructuring of social security systems. At the same time *Business Europe* (2009a: 6) suggested that a major cause for the failure of the Lisbon Strategy was the failure to implement strict supervisory and enforcement instruments in economic policy coordination. In addition, it pleaded for greater efforts by the EU to liberalize international trade relations. And, as a leading player in *Business Europe*, the *Federal Association of German Industry* (BDI 2009; BDI/ BDA 2010) has also supported the intensification of European integration through domestic budget consolidation and tax reforms to increase competitiveness.

In short, transnational profit-producing capital had already used the Eurozone crisis as a chance to promote and justify its strategic interests through appropriate crisis interpretations. And these are translated by European Institutions into a comprehensive growth strategy that reinforces the Lisbon Agenda and aims to boost Europe's global competitiveness by extending the internal and external prominence of EU institutions, that is, in terms of shaping relevant policy areas in member states as well as negotiating external free trade agreements. *Pace* the constructionist argument that interpretations determine policies, we see rather that the strategies of dominant social forces construct the (crisis) interpretations. Nonetheless the process of translating these interpretations into European policy is shaped by agential selectivities and thus open to political, economic and discursive contestation.

The implementation and selectivity of European crisis management

The EU has a complex multi-spatial governance regime that is also part of a wider set of governance regimes that cross-cut the EU, integrate it into higher order governance regimes and connect it to other parallel power networks. This leads to a set of selectivities that distinguish the EU scale of policy deliberation, formation and implementation from national, regional or cross-border constellations without necessarily making the EU scale dominant in all respects within what is often a tangled hierarchy of competences and powers. Different policy fields are more or less integrated at the EU level and the extent to which this occurs depends on more or less stable and institutionalized supranational, but always contested, compromise structures as well as on the extent of EU-wide interdependencies in these fields.

Critical research on Europe has shown that, in the EU, it is above all profit-producing capital, more exactly globally oriented and transnationally organized capital groups (for example, those represented by the European Round Table of Industrialists), that has the most influence on 'agenda-setting' and decision-making (van Apeldoorn 2002). Even if these capital groups have become economically and politically interwoven with other capitals that provide simple financial intermediation and risk-management and/or engage in financial speculation and risk-taking in an emerging regime of finance-dominated accumulation, the principal coalitions and alliances of social forces remain, at least at the European level, heavily determined by the productive side of these alliances (see Caroll *et al.* 2010). The claims of transnational profit-producing capital go well beyond the pure defence of the (national) production conditions. They concern a comprehensive reorganization of national and regional accumulation regimes, modes of regulation and governance structures to increase their own global competitiveness and their share in global surplus value. In contrast, interest-bearing capital, especially in its speculative form, has far less privileged access to European interpretation and decision structures (cf. Woll 2012). While financial capital is often well-positioned politically at the national level, most financial institutions are less transnationalized and politically organized in relation to EU governance. Hence they can often only engage in (belated) lobbying efforts and resort to national channels (for example, through the European Parliament) to codetermine and reorient EU policy for their purposes.

These agential selectivities are also reflected in the different policy areas of European crisis management and prompt significant conflicts during the translation of dominant crisis construals into effective policy measures. In this regard three major policy areas with different underlying dynamics and compromise structures are relevant to management of the euro crisis: (1) the European rescue and guarantee measures for EU states that face payment difficulties; (2) the

ECB's increasingly expansionary monetary policy; and (3) reforms of European governance structures to ensure fiscal discipline and global competitiveness by reducing macroeconomic imbalances.

First, the European bailouts are especially marked by intergovernmental dynamics and by conflicts of interest and strategies among EU member states. This is not least due to an absence of any uniform institutionalized European crisis-management procedure in this policy area and, hence, a lack of supranational coordination mechanisms and routines. Correspondingly the negotiation process of European rescue and stabilization measures primarily reflects strategies of European banks and creditor nations (mainly France and Germany, but also the United Kingdom) based on ad hoc decisions and compromises (cf. Bieling 2011). The bilateral bailout packages for Greece in March 2010, as well as the establishment of the European Financial Stability Fund and later the European Stability Mechanism reflect a far-reaching compromise between France and Germany as the leading political advocates of the deficit and surplus countries respectively. At the same time the representatives of interest-bearing capital in the form of large European banks that had previously invested heavily in the European periphery, were represented directly at the negotiating table by the *International Financial Forum*. It was these actors that campaigned for rescue measures in the form of guarantees for private banks and also blocked a serious debt cut that would benefit deficit countries in the first instance (cf. Stuchlik *et al.* 2011).

Second, in contrast, the ECB's crisis-management strategy is primarily structured through supranational dynamics and selectivities, which encourages the ECB to interpret its role as acting as lender of last resort to European capital and credit markets (cf. Richter and Wahl 2011). Thus, the expansionary monetary policy of the ECB is not only concerned to unburden European bond markets but also to stabilize transnational European credit relations. This does not, as is often thought, contradict the strategic interests of transnational profit-producing capital because it also benefits from market stabilization and low interest rates (Business Europe 2009b: 3). But there is a growing contradiction with the tight monetary policies that were crucial to national accumulation strategies that depend on deflation and that were privileged in the restrictive financial models that targeted internal price stability and characterized EU policies in the pre-crisis period. While this has, unsurprisingly, drawn fierce criticism from German central bankers, their criticism has found little resonance on the EU level, where the ECB's policies reflect European-wide concerns. It remains to be seen whether the bank maintains this newly accustomed role after the crisis or will then revive old routines that favour the interests of export-oriented member states.

Third, and finally, the reforms of EMU governance are embedded mainly in supranational mechanisms and compromise structures and are therefore imprinted above all by transnational selectivities and the transnational balance of power. The far-reaching transformations through the 'Europe 2020' strategy (European Semester), the so-called six pack, the Euro-Plus Pact and the fiscal compact all aim to increase the global competitiveness and the role of the EU through an expansion of the neo-liberal strategy of competitive deregulation and consolidation of austerity policies throughout the entire European economic area. The (authoritarian) expansion of the internal and external organizational power of the European level, which is construed to be necessary for the pursuit of this strategy, does reflect the strategic interests of transnational profit-producing capital. As such, it is also actively supported by the relevant transnational actors (especially the ERT and Business Europe), promoted via their privileged access to the European institutions in the relevant decision-making processes (cf. CEO 2011, 2012).

Faced with the demands of managing the euro crisis, transnational business associations have demanded a – more or less – strict regulation of interest-bearing capital (especially in its fictitious forms) as well. With the aim to improve its position in international competition and to align finance activities with the strategies of profit-producing capital, demands are being made to prevent interest-bearing capital from engaging in financial speculation and risk-taking and limit its activities to the more traditional functions of financial intermediation and risk management in line with the interests of profit-producing capital (see BDI 2013; Business Europe 2009c; ERT 2010). Thus, while there is strong support for a liberalization of financial services that would benefit interest-bearing capital as well as reduce the costs of profit-producing capital, the latter also back measures to address the Eurozone crisis that would constrain interest-bearing capital. These measures include strong macro-political financial market regulation, stress tests, tougher capital requirements, a financial transaction tax, debt write-downs, and tough resolution measures for insolvent banks. In other words, there is an overlap between reforms in the EU governance regime that derive from efforts to manage the Eurozone crisis and proposals oriented to a (possible) re-regulation of European financial markets. These proposals are far more contested on a European level than initiatives concerned with European money, competition and fiscal policy; they are also less well institutionalized and, therefore, less likely to endure even when introduced. At this stage of the crisis, therefore, in the absence of sedimented meaning-systems, stable compromise structures and established and well-oiled coordination mechanisms, it is increasingly evident that there are conflicts of interest over crisis-management and exit strategies. Above all these concern the conflicts between, first, transnational productive capital and national (financial) capital fractions (especially in its speculative form) and, second, export-oriented and finance-dominated accumulation regimes. This is evident in the failure to date to integrate the fiscal compact into primary European law, because of the opposition from the UK government and British business leaders, who fear creeping regulation of speculative money and credit capital operating from the City of London – activities that are central to Britain's accumulation strategy and backed by all three leading political parties in England.

Conclusion: the crisis of crisis management in Europe

In the current configuration of the EU, the challenges of crisis management have been aggravated by poor institutional arrangements and the asymmetries in the European economic area. A transnational export-oriented strategy that is based primarily on the competitiveness of increasingly Europeanized capital does not allow deficit countries to break out of the cycle of rising debt and economic weakness. Indeed, a debt-default-deflation spiral threatens the entire EMU because this exit strategy depends on a massive extension of pan-European exports for which there is as yet insufficient international demand (cf. Aglietta 2012: 34). Our CPE-inspired analysis of the euro crisis indicates that the limits on effective crisis management can be traced back to selective interpretation patterns and imaginary worlds as well as to the differential power of specific economic interests. The dominant economic interpretations in the euro crisis derive from a liberal market competitiveness discourse, which seems able to contain in a European compromise structure the different interests within the transnational European power bloc as well as those of various national (financial) capital fractions (cf. Macartney 2010: 157).

This said, there are still unmistakable tensions in specific European policy fields that require more specific solutions than a general, long-term working out of trade-offs in competition and fiscal policy. These tensions can be seen in issues such as the tasks of the ECB as the lender of last resort, calls for a transfer Union, proposals for euro-bonds, and the progressive integration of European financial markets. They stem above all from the contradictions between (1) the transnational profit-producing fractions of capital active on the European and global market and (2) internationally oriented speculative financial capital. On the European level, the former still enjoy the hegemonic interpretive power and links to authoritative bodies with power to act. In the guise of removing European imbalances, these fractions now also aim to curb speculative interest-bearing capital. Yet interest-bearing capital remains 'ecologically dominant' at the global scale and retains more than enough structural power at the national level and in the European Parliament to block such approaches, which enables them to water down European directives aimed at curbing financial speculation, prohibiting naked short selling and imposing more robust supervision of hedge-funds and rating agencies.

The conflicts of interest between interest-bearing and productive capital are reflected in the primarily finance-dominated and primarily export-oriented member states of the EU. Thus, the euro crisis as a whole revealed that the EU (still) lacks political leadership that might be able to unite the antagonistic interests of European capital fractions and of member states in a long-term pan-European vision that goes beyond the mere strengthening of an internal global competitiveness strategy to affect the EU's influence within the Dollar-Wall-Street Regime. Thus, regarding the EU's role in shaping international and financial relations and, ultimately, the fundamental character of the EU, European elites and member states have been at loggerheads since the early 1990s and, in the light of the crisis, seem to have moved ever further apart (cf. Schmidt 2012).

This reflects a progressively unfolding 'post-Maastricht crisis' of the EU since the 1990s and thus a growing social crisis of European integration (Deppe 2011: 20). While the EU in the 1970s could still legitimate itself primarily through its economic success, this 'permissive consensus' is dissolving *pari passu* with changes in the mode of European integration. Today, the EU appears not only as a major source of crisis tendencies but also, through its unilateral management of the euro crisis, it is revealing ever more clearly the class character of European politics. This makes it harder to handle the crisis in a legitimate manner. The costs of the crisis have been dumped so far mainly on the population in the European periphery together with the squeezed middle, precarious workers and social service and welfare recipients. This is leading to social and political criticism of national and European policy alignment as well as to more general criticism of the state of affairs in the European Union. The combination of discursive and agential selectivity in EU crisis management seems to be culminating in a far-reaching social crisis of crisis management in Europe.

In sum, the CPE approach adopted here indicates that the translation of the dominant interpretations of the crisis into political initiatives has not only blocked effective economic and political crisis-management initiatives but also provoked a series of crises of crisis management and political and social conflicts. This results not only from the basic structural contradictions in the EU but also from the effects of discursive, technological and agential selectivities on crisis management. It relates competing interpretations and alternative economic imaginaries to different accumulation strategies, state projects and hegemonic visions and, in this context, to the differential power of economic, social and political forces to shape meanings and control interpretations. In this way it can also contribute to the critique of ideology and domination by exposing contradictions in the reciprocal reproduction of semiotics and structure, ideology and rule as a (necessary) complexity reduction within the existing antagonistic configuration of the EU to the handling of the crisis.

Notes

1 Writing this text was facilitated by a Professorial Research Fellowship (Jessop) and Research Studentship (Heinrich) from the *Economic and Social Research Council*. The case studies of policy are drawn from Heinrich's ongoing research. We also thank the Rosa Luxemburg Foundation for its financial and intellectual support and Hans-Jürgen Bieling and Amelie Kutter for stimulating discussions and helpful comments. This chapter draws in part on Heinrich and Jessop (2013).
2 These include money-dealing capital, stock-dealing capital and bank capital. Note that profit-producing capital may lend idle money capital to earn interest before it is reinvested in profit-generation. This anticipates later forms of financialization in which non-financial firms earn a growing share of their total profits from financial activities.

References

Aglietta, M. (2012) The European vortex, *New Left Review*, 75: 15–36.
Amato, L., Doria, M. and Fantacci, L. (eds) (2010) *Money and Calculation: Economic and Sociological Perspectives*, Basingstoke: Palgrave Macmillan.
Bundesverband der deutschen Industrie (BDI) (2009) *Expanding Europe's Strengths. Recommendations for Action for the Coming Years*. www.bdi.eu/download_content/ Publikation_Europas_Staerken_ausbauen.pdf, accessed on 20 February 2013.

Bundesverband der deutschen Industrie (BDI) (2013) *Opinion: Draft of National Reform Programme 2013*. Berlin, 19 February.

Bundesverband der deutschen Industrie and Bundesvereinigung der Arbeitgeber-verbände (BDI/BDA) (2010) *BDI/BDA Statement on the Public Consultation of the European Commission on the 'EU 2020'-strategy*, Brussels.

Becker, J. (2011) EU: von der Wirtschafts- zur Regulationskrise, *Z Zeitschrift für Marxistische Erneuerung*, 85: 10–29.

Bellofiore, R., Garibaldo, F. and Halevi, J. (2010) The great recession and the contradictions of European neomercantilism, *Socialist Register 2011*: 120–46.

Bieling, H.J. (2010) *Die Globalisierungs- und Weltordnungspolitik der Europäischen Union*, Wiesbaden: VS Verlag.

Bieling, H.-J. (2011) Vom Krisenmanagement zur neuen Konsolidierungsagenda der EU, *Prokla*, 41(2): 173–94.

Business Europe (2009a) *Putting Europe Back on Track: European Growth and Jobs Strategy post 2010*. Brussels, September.

Business Europe (2009b) Priorities for European economic recovery. Meeting with Michael Glos. Brussels, 16 January.

Business Europe (2009c) *Business Perspective on Financial Market Reforms: Towards Financial Stability and Sustainable Growth*. Brussels, September.

Carroll, W.K., Fennema, M. and Heermskirk, E. (2010) Constituting corporate Europe: a study of elite social organization, *Antipode*, 42(4): 811–43.

Corporate European Observatory (CEO) (2011) *Corporate EUtopia: How New Economic Governance Measures Challenge Democracy*, Brussels: CEO.

Corporate European Observatory (CEO) (2012) *Business Against Europe*, Brussels: CEO.

European Commission (COM) (2010a) *EUROPE 2020: A European Strategy for Smart, Sustainable and Inclusive Growth*, Brussels: COM(2010) 2020.

European Commission (COM) (2010b) *Proposal for a Regulation of the European Parliament and of the Council on Enforcement Measures to Correct Excessive Macroeconomic Imbalances in the Euro Area*. Brussels: COM(2010) 525 final.

European Commission (COM) (2010c) *Europe 2020 – Public Consultation. Overview of Responses*. Staff working document. Brussels: SEC(2010) 246 final.

European Roundtable of Industrialists (ERT) (2010) *ERT's Vision for a Competitive Europe in 2025*, Brussels: ERT.

European Roundtable of Industrialists (ERT) (2009) *ERT Message to the Informal European Council Meeting*. Brussels, 24 February.

Deppe, F. (2011) Der Weg in die Sackgasse. Eine Kurzgeschichte der europäischen Integration, in J. Bischoff *et al.* (eds), *Europa im Schlepptau der Finanzmärkte*, Hamburg: VSA Verlag.

Financial Times (FT) (2010a) Lagarde criticises Berlin policy. Interview transcript, 14 March.

Financial Times (FT) (2010b) Barroso demands solidarity on Greece. Interview transcript, 24 March. www.ft.com/cms/s/0/36484548–35c4–11df-963f-00144feabdc0.html#axzz2L SLPyC4E, accessed on 24 February 2013.

Frankfurter Allgemeine Zeitung (FAZ) (2010a) Erst die Strafe, dann der Fonds, in conversation with Wolfgang Schäuble. 24 May, www.faz.net/aktuell/wirtschaft/europas-schuldenkrise/im-gespraech-wolfgang-schaeuble-erst-die-strafe-dann-der-fonds-1954060. html, accessed on 24 February 2013.

Frankfurter Allgemeine Zeitung (FAZ) (2010b) Manchmal haben Krisen auch ihr Gutes, in conversation with José Manuel Barroso. 25 May, www.faz.net/aktuell/wirtschaft/

europas-schuldenkrise/im-gespraech-jose-manuel-barroso-manchmal-haben-krisen-auch-ihr-gutes-1980525.html, accessed on 24 February 2013.

Gowan, P. (1999) *The Global Gamble: Washington's Faustian Bid for World Dominance*, London: Verso.

Heinrich, M. and Jessop, B. (2013) Die EU Krise aus Sicht einer kulturellen Politischen Ökonomie. Krisendeutungen und ihre Umsetzung, *Das Argument*, 301: 19–33.

Lapavitsas, C. (2013) The Eurozone crisis through the prism of world money, in M.H. Wolfson and H.A. Epstein (eds), *The Handbook of the Political Economy of Financial Crisis*, Oxford: Oxford University Press.

Macartney, H. (2010) *Variegated Neoliberalism: EU Varieties of Capitalism and International Political Economy*, London: Routledge.

Richter, F. and Wahl, P. (2011) *The Role of the European Central Bank in the Financial Crash and the Crisis of the Euro Zone*. WEED report.

Schmidt, V.A. (2012) European member state elites' German visions of the European Union, *Journal of European Integration*, 34(2): 169–90.

Stockhammer, E. (2009) The finance-dominated regime of accumulation, income distribution and the present crisis, *Papeles de Europa*, 19: 58–81.

Strange, S. (1971) The politics of international currencies, *World Politics*, 23: 215–31.

Stuchlik, S., Otto, K. and Orth, A. (2011) Steuermilliarden – wie sich die Banker in Brüssel die Regeln selber machen. *Sendungsbeitrag Monitor* No. 624, 25 August.

Sum, N.L. and Jessop, B. (2013) *Towards a Cultural Political Economy: Putting Culture in its Place in Political Economy*, Cheltenham: Edward Elgar.

Van Apeldoorn, B. (2002) *Transnational Capitalism and the Struggle over European Integration*, London: Routledge.

Woll, C. (2012) Lobbying under pressure: the effect of salience on European Union hedge fund regulation, *Journal of Common Market Studies*, 51(3): 555–72.

Young, B. (2011) Economic governance in the Eurozone: a new dawn?, *Economic Sociology*, 12(2): 11–16.

15 Mark my words

Discursive central banking in crisis

Daniela Gabor and Bob Jessop

The collapse of Lehman Brothers in September 2008, initiating the biggest bankruptcy in US history, introduced massive uncertainty into the principles and future of monetary policy. The conduct of this policy had been applauded widely until then for its contribution to what was called 'the Great Moderation', that is, the period of price stability and steady expansion that lasted from the mid-1980s to 2007.[1] The ensuing crisis challenged central bank officials to abandon the inherited wisdom of New Keynesian policy models dominating the pre-crisis period and to play instead a more interventionist, overtly political role in financial markets and the conduct of fiscal policy.

Yet, as the timeline of crisis responses in the advanced (neoliberal) capitalist countries that were most affected by the 'global financial crisis' has unfolded, it seems that all the compromises, inconsistencies, and contradictions that generated the global financial crisis have yet to produce a crisis *of* neoliberalism (cf. Mirowski 2013). Just as the 1990s' Anglo-American recession or the Asian crisis transformed, rather than subverted, neoliberal paradigms of macroeconomic governance (Peck and Tickell 2002), the 2007–2013 (and continuing) crisis has also transformed rather than destroyed neoliberalism. The crisis in financialized globalization is thus being explained increasingly as a failure of regulation rather than being attributed to economic policies or finance-led accumulation regimes; and, correspondingly, central banks have stepped in (through quantitative/credit easing) to restore finance-led growth regimes. Overall, this permits (or justifies) a return to business as usual. The IMF and central banks are in mutual agreement that there will be a return to the New Keynesian inflation-targeting consensus with a more explicit focus on systemic regulation once unconventional policy measures have produced the desired outcome (Blanchard *et al.* 2010).

For scholars of crises who work in one or another political economy tradition, these attempts to re-normalize are a puzzle. Junctures of unwonted radical uncertainty typically disturb established theoretical and policy paradigms, producing shifts in economic imaginaries (see Heinrich and Kutter 2013; Jessop 2014; Young, this volume). The pre-crisis imaginary of the central bank conceived it as a policy actor that simply altered its 'signals' and ensured that the 'market' interpreted them correctly by anchoring expectations (Woodford 2007). This amounted to a neoliberal enlisting of efficient markets to do the central bank's job (see Krippner 2007). Central banks and monetary economists dedicated their energies to denying the importance of institutional relationships beyond the discursive realm of managing expectations, whether these relationships were to financial institutions or governments. Indeed, in the accounts offered before the crisis, what matters for central banks are the models employed to guide interest rate decisions. The decisions are then implemented, in a frictionless manner, in money markets. Implementation (liquidity management in central banking jargon) is irrelevant to story-telling, as is the nature of money or the institutional embedding of financial markets. Sharing a 'scientific' interpretative framework with financial markets, i.e. belonging to one epistemic community, does the job of monetary policy.

The idea of discursive central banking is embedded not only in the corpus of mainstream monetary economic thought but also in recent contributions from anthropology and sociology. These view central banking as primarily discursive because central banks are in the business of stabilizing expectations in a climate of uncertainty defined as lack of knowledge about 'fundamental structures' of the economy (Pigeon 2011; Holmes 2013; Katzenstein and Nelson 2013). By privileging the 'story-telling' element, the discursive approach thus converges with the mainstream economics account of monetary policy in rendering the practices of central banking analytically invisible. While accepting that independent central banks may not be the objective technocrats that mainstream economics assumes them to be, the discursive approach assumes them to be political in devoting their energies to domesticating uncertainty in financial markets, assumed homogeneous and therefore analytically irrelevant. Thus, this discursive approach reinforces the economic imaginary of a central bank disembedded (and distanced) from financial markets and the structural changes these may experience.

This chapter is premised on the claim that central banking is a deeply political process; and that its political character does not solely arise from its story-telling dimension, but also from the how central banks imagine and conduct the relationship with financial institutions and with governments. It thus stresses the importance of competing fisco-financial imaginaries and alternative narratives in shaping economic policy, crisis-management, and exit strategies. Following Karl Niebyl (1946), the political economy of central banking must pay equal attention to policy argumentation and institutional configurations. This is also in large measure the argument of cultural political economy. At the same time, however, it indicates the limits to constructivist accounts by highlighting the constraints imposed on policy-making and policy implementation by the nature of money and debt and the interdependencies that exist in the European and world economies. It also indicates the importance of struggles over alternative imaginaries as part of the process of learning in, about, and from crises (Jessop 2014).

We develop this argument in the following pages by proposing that the crisis-induced central bank interventions illustrate a different economic imaginary that reflects profound structural changes in the nature of debt relationships, elsewhere described as shadow banking (see Pozsar 2011; Gabor 2013). This financial imaginary is ruled by collateral produced by governments rather than the discursive mediation of the central bank's short-term interest rate. It raises serious problems of legitimacy for central banks, undermining their privileged positions in institutional architectures. From this perspective, exit narratives constitute strategies to re-instate the pre-crisis imaginary.

A critical political economy of monetary policy

It is hardly novel to note that monetary policy is political (Kirshner 2003; Gabor 2010). Even the mythical maestro, Alan Greenspan, recognized this in late 2008 when he was asked by Representative Henry Waxman (D-Cal): 'Do you feel that your ideology pushed you to make decisions that you wish you had not made?' Greenspan replied that everyone inevitably had an ideology, that is, a model of reality, on which he/she based decisions. The real issue, he added, was whether it was accurate or not. And, following the crisis, he had discerned a flaw in the model on which he had based his decision-making at the Federal Reserve, namely, the efficient market hypothesis (Greenspan 2008).

Waxman's question and Greenspan's answer are illuminating because they reveal how crises lead to the questioning of taken-for-granted assumptions and, in particular, challenge a fundamental premise in recent monetary policy: the objectivity of technocratic policy-makers and the models on which they base their policy decisions. They suggest that, beneath the cloak of objectivity surrounding monetary policy, there lurk many questions of power, ideology, and politics (Gabor 2011). In particular, monetary policy does not first become political only when governments impose their political agendas onto an otherwise objective, apolitical field of policy formulation by experts. Rather than being grafted onto policy, politics and power are constitutive of it. This is because policy arises through contestation between actors with competing interests and rival agendas (Keeley and Scoones 1999).

We can develop these arguments by returning to the neglected work of Karl Niebyl on theories of money. His *Studies on the Classical Theories of Money* (1946) suggested that an account of central banking should involve three dimensions: monetary theorizing, policy-making, and reality. 'Reality', in his account, captured the specific historical features of relations of production and finance. In other words, theorizing an economy dominated by commodity money is different from theorizing an economy with highly complex debt relationships. At different junctures, some monetary theories are better than others at capturing the nature, embeddedness, and complexity of financial markets.

Thus, for Niebyl, monetary theories and policies are embedded in particular institutional structures associated with the productive and/or financial sectors. Continued support and implementation for an economic doctrine depends on its interpretive and material adequacy, that is, its capacity to represent and explain reality. However, Niebyl did not claim that a theoretical approach becomes dominant simply because, and in so far as, it provides the most accurate, scientifically verifiable account of prevailing economic conditions. Rather, he stressed that theoretical hegemony primarily relies on particular (productive and/ or financial) interests and shifting power relations. In other words, specific institutional configurations and the balance of forces, rather than 'objective' criteria, can shape the theory and policy prescriptions applied to an economic problem.[2]

Karl Niebyl's work has implications not only for the history of economics but also for studies of central banking. In particular, it differs radically from the conventional instrumental view according to which policy-makers engage in rational problem-solving and then control the way in which rational policies are implemented in a frictionless, linear manner (for a critique of this view, see Mosse 2005: 2). His approach suggests that, while a particular economic model and its associated policy narrative may frame the interpretation of events, the model and policy narrative may not be fully translated into practice thanks to the frictions of institutional structure and the vagaries of shifting power relations.

So we cannot presume a one-to-one relationship among theory, policy narratives, and central-bank practices. In other words, as Niebyl might have phrased it today, policy models (informed by a given theoretical conceptualization) might not shape practice in the way they claim, nor do they generally offer an accurate guide to policy implementation and effects. On the contrary, as Mosse concluded from his ethnographic work on economic development projects, the causality might run in the opposite direction: 'what if, instead of policy producing practice, practices produce policy, in the sense that actors in development devote their energies to maintaining coherent representations regardless of events?' (2005: 2).

Applying this perspective, central banks could be analysed in terms of: (1) what they *do* (practices of monetary management); (2) what they *say* (policy narratives); and (3) the discursive and material connection between practices and narratives (including their mutual consistency, sequencing, and modes of influence). From this perspective one cannot rely, as both discursive and economic mainstream approaches do, on hegemonic central bank narratives alone to illuminate 'the implementation black box' of instrumentalist approaches. Rather, central bank interventions in financial markets are distinctly, and analytically, relevant. Then, interpretive policy analysis should be combined with questions about the systemic implications of financial innovation and 'traditional tools' – empirical analysis – in order to produce an adequate account of how practices are reconfigured in response to changing structural conditions in financial markets.

Thus, if policies work, it is not necessarily because they are well-designed but because of more contingent factors that happen to facilitate their realization. For example, scholarly debates on the impact of globalization on monetary policy explore whether a 'divine coincidence' (or the Chinese impact on global prices and wages) rather than more credible central bank policies account for the Great Moderation period (see Woodford 2007; Papademos 2008). Likewise, coherent policy narratives may serve to disguise these contingencies during normal periods (Mosse 2005: 230) – making it even more disorienting when crises eventually occur.

That policy is the product of discursive struggles – and that there is no one-to-one correspondence between theoretical/policy paradigms, institutional orders, and policy practice – is most evident during times of crisis. Régis Debray describes crises as historical conjunctures that are objectively overdetermined but subjectively indeterminate (Debray 1973: 113). Reinforcing this point, the Slovenian philosopher, Slavoj Žižek (2009), presents them as moments of *extraordinary* politics that disrupt 'existing cognitive mappings', opening the space for ideological struggle over how to interpret events and imagine solutions. In other words, policy responses do not develop out of technical, objective analysis of options but derive from a political struggle over how to represent the crisis, what lessons to draw from them, and what opportunities they offer. Colin Hay (1999) drew a Kuhnian analogy between periods of 'normal' policy-making, when a dominant interpretation demarcates the boundaries of what is possible in policy, and periods of 'exceptional' policy-making, marked by a shift in the parameters of what is accepted as rational policy. For central banks in the business of establishing certainties, then, crises demand particularly intense interpretative efforts.

Thus crises may reveal the limits to how a dominant construction of the 'problem' gets stabilized and becomes hegemonic. As the 'legitimate' policy issues come under greater and more intense contestation, it becomes increasingly apparent that policies are 'shaped by competing narratives, informed by divergent interests' (Scoones 2003: 1). Indeed, narratives, defined as vehicles 'for transmitting and making accessible a framework of meaning, that is discourse' (Hajer 1995: 23) have long been advocated as a valuable analytical tool for exploring moments of dislocation (Roe 1991). Framing is essential in all policy-making, providing the tools with which narratives are constructed and 'cannot be settled by instrumental rationality precisely because it frames that' (Apthorpe and Gasper 1996: 6). By imposing a certain meaning and order onto a series of disjointed events, policy narratives provide a method for creating categories and spaces amenable for interventions, stabilizing the assumptions needed for policy-making while marginalizing competing approaches and closing down policy spaces (Keeley 1997). Essential to any policy narrative is its complicity with politics, what Currie (1998) called the ideological function: not what it includes, but what it leaves out of the story. Before the collapse of Lehman, financial markets were virtually absent from central bank imaginaries, while governments were threateningly present as potential agents of inflation should there be any challenge to central bank independence.

Re-imagining central banking: the return to pre-crisis imaginaries

In Great Moderation models, central banks operated under a narrow remit: to achieve price stability. Despite the narrow remit, central banks were portrayed as the most important institutions in the institutional framework underpinning macroeconomic management (Gabor 2010). This hegemony relied on two distinctive premises-cum-promises: independence from financial markets (market neutrality) and independence from politics (political neutrality, in the sense that monetary policy should be conducted in line with defined economic objectives without (direct, detailed, continuous) interference from the legislature or executive branches). Given these premises-cum-promises, the conduct of monetary policy by central banks could be represented as a rules-based, scientific exercise in which interest rates would be set to deliver price stability (Clarida *et al.* 1999).

The *market neutrality principle* established that, in seeking to influence interest rates, central banks should intervene in only one market segment: the interbank market where banks trade liquidity with each other. Rational expectations and arbitrage would then transmit central bank influence via *the* price of liquidity as is established in the interbank market to asset prices and long-term interest rates (Woodford 2007). Interventions in other asset markets are (1) *redundant*, since arbitrage already links short-term to long-term interest rates and (2) *ineffective*, because, as assets are perfectly substitutable, any interventions in private or government asset markets will not change interest rates or prices there (Eggertsson and Woodford 2003). Hence central bank intervention in financial markets cannot have distributive consequences (Cecioni *et al.* 2011). Conversely, the collateral policies of the central bank cannot influence significantly the markets where collateral trades (Cheun *et al.* 2009).

Put differently, central banks cannot 'make' or 'move' markets other than the interbank market. This is how New Keynesianism is compatible with discursive studies of central banking: the story-telling dimension has a crucial function in that provided that expectations about short-term interest rates are firmly anchored, efficient financial markets would realize the aims of central banks with minimum interference.

The *political neutrality principle* enshrined in turn the idea that monetary policy should be protected from political interference and sovereign debt management. The theoretical case for a clear and strict separation between monetary and fiscal policies rested on demonstrating how attempts to coordination may have adverse consequences for macroeconomic stability by distorting the system of incentives that govern (fiscal) policy-making. First, the literature recognized that the objectives of monetary and fiscal policies may overlap, producing externalities and spillovers that rendered the question of coordination a valid theoretical pursuit (Issing 2002). But New Keynesian research quickly dismissed the benefits, arguing that coordination with fiscal policies would be harmful because this practice confused accountability and transparency, engendering a form of moral hazard through the implicit endorsement of fiscal authorities' well-documented tendency to prefer short-run political gains (Leeper 2010a). The central bank's involvement in the fiscal domain undermined fiscal discipline (Alesina *et al.* 2001), particularly in monetary unions without common fiscal authorities (Issing 2002).

Even where sympathetic accounts accepted that fiscal policy could be more potent than assumed in Great Moderation models, the divergent pace of theoretical innovation drove a further wedge between monetary and fiscal policy analysis.

Whereas New Keynesianism made claims to science by incorporating dynamics, expectations, and micro-foundations into models of monetary policy (Clarida *et al.* 1999), research on fiscal policy retained the old Keynesian concerns (and the overt politicization) with fiscal multipliers, prompting Leeper (2010b) to contrast 'monetary science' with 'fiscal alchemy' and to lament the lack of a scientific approach that would isolate fiscal decisions from political cycles.

Together these two principles involve a double depoliticization of monetary policy – its *policy neutrality* vis-à-vis different (financial) markets and the *institutional separation* of the logic of the (financial) market from the (partisan) logic of the political. In turn this implies that the conduct of monetary policy can be left to rules-based, scientific, or technocratic institutional practices. Yet this produced a strange paradox in the role attributed to central banking in the conduct of policy and in the institutional framework of economic governance. For the Great Moderation model of central banking, and the institutional architecture it shaped, engendered what Mann (2010) termed a 'discursive ambivalence'. On the one hand, it proclaimed the hegemony of monetary policy in the macroeconomic management toolkit; and, on the other hand, it posited that successful management depended critically on careful observance of the principles of neutrality from both fiscal policy/sovereign debt management and from financial markets. Successful monetary policy entailed careful signalling of the central bank and adequate interpretation from financial markets. Central banks or academic economists saw no reason why the rapid pace of financial innovation – such as the rise of shadow banking – would have any significant consequences for this interpretative game.

Back to the discursive: abandoning and re-claiming neutrality

> It is also sound policy to limit the discretionary ability of central banks to engage in policies that fundamentally belong to fiscal authorities or private markets
>
> (Charles Plosser, president of the Federal Reserve
> Bank of Philadelphia, 2012)

The collapse of Lehman Brothers radically undermined this double depoliticization of central banking and its requisite supportive institutional framework. The bank's collapse forced central banks to depart from both principles of neutrality. Story-telling no longer worked to restore market confidence. First, market neutrality was abandoned as soon as central banks adopted unconventional policies in the forms of outright purchases of private assets (see Gabor 2014). In other words, it was deemed necessary for policy to favour specific financial markets and/or actors. For example, the ECB initiated the Covered Bond Purchase programme in 2009, buying bonds mainly issued by Spanish and German banks. Second, with the generalized shift to quantitative easing, which involved purchases of government bonds, central banks could no longer pretend that monetary policy could be conducted without regard to fiscal policy (Moessner and Turner 2012). Indeed, on the fourth anniversary of the collapse of Lehman Brothers, the US Federal Reserve announced its third round of quantitative easing, committing to purchase USD 40 billion worth of agency mortgage-backed securities and USD 45 billion worth of government bonds every month. In parallel, the European Central Bank announced its Outright Market Transactions programme, committing to step into European government bond markets at any sign of potential turmoil (Gabor 2014).

A further paradox is that *this double leap into the unknown has not triggered a paradigmatic shift in how central banks or mainstream academia conceptualize monetary policy or its leading role in the macroeconomic management toolkit.* Indeed, although the crisis prompted scholarly reflection on how and why the Great Moderation model of central banking failed to identify and address the sources of financial instability and, in addition, prompted reflection on the lessons to be learnt (witness the rapid ascendance of macroprudential policies), central banks have continuously emphasized that these extraordinary measures should be timely, targeted, and temporary – with 'unwinding' and 'exit' occurring at the earliest opportunity (see Trichet 2009; ECB 2010; Plosser 2012).

The return to central banking business as usual, it is argued, is important precisely because an independent monetary policy, conducted beyond political or market pressure, is the only way to avoid inflation, future financial instability, or moral hazard (Belke 2010; Yamaoka and Syed, 2010). These risks indicate the need for an exit strategy from policies pursued during a state of economic emergency. In this context exit is defined as a 'return to conducting central banking in a market neutral manner' (Zorn and Garcia 2011). Exit means re-instating the short-term interest rate as the key policy instrument and reviving the two neutrality principles underpinning the pre-crisis model of central banking. This reflects the idea that exceptional measures of crisis management should be targeted, timely, and *temporary*, that is, should be conducted in such a way that a return to 'neutral' business as usual can occur as soon as practicable.

However, on close scrutiny, re-establishing the pre-crisis boundaries is more difficult than one might have expected in the light of the technocratic Great Moderation model of central banking. This, it will be argued in the next sections, is because sovereign and private debt markets have become inextricably connected through the practices of collateralized finance. This observation reinforces my opening remarks about the importance of the institutional framework and mediation of policy alongside the role attributed to specific theoretical and policy paradigms. To substantiate this argument, this chapter turns to institutional issues by exploring how a collateral-based financial system creates exit policy dilemmas that continue to complicate efforts to re-normalize central banking.

A taxonomy of crisis-based policies

By intervening directly in government bond markets, central banks abandon simultaneously the political neutrality and market neutrality principles. Outright purchases of government debt blur the boundary between monetary and fiscal policy as the central bank assumes 'quasi-debt management' functions (Borio and Disyatat 2009). So why intervene when interventions threaten the legitimacy and independence (read political power) of the central banks? The next sections first describe the practices of central bank interventions during crisis to argue, in line with Niebyl's ideas about the importance of 'reality' understood as contingent structural characteristics of financial markets and institutions, that unconventional interventions reflect a different collateral-based imaginary underpinning the rise of shadow banking activities, problematic for central banks.

In the traditional model of financial intermediation, central banks could preserve market neutrality even during a financial crisis. The immediate effect of a financial crisis is to increase the preference for holding highly liquid assets – the most liquid of which is money – in order to preserve funding liquidity, that is, the ability of banks to meet liabilities or settle positions (BIS 2011). The increased liquidity preference translates into higher interest rate on the market where banks trade reserves – the interbank market – moving interbank rates away from the official policy rate. The central bank is the only institution that can mitigate the systemic risk associated with funding liquidity problems because it has (theoretically unrestricted) monopoly power to issue the most liquid asset – bank reserves (under the lender of last resort facility, against quality collateral, Woodford 2007) – until the preference for liquidity normalizes. Liquidity policies would be thus conducted in the usual manner, to realign interbank interest rates with the policy rate, as most central banks did in the aftermath of the collapse in the subprime mortgage market in August 2007.

Yet by March 2009 large central banks went much further. With interest rates rapidly brought down to the lower, (zero bound and ample evidence that the 'normal' transmission mechanism would not be restored by the traditional lender of last resort liquidity provision (already in place on a large scale throughout early 2008)), central banks became market-makers of last resort, intervening first in private and then government bond markets (Mehrling 2012). The interventions were attributed to two key motivations (Stone *et al.* 2011):

- *Macroeconomic stabilization*: aimed to ease credit conditions or to restore the transmission mechanism disrupted by shocks to particular market segments.
- *Financial stability*: central banks recognized that the traditional crisis mandate of preserving funding liquidity had to be expanded to take into account market liquidity, defined as the ability to trade (large volumes) of debt instruments with a small impact on price, as the increasing importance of collateral-based finance left financial institutions dependent on their portfolios of marketable collateral in order to raise market finance.

The crisis toolkit was expanded to include three distinctive types of measures: outright purchases of private and sovereign debt, bank-based liquidity injections, and collateral based measures. The first and third type of measures, it will be argued, indicate a different financial imaginary ruled by collateral rather than the central bank's short-term interest rate.

Outright purchases were conducted either through direct interventions in private debt markets to restore market liquidity and thus increase the availability of credit (the MBS purchases in the US and UK) or in government debt markets. Central banks invoked the theoretical guidance of the portfolio-rebalancing channel: once assets are not perfectly substitutable (as for instance in Culbertson's (1957) 'preferred habitat theory' that proposes distinct investors preferences for certain maturities), central bank interventions can trigger yield changes and modify investors incentives away from (low yielding) government debt to (higher risk-higher yield) private debt instruments (Lenza *et al.* 2010; Cecioni *et al.* 2011). Scholars in the mainstream monetary tradition, such as Curdia and Woodford (2010), challenged the effectiveness of this rebalancing channel, arguing that unconventional monetary policies, just as 'normal' policies, can only work discursively. In other words, the central bank need not do anything beyond lowering its policy rate to zero. Through the signalling channel, the central bank reduces uncertainty, promising to keep interest rates low until economic activity normalizes. The interpretative cooperation with financial markets is restored to pre-crisis coordinates.

Bank-based liquidity injections are an extension of the normal Open Market Operations: central banks inject bank reserves against collateral but vary the collateral requirements (accepting illiquid private instruments), the volume (full allotment or predetermined volumes), the counterparties (extending the range of eligible institutions), and the maturity (extending it, as the ECB did, to up to three-year loans). Since the start of the subprime mortgage market tensions[3] and until the collapse of Lehman, most large central banks engaged in bank-based liquidity injections in response to interbank market tensions (see Cecioni *et al.* 2011 for a detailed account), while after Lehman the ECB deployed it as the primary tool for unconventional market interventions, invoking the bank-based nature of its financial system (Gabor 2012).

Long-term refinancing operations (LTROs) of the type announced by the ECB in May 2009 similarly entailed a well-defined maturity and predetermined auction dates, although the volume of reserves injected was demand-driven, depending on private banks' portfolio of acceptable collateral. The ECB re-introduced LTROs when, towards the end of 2011, European banks' funding conditions had deteriorated enough to raise concerns of a system-wide banking crisis (ECB 2010; Gabor 2012). The ECB changed the qualitative conditions of its subsequent LTROs by relaxing collateral requirements.

The third type of intervention, **collateral swaps**, is unusual because unlike the previous two approaches, it involves no additional creation of central bank money. It instead requires close coordination with the government's debt management office. The Securities Lending Facility (BoE) and the Terms Securities Lending Programs, both introduced in early 2008 and unwound in 2011, shared the same mechanism: the central bank offered highly liquid Treasury debt in exchange for high quality, temporarily illiquid, private debt instruments (mostly MBS). Banks could use sovereign debt as collateral to access short-term collateralized funding markets. These schemes involved direct coordination with the Treasury's debt management offices. The US Fed exchanged sovereign Treasuries for investment grade debt securities, on a 28-day maturity, at monthly auctions (Fleming *et al.* 2009). At its peak, the facility injected USD 250 billion of US Treasuries, around a fourth of the overall QE purchases. In the British case, nine-months Treasury bills were specifically issued for the SLS with up to three-year maturity, and by the end of the scheme in January 2009, banks had acquired £185 billion, double the pre-crisis volume of the Bank of England's balance sheet and close to the £200 billion QE programme announced in March 2009 (John *et al.* 2012). It is important to note that the ECB did not adopt collateral swaps for two reasons: its holdings of sovereign debt were relatively small pre-crisis (around 10 per cent of overall assets, see Cheun *et al.* 2009) and it faced political difficulties of pursuing coordinated policies with member states' sovereign debt management offices.

Although the specific framework for collateral swaps varied across individual central banks, they were designed as very temporary measures to mitigate stress in funding markets. The Bank of England's SLS did not seek to ease credit conditions so defined acceptable collateral as the 'overhang of illiquid assets' produced through the securitization of loans extended prior to 31 December 2007. The swaps had a predefined 'drawdown window' in which banks could take illiquid collateral to BoE; initially to close on October 2008, extended to 30 January 2009 in response to Lehman's collapse. The TSLF in turn entailed minimum fees set higher than the cost of the same collateral swap in private markets, giving it an automatic unwinding once funding conditions improved (Fleming *et al.* 2009). Both facilities expired by early 2011.

Crisis policies: imagining a collateral-based world

Since the onset of the financial crisis, a rapidly growing scholarship has drawn attention to the importance of collateral-based finance and its implications for macroeconomic management, particularly in what concerns the relationship between monetary policies and collateral markets (Hrung and Seligman 2011; Singh 2011; Avouyi-Dovi and Idier 2012; Gabor 2012; Singh and Stella 2012). The rapid expansion in credit intermediated by the shadow banking sector relied on collateral-based funding obtained in wholesale (repo) markets (Pozsar 2011).

Repos constitute an important funding instrument for banks that move away from the traditional balance sheet structure where assets are dominated by loans to non-financial corporations and liabilities by retail deposits. Take for example the European banking figures for 2012: loans to non-financial corporations only accounted for around 30 per cent of bank assets, with deposits of non-financial institutions amounting to around 30 per cent of total liabilities, with some heterogeneity depending on the size and degree of internationalization of the banking group (ECB 2012; see also Hardie *et al.* 2013). In other words, banks financed their non-loan assets (securities, derivatives, and other financial instruments) by relying on wholesale money markets, in particular the repo market. Indeed, through the repo market, banks can use tradable assets as collateral to borrow from cash-rich financial institutions (other banks, money market funds, etc.). In other words, repos are crucial to a leverage-reliant business model for financial institutions (BIS 1999; Adrian and Shin 2010; Financial Stability Board 2012; Gabor 2013). Thus, banks can purchase securities or borrow them (through the securities lending market), and repo them out to obtain the cash necessary to fund that purchase, rather than rely on retail deposits. This, the BIS (1999) stressed, makes the repo instrument 'special', since it is the cheapest source of leverage in modern financial systems.

Indeed, large European banks made extensive recourse to repos to grow balance sheets: by 2008, around 80 per cent of repo transactions were undertaken by the 20 largest European banks (Hordahl and King 2008; Gabor 2012). Repo-reliance is thus a distinguishing feature of global systemically important banking, making them systemic players in the shadow-banking universe (see BIS 2011; Singh 2011; Singh and Stella 2012; Gabor 2013).

Collateral-based finance expands the basis for private liquidity creation from bank reserves under the traditional intermediation model to include marketable collateral that similarly satisfies funding and liquidity needs. To understand collateral-based liquidity creation, and the challenges this raises during times of market stress, Singh and Stella (2012) distinguish between bank reserves (termed D) and collateral (C): assets trading in markets with high liquidity and low price volatility, such as government bond markets. Central banks have full control over D through its market interventions, whereas C can be influenced by collateral management strategies of global banks (Singh 2011), by fiscal policies of the government, and by central bank collateral policies (see Gabor 2012, 2014).

During periods of normal market conditions, D and C are very close substitutes. Financial institutions tend to economize on bank reserves since these provide no returns and prefer C because (1) it is eligible for central bank operations (easily substitutable for D) and (2) satisfies preference for safety of principal and yield. The process of collateral-based money creation is similar to the bank-based system: collateral acts as the shadow parallel of reserves created by the central bank. Financial institutions can repo assets repeatedly, a process of rehypothecation that creates pyramid of debt claims (see Pozsar 2011; Singh 2011; Financial Stability Board 2012; Gabor 2014). The longer the intermediation chains supported by the same collateral, the higher the velocity of 'shadow reserves' (Singh 2011). The stock of liquid collateral, private and sovereign, is then key to the pace and scope of shadow-based financial intermediation. For example, Pozsar (2011) argues that constraints on velocity of government debt collateral triggered a supply response from shadow banks. In other words, securitization was not driven by the search for high-risk, high-yield tranches but can also be conceived as private creation of high-quality collateral (the AAA tranches) demanded by large institutional investors that required money-like instruments that offered the protection similar to bank deposits.

Yet if C provides the same liquidity as D in 'normal' times, this may change dramatically under market distress. The 'moneyness' of an asset depends on two distinct characteristics of a collateralized-repo transaction:

1   **Haircut**: the cash lender in a repo transaction requires the nominal value to be higher than the cash provided in order to minimize market risk (the risk of price volatility). Lower quality collateral then requires higher haircuts.
2   **Liquidity**: perceptions of collateral liquidity are important because of the practice of daily re-valuation of collateral portfolios. Collateral is marked-to-market, if its market price falls the cash borrower may be required to post additional collateral, increasing repo costs. The liquidity of collateral markets becomes essential: very liquid markets have less price volatility, whereas price (and thus repo collateral costs) can vary widely in illiquid markets.

Since the crisis, the growing scholarship on the economics of collateral stresses that perceptions of quality and liquidity of collateral are procyclical (Brunnermeier *et al.*, 2011; ECB 2010). During normal times, haircuts are low (and liquidity high) for both private and sovereign assets used as marketable collateral. But market distress and the increased preference for liquidity is accompanied by a segmentation or tiering of collateral markets. In other words, financial crisis creates two distinctive types of collateral. Some collateral preserves its 'money-ness' (for example US-issued sovereign bonds) and some doesn't. For example, crisis-induced price volatility for assets in illiquid markets (as for instance with mortgage-backed securities) translates into haircut increases and margin calls, thus reducing their attractiveness as marketable collateral. Singh and Stella (2012) capture the first category into C1 (easily substitutable for D overnight) and the second into C2 (possibly substitutable depending on central banks' unconventional measures), a distinction that is analytically useful for exploring the politics of collateral-based central banks.

For Singh and Stella (2012), the distinction between C1 and C2 should be approached from a 'substitutability angle' that indicates the extent to which unconventional monetary policies 'provide liquidity relief' (see Table 15.1). Thus, outright purchases of high quality sovereign bonds (under quantitative easing programmes) simply substitute two highly liquid forms of money: D and C1. In contrast, outright purchases of C2 (as in the US, UK) or LTROs on easy collateral requirements (C2) inject central bank money (D) and thus provide effective liquidity relief. The most effective method to provide collateral liquidity is through collateral swaps that exchange C1 for illiquid C2. The central bank thus performs a key function in a crisis-ridden collateral-based system: it injects unencumbered collateral into the financial system and mitigates the adverse consequences of the shortage of safe assets. Collateral policies affect directly the overall degree of market and funding liquidity: collateral-based finance ties these together.

Yet the focus on 'substitutability' downplays the politics of the process, as if monetary policy has no direct effect over the movements of an asset from C1 to C2 (and vice versa). In other words, the move between the 'good' and 'bad' collateral states of an asset are more porous than the collateral literature recognizes. According to Gorton and Ordunez (2012), the distinction runs along information lines: information insensitive collateral – i.e. sovereign bonds – preserves its 'money-ness' irrespective of market conditions. However, membership of the exclusive C1 club is neither automatic nor irrevocable for sovereigns because concerns about banks' funding liquidity may spill over into collateral markets, including government bond markets, in a collateral-based financial system.

For instance, Bolton and Jeanne (2011) persuasively argue that monetary unions with integrated banking systems generate externalities that benefit high rated sovereigns that issue safe-haven assets but also spread collateral discrimination among lower-rated sovereigns that eventually moves that collateral from C1 into C2. From this perspective, how the central bank responds to such possible moves makes a different. Outright purchases of government bonds contribute to preserving the function of C1 as marketable collateral, whereas bank-based interventions and collateral swaps may not.

With outright purchases, the central bank suggests that it stands ready to intervene in sovereign bond markets when concerns about the crisis implications for public debt sustainability may reduce collateral-driven demand. Indeed, the success of the ECB's OMT in stabilizing European financial markets, including government bond markets, without the ECB having to purchase *any* government bonds, offers a powerful indication that collateralized-based finance needs outright interventions during periods of collateral stress.

In turn, bank-based liquidity injections (LTROs) can only offer indirect influence over the shifts between distinct collateral states. Influence is contingent on private banks' collateral management strategies, what two ECB researchers described as outsourcing 'decisions determining demand and supply in capital markets' to the banking sector (Cour-Thimann and Winkler 2012: 800). In other words, demand for C2 assets depends on private banks' preferences for risk/return *and* their assessment of future market liquidity for these assets. High risk/high return collateral – for example Italian bonds – is 'cheapest to deliver' in repo markets (because prices are low). Thus, private banks may demand and use C2 assets for collateral as long as expectations are that market liquidity will improve. For example, throughout 2009, private banks appeared to have successfully restored the C1-collateral status of Irish, Greek, and Portuguese sovereign bonds (see BIS 2011), using cheap ECB liquidity to purchase these instruments as both the ECB and European governments shared a consensus that fiscal stimulus, and liquidity policies supportive of this stimulus, were necessary to address the European crisis. Banks interpreted this consensus to signify a clear political will to overcome market tensions.

Collateral swaps do provide liquidity relief but have no direct consequences for the movements between the two types of collateral, although indirectly an injection of C1 collateral may bring funding stability that restores confidence and prompts portfolio realignments into riskier asset classes (C2).

Table 15.1 Through the collateral lens: collateral consequences of adoption and exit

Types of balance sheet policies		UMP measures	Implication	Exit strategies	Implication
Outright purchases	private/low rated sovereigns	D↑, C2↓	+: liquidity relief ? may contribute to C2 → C1	C2↑ D↓	
	sovereign bonds	D↑, C1↓	–: no liquidity relief +: preserves 'money-ness' of C1, prevents C1 → C2	C1↑; D↓	C1 → C2?
Bank-based measures		D↑, C2↓	+: liquidity relief +? C2 → C1 contingent on banks' collateral management strategies	D↓, C2↑	C1 → C2?
Collateral swaps		C1↑, C2↓	liquidity relief	C1↓, C2↑	–

Note
The ↓ indicates that the central bank absorbs collateral/bank reserves from the formal system of financial intermediation (and vice versa).

Similarly, exit from unconventional policies may trigger movements from C1 into C2 if the central bank does not attribute any policy significance to stabilizing both illiquid and liquid collateral values. Gabor (2014) for example argues that the ECB's decisions to suspend its first round of long-term liquidity injections in December 2009 – when the Greek government bond market came under increased pressure – triggered a crisis of shadow banking in the European repo markets and the asset markets that provide collateral for repo transactions.

Automatic exit from LTRO-type measures may have negative consequences because it requires banks to replace C2 with C1 collateral in order to substitute central bank funding with market funding. The ensuing scramble for safe assets and the collateral scrutiny this may trigger could push some low C1 collateral into C2 – as happened in the Eurozone, when the ECB's refusal to intervene in collateral markets during the first stage of the Greek crisis (May 2010) in the context of the expiry of the first one-year LTRO dramatically reduced the use of Portuguese/Irish/Greek bonds in repo transactions (see BIS 2011); a story later re-enacted for Italy and Spain in 2011. In contrast, the Bank of England and the US Federal Reserve designed collateral swaps specifically to avoid unwinding *before* liquidity was fully restored in markets for collateral – the pricing mechanism ensured financial institutions would continue to tap that source of collateral only until private wholesale funding became cheaper.

In sum, the shift to collateralized finance brought a qualitative change in the relationship between the two neutrality principles. Indeed, central banks cannot abandon one and uphold the other where funding and collateral market liquidity are closely connected. The ECB's example illustrates this dilemma clearly: whereas its bank-based measures did depart from the market neutrality principle, its difficulties in coordinating with sovereign debt management authorities prevented it successfully stabilizing funding conditions for European banks (Gabor 2012).

Collateral-based finance: towards a new imaginary of central banking

Collateralized financed has undermined progressively both the authority and the policy instruments of central banks. The insistence on 'exit' should be understood as an attempt to meet its growing challenges by regulatory rather than macroeconomic policy means. Indeed, the consensus appears to be that a careful regulation of global banks and the Financial Stability Board work on tackling the systemic implications of repo markets (FSB 2013) can and should allow central banks to re-draw the pre-crisis boundaries. Yet central banks have to confront three sets of questions in this attempt:

1 *The theoretical foundations for interest-rate policies: is a return to the efficient market hypothesis possible?* The pre-crisis imaginary premised a nationally bounded set of financial relationships governed by rational expectations about the path of the central bank's short-term interest rates. However, recent debates on tapering by the US Fed question this methodological nationalism: the

relevant unit of analysis is global financial architectures, with global banks headquartered in high-income countries acting as key nodes in these networks (Haldane and May 2011; Singh 2011; Bruno and Shin 2012). How can short-term interest rate manipulation be reconciled with a collateral-based imaginary where liquidity conditions in any country are heavily influenced by cross-border flows and the collateral management of large global banks?

2   *The practice of central banking: shifting interest rate policy on collateralized funding markets?* A few (as yet isolated) voices working in the research departments of central banks have highlighted the policy implications of a collateral-based world. Klee and Stebunov (2011) argued that central banks should shift to targeting the interest rate on the repo market, thus abandoning the framework of varying bank reserves in order to influence unsecured short-term market rates.

3   *Central banking in crisis: the institutional framework for preserving liquidity of collateral.* Since it is now recognized that unconventional monetary policies have distinctive impacts on collateral markets depending on whether the central bank chooses to intervene directly or through the banking sector (Gabor 2014), it is crucial to ask whether such interventions should be normalized into a crisis framework. In a collateral-reliant global financial system, central banks will continue to have to deploy policies that preserve the liquidity of collateral during times of crisis.

Once more on the (cultural) political economy of central banking policies

Monetary policy choices are inevitably political under any economic or political paradigm and policy regime. Central banks cannot vanish from 'technocratic' policy processes, as either automatic adjustment narratives or the rhetoric of free markets triumphantly suggest. Instead, the central bank functions within, and works to reproduce, ideologically informed strategies of economic management. This is especially clear during periods of crisis. Critical to substantiating this claim is to integrate conventional economic analysis with a discursive approach that treats policies as contested and contingent, linking struggles over the construction of the 'crisis' and its 'solutions' to configurations of power and interest groups in policy spaces. Such a redefinition allows conceptual precision by acknowledging that policy and 'reality' are mutually constitutive, while retaining Niebyl's fundamental insight that policy does not arise from rational choices between various scenarios. As a methodological tool to this epistemological position, a narrative approach allows mapping the discursive frames involved in the production of a crisis. Narratives have homogenizing effects, imposing a certain order of interpretation over a collection of events. Its ideological function, then, resides not in what it includes but in what it leaves out of the story. In the global financial crisis, central banks have sidelined collateral-based finance in their narratives of monetary policy because of the institutional and political challenges these underpin.

Notes

1 Sir Mervyn King, the Governor of the Bank of England, referred to the Great Moderation as the NICE decade, i.e. ten years of non-inflationary, constant expansion (King 2003: 3–4). In 2010, he recognized the need for a SOBER decade, i.e. 'a decade of *s*avings, *o*rderly *b*udgets, and *e*quitable *r*ebalancing' (King 2010). Some commentators regard the coming decade as more likely to be VILE (*v*olatile *i*nflation, *l*ess *e*xpansionary) (Giles 2010).
2 While Niebyl's argument has its own theoretical foundations and logic, this argument can be seen to anticipate what the editors to this volume have presented as cultural political economy. Here we engage with Niebyl rather than with the full range of arguments encompassed within CPE.
3 During the Gold Standard, the Bank of England for instance often responded with both larger liquidity injections and interest rate increases to tensions on the interbank market. Interest rate increases sought to prevent capital (gold) flight or to attract capital inflows.

References

Adrian, T. and Shin, H.S. (2010) Liquidity and Leverage, *Journal of Financial Intermediation*, 19(3): 418–37.

Alesina, A., Galí, J., Giavazzi, F., Uhlig, H., and Blanchard, O. (2001) Defining a Macroeconomic Framework for the Euro Area, *Monitoring the European Central Bank*, No. 3, London: Centre for Economic Policy Research.

Apthorpe, R. and Gasper, D. (1996) *Arguing Development Policy: Frames and Discourses*, London: Frank Cass.

Avouyi-Dovi, S. and Idier, J. (2012) The Impact of Unconventional Monetary Policy on the Market for Collateral. The Case of the French Bond Market, *Journal of Banking and Finance*, 36(2): 428–38.

Bank for International Settlements (BIS) (1999) *Implications of Repo Markets for Central Banks*, Basel: BIS. 9 March. www.bis.org/publ/cgfs10.pdf.

Bank for International Settlements (BIS) (2011) The Impact of Sovereign Credit Risk on Bank Funding Conditions, *Committee on the Global Financial System Paper*, No. 43.

Belke, A. (2010) Financial Crisis, Global Liquidity and Monetary Exit Strategies, *DIW Discussion Paper*, No. 995.

Blanchard, O., Dell'Ariccia, G., and Mauro, P. (2010) Rethinking Macroeconomic Policy, *IMF Staff Position Note*, www.imf.org/external/pubs/ft/spn/2010/spn1003.pdf.

Bolton, P. and Jeanne, O. (2011) *Sovereign Default Risk and Bank Fragility in Financially Integrated Economies*, www.econ2.jhu.edu/people/Jeanne/ARC031611.pdf.

Borio, C. and Disyatat, P. (2009) Unconventional Monetary Policies: An Appraisal, *BIS Working Paper*, www.bis.org/publ/work292.pdf.

Brunnermeier, M.K., Gorton, G., and Krishnamurthy, A. (2011) Risk Topography, *NBER Macroeconomics Annual 2011*, 26: 149–76.

Bruno, V. and Shin, H.S. (2012) Capital Flows, Cross-Border Banking and Global Liquidity, http://ssrn.com/abstract=2020556 or http://dx.doi.org/10.2139/ssrn.2020556.

Cecioni, M., Ferrero, G., and Secchi, A. (2011) Unconventional Monetary Policy in Theory and Practice, *Banca D'Italia Occasional Papers*, No. 102.

Cheun, S., Von Köppen-Mertes, I., and Weller, B. (2009) The Collateral Frameworks of the Eurosystem, the Federal Reserve System and the Bank of England and the Financial Market Turmoil, *ECB Occasional Paper*, No. 107.

Clarida, R., Gali, J., and Gertler, M. (1999) The Science of Monetary Policy: A New Keynesian Perspective, *Journal of Economic Literature*, 37(4): 1661–707.

Cour-Thimann, P. and Winkler, B. (2012) The ECB's Non-Standard Monetary Policy Measures: The Role of Institutional Factors and Financial Structure, *Oxford Review of Economic Policy*, 28(4): 765–803.

Culbertson, J. (1957). The Term Structure of Interest Rates, *Quarterly Journal of Economics*, 71: 485–517.

Curdia, V. and Woodford, M. (2010) Conventional and Unconventional Monetary Policy, *mimeo*, Federal Reserve Bank of New York and Columbia University.

Currie, M. (1998) *Postmodern Narrative Theory*, Basingstoke: Macmillan.

Debray, R. (1973) *Prison Writings*, London: Allen Lane.

Eggertsson, G. and Woodford. M. (2003) The Zero Bound on Interest Rates and Optimal Monetary Policy, *Brookings Papers on Economic Activity*, 1: 139–233.

European Central Bank (ECB) (2010) The ECB's Response to the Financial Crisis, *ECB Monthly Bulletin*, October, 59–74. https://www.ecb.europa.eu/pub/pdf/other/art1_mb201010en_pp59-74en.pdf.

European Central Bank (ECB) (2012) Financial Integration in Europe, April, Frankfurt am Main. www.ecb.europa.eu/pub/pdf/other/financialintegrationineurope201204en.pdf

Financial Stability Board (FSB) (2012) Global Shadow Banking Monitoring Report, 18 November, www.financialstabilityboard.org/publications/r_121118c.pdf.

Financial Stability Board (FSB) (2013) Policy Framework for Addressing Shadow Banking Risks in Securities Lending and Repos, www.financialstabilityboard.org/publications/r_130829b.pdf.

Fleming, M., Hrung, W.B., and Keane, F. (2009) The Term Securities Lending Facility: Origin, Design, and Effects, *Federal Reserve Bank of New York Current Issues in Economics and Finance*, 12 February.

Gabor, D. (2010) The IMF and its New Economics of Crisis, *Development and Change*, 41(5): 805–30.

Gabor, D. (2011) *Central Banking and Financialization: A Romanian Account of How Eastern Europe Became Subprime*, Basingstoke: Palgrave-Macmillan.

Gabor, D. (2012) The Power of Collateral: The ECB and Bank Funding Strategies in Crisis, *SSRN eLibrary*, 18 May.

Gabor, D. (2013) Shadow Interconnectedness: The Political Economy of European Shadow Banking, http://ssrn.com/abstract=2326645 or http://dx.doi.org/10.2139/ssrn.2326645

Gabor, D. (2014) Learning from Japan: The ECB and the Sovereign Debt Crisis, *Review of Political Economy*, 26(2), pp. 190–209.

Giles, C. (2010) Mervyn King: Sober or Vile?, *Financial Times*, 19 October, http://blogs.ft.com/money-supply/2010/10/19/mervyn-king-sober-or-vile/.

Gorton, G. and Ordonez, G. (2012) Collateral Crises, *NBER Working Paper*, No. 17771.

Greenspan, A. (2008) Evidence given on 23 October 2008, Washington, DC: House Committee on Oversight and Government Reform.

Hajer, M. (1995) *The Politics of Environmental Discourse*, Oxford: Oxford University Press.

Haldane, A.G. and May, R.M. (2011) Systemic Risk in Banking Ecosystems, *Nature*, 469 (7330): 351–5.

Hardie, I., Howarth, D., Maxfield, S., and Verdun, A. (2013) Banks and the False Dichotomy in the Comparative Political Economy of Finance, *World Politics*, 65: 691–728.

Hay, C. (1999) Crisis and the Structural Transformation of the State: Interrogating the Process of Change, *British Journal of Politics and International Relations*, 1(3): 317–44.

Heinrich, M. and Kutter, A. (2013) A Critical Juncture in EU Integration? The Eurozone Crisis and its Management 2010–2012, in F.E. Panizza and G. Philip (eds), *The Politics of Financial Crisis: Comparative Perspectives*, London: Routledge.

Holmes, D.R. (2013) *Economy of Words: Communicative Imperatives in Central Banks*, Chicago: University of Chicago Press.

Hordahl, P. and King, M. (2008) Developments in Repo Markets during the Financial Turmoil, *BIS Quarterly*, December.

Hrung, W. and Seligman, J. (2011) Responses to the Financial Crisis, Treasury Debt, and the Impact on Short-Term Money Markets, Staff Reports *481*, Federal Reserve Bank of New York.

Issing, O. (2002) On Macroeconomic Policy Co-ordination in EMU, *Journal of Common Market Studies*, 40(3): 345–58.

Jessop, B. (2014) Repoliticizing Depoliticization: Theoretical Preliminaries to an Account of Responses to the American and Eurozone Fiscal Crises, *Politics & Policy*, 14(2), 207–223.

John, S., Roberts, M., and Weeken, O. (2012) The Bank of England's Special Liquidity Scheme, *Bank of England Quarterly Bulletin*, 52(1): 57–66.

Katzenstein, P. J. and Nelson, S.C. (2013) Reading the Right Signals and Reading the Signals Right: IPE and the Financial Crisis of 2008, *Review of International Political Economy*, 20(5): 1101–31.

Keeley, J. (1997) Reconceptualising Policy Processes: The Dynamics of Natural Resource Management and Agricultural Intensification Policy-making in Ethiopia, 1984–97. MPhil Dissertation, Brighton: Institute of Development Studies, University of Sussex.

Keeley, J. and Scoones, I. (1999) Understanding Environmental Policy Processes: A Review, *IDS Working Paper*, No. 89, Falmer: Institute of Development Studies.

King, M. (2003) Speech at East Midlands Development Agency/Bank of England Dinner, 14 October, www.bankofengland.co.uk/archive/Documents/historicpubs/speeches/2003/speech204.pdf.

King, M. (2010) Speech at Black Country Chamber of Commerce, West Midlands, 19 October, www.bankofengland.co.uk/archive/Documents/historicpubs/speeches/2010/speech454.pdf.

Kirshner, J. (2003) Money is Politics, *Review of International Political Economy*, 10(4): 645–60.

Klee, E. and Stebunov, V. (2011) A Target Treasury General Collateral Repo Rate: Is a Target Repo Rate a Viable Alternative to the Target Federal Funds Rate? Board of Governors of the Federal Reserve System, September (preliminary draft).

Krippner, G.R. (2007) The Making of US Monetary Policy: Central Bank Transparency and the Neoliberal Dilemma, *Theory and Society*, 36(6): 477–513.

Leeper, E.M. (2010a) Anchors Away: How Fiscal Policy can Undermine 'Good' Monetary Policy, in *Monetary Policy Under Financial Turbulence, 13th Annual Conference of the Central Bank of Chile*. Santiago: Banco Central de Chile.

Leeper, E.M. (2010b) Monetary Science, Fiscal Alchemy, Federal Reserve Bank of Kansas City's Jackson Hole Symposium, 'Macroeconomic Policy: Post-Crisis and Risks Ahead', 26–28 August.

Lenza, M., Pill, H., and Reichlin, L. (2010) Monetary Policy in Exceptional Times, *Economic Policy*, 62: 295–339.

Mann, G. (2010) Hobbes' Redoubt? Toward a Geography of Monetary Policy, *Progress in Human Geography*, 34(5): 601–25.

Mehrling, P. (2012) Three Principles for Market-Based Credit Regulation, *American Economic Review*, 102(3): 107–12.

Mirowski, P. (2013) *Never Let a Serious Crisis go to Waste*, London: Verso.

Moessner, R. and Turner, P. (2012) Threat of Fiscal Dominance? Workshop Summary, in Bank of International Settlements (ed.), *Threat of Fiscal Dominance?* BIS Paper 65, www.bis.org/publ/bppdf/bispap65.pdf.

Mosse, D. (2005) *Cultivating Development: An Ethnography of Aid Policy and Practice*, London: Pluto Press.

Niebyl, K.H. (1946) *Studies in the Classical Theories of Money*, New York: Columbia University Press.

Papademos (2008) Globalization and Central Bank Policies. Speech at the Bridge Forum Dialogue, Luxembourg, www.bis.org/review/r080125e.pdf.

Peck, J. and Tickell, A. (2002) Neoliberalizing Space, *Antipode*, 34(3): 380–40.

Pigeon, M.A. (2011) The Wizard of Oz: Peering Behind the Curtain on the Relationship Between Central Banks and the Business Media, in D. Winseck and D. Yong Jin (eds), *The Political Economy of Media: The Transformation of the Global Media Industries*, New York: Bloomsbury Academic.

Plosser, C. (2012) Re-Examining Central Bank Orthodoxy for Unorthodox Times: Inaugural Meeting of the Global Society of Fellows of the Global Interdependence Center, www.philadelphiafed.org/publications/speeches/plosser/2012/03–26–12_global-interdependence-center.pdf.

Pozsar, A. (2011) Institutional Cash Pools and the Triffin Dilemma of the US Banking System, *IMF Working Paper*, No. WP/11/190.

Roe, E. (1991) Development Narratives; or, Making the Best of Blueprint Development, *World Development*, 19(4): 287–300.

Scoones, I. (2003) Making Policy in the 'New Economy': The Case of Biotechnology in Karnataka, India, Brighton: *IDS Working Paper*, No. 196.

Singh, M. (2011) Velocity of Pledged Collateral: Analysis and Implications, *IMF Working Paper*, No. 11/256.

Singh, M. and Stella. P. (2012) Money and Collateral, *SSRN eLibrary* (April), http://papers.ssrn.com/sol3/papers.cfm?abstract_id=2050268.

Stone, M., Fujita K., and Ishi K. (2011) Should Unconventional Balance Sheet Policies be added to the Central Bank Toolkit? A Review of the Experience So Far, *IMF Working Paper*, No. 11/145.

Trichet, J-C. (2009) The ECB's Enhanced Credit Support. Keynote Address at the University of Munich, 13 July, www.ecb.int/press/key/date/2009/html/sp090713.en.html.

Yamaoka, H. and Syed, M. (2010) Managing the Exit: Lessons from Japan's Reversal of Unconventional Monetary Policy, *IMF Working Paper*, No. 114.

Woodford, M. (2007) Globalization and Monetary Control, *NBER Papers*, No. 13329.

Žižek, S. (2009) Lunch with FT, *Financial Times*, 6 March.

Zorn, L. and A. García. (2011) Central Bank Collateral Policy: Insights from Recent Experience, *Bank of Canada Review 2011*: 37–45.

Index

Page numbers in *italics* denote tables, those in **bold** denote figures.

For Product Safety Concerns and Information please contact our EU
representative GPSR@taylorandfrancis.com Taylor & Francis Verlag GmbH,
Kaufingerstraße 24, 80331 München, Germany

Printed and bound by CPI Group (UK) Ltd, Croydon, CR0 4YY
12/05/2025
01866861-0001